FOR THE HELL OF IT

Jonah Raskin

FOR THE HELL OF IT

The Life and Times of Abbie Hoffman

Jan 7, 2000
For Elvis,
In honor of the
spirit of that strange
era that brought out the
best and the worst in us
(the "rebels"): troubled times,
yet the world was magical
and young again — so unlike
today and possible.
Happy B,)

University of California Press
Berkeley   Los Angeles   London

University of California Press
Berkeley and Los Angeles, California

University of California Press, Ltd.
London, England

First Paperback Printing 1998

Library of Congress Cataloging-in-Publication Data

Raskin, Jonah, 1942–
    For the hell of it : the life and times of Abbie Hoffman /
Jonah Raskin ; with a foreword by Eric Foner.
        p.   cm.
    Includes bibliographic references and index
    ISBN 0-520-21379-3 (pbk : alk. paper)
    1. Hoffman, Abbie.   2. Radicals—United States—
Biography.   3. Radicalism—United States—History—20th
century.   I. Title.   HN90.R3R37   1996
    303.48′4—dc 20
[B]   95-52181

Printed in the United States of America

9 8 7 6 5 4 3 2 1

The paper used in this publication meets the minimum
requirements of American National Standard for Information
Sciences—Permanence of Paper for Printed Library Materials,
ANSI Z39.48-1984. ⊗

CONTENTS

ILLUSTRATIONS

PERSONS
INTERVIEWED

Joe Aboody
Judy Clavir Albert
Stewart Albert
Dorothy Altman
Nelson Ambush
John B. Anderson
David Aronson
William Ayers
D'Army Bailey
Robert Baker
Stu Ball
Frank Bardacke
Dana Beal
Lincoln Bergman
Jesse Berman
Paul Berman
Sharon Berman
Bob Bloom
Dean Blowbaum
Anne Boster
Richard Bovenzi
Donald Brennick

Dr. Donald Broverman
Anna Bullard
Kathleen Bursley
Lisa Callamaro
Marty Carey
Susan Carcy
Peter Carroll
Clay Carson
Ron Carver
Joe Casdin
Chris Cerf
Henry Chaiklin
Kathy Chaiklin
Paul Chevigny
Charlotte Cohen
Joyce Cole
Lewis Cole
Peter Coyote
Walter Crockett
Coca Crystal
Patsy Cummings
Dennis Dalrymple

Bruce Dancis
Linda Davidoff
R. G. Davis
David Dellinger
Daniel Dick
Marjory Dick
Bernardine Dohrn
Angela Dorenkamp
John Dorenkamp
Doug Dowd
Claudia Dreifus
Don Epstein
Jason Epstein
Catherine Fallon
Bob Fass
David Fenton
Greta Finger
Joseph Fink
Jim Fitzgerald
James Forman
Jim Fouratt
Bart Friedman
Robert Friedman
Marshall Ganz
Ann Gefell
Father Bernard Gilgun
Allen Ginsberg
Al Giordano
Todd Gitlin
Art Goldberg
James Goldman
Sherman Goldstein
Donald Gonynor
Arlene Gordon
Hal Gordon
Jeanne Gough
Wavy Gravy

Donald Gropman
Barbara Haber
Anne Halliwell
Steve Halliwell
Chester Hartman
Casey Hayden
Tom Hayden
Irene Heinstein
Mark Hertsgaard
america Hoffman
Andrew Hoffman
Anita Hoffman
Jack Hoffman
John Holmstrom
Len Holt
Freeman House
Gerry Howard
H. Stuart Hughes
Steve Ben Israel
Dr. Oscar Janiger
Joyce Johnson
Jeff Jones
Fred Jordan
Pauline Kael
Paul Kantner
George Katsiaficas
Aaron Kay
John Kifner
Jeff Kisseloff
Bill Kunstler
Ken Kelley
Michael Kennedy
Marty Kenner
Lanny Kentfield
Jim Klee
Rabbi Joseph Klein
Ron Kovic

Larry Kramer
Janet Kranzberg
Paul Krassner
Janet Kraybill
Ron Kuby
Tuli Kupferberg
Bernice Salomon Kurchin
Nancy Kurshan
Greg Lago
Karen Lago
Ira Landess
Tim Leary
Gerald Lefcourt
Aryay Lensky
Tom Lesser
Julius Lester
Jay Levin
Bernard Levine
John Lewis
Joe Lo Guidice
David Lubell
Jonathan Lubell
Lynn Luria-Sukenick
Dickie Magidoff
Elaine Markson
Elizabeth Martinez
Ellen Maslow
Angela Massimo
Doug McAdam
Paul McIsaac
Daphne Merkin
Ellen Meyers
Mike Miller
Sara Miller
Herb Mills
Cynthia Morin
Bob Moses

Paul Mullaney
Ray Mungo
Jack Newfield
Jeff Nightbyrd
Carl Oglesby
Gloria Orenstein
Robbie Osman
Roz Payne
Abe Peck
Martin Peretz
Diane Peterson
Terri Priest
Ann Forer Pyne
Harold G. ("Dutch") Rader
Carol Ramer
Gail Randall
Gus Reichbach
Bonnie Jean Romney
Alan Rosenberg
Mark Rosenberg
Bob Rosenthal
Bob Ross
Gabrielle Schang-McCusker
Rabbi Alexander Schindler
Eli Schleifer
Emanuel Schreiber
Bobby Seale
Allen Secher
Jill Seiden
Franklin Siegel
Ronald Siff
Jonathan Silvers
Daniel Simon
John Simon
Jan Simonds
David Sinclair
Larry Sloman

Camilla Smith
Albert Southwick
Rick Spencer
Eleanor Stein-Jones
Don Stotler
Olga Talamante
Steve Tappis
Elizabeth Tomlinson
Michael True
Jack Tubert
Kwame Turé
Mayer Vishner
Viva
Nicholas von Hoffman

Jerome Washington
Harvey Wasserman
A. J. Weberman
Rex Weiner
Len Weinglass
Paula Weinstein
Sue Williamson
Louise Yellin
Allen Young
Quentin Young
Art Zellman
Bob Zellner
Dottie Zellner
Howard Zinn

Note to Readers: Whenever I use information or quote from someone I have interviewed, I use the word *remembered* or *recalled*.

FOREWORD

ERIC FONER

Jonah Raskin's biography of Abbie Hoffman is a major contribution to our knowledge of the 1960s—one of the most pivotal, controversial, and misunderstood decades in all of American history. Few figures of that remarkable era exemplify its qualities, for better and worse, more fully than Hoffman. Few, indeed, were present at so many of the decade's defining moments, from the 1960 demonstrations in California against the House Un-American Activities Committee to the Chicago Democratic convention of 1968 and the conspiracy trial that followed. Among Raskin's more impressive accomplishments is to place Hoffman firmly within the context of his times, thus illuminating not only his remarkable and, in the end, tragic life, but also the turbulent years in which he lived.

Too often, the literature on the 1960s—much of which was written by participants in the Students for a Democratic Society—privileges the history of SDS over other manifestations of New Left radicalism. In Raskin's account, Hoffman's career offers a different way of viewing the rebellion of the young, one centered not on SDS politics and campus radicalism during the first half of the decade, but on the far broader generational revolt of the mid- and late 1960s. After all, the peak of New Left protest did not come until 1970, after SDS had self-destructed, when half a million people rallied in Washington against the war in Vietnam and a strike paralyzed scores of college campuses throughout the nation, including institutions far removed from the elite centers of earlier student activism. (The most violent assaults on student protest came not at Columbia or Berkeley but at the mainstream state universities located at Orangeburg, South Carolina, and Kent, Ohio.)

Unlike the authors of SDS's Port Huron Statement, Abbie Hoffman had little interest in offering a blueprint for a new society or developing a carefully worked out critique of American life. His was a radicalism of deed, not word. Yet, as Raskin makes clear, Hoffman read widely and struggled to formulate a new approach for radicals, one that would take into account the ways in which American life had been transformed since World War II. He grasped that the young represented a far more distinct and powerful segment of society than ever before and that their discontents were not the economic deprivations that had catalyzed the Old Left but an alienation born of a lack of social purpose and of individual happiness despite material abundance. Generational conflict, Hoffman recognized, had the same potential to disrupt society as class conflict had possessed in the 1930s. A self-proclaimed "cultural revolutionary," he was ready to act when established liberal leaders abdicated their responsibility by supporting the Vietnam War and the torch of radicalism passed for the first time in American history into the hands of students and the young.

Hoffman challenged the way the Left had traditionally communicated with a mass constituency, introducing humor, theatricality, and studied irreverence into the repertoire of protest. Better than any other figure of the period except Dr. Martin Luther King, Jr., Hoffman understood how the mass media had transformed political communication, offering radical movements the opportunity to reach a mass audience through carefully staged (though apparently spontaneous) events that dramatized the injustice, pretensions, and hypocrisy of American society. Like King's Selma march and Birmingham demonstrations, Hoffman's actions—such as flinging dollar bills onto the floor of the New York Stock Exchange, nominating a pig for president, and wearing an American flag to a Congressional committee hearing—were calculated to attract media attention and galvanize public sentiment.

Hoffman saw styles of dress, music, and drugs as elements of rebellion, while at the same time believing that they must be given a political focus. He also recognized that personal liberation had become a mass movement rather than the privilege of small cadres of bohemians like those in Greenwich Village before World War I. Many called him an egomaniac—with some justice—yet Hoffman did not even put his name on his first book, *Revolution for the Hell of It*. The author was listed simply as "Free"—the motto of the countercultural rebellion and its quest for personal authenticity. Yet, as Raskin makes clear, Hoffman also exemplified the pitfalls of substituting theatricality for careful political analyses and elevating personal liberation to the end-all and be-all of politics. His penchant for self-destructive behavior, his thoughtless use of drugs, and the machismo that governed his relationships with women reveal larger failures of sixties radical culture. Raskin does not romanticize Hoffman; he insists, however, that without coming to terms with him, one can understand neither the 1960s nor our own time, when people feel free to conduct their personal lives in ways far more diverse than before the countercultural rebellion.

Like the movement itself, Hoffman lost his sense of direction after 1970. Raskin makes a real contribution in exploring Hoffman's life in the seventies and eighties. He does not gloss over Hoffman's excesses or dishonesty, but at the same time shows how his participation in the environmental movement and the struggle against American intervention in Nicaragua exemplify the many channels into which sixties radicalism eventually flowed. Toward the end of his life, Hoffman reemerged on college campuses, this time as a commodified version of his former self, a living icon of the sixties (commanding high appearance fees, to boot). But the man and the times no longer fit as perfectly as they had two decades earlier, and Hoffman's suicide reflected not only the denouement of a troubled life, but also the exhaustion of a movement he had done so much to shape.

"I'M ABBIE HOFFMAN"

> Myths are the only news, and the only thing
> that stays true all the time is a lie.
>
> *Abbie Hoffman, 1968*

Cultural Revolutionary

I knew Abbie Hoffman—whom I think of as the quintessential spirit of the sixties—for almost twenty years, and for much of that time I wasn't sure when he was acting, when he was for real, and when he was acting for real. I suppose that's why I have such contradictory feelings about him. Looking back at Abbie from the vantage point of the nineties, it seems to me that he was the first American cultural revolutionary in the age of television. He was a very funny and a very sad character who saw his life and times as a story that he could tell and retell again and again as he went along. The point, of course, was to inflate himself and deflate the established order. What most of us think of as "objective reality" didn't exist for him; while he managed to outwit it time and again, it finally caught up with him. In the end, Abbie the comedian became a tragic figure. He also embodied the sensibility called postmodern. Nowadays, postmodernism is a cliché that has lost most of its clout. But long before it entered the academic world, Abbie was a walking, talking postmodernist. A great many critics have tried to define the term, but no one, it seems to me, has done it as well as the writer E. L. Doctorow, who published Abbie's first book, *Revolution for the Hell of It,* when he was an editor at Dial Press, and who created an Abbie Hoffman–like character named Artie Sternlicht in his radical novel *The*

Book of Daniel. "There is no fiction and no nonfiction as we commonly understand the distinction: there is only narrative," Doctorow asserts in his essay "False Documents." Moreover, he explains, "history is a kind of fiction in which we live and hope to survive, and fiction is a kind of speculative history." Abbie would have agreed. Almost all of Abbie's books, including his unreliable autobiography, *Soon to Be a Major Motion Picture,* are "false documents" in Doctorow's sense of the term. All of them blend fiction and history, news and entertainment.

Moreover, Abbie's dramatic life itself is a "false document": a fabulous story that blurs the line between fact and fiction, reality and fantasy, autobiography and mythology. While it makes for fascinating reading, it also creates nightmares for fact-hungry biographers. After his suicide in April 1989, at the age of 52, the *New Yorker* observed that "Abbie Hoffman led three lives . . . social activist, yippie anarchist and white-collar impostor." By my count he led more than half a dozen lives. Abbie was orphan, imp, outlaw, martyr, patriarch, prodigal son, lost soul, and tragic hero. Moreover, he consciously tried to be Prometheus, Dionysus, Wandering Jew, Ulysses, Faust, Robin Hood, Pied Piper, and Road Warrior. He was like a contemporary incarnation of Proteus, the god who was continually changing his form—who ought to have served as the deity of the sixties, an era of unprecedented transformation and metamorphosis. "The thing about movements is that they move," Abbie explained in an interview with the *East Village Other* in May of 1969, near the apex of the political and cultural movement of the sixties. "That's what a movement does—it moves and if you are a part of a movement, you have to recognize that . . . you and your tactics have to change and at that very rapidly." Like the sixties themselves, Abbie was constantly moving and always in motion, which is why I see him as the quintessential spirit of the era.

Elusive, mercurial, and ambiguous, he was and still is hard to pin down, hard to define. He believed his lack of definition meant he couldn't be co-opted by the "square" culture he wanted to transform. While he was still young and energetic, he seemed capable of changing forever. As he aged, however, he became increasingly locked in habitual gestures, and his inability to give rebirth to himself depressed him. The manic boy wonder turned into a cranky old man.

The first time I saw him, I was on a panel with Susan Sontag at the

Socialist Scholars Conference in New York. It was 1967 and the topic was the moral and political responsibility of intellectuals vis-à-vis the war in Vietnam. Abbie showed up in the audience as a cowboy, firing off a toy cap gun and complaining that in the movement there was too much analysis and too much intellectualizing, and not enough socialism or direct action. The next time I saw him was on the campus of the State University of New York at Stony Brook, where I was an assistant professor of English and American literature. He was again in costume, but this time he was accompanied by Jerry Rubin, his on-again, off-again sidekick during the cultural revolution of the late sixties and early seventies. Abbie and Jerry and a few friends had just created the Youth International Party, better known as the Yippies, a kind of roving anarchist theater group whose antics were designed to make the powers-that-be sit up and pay attention. Driving cars they had made to look like police vehicles, and wearing the uniforms of Keystone cops, Abbie, Jerry, and the Yippies descended on the campus and announced they were looking for drugs. The loony performance was in protest of a drug raid by the Suffolk County Sheriff's Department that had been staged for television to make students look like drug-crazed freaks.

Over the next year or so I saw Abbie several times on the stage of the Fillmore East on the Lower East Side. On one occasion he described how he'd been arrested by the Chicago police, shortly after the riots at the 1968 Democratic National Convention, for carrying a concealed weapon: a penknife. Pacing across the stage, and talking nonstop, he casually tossed the weapon in the air—with blade open—and caught it in his bare hand. On another occasion he appeared onstage wearing a white shirt, tie, and jacket, and explained how he'd evolved from his existence as a mundane salesman for a pharmaceutical supply company in Massachusetts into a bona fide long-haired, pot-smoking hippie in Manhattan. As he talked, he changed his clothes to emphasize the possibilities for change. By the end of the performance he was wearing a T-shirt, jeans, and boots; his long curly hair, which had been carefully held down, was now unruly.

For years we were at the same places at the same times, but so were thousands of others. We were at the March on the Pentagon in October 1967 to protest the war in Vietnam, and we were arrested during the student takeover of Columbia University in April 1968, but we never met. Then, in 1969, I reviewed Hoffman's second book, *Woodstock Nation,* for Liberation News Service, the movement's self-styled answer to the Associated Press. Soon thereafter, Abbie called to say he appreciated my favorable comments.

We finally met face-to-face at the Law Commune, an office of radical attorneys who were defending the Black Panthers, Yippies, and Columbia students who had been arrested for occupying campus buildings to protest the university's discriminatory policies. From time to time we saw one another at political events and parties on the Lower East Side, and at "hip" restaurants like Max's Kansas City in Union Square. We didn't become friends, however, until the winter of 1970, when he was 34 and I was 28. By then the Chicago Conspiracy trial was over, and Abbie was a media celebrity and the movement's male sex symbol, an icon of the revolution. For countless young men who wanted to defy the system and at the same time become famous, Abbie was a flesh-and-blood role model. By then, too, I was no longer a straight-and-narrow academic. I had been arrested and pummeled by a dozen or so New York City policemen after a demonstration to protest the murders of two Chicago Black Panthers, Fred Hampton and Mark Clark, and the *Village Voice* had splashed my picture on the front page with the caption "Moratorium Man Beaten." I'd taken a leave of absence from teaching to write a book about the British empire and British literature, and when I wasn't in the library I was a reporter and activist in the movement. Among other tasks, I carried messages between members of the Weather Underground, who envisioned themselves as armed revolutionaries, and their aboveground contacts, including organizers, journalists, lawyers, family members, and friends.

One afternoon at Macy's I received an envelope and was asked to deliver it to 114 East Thirteenth Street in Manhattan. Under no circumstances was I to engage in conversation with the individual who answered the door. The document was, of course, for Abbie, and I soon learned that it outlined how he might help the underground. It also inadvertently served as a letter of recommendation for me and proof of my radical credentials. As a professor I didn't carry much weight in Abbie's scale of nonconformist values, but as a courier who had access to the underground I was a force to be reckoned with, at least in his eyes. Without a moment's hesitation he invited me into his rooftop apartment, introduced me to his wife, Anita, who was making stuffed mushrooms, and gave me a tour of his clean, cozy rooms. This bourgeois scene was hardly what I would have imagined for the King of the Yippies, but it made me feel more comfortable. Abbie opened the letter and read it, laughing as he did. Then he handed it to me, knowing that he was breaking the underground's rules. Matter-of-factly, Abbie explained that he was the Howard in "Dear Howard." Howard was his alias as well as his real middle name: Abbott Howard Hoffman was his full, legal name. The "Molly" who signed the letter, he told me, was none other than Bernardine Dohrn, a graduate of the University of Chicago who had been a key organizer for both the National Lawyers Guild and Students for a Democratic Society (SDS), the leading radical organization on college campuses in the mid and late sixties. Now Bernie, as Abbie liked to call her, was the leader of the Weather Underground, and her "Wanted" poster appeared in post offices from coast to coast.

Soon after I delivered the letter to Abbie, I not only converted to the irreverent Yippies, but even became the Yippie minister of education. Jerry Rubin, Abbie Hoffman, and I were driving together in the Bronx one day when I suggested that the Youth International Party, as the Yippies were now calling themselves, needed a minister of education and a series of provocative manifestos for students on the subject of schooling. Jerry and Abbie agreed and immediately conferred upon me the title Youth International Party Minister of Education. Wasn't it necessary to conduct a discussion or hold an election by the general membership? I asked. Not at all, they insisted. If I said I was the minister of education, that was good enough—not only for them but for all the Yippies. Soon thereafter I began to define myself as the Yippie minister of education, a title that I took to be part put-on, part real. The straight world took it at face value, and when my book about culture and empire was reviewed in the press, I was described solemnly in the *Times Literary Supplement* as the Minister of Education for the Youth International Party.

For years I had defined myself as a Marxist intellectual. I had assumed that there was a real world, that it was governed by certain immutable, historical laws, and that it could only be changed by a revolution engineered by a disciplined party, a working class, and its allies.

Now, slowly but surely I began to shed my Marxist skin, and to accept the notion that "reality is made up," as Abbie put it: that everything is a fiction. I came to accept the idea that generational rather than class conflict was crucial for historical change, and that cultural rather than political or economic revolution was the key to the transformation of society. Moreover, I accepted the idea that radicals could use the mass media to transform consciousness and change institutions and values. Though these ideas weren't original with Abbie, he popularized and exploited them more effectively than anyone else. For a while in the late sixties and early seventies, his movie—his version of reality—seemed more compelling than anyone else's, not only to me but to an entire generation of young, white men.

Life proved to be a lot more of a lark for me as a Yippie than as a left-wing intellectual. There were games to play on the basketball court and at peace movement meetings. Abbie and I were pals. We watched TV together, made the rounds of law and magazine offices, and schmoozed in bookstores and restaurants. On Saturday mornings we made our weekly pilgrimage to the Luxor Baths and kibitzed with the middle-aged businessmen who were sweating it out in the sauna and the steam room, and who approached Abbie as though he was a Mafia don who could solve their problems. "They ask *me* for advice about their kids," he chortled. "They want *me* to tell them how to keep them in school and off drugs." The irony of the situation delighted him immensely: he was being asked to conspire with the fathers and to bridge the very generation gap that he wanted to widen.

It was the seventies now, but the sixties hadn't ended. We organized antiwar protests, demonstrated in the streets, and marched outside courthouses to demand freedom for the Black Panthers, including Bobby G. Seale, their chairman and cofounder (with Huey P. Newton), who was on trial in New Haven, Connecticut. Abbie and I traveled to Europe together; we met with the French Yippies and with Parisian editors and publishers who were looking for hot American literary properties like Abbie's *Revolution for the Hell of It* and Jerry Rubin's *Do It!*

In Algeria a Yippie delegation that included myself, Abbie's wife Anita, and Bernardine Dohrn's younger sister Jennifer conferred with Timothy Leary and Eldridge Cleaver and tried to create a new, all-encompassing international organization that would harbor Yippies, hippies, Weathermen, and Black Panthers. But there were too many conflicting egos, too many political disagreements, and, much to Abbie's dismay, the megaorganization never got off the ground.

Underground Fiction

For a while we lost track of one another. Then, in the summer of 1973, Abbie was arrested for selling three pounds of cocaine to undercover narcotics agents in Manhattan, and once again we were in cahoots. He had never even hinted that he'd been involved with the cocaine trade, but now that he'd been caught, he wanted me to know that he was guilty and that he needed help. He was desperate to go underground and avoid what he felt would be an embarrassing media trial, conviction, and long prison term. There was nothing for him in prison, he felt, no way to create a new identity for himself. The underground, he insisted, offered the possibility to generate another persona. The Weather people had provided Abbie with fake identification papers, and I helped him rehearse what he thought was going to be his new role: a college professor, an expert on Walt Whitman's erotic poetry. We met in out-of-the-way restaurants in the Village and planned his getaway, where he'd live, and how he'd survive. He was wearing slacks and Harris tweed jackets now, and he'd exchanged his trademark Massachusetts accent for the generic voice of academia. One day at the Bronx Zoo he asked me to contact a lawyer in midtown Manhattan and pick up an envelope containing ten thousand dollars in cash. I remember being impressed that he'd managed to stash away that much money, and when I handed it over, I said good-bye, thinking I'd never see him again.

Then one day in April 1975, he was on the telephone with me again as though he'd never been away. He was in Los Angeles. I was on my way to Mexico City to write a book about B. Traven, the German anarchist who settled in Mexico in the 1920s, where he wrote a number of books, the best known of which is *The Treasure of the Sierra Madre*. We met at a hotel near the L.A. airport, and the first thing Abbie did was to lift his T-shirt and urge me to hit him in the stomach as hard as I could, an offer I easily declined. He was Barry now: he was physically fit and working as a Hollywood screenwriter and producer about to make his first blockbuster movie. That afternoon, Ken Kelley, a former underground newspaper editor who was now working for *Playboy,* interviewed Abbie about his underground adventures. We watched on television as helicopters lifted frantic survivors from the roof of the American Embassy in Saigon and drank champagne to celebrate the end of the war in Vietnam, which had seemed so endless that it had come to define our lives.

Abbie explained that he'd had an operation for hemorrhoids and was in a great deal of physical pain. Indeed, he was unable to sit down, even on a toilet, and much to my alarm he was popping pills and snorting cocaine. He claimed to have sold the idea for a movie about two fugitives, a Black Panther and a Yippie, who travel incognito down the Mississippi River to New Orleans, and from there to Havana and Fidel Castro's protection. The story sounded a lot like Mark Twain's classic American novel with Abbie as Huck Finn and Huey Newton as Jim, but Abbie had added his own upbeat ending: his fugitives would join a Cuban baseball team and defeat the New York Yankees in Yankee Stadium. In the film's last scene, the governor would pardon them. It was the kind of resolution he hoped to write for his own problems with the law.

It was hard to tell how much he was acting and how much he was for real, but he seemed to be in much psychic pain brought on by the death of his father, John. His grief took me by surprise. For as long as I'd known him, he'd spoken of his father as though he was the enemy: the epitome of blind authority and the stereotype of the raging bull. Now he was expressing a sense of loss for his dearly beloved "Papa." He was angry that he'd been unable to attend his father's funeral in Worcester; if he had gone, he'd have been arrested. Agents from the Federal Bureau of Investigation (FBI) had swarmed all over the synagogue, expecting him to put in an appearance and hoping to arrest him. He had known his father was going to die, so he'd packed a "funeral suit," as he called it, and schlepped it across the underground. As though to prove the depths of his devotion, he flung open the doors to the closet, and pointed to the rather ordinary-looking suit he would have worn. When the news of his father's death finally arrived, it was too late to go home, he explained. No one in his family had bothered to tell him in time. Even worse, his father's brothers were blaming him for John's fatal heart attack. If only he hadn't been busted for cocaine, they were saying. If only he hadn't gone underground and broken his poor father's heart.

The underground had become a prison for Abbie, but it was also a playground. He explained that he had recently remarried and showed me photos of what looked like a wedding ceremony. He said that since he hadn't divorced Anita he was now a "monogamous bigamist." I could see that the idea tickled him tremendously, and he liked the idea, too, that his new wife had met him and fallen in love with him as "Barry," the pauper of the underground, rather than with Abbie, the prince of the sixties. Once again he was telling tall tales. His wife's code name was "Jane," but her real name was Johanna Lawrenson, and not only was she was a shiksa, he said, but a world-class model whom he'd spotted and fallen in love with on a fashion runway in Mexico City.

Abbie often made Johanna out to be apolitical and anti-intellectual, but that wasn't the case. She had been raised in a highly intellectual and very political family, and much of that background and breeding showed. Her father, Jack Lawrenson, had been a Communist and a leading trade union organizer in the thirties and forties, and she identified with the workers of the world. Her mother, Helen, whom Abbie had met under his alias, wrote for *Esquire* and *Vanity Fair* and had made a reputation for herself on the basis of two articles, "Latins Make Lousy Lovers" and "In Defense of the American Gigolo." It had been a difficult act for Johanna to follow, but by living on the lam with Abbie, she was doing her best to emulate her legendary mother. When I met Johanna on the way to Las Vegas, I felt that I had as much in common with her as with Abbie since, like me, she'd grown up in the culture of the Old Left during the heyday of McCarthyism in the fifties. She had grown up feeling un-American, while Abbie had been an all-American kid in an all-American family, playing sports and collecting trophies. But now, in the underground, Abbie had adopted a new family and embraced a new set of parents. He wasn't a Hoffman anymore but a Lawrenson, and he was thrilled to belong to a family of communists and bohemians, literary and political celebrities.

In the neon world of Las Vegas, mild-mannered Barry vanished and flashy Abbie came alive again. At the Hilton Hotel he registered under a pseudonym, and after settling in our suite, we took a sauna in the basement, "just like old times at the Luxor Hotel," he said. But before we could work up a sweat, Abbie vanished, and by the time I caught up with him, he was back in the room, fully dressed. He was standing as though paralyzed, holding suitcases in both hands. He had been recognized in the sauna, he insisted, and it would only be a matter of time before the police arrived to arrest him. It didn't do any good to tell him that we had been alone in the sauna. His mind was made up: he had to get out. When Johanna returned from her own sauna, we made plans to escape from the police, whether they were coming or simply a figment of Abbie's paranoid imagination. The situation might have been hilariously funny, but instead it was terribly frightening. I used a pay phone in the lobby (since the phone in the room was undoubtedly tapped) and spoke to one of Abbie's lawyers, who promised to send reinforcements. Then I went back to the room and began to load the luggage into the van. Abbie was talking nonstop now, but I didn't understand what he was saying or what he meant to say. It was all hieroglyphics.

The last night in the hotel he became violent and menacing. He slapped me across the face, and my glasses flew across the room. Then he whacked Johanna across her face and pulled her hair so hard that she screamed. We held him down in the bed, and Johanna tried to soothe him, but he tossed us off his back, then dashed out of the room in his underwear and a T-shirt, screaming "I'm Abbie Hoffman! I'm Abbie Hoffman!" A few guests in the hall heard him, but no one seemed to care. It didn't matter to me whether he was for real or acting, crazy or sane. I wanted out. I don't think that Johanna ever forgave me for leaving her with Abbie, but I had my own life to save. I grabbed my suitcase, took a cab to the airport, and flew to Mexico City, pausing only long enough to leave my address and to have Johanna write down their address and phone number in Teopotzlán, a small village not far from Cuernavaca. I remember thinking that Abbie had taken an immense fall from his triumphant days. His behavior was aberrant and deranged. It was also reminiscent of other sixties figures—such as Tom Hayden, Jerry Rubin, and Rennie Davis—who had lost their way now that the revolution was over.

Three weeks later, I met up with Abbie again. Only this time he was a different person: apologetic, polite, and anxious to be my friend. He was speaking Spanish as much as English. He'd turned into just another North American tourist who had fallen in love with Mexico. What he wanted to tell me most of all was that the incident in Las Vegas would never, could never, happen again. He had it all under control now. He had it all figured out: he had cracked up at the very moment that the American Empire was falling apart in Vietnam. It didn't make sense to me, but it did to him. For years, he said, he'd been preoccupied with the war, and now that it had ended, his own identity had come unraveled. He had allowed himself to go crazy, and in going crazy he had regained his sanity, or so he insisted. Shouting out his real name was self-destructive, he admitted. It was as though he *wanted* to be recognized, apprehended, and incarcerated so that he could escape from his fugitive life. I could see his argument, of course, but to me what seemed apparent was his inability to adapt to the underground and to the undramatic life of the seventies. He wanted to be Abbie Hoffman, the media personality and the star of the sixties, all over again. Though he'd changed his name and his appearance, he'd been unable to make more fundamental changes in his personality, and that was sad. It also seemed to me that crying out his name had been an existential act of defiance and rebellion, a refusal to play by the rules of the fugitive game, even if it meant that he'd be captured. He was *Abbie Hoffman.* He wasn't going to deny his name or his identity. He wasn't going to shut up, be invisible, remain anonymous. Years later he appeared on the TV show *20/20* with Barbara Walters and described the crack-up in Las Vegas as "the most painful thing in my life." He persuaded me to go on TV, too, and describe the incident. Soon Las Vegas became an archetypal place in the odyssey of Abbie Hoffman: a place of ultimate pain, but also a place where he'd made a crazy declaration of his own independence.

Abbie and I spent time together in Mexico and in California in the mid- and late seventies. In Mexico we visited landmarks of the revolution and milestones in the life of Emiliano Zapata. We wandered through the labyrinth of Mexico City, visited museums to see the work of Diego Rivera and Frida Kahlo, explored ancient ruins, and drove to small towns in the countryside. We played at being exiles and gringos, hungry for new food, new landscapes, a new culture. There was a constant stream of visitors from the United States, most of them sixties people, and more often than not it was the sixties that we talked about.

Abbie was also writing about the sixties in his autobiography, which had the working title "Kiss and Tell." I watched him as he created a "false document" about his own life, and I was fascinated. I listened to him talk about himself, then read chapters in which he exaggerated, aggrandized, and embellished on his activities—for example, in the civil rights movement in the South. Anxious to get to the truth of the matter, I interviewed him. When he was growing up, were his parents middle-class? I wanted to know. "Ruling-class," he said, smirking. "How many cars did your parents have?" I asked. "Too many," he said, without missing a beat. His answers to my questions about his background and his past were almost always ambiguous and playful. When he insisted that he was now living a working-class life, I pointed out that he had an apartment in Mexico City and a large house with a swimming pool and horses in the countryside. Wasn't that rather aristocratic? I asked, only to learn that I'd hurt his feelings.

It was a transitional time for Abbie. Little by little, he began to see how he could use the underground to break into new territory. Inspired by B. Traven, whom he called "the world's greatest fugitive" and "the best working-class writer that ever lived," he created his own fugitive personae. Traven had taken other names and other identities, including T. Torsvan, the Norwegian anthropologist, and Hal Croves, the American literary agent. Abbie took the names and identities of Barry Freed and Howard Samuels, among others, and began to develop a career for himself as a political activist.

He also began to write articles about his adventures in the underground—such as his trip to Los Alamos, the birthplace of the atomic bomb—that were part fiction, part nonfiction, though he no longer seemed able to tell the difference. In 1976 I moved to California and kept in touch with Abbie by mail. Later he and Johanna stayed briefly in San Francisco at the home of Paul Kantner of the Jefferson Starship, then, in the winter of 1979–80, moved into my house in Sonoma County. Abbie was finishing his autobiography and preparing to turn himself in to the authorities. I learned that a psychiatrist had diagnosed him as suffering from manic-depressive illness and that he was taking lithium for his mood swings, but I'd long observed that he could be down as well as up, so the medical terms didn't mean much to me. I remember a conversation about the eighties that suggested the distance between us. Abbie thought that the decade ahead was going to be a replay of the sixties, but I foresaw years of conservatism. Soon he was accusing me of cynicism, and I was accusing him of hiding from his own despair. He was happy, he said, and showed me a treatment for a movie about himself and Johanna, which he insisted was "completely true to life," though almost none of it was. He was Billy. She was Sally. They were ecowarriors in love and on the run from the FBI. In the proverbial nick of time they would elude the dragnet and escape to Hollywood, where they would sign a contract for a blockbuster romantic comedy about themselves, then literally walk into the sunset and live happily ever after.

As it turned out, the eighties weren't very funny or romantic for Abbie, though he put up a good front and insisted in public that they were better than the sixties. His story definitely didn't have the conventional happy ending. In April 1989, when I heard the news that he had committed suicide, I had the strange feeling that he had cried out one last time, *"I'm Abbie Hoffman!"* and that his cry exuded not only the optimism and joy of the sixties but also its darkness and despair. His suicide by a drug overdose surprised me but also seemed a fitting way for him to die, much as Huey Newton's death by an assassin's bullet in the streets of Oakland later that year seemed also appropriate, given the violence of his life. For years Abbie had talked about committing "revolutionary suicide"—consciously borrowing the phrase from Newton— of dying on the barricades in battle against the system. But he was never a violent revolutionary, and most of his political and cultural confrontations with the system were symbolic. I remembered that in Mexico in 1975, Abbie had borrowed *The March to the Montería,* one of B. Traven's proletarian novels, and when he finished it had explained that he wanted to exercise the ultimate power, which to him meant choosing "the moment to die."

I was disappointed that his family members denied the clear evidence of his suicide. "They found no drugs around him," his 83-year-old mother, Florence, told reporters from the home in Worcester, Massachusetts, where Abbie had been raised. "I think suicide may be ruled out," she added. Florence's youngest son, Jack, explained to the media that Abbie had merely been "careless with pills." His death was an accident, not a deliberate, willful act, Jack insisted. Many radicals from the sixties were also in denial about Abbie's death, reflecting the movement's failure to confront grief, acknowledge personal tragedy, and accept loss. Dave Dellinger, a pacifist and one of Abbie's codefendants at the Chicago Conspiracy trial, told the *New York Times,* "I don't believe for one moment the suicide thing." No suicide note had been found, Dellinger pointed out. But to Jerry Rubin the absence of a note was entirely in character. It was, Rubin suggested, a way of "making a statement and stirring discussion through the mystery." Many people were determined to create a murder mystery about Abbie's death. Others found the notion that he might have been murdered enticing. "Who or what killed Abbie?" Bruce McCabe asked in an article entitled "Why did Abbie Hoffman die?" that appeared in the *Boston Globe* and gave rise to far-fetched speculations about his death.

From my perspective there was little if anything that was mysterious about Abbie's suicide. The big question wasn't why he died, but why he had lived. Who, in fact, *was* the man who cried "I'm Abbie Hoffman!"? What did his life have to say about the life of the sixties and sixties people? Were we really self-destructive and suicidal? This book is an attempt to answer those questions. I have drawn on my own memories, recollections, and interviews with Abbie, but this book is also based on over 250 interviews with Abbie's friends, comrades, and family members as well as on FBI files, public documents, newspaper accounts, court records, letters, and TV and radio broadcasts. *For the Hell of It* is Abbie's biography, but I have also viewed it as a historical interpretation of the times. In that sense it is a contribution to what Tom Hayden described in his memoir, *Reunion,* as "an ongoing struggle today to define the sixties," an enterprise that has now been highly contested for three decades.

While Abbie appears in documentary films about the era, and while Abbie and Abbie-like characters have appeared in Hollywood films (such as *The Big Fix* [1978], in which F. Murray Abraham plays "Abbie"), Abbie the historical figure has been largely omitted from books about the sixties. For example, Todd Gitlin's *The Sixties: Years of Hope, Days of Rage* unfairly lumps Abbie together with Jerry Rubin and does both of them a disservice by describing them as "public nuisances." The neglect of Abbie is unfortunate but understandable. As the American historian and civil rights activist Staughton Lynd observed in an inter-

view with me, "sixties history tends to get written as the history of
Students for a Democratic Society [SDS] and the Student Nonviolent
Coordinating Committee [SNCC], and since Abbie was never a mover
or a shaker in SDS or SNCC, that made him prima facie left out." By
focusing on organizations like SDS and SNCC, the historians of the
sixties often make the activism of the era seem much better organized
and more carefully directed by political leaders than it really was. Focusing on Abbie reveals the sixties as a rough-and-tumble era that was
messy, unpredictable, wildly imaginative, and more than a little bit
crazy. Focusing on Abbie also shows that certain individuals really did
alter the course of history.

In his biography of Hoffman, Martin ("Marty") Jezer, a long-time
sixties pacifist, observes that "Abbie played the youth revolt like a mae-
stro, pitting the hip counterculture against the straight mainstream culture with spectacular effect." He goes on, however, to note that "cultural issues . . . are always explosive" and that "Abbie's Yippie years are
a warning against fighting political battles on cultural turf." But criticizing Abbie Hoffman for waging cultural warfare when he should have
engaged in political campaigning is like criticizing a leopard for having
spots, or a fish for swimming in water. Cultural revolution is what
Abbie Hoffman did best, and cultural rather than political or economic
revolution was what the sixties were largely about. Granted, sixties protest resulted in profound social change. It ended legal segregation in the
South, gave birth to contemporary feminism, and together with an international protest movement helped end the war in Vietnam. But the
sixties did not bring about the fundamental redistribution of power or
wealth achieved in other revolutions, whether in France, China, Russia,
or eighteenth-century America.

The sixties did usher in revolutionary changes in the ways we think
about the world and about ourselves: black and white, male and female,
gay and straight, Anglo and Latino, working-class and ruling-class.
Abbie was a major figure in that revolution in consciousness. As John
Simon, one of his editors at Random House, observed, "Abbie knew
that once you got into peoples' heads, you could change their minds."
The sixties were mind-blowing, as we used to say. They made revolution a popular idea again in a society that had come to think of revolution as something to be feared and destroyed—something un-

American. Abbie helped to recapture the word and the concept of revolution. Why not have a revolution that was not for peace, bread, and land or for liberty and equality, but was a revolution that Americans could understand and take part in, a revolution of the sixties, by the sixties, and for the sixties: a revolution just for the hell of it.

chapter one

BAD BEHAVIOR

The Rebels

Abbie Hoffman belongs to a distinct generation of American radicals born in the mid- to late thirties who became synonymous with rebellion and insurrection, feminism and black power, and the antiwar and youth movements of the sixties. Abbie was born in 1936, the same year as Bobby Seale of the Black Panthers. Gloria Steinem was born in 1934, Eldridge Cleaver in 1935, Jerry Rubin in 1938, and Tom Hayden in 1939.

Unlike a great many of the radicals of the twenties and thirties, Abbie's generation had little if any direct experience with crushing poverty, no memories of Europe, and none of the cultural and psychological dislocation associated with the immigrant experience. Abbie Hoffman, Jerry Rubin, Tom Hayden, and Gloria Steinem grew up with American values in the midst of unprecedented America prosperity. While they were old enough to be aware of the Cold War and McCarthyism, it was the cultural vacuity of middle-class society more than direct political repression or economic deprivation that informed their rebellion.

Abbie described the emptiness of this world in an essay entitled "Thorns of the Flower Children," which was published in *Woodstock Nation* (1969). There was a common experience for young people, he explained. The sons and daughters "saw their fathers disappear behind the corn flakes box and hurry off to his other life in a distant land called DOWNTOWN. . . . They heard from their mothers over and over again about being *respectable* and *responsible* and, above all, *reason-*

able. . . . They monopolized the TV set with Bob Hope, baseball games, situation comedies about people like them and of course Ed Sullivan. They liked to 'keep up' so they read *Time* Magazine and the N. Y. *Times* on Sunday. . . . If there ever was a Desolation Row it climbed into the front seat of the Oldsmobile on Monday morning, checked its passport and headed DOWNTOWN."

Abbie's generation shared much the same cultural experience with the generation that was born after World War II and that came to be known as the baby boomers, but his was a transitional generation. Though they were supposed to belong to the "silent generation," they began to speak up by the time they reached college. Moreover, though they came a decade or so after the Beats, they were still young enough in age and close enough in spirit to appreciate the Beat movement first-hand. Then, too, most of them were shaped directly and profoundly by existentialism—by the notion that they could choose not to collaborate with the system of oppression and could instead become self-conscious rebels. Though Abbie and his contemporaries weren't the cultural and political fathers and mothers of the sixties, they were certainly the older brothers and sisters of the decade of defiance. They paved the way for the full-fledged rebellion of the baby boomers.

They grew up in the North and in the South, in black neighborhoods and white neighborhoods, in working-class and middle-class families, with Catholic, Jewish, and Protestant parents. The common denominator wasn't race, class, geography, or religion but a moment in history when the Pax Americana broke down, and when the underlying realities of the society—poverty, racism, and spiritual impoverishment—emerged from behind the facade of material comfort, family togetherness, and glib happiness. They came, for the most part, from the big cities and urban centers of New York, Little Rock, Dallas, and Cincinnati, but they came as well from towns like Royal Oak, Michigan; White Fish Bay, Wisconsin; and Worcester, Massachusetts. Some of their notable contemporaries in the worlds of entertainment, literature, and film included Elvis Presley, Ken Kesey, Thomas Pynchon, Jack Nicholson, and Francis Ford Coppola—all of whom were rebels, mavericks, and outsiders who translated their idiosyncratic styles and defiant stances into establishment success. They helped to create a popular culture that defied the old Hollywood system, the music industry, and the literary elite, but their dissident images became a part of the very system they confronted. They were rebellious, yet they belonged to the world of privilege. They celebrated the common woman and the common man, but they themselves were uncommon celebrities. Abbie shared the ability to make rebellion an acceptable—almost an obligatory—part of mainstream culture. In a world of competing media icons, he fashioned himself into a genuine icon of the American revolutionary.

In the late sixties, Abbie liked to say that he had been born in 1960—at the precise moment that the era of the sixties was born—and that he had been abandoned by a culture that had turned its back on its own children. Years later, he liked to say that he had been reborn in 1980, when he returned from the underground to begin a new life at the start of a new decade. The new, the timely, and the contemporary counted heavily in his scheme of things, and he continually aimed to give rebirth to himself, but there was also something old-fashioned about him. For all his rebellion and nonconformity, he was patriarchal, conservative, and respectful of traditional ways and family togetherness. Though he had a strong nihilistic streak and an apocalyptic imagination, he also had, paradoxically, a profound longing to venerate the past, and an impulse to preserve and to maintain the world as it was. Having roots was essential.

He satirized Worcester, his birthplace and his hometown; among friends he called it the city of "seven hills and no thrills," a cultural wasteland that was "half way between Boston and nowhere." But he also loved Worcester and clung to it tenaciously. Until 1966, when he turned 30, it was at the heart of his universe. When he went away to college, it was to Brandeis in nearby Waltham, Massachusetts: so close he often went home for weekends.

Abbie rebelled against his parents, but he visited them and maintained close contact with relatives and friends from the neighborhood. From 1960 to 1966, when he and his first wife, Sheila Karklin, lived in Worcester, they lived only a short distance from the home in which he had been raised, where his parents still lived. After he left Worcester in 1966 and settled in New York, his hometown remained a haven, and he visited there repeatedly. Even when he was a fugitive in the seventies, he slipped back into town, ate at his favorite restaurant, El Morocco, and visited old friends. The old saw "you can't go home again" simply didn't apply to Abbie. "I've never left Worcester," he told reporter Kristen Duran in 1987. That was part of the mythology he disseminated about himself. Long after he had become internationally famous, he still wanted to be thought of as the local kid who'd made good in the big world. He had, of course, moved away from Worcester, but he had taken his hometown with him. Worcester provided him with his view of society and his way of dealing with the world.

Born Troublemaker

There was nothing extraordinary about the circumstances of Abbie's birth on November 30, 1936, but over the years he created a mystique about them. After all, he was a hero, and his birth had to have heroic reverberations. He had been born a troublemaker, he insisted. He had arrived in the world, he explained to Duran, "half way between the gun factory and the circus," which seemed chosen by fate to be "exactly the right place" for a future antiwar activist opposed to weapons of destruction and a countercultural clown who made all the world his circus. In *Revolution for the Hell of It* he boasted, with characteristic hyperbole, that "as far as the revolution goes it started when I was born."

In his autobiography, Abbie suggested that his Russian ancestors had been revolutionaries and that he had inherited "traces of Bolshevik blood." But this was more fantasy than fact; there is no clear evidence of any family member who took part in the Russian revolutions of 1905 or 1917. Although his grandparents had emigrated from Russia, they had not been revolutionaries. His parents, John and Florence Hoffman, steered clear of radicalism and avoided the major left-wing organizations of the day, including the Socialist and Communist Parties, which claimed the loyalties of so many European working-class Jews who had fled to America in the late nineteenth and early twentieth centuries. John and Florence embraced the values of Main Street, and they expected their three children—Abbie, the oldest; Jack, the middle child, born in 1939; and Phyllis, the youngest, born in 1941—to work hard, honor their parents, and never bring public disgrace or scandal to the family.

If radicalism wasn't in Abbie's blood, as he claimed, it wasn't spawned by poverty, either: the Hoffmans were upwardly mobile and solidly middle class. Nor was it engendered by ethnic discrimination, although there was anti-Semitism in Worcester: a great many of the Irish Catholic kids who grew up and went to school with Abbie believed that Jews were rich and that they controlled the political life of the city. As a child, Abbie felt self-conscious about his Jewishness among so many Catholic schoolmates, and occasionally he even tried to pass for a Catholic. But while his uncles had had to defend themselves against physical attack from Irish and Italian kids, he was never menaced or assaulted because of his Jewish identity.

His mother, Florence, noted that he was "a difficult child to bring up": he was intensely jealous of, and often hostile toward, his younger brother Jack, and as a child he had few friends. His father, John—known to friends and family members as Johnnie—described him as "Hell unleashed," and while he derived a modicum of pleasure from his son's rambunctiousness, he was also disturbed by it. Johnnie simply couldn't understand Abbott, as he called him, because he went against everything Johnnie stood for. Johnnie had grown up hungry; Abbott's plate was full every night of the week, yet he often refused, perversely (it seemed), to eat anything. Johnnie repeatedly banished him to his room as punishment, and Abbie continually refused to knuckle under.

Very early in life Abbie expressed an almost instinctive dislike of "blind authority" and showed a penchant for causing trouble. To his parents, he was "the ultimate in Jewish nightmares" (or so he liked to think): the firstborn son who wouldn't obey the rules or follow the blueprint for his own preordained success. Johnnie Hoffman had done his lifelong best to stay out of trouble and out of the public eye. Notoriety was the last thing he wanted. Given the anticommunist crusade of the day, it's not surprising that he rarely spoke of his own birth in Russia shortly after the failed revolution of 1905, and Abbie grew up in the dark about his own family history. It was only when he was writing his autobiography in the seventies that he began to learn the history of the Hoffmans, and by then a great many memories had been lost and replaced by mythologies.

He was then told that in nineteenth-century Russia the Hoffmans had gone by the name Shapoznikoff, and that they had been lower-middle-class shopkeepers who were unhappy under the czar's repressive regime and anxious to migrate to America. Jacob Shapoznikoff, one of Johnnie's uncles, purchased or perhaps purloined (the details in the "family mythology," as Abbie called it, are sketchy) the papers of a German named Hoffman and became the first member of the family to reach America. Abbie, of course, was delighted by this tale of an ancestor who had taken on a different name and identity and had traveled under false documents.

In disguise and under the name Jacob Hoffman, Abbie's grandfather had traveled via Siberia and Japan to California and then to New York, where he sent word to the rest of the family to follow him to the promised land. Morris and Anna Shapoznikoff, Abbie's grandparents on his father's side, came to America about 1910, settling first in Malden, near Boston, and then in Worcester, which was then and still is the second largest city in the state. An industrial and manufacturing city in the late nineteenth century, with a population drawn from all across Europe, Worcester was home to a large community of Polish and Russian Jews, and it could boast a dozen or so thriving Orthodox synagogues—a major attraction for the Shapoznikoff-Hoffmans.

Worcester itself had a remarkable past that Abbie knew little about. Founded in the early eighteenth century, it became a center of the antislavery and feminist movements in the mid–nineteenth century. Henry David Thoreau spoke there in defense of John Brown and his raid at Harper's Ferry. Emma Goldman and Alexander Berkman, the celebrated anarchists, made Worcester a brief refuge several decades later, and there were vigorous socialist and trade union movements. Eugene V. Debs spoke in Worcester, and so did Sigmund Freud. The city was hardly provincial.

Indeed, it was "zippy and exhilarating," Samuel N. Behrman wrote in *The Worcester Account,* a chronicle of his early years. Behrman, who was born in Worcester in 1893 and went on to become a successful Broadway playwright, Hollywood screenwriter, and contributor to the *New Yorker,* was—until Abbie's rise to fame in the sixties—Worcester's most famous native son. Abbie's grandfather, Morris Hoffman, had, however, known little if anything about the "zippy and exhilarating" world of Worcester. A street peddler who sold fruits and vegetables from a horse-drawn cart, he later became the proprietor of a small candy store, where he kept his eyes on the cash register, not on cultural improvements or the lecture circuit.

Like their Russian ancestors, the American Hoffmans were lower middle class, but they worked hard, saved their money, and planned for a better life for their children. At home they spoke Yiddish, which Abbie called "the language of survival . . . half insults, half complaints," but they mastered English, learned their civic lessons, became American citizens, and bought into the American dream. By his own report, Johnnie Hoffman was a devoted son, a diligent student, and a hard worker who made sure to contribute his meager earnings as a newspaper-delivery boy to "the family pot." Like his son Abbie, Johnnie had a flair for storytelling and mythmaking, and in his own telling of the tale he was a Horatio Alger figure who climbed the ladder of success, rising from ghetto rags to suburban riches through sheer perseverance.

After high school Johnnie attended the Franklin Institute of Pharmacy in Boston and then worked in an uncle's drug store in Worcester, hoping to be taken in as a partner or to inherit the business. When the uncle died and Johnnie was read out of the will, he was resentful, or so Abbie claimed. He started his own business, the Worcester Pharmaceutical Supply Company, and made a good living selling "bedpans, Band-Aids and barbiturates in bulk" to doctors and hospitals and to the medical facilities in the city's booming factories.

A mainstay in the Reform congregation at Temple Emanuel, Johnnie belonged to the rabbi's Sunday Ayem Breakfast Club and to the Worcester lodge of B'nai B'rith and served on the Board of Directors at the Jewish Home for the Aged. In spite of his well-defined position within the Jewish community, there was a certain ambiguity about his identity beyond the synagogue and the social milieu of the Jews. When he attended Holy Cross football games, he blended in with the Catholic crowd. Abbie also remembered that his father would conveniently deny being a Jew at resorts that didn't accept Jews.

Johnnie wanted to be embraced by Gentiles and to move freely in their world, so he joined the Worcester Rotary Club and other like-minded civic organizations. In the world of electoral politics he was clearly uncomfortable, and he rarely discussed his beliefs or his party affiliations. The subject of politics was as taboo as sex or money. If in the fifties Johnnie was a Republican, as Abbie suspected, it wasn't because of a strong ideological identification with the party of big business and anticommunism, but because he thought that voting for Eisenhower and Nixon would be good for his own business and for the well-being of his family. Abbie's mother, Florence, was even less comfortable than her husband in the political waters of the fifties, and like many women of her generation she voted exactly as her husband told her to vote.

Florence and Johnnie were "two different kinds of people," as she put it. She was a "homebody," content to make an evening with her husband and children in the living room, while Johnnie was a mixer and a joiner, anxious to have a drink in town and to schmooze with friends. In Abbie's view, Florence was affirmative and validating, while Johnnie was negative and denigrating. Florence built him up; Johnnie knocked him down.

In fact, by almost all the reports, including Abbie's, Johnnie consistently beat him—whipped him, punched him, belted him—and, according to his brother Jack, once "threw us both down the stairs." The constant beating at the hands of his father was, it seems to me, the single most important experience of his childhood. In his autobiography Abbie noted that his relationship with his father was "one continuous, raging battle, with me refusing to cry and him huffing and puffing. . . . After a few years, I learned that dungarees absorbed all the whammy out of a whipping." Still, the beatings must have hurt. When he turned fifty, a young filmmaker named Nancy Cohen, in her film *My Dinner with Abbie* (1989), asked him whether he had raised his own children— Andrew, Amy, and america—differently from the way he'd been raised. "I don't kick the shit out of them," he replied with bitterness.

Alice Miller, the German psychologist who has studied the "roots of violence," argues that a child who is beaten will very likely turn into an authoritarian adult. This certainly wasn't the case with Abbie. If anything, physical abuse seems to have made him more rebellious. Sam Keen, a psychologist and author of the best-selling book *Fire in the Belly,* claims in *Hymns to an Unknown God* that "a man beaten as a child forms his body into a permanent stance of cringing or defiance," but that description doesn't do Abbie justice either. He certainly didn't cringe, and while he did adopt a stance of defiance, he did so with a sense of humor and flexibility. What Abbie's beatings taught him was how to taunt authority figures, how to provoke them into rage so that they overreacted. Then he could sit back and point out how irrational and unethical they were.

His mother's ancestors, the Schanbergs, were Orthodox Jews from Austria, but Florence was born in Clinton, Massachusetts, and her American birth gave her an edge that her Russian-born husband didn't have. Florence had nothing to prove, whereas Johnnie always had to show how good he was, that he was an American and one of the guys. To Abbie, the Schanbergs and the Hoffmans seemed a study in contrasts: the Hoffmans were of the old world, the Schanbergs of the new; the Hoffmans were serious, the Schanbergs fun-loving. The world at large seemed an even bigger study in contrasts: there were Orthodox Jews and Reform Jews, preppies and greasers, outsiders and insiders, New England Yankees and everyone else. Growing up in Worcester meant straddling different worlds, cutting across different cultures and ethnic groups.

As a young woman, Florence Schanberg had followed an unconventional path that was opposite the beaten trail that her hard-working husband had taken. Florence was playful: she was an avid gymnast and an adept performer, and in the early thirties she traveled throughout the Northeast to compete. Once she watched and listened in stunned silence as a group of German gymnasts shouted "Heil Hitler!" "I didn't know what to do," she told reporter Fred Bernstein, who included his interview with her in a book entitled *The Jewish Mothers' Hall of Fame*, "so I just left."

Florence lived briefly in New York City, rooming at the YWCA while working as a bookkeeper and secretary, but the pace of life in Manhattan was too hectic for her, and she returned home. Family legend has it that she met Johnnie Hoffman, who was younger than she, at a bowling alley in Worcester. She fell in love with him—though neither he nor she was comfortable using words like "love"—and they were married on October 21, 1934, in the middle of the Depression.

According to Florence, she named her son Abbie after her brother Abraham (Abie) Schanberg, who had died from injuries sustained in an automobile crash on the Massachusetts Turnpike while en route to Boston to buy a diamond ring for his fiancée. Abbie knew, of course, the story of his uncle's tragic death, but he doesn't seem to have been moved by it. In his autobiography, for example, he describes his namesake Abraham simply as "One of my mother's brothers." He was haunted, however, by the story of his Aunt Rose, Abraham's sister— "Crazy Rose," Abbie called her. Rose had been a student at Middlesex

Medical College but had a nervous breakdown when she heard the news about her brother's death. Institutionalized at Worcester State Hospital, she was given a frontal lobotomy, then came home, never to realize her dream of becoming a doctor. Aunt Rose was a living reminder to Abbie of human frailty and the thin line separating sanity from insanity.

As Abbie grew up, the family moved up in the world, literally as well as figuratively, from a small apartment at 264 Chandler Street to a larger apartment at 5 Geneva, and then to a comfortable house of their own at 6 Ruth Street, with each home higher than the previous one in the hills of Worcester. Like the Hoffmans, most of the other Jewish families also moved up the social ladder in the forties and fifties, from the working and lower middle classes to the middle- and upper-middle-class ranks. Like many of the middle-class Jews of Worcester, the Hoffmans attended Temple Emanuel, the most popular synagogue in the city. A red-brick building with stately white pillars, it looked then and now like it was trying to pass for a Yankee institution, just as many of the Jews were trying to assimilate into American life. This assimilationism disturbed Abbie as a young boy. "Slowly, my parents got sucked into the social melting pot, where they were to simmer uncomfortably for the next thirty years," he wrote in his autobiography.

Johnnie and Florence insisted that their son attend synagogue, and though he didn't like the idea, he went along with the scenario. In 1949, on his thirteenth birthday, he was bar mitzvahed in Temple Emanuel. The ceremony went smoothly, much to the family's delight, and afterward he posed for photos with Anna and Morris, looking like a near-perfect bar mitzvah boy in his suit and tie.

For the most part, Abbie's boyhood was untroubled by war, poverty, social injustice, or political upheaval. His own family life was often stormy—the beatings were certainly painful—but he grew up in a social environment that was relatively tranquil. Decades later, he would define himself as a child of the atomic age. "The world really began for us on March 6, 1945," he would say, using the collective "us" to describe the postnuclear generation of baby boomers with whom he would identify. Though he was nine years old at the time and mature enough to grasp the significance of Hiroshima and Nagasaki, the dropping of atomic weapons on Japan didn't impinge on his boyhood world or his youthful imagination, and neither did the concentration camps at Auschwitz and Buchenwald.

As an adult he would resent the fact that neither his teachers nor his parents had told him of the trial and execution in 1953 of Julius and Ethel Rosenberg as atomic spies for the Soviet Union. He was incensed, too, that no one had told him about the mob lynchings of black men in the South, which took place as late as the fifties, or about the "race riots" by blacks in the forties to protest segregation and inequality. Nor had his textbooks mentioned the extermination of Native Americans, though he had been taught everything there was to know about the historic battles of the American Revolution at nearby Lexington and Concord.

His battles with his father aside, he seemed to grow up happy and carefree, perhaps as happy and as free as an American boy could be in the forties and fifties. "There will never be a time like the late Forties," he wrote in a 1971 article for *Esquire* entitled "Yo-Yo Power!" Indeed, it was an extraordinary historical moment to be a middle-class, white man-child, when the troubles of the world could be shut out, and when all the world seemed to be contained on the baseball diamond or at the park. He played baseball, football, tennis, basketball, and Ping-Pong. He bowled, roller-skated, and became a yo-yo champion, performing all the tricks, from cat's cradle and skin-the-cat to shoot-the moon and monkey-on-a-pole. With Johnnie he went fishing and to Fenway Park and the Boston Garden to watch the Red Sox and the Celtics, bringing home photos of his athletic heroes, which he put up on the walls of his bedroom. When Babe Ruth died in 1949, Abbie thought the world would never be the same.

Abbie often seemed to be the epitome of the nice Jewish boy. He sang in the glee club, took dancing lessons, learned the fox-trot and the waltz, and at social gatherings was a latter-day version of Little Lord Fauntleroy. That is precisely his persona in many of the family photos from the mid-forties. In a white shirt and tie, a neatly folded handkerchief poking out of the pocket of his jacket, and his hair combed across his forehead, he looks like a perfect young gentleman. But Abbie was also moody and introverted. He would disappear behind the locked door of his bedroom with a stack of library books—to read, his mother assumed, but just as often he'd daydream or lose himself in thought instead of reading. Then, too, there was another side to Abbie, especially as he approached adolescence: he liked to have devilish fun, to play trick-or-treat on Halloween and perform wild pranks just about every day of the year. Most of his activities were harmless. But before long, as a teenager, he began getting into more serious trouble, stealing license plates from cars parked in the street, smoking stolen cigarettes, and using his peashooter and his slingshot to annoy the neighbors.

"He was the kind of kid who, if you said 'don't do it,' he did," his Aunt Dorothy remembered in an interview. There was a story, perhaps apocryphal, that he once mounted a horse and rode it bareback into his parents' house on Ruth Street. Needless to say, his horseplay got him into trouble with his parents, especially his father, who thought that physical force was necessary to control his wild son. Abbie was "stubborn" and "never changed his attitude," even when he was spanked, Johnnie complained in 1968 to James Gourgouras, a reporter for the *Worcester Telegram and Gazette*. "He always had to show off."

Much to Johnnie's chagrin, Abbie insisted on being the star of the Hoffman family situation comedy on Ruth Street, and he demanded, by Johnnie's standards, an inordinate and unhealthy amount of attention. Indeed, for Johnnie, who had made it his business to go through life without notoriety, his son's need for constant attention—which seemed to outstrip by far his need for food—was profoundly disturbing and ultimately inexplicable. Florence was less severe and far more forgiving, but she too noted that Abbie "demanded a lot of attention." Almost everyone in the Hoffman clan noted Abbie's urge to perform and to be noticed. One cousin recalled that as a boy Abbie continually "mugged for the camera." When Abbie acted up at home, Florence called Johnnie at work and asked him to come home and discipline their son. Long after her son had grown up, she placed the bulk of the blame for his bad behavior on herself and her husband. "I don't think we really communicated," Florence told reporter Fred Bernstein. "There was nobody to give Abbott direction."

A Cut-Up

When he cut up at home, he was spanked and banished to his room. When he cut up at school, he was ordered to the principal's office. But the more he was punished, the more he seemed to act up and act out.

Rebuke and recrimination made him even more rebellious. "He was a rebel without a cause—before the movie," his Aunt Dorothy remembered. He carved his initials on school property, put snakes in teachers' desks, cracked jokes in the classroom, used four-letter words, and called teachers by their first names or else by their last names without the polite "Mr." or "Miss." He smoked in the lavatory, bullied younger kids on the playground, and generally turned into a juvenile delinquent.

In turning to delinquency he wasn't alone, of course. In the early to mid-fifties, a generation of young men began to express their boredom, frustration, and hostility, and the commercial culture reflected their attitudes and behavior in movies like *The Wild One*, on TV shows like *American Bandstand*, in *Mad* magazine, and in Elvis Presley's early recordings. Like the hoodlums of the day, Abbie wore a black leather jacket, pointed shoes, and pegged trousers. He rode a motorcycle, drag raced, picked up girls, and took them to drive-in movies.

By today's standards his bad behavior seems tame, but in Worcester in the late forties and early fifties his rebellion from middle-class Jewish traditions and values was unusual. Everyone in the neighborhood and at his high school knew about Abbie's wild exploits, and everyone knew that he was giving the family a bad name. By the time he was a high school sophomore, his adventures were the stuff of legends, and like most legends they had a way of snowballing. To his cousin Sydney Schanberg, who went on to become an award-wining reporter for the *New York Times*, he was a larger-than-life figure who seemed to have stepped out of a movie.

Abbie and his friends—who called him "The Abs" and considered him "Mr. Cool"—formed the "Ruth Street Stomping Society." Abbie and the gang played cards, rolled dice, and gambled at the racetrack. They wore pegged trousers and pointy shoes, just like the "hoods" they read about in *Life* and *Look* and in books like Harold Robbins's *A Stone for Danny Fisher*, which was published in 1952 when Abbie was 16, and which he claimed was a major influence on him at this point in his life.

Eventually he crossed the line that divides legal mischief from blatantly illegal enterprise. He hot-wired cars and went joyriding, participated in violent gang fights, and got into trouble with the law for speeding on the streets of Worcester and driving without license or registration. By most reports, Johnnie fretted about his son—who was "on everyone's tongue" for all the wrong reasons—but he continually came to his son's rescue, hoping he'd eventually go straight.

Abbie's freshman and sophomore years were spent at Classical High, the public school for college-bound students. His junior and senior years were spent at Worcester Academy, a private school on the other side of town. How and why he made the switch from Classical to the Academy isn't clear. The details of the story changed with each telling, year after year, but Abbie always insisted that he had been expelled from Classical because of his bad behavior. In one account he explained that he had hit one of his teachers and was "thrown out of high school." In another account, he claimed that he had written a paper "questioning the existence of G-dash-D," and his English teacher called it "heresy" and "ripped it up." In still another account, he claimed to have been ejected for writing an essay in which he argued that "God fucked up a lot."

In his autobiography, he explained that in June 1953, when he was sixteen years old, he wrote a paper that questioned "the concept of a Supreme Being." Abbie argued (or so he claimed) that there really couldn't be a God, because if God existed he would dispense rewards and punishments fairly and justly, and obviously that wasn't the case. Mr. Brooks, his English teacher, called him a "little communist bastard," tore up the paper, and hurled the "confetti at me," Abbie wrote. He overturned Mr. Brooks's desk and tackled him before he could be restrained. He later told me that this incident had been his "first rupture with the establishment," a turning point in his life, and a premonition of bigger things to come. By his own calculation, he was "the only Jew in the history of Classical High School to be expelled," and maybe he was. By the early sixties, other students, including Jews, would be expelled for violating school infractions—such as wearing long hair and jeans—but Abbie was ahead of the times. Whether the encounter with Mr. Brooks took place as Abbie claimed, however, is uncertain. There are no school records, no eyewitnesses to corroborate Abbie's tale, and no copy remains of the essay in question. Moreover, no Mr. Brooks has come forward to affirm or deny the allegations. Alfred Cravadi, Abbie's math teacher, remembers that Abbie and Mr. Brooks "had words," as he put it, but that is all he recalls. What is clear is that Abbie wanted to mythologize himself as a troublemaker and rebel, a teenage Prometheus, who stood out from the crowd by questioning not only the teacher's authority and power but even the status of the Almighty.

After the "expulsion" from Classical—the fall from the good graces of the public school system—Abbie discovered Worcester's downtown pool halls, and the older men who spent their lives there smoking, drinking, and gambling. In his own downward mobility he defied his father's upward mobility. For the first time he saw the city from the bottom up, providing an enlightening perspective on class and status and an identification with outcasts and losers. In Abbie's eyes, the pool-hall hustlers were spiritual warriors and high priests; they carried their cue sticks like "rifle butts" and took on the identity of "old Buddhas" engaged in "ritualistic dances," he wrote in *Revolution for the Hell of It*. Here were father figures with whom he could identify, and here was a place where—unlike school, temple, or his parents' house—he could feel at home and like a man. For the rest of his life he would feel comfortable in a pool hall, even in places like Chicago during the riots at the 1968 Democratic National Convention or in the various places he frequented during his time underground in the seventies. Moreover, he would celebrate the pool hall as the institution that had taught him how to size up a situation, how to read the moment, and how to be ready to meet the world.

When he went back to school in the fall of 1955, he was a lot wiser and a lot more shrewd. He had indeed learned how to play the game. This time his parents enrolled him at Worcester Academy, which had once served only the sons of the Anglo-Saxon elite; by the mid-fifties, barriers had been broken, and it was accepting Jews. "Yids were pouring into the place like the eleventh plague," Abbie would say. The inclusion of middle-class Jews in the world of the Yankees taught him that "money is power"; his particular admission into the Academy may also have shown him that rebellion had its rewards.

Worcester Academy wasn't a top-name prep school, but it was a step up in the world from Classical High, and Abbie had no inhibitions about flaunting his newfound status in the world of the preppy Holden Caulfields. Now he was part of the "in" crowd. The school yearbook tells us that he joined the chess club, played on the tennis team, and at five feet, six inches tall and 135 pounds was a scrappy halfback on the junior varsity football team. His grades were so good that Johnnie helped him buy him a '52 Ford, though he complained that his "brilliant" son "wouldn't crack a book."

The good student wasn't prepared to give up his role as bad boy. He broke the school's rules by drifting downtown for "wild escapades," until he was finally caught and placed on "indefinite bounds and probation," according to the 1955 school yearbook. He affected what he later called "a Jewish drugstore cowboy persona," greasing his hair and combing it back in the manner of rock singer and actor Sal Mineo, who appeared in *Rebel without a Cause* (1955). He was "a real bee-bop-a-luba," his brother Jack remembered: he loved listening to rock 'n' roll and to disc jockeys like Alan Freed, who played the music of Fats Domino, the Drifters, and Elvis Presley.

Oedipus in Worcester

In his autobiography, Abbie describes an endless war between himself and his father. From his own account it seems as though they were in a continual state of rage. Abbie says that as a boy he had resented the fact that Johnnie had been classified as "4-F"—physically unfit—and rejected from military service. He was disturbed that his father had not taken up arms to stop Hitler's war "to get the Jews," as he called it, and he thought of his father as a coward. He had been embarrassed by his father's continued presence in the home while other adult men were overseas. He was also angry that his father "never spoke of family history," never confided in him, and "never spoke of intimate things." He was saddened and disappointed, too, that Johnnie didn't take more notice of him, didn't accept or approve of him. Moreover, he was angry that his father imposed rules and regulations about almost everything, from the right way to eat and sleep to the right way to walk and talk. In the end Abbie seems to have been angry at Johnnie simply because he was there, blocking his way, dominating him, and making him feel small and insignificant. The timeless Oedipal conflicts between father and son played themselves out in the house at 6 Ruth Street. Moreover, Abbie's childhood rebellion against Johnnie was a rehearsal for his adult rebellion against the establishment. In the sixties, when he urged kids to dismantle the "parent culture," burn down their parents' homes, break down the nuclear family, and "kill parents," he was magnifying and projecting the anger that had its origins in his own turbulent boyhood.

Abbie was usually resentful when scholars suggested that his own rebellion, and the rebellion of the sixties, was motivated by psychological rather than social, political, and cultural conditions. But occasionally he admitted that psychology had played a part. His early relationship with his father, he explained, established a pattern that was to be repeated in his encounters with authority figures later on. "I used to see everything as a struggle with my father, just transferred to various institutions," he wrote in his autobiography.

The anger and rage that he felt toward Johnnie were only a part of the psychological picture, however. As a kid, he had marveled at his father's apparently magical ability to score bubble gum and bring home meat from the butcher when government rationing was in effect and other families were going without. As an adult, he liked his father's talent for schmoozing, his skill as a finagler and a wheeler-dealer. Then, too, he admired his father's skill at crossing social boundaries: his ability to penetrate the world of the Yankees and of the goyim.

As a child, Abbie had identified strongly with his mother's brother, Sam "Schmully" Schanberg, who was even more patriotic, more American, and more middle-class than Johnnie. In the forties, Schmully was Abbie's real-life all-American hero. "He was a Jew accepted and liked in the most redneck Polish-Irish town imaginable," Abbie boasted in his autobiography. "They even made him head of the American Legion Post." Not only was Schmully prosperous, but he flaunted his prosperity, driving a pink Cadillac. Moreover, he married a shiksa, a "snazzy dame with flaming red hair and a thick Irish brogue." Abbie loved the fact that Schmully and his wife "were in love and showed it—unlike my other relatives who hid their affections."

There was a strong part of Abbie that wanted to assimilate into mainstream America, as Schmully and his father had done, but he never gave up his identity as the Jewish outsider, exile, and wanderer. "I came into this world acutely aware of being Jewish and am sure I'll go out that way," he wrote with characteristic hyperbole. For Abbie, being Jewish meant having to face awful dilemmas and make difficult choices.

"Jews, especially first-born male Jews, have to make a big choice very quickly in life whether to go for the money or go for broke," he wrote in his autobiography. Most Jews, he said, want to fit in, to become "'better' Americans." Then there were the other Jews, the "wiseguys who go around saying things like 'Workers of the world unite,' or 'Every guy wants to screw his mother,' or 'E = mc².'" Even as a young adult Abbie wanted both—to go for broke and to go for the money, and those double desires generated a lifelong sense of ambiguity.

Being Jewish, he would explain, meant surviving by "ambiguous gestures" and "ethical ambiguities." It meant anxiety, guilt, uncertainty, unhappiness, and the sense of impending doom that we associate with the prophets, the patriarchs, and the rebels of the Old Testament: the defiance of David against Goliath, the blindly destructive yet liberating rage of Samson. Being Jewish also meant laughing at anxieties and making jokes about death and dying: the humor of Lenny Bruce, Woody Allen, and the borscht belt tummlers, comedians whose jokes were half in Yiddish and half in English, and who made the rounds of the Catskill resorts.

"The person who could tell my story better than anyone was Isaac Bashevis Singer," Abbie wrote in a 1978 essay entitled "Bye-Bye Sixties, Hollywood-Style" (collected in *Square Dancing in the Ice Age*). He was indeed much like many of the Jews in Singer's novels: haunted, superstitious, and impish. Moreover, like Singer's tormented heroes, he would grow into manhood wrestling with his own private demons, trying to do the right thing and to be a real mensch in a time of unfolding troubles.

chapter two

A THOUSAND FACES

College Testing

In the Fall of 1955, during freshman orientation at Brandeis College, Abbott Hoffman, like all incoming students, was required to take a standard Rorschach test, which involved looking at a dozen abstract designs and explaining to the psychology graduate students who administered the test what he saw. The ostensible point was to determine how the student functioned emotionally and intellectually, and to ascertain whether or not he or she had an integrated personality. For Abbie the Rorschach provided an excellent opportunity to test Brandeis and to turn the university's traditions inside out, a trait for which he would soon become famous.

What Abbie said he saw in the abstract designs were male and female genitalia, according to the recollections of his college roommate, Emanuel ("Manny") Schreiber. "That could be a penis," he would say, or "That looks like a vagina," all the while maintaining a straight face. Only when he was asked to come in for further interviewing did he let on that he had been kidding them. It was all meant in good fun, he explained, and since the college prank was a way of life at Brandeis, Abbie was accepted as just another practical joker.

Looking at the composite picture of Abbie when he was at Brandeis is like looking at a cubist portrait of a human figure. He offered so many different angles to the world and presented so many facets of himself— as entrepreneur, jock, playboy, and rebel without a cause—that no individual saw all of them, at least not all at once. Each person perceived him differently; from Abbie's outlook it was subjective perceptions that mattered most, in any case. Years later, in the chapter in his autobiography entitled "America Has More Television Sets Than Toilets," he would write, "All is subjective, all is information molded by distortion, selection, exaggeration, emphasis, omission, and every other variable of communication." Though he didn't know this intellectually when he entered Brandeis, he knew it intuitively. It wasn't what was *in* the abstract Rorschach designs that counted, but what was in the eye of the beholder.

Like most incoming freshmen, Abbie arrived on campus with his parents—who, like most other parents, were paying tuition and expenses. Abbie, however, didn't seem like just another college kid in the tow of Mom and Dad; he didn't dress, or talk, or act like everyone else. At nineteen he was a couple of years older than most freshmen, and he had what his friends called "street smarts": a working knowledge of the real world that gave him a psychological edge in dealing with students and teachers.

Abbie wore a flashy leather jacket with a slash in the back that he claimed was from a knife fight. Moreover, a rumor spread across Brandeis that he had been kicked out of high school for fighting with a teacher. To many of his classmates, he didn't seem to belong on campus at all; Ira Landess, who would become a close friend, remembered that at first he had thought Abbie was a townie—an invader and interloper in the academic world—a perception that Abbie encouraged. James Dean was the big hero on campus, and Abbie borrowed some of Dean's magic.

Beneath the leather jacket there was also a career-minded young man. He took all the tests, received high grades, and even made Dean's List. Like almost everyone else, he played the academic game. His refusal to fit into any single campus group was striking, but it wasn't unusual. Abbie's circle of friends weren't then and still aren't easily pigeonholed, as he himself realized. In his words, they were "semi-bo-rah-Libs": they were bohemians, they cheered at athletic events, and they were also liberals.

Though they didn't think of themselves as political activists, they grumbled about the hefty spending for college athletics and for campus expansion. Indeed, they were irate when old apple trees were cut down to make room for new buildings. They didn't join liberal or left-wing organizations, but they admired Eleanor Roosevelt and the liberal humanists of the day who spoke on campus. They certainly weren't revolutionaries or even radicals, but in the spring of 1959 they flocked to Harvard Stadium to hear the Cuban guerrilla leader Fidel Castro, who was "young and flashing in his green army fatigues," Abbie would write in his autobiography. They idolized Fidel, as they called him, as much for his charisma and spunk as for his military prowess or his Marxism. For Abbie, Fidel would always be a Latin American sex symbol.

Abbie and his circle didn't follow the Beats into the byways of "blackmarkets, bebop, narcotics, sexual promiscuity, hucksterism and Jean-Paul Sartre"—as listed by John Clellon Holmes in his 1952 *New York Times Magazine* article "This Is the Beat Generation"—but they were intrigued by drugs, sex, existentialism, con artists, and jazzmen. Abbie and his circle went to Cambridge coffeehouses where they listened to poetry and to folk musicians like Pete Seeger and Joan Baez, but they stopped short of going on the road and casting their lot with the Beats. Like his classmates, Abbie resisted sociological labels. Like them, only with more verve and panache, he threw himself into a variety of cultural trends and fads. He straddled worlds and experimented with lifestyles: Zen Buddhism, bohemianism, gamesmanship, and salesmanship. In a society that looked as though it was becoming faceless and nameless, Abbie affirmed his own individuality. He wanted to stand out, not blend in. Like his peers, he wanted to find himself and to define his identity, and at the same time to situate himself in a larger community that would provide a sense of fulfillment and meaning beyond the self. Before the end of his senior year, he would dream about a utopia of spiritual abundance that would fulfill the soul and a paradise of material plenty that would satisfy basic human needs.

Twentysomething

Historians have rarely been kind to the generation that attended college in the fifties. Media pundits called it the "Silent Generation" because almost no one who was white and middle class spoke out loudly and clearly on the political issues of the day, from nuclear testing to racial segregation. The poet Karl Shapiro, who had reached adulthood in the more radical thirties, called it the "Brainwashed Generation" because its members appeared to be incapable of independent thought. The journalist Jack Newfield, who was born in 1934 and began his own college career in 1956, called his peers the "Un-generation"—a forerunner of "Generation X," one might say—and lambasted what he termed the "campus catatonics of the 1950s."

The years of Dwight David Eisenhower's presidency (1952–60) were difficult for Abbie and his contemporaries, in part because they saw the glaring disparity between official values and social realities. Americans were supposed to live by and live up to the high moral values expressed in the twin watchwords "teamwork" and "togetherness." Officially, of course, it was the hour of the organization man, dressed impeccably in his gray flannel suit; at his side was his cheerful, attentive housewife and helpmate. But something disquieting was going on beneath the appearance of suburban calm and corporate efficiency; their silence notwithstanding, many young Americans had an unspoken awareness of the uneasiness, the hypocrisy, the brittle facade of happiness.

The fifties were the chronological halfway point in the twentieth century, but they were also a real watershed in American history, and college students had a unique vantage point from which to watch the social tremors and record the aftershocks in their own sensibilities. Abbie's generation learned that the American military had been brought to a stalemate in the Korean War. They saw Senator Joseph McCarthy's career come unglued on television during the Army–McCarthy hearings of 1954, which made America's leading anticommunist crusader look like a bad-mannered bully while the Army's attorney, Joseph Welch, seemed a genteel hero. They followed the path of the orbiting Russian Sputnik in space and noted that their parents, teachers, and political leaders reacted, as Professor Eric Goldman observed in *The Crucial Decade,* with "alarm, exasperation, humiliation, and confusion." They read the handwriting on the wall in the 1954 Supreme Court ruling in the landmark *Brown v. Board of Education* case that segregation in public schools was unconstitutional. And they were amazed by the quiet valor of a black woman named Rosa Parks who boarded a bus in Montgomery, Alabama, and refused to sit in the colored section in the back. With the society shifting suddenly under their own feet, it was no wonder that fifties college students were a cautious lot, unwilling to cast themselves with causes and wise enough to play the full length of the social field.

Martin Peretz, one of Abbie's classmates and later the publisher and editor of the *New Republic,* suggested that "the '60s happened at Brandeis in the '50s." Indeed, there were students who smoked marijuana and even a few who were openly homosexual. There were *signs* of the sixties in the fifties at Brandeis, but the decade of defiance was still a decade away. What radicalism there was on campus was as much a legacy of the past as a harbinger of the turmoil to come. Barbara Haber, another Brandeis student, remembered that there was "socialist ferment" at the college and that the sons and daughters of thirties Reds colored the campus atmosphere. Like Berkeley and Columbia, Brandeis would have to wait another decade for campus sit-ins, violent political demonstrations, and agitation for student power. For Abbie, Brandeis was *alma mater,* a true "fostering mother." Unlike the radical students of the sixties, he had no intention of going on strike and shutting down the institution. And unlike them, he identified thoroughly with his professors and adopted them as his intellectual father figures.

Brains and Bravado at Brandeis

Students were more complacent in the fifties than they had been in the thirties or would be again in the sixties, and that was no historical accident. McCarthyism and the climate of the cold war chilled the intellectual atmosphere of the ivory tower much as it chilled almost every other major institution of American life, from Hollywood studios to heartland factories. Along with antifascist screenwriters and trade union militants, dozens of left-wing professors were fired, and many others—including liberal Democrats as well as closet socialists and outright communists—were terrified of losing tenure and of banishment to second-rate colleges in the provinces.

In these intolerant times, when books were burned and professors were fired, Brandeis University was an oasis of intellectual freedom and a haven for radical intellectuals. Founded in 1948, it was named after Louis Brandeis, one of the most liberal of Supreme Court Justices, and it remained true to its roots. There were lively debates about communism and anticommunism, the Hungarian Revolution of 1956, the cold war, and political conformity. There were controversial speakers from off campus, including Dorothy Day, the editor of the *Catholic Worker,* and Dr. Martin Luther King, Jr., who brought the latest news of the civil rights movement in the South.

When James Wechsler, the editor of the *New York Post* and an ex-communist, spoke at Brandeis, a group of students berated him for providing the names of former comrades to congressional investigators. While most American campuses refused to allow speakers who were procommunist, Brandeis provided them, albeit tentatively, with a podium. There was a spirit of nonconformity and the freedom to poke fun even at the university itself. Abbie joked about the construction boom on campus, which he dubbed the "enormous edifice complex," and on St. Patrick's Day he and his friends poured green dye into the fountains to satirize the school's obsession with its own Jewishness.

Irving Howe, who was a professor at Brandeis in the 1950s, described the extraordinary character of the institution in his autobiography, *A Margin of Hope:* "While I have taught at more distinguished schools, never have I known any place where the life of the mind was engaged with such passion." The faculty could boast of intellectual heavyweights like Herbert Marcuse, a European Marxist and a refugee from German fascism, and Abraham Maslow, a Brooklyn-born psychologist influenced by the work of Erich Fromm and Karen Horney who emphasized "healthy motivation" rather than neurosis.

There were other outstanding professors who shaped Abbie's intellectual growth and development: Frank Manuel, a wounded veteran of the Spanish Civil War who lectured on the history of ideas; Maurice Stein, who taught a class on mass psychology and mass culture and urged undergraduates to get out of the library and into the field; and James Klee, who emphasized the importance of myth, dream, and symbol and assigned readings in Joseph Campbell's 1949 groundbreaking study of ancient mythologies and universal archetypes, *The Hero With a Thousand Faces.*

There were famous instructors like Max Lerner, a quintessential liberal and one of the *New Republic's* regular commentators on contemporary affairs. Abbie didn't approve of Lerner, but Lerner was a living reminder that academic concerns had immediate social implications.

There were less famous but equally inspiring teachers like Marie Syrkin and Philip Finklepearl, who helped Abbie understand his own experiences and make the transition from the middle-class world of his parents to the world of ideas, ideologies, and intellectuals. In Syrkin's class Abbie wrote an interpretative essay in which he applied his own prowess as a pool-hall hustler to James T. Farrell's hoodlum hero "Studs" Lonigan. In Finklepearl's class he wrote an irreverent paper entitled "How to Bluff Your Way through College," in which he offered practical suggestions for academic success without stress.

Abbie often made a bluff of anti-intellectualism, but underneath the cool posture he was swept away by intellectual passion. "Every new idea hit like a thunderclap," he wrote in the chapter from his autobiography entitled "From Bum to College Boy." Granted, he didn't read every textbook, and he did not like to be seen in the library (which would have been bad for his image), but he stayed up late wrestling with ideas and discussing books, plays, and movies: *Hamlet*, Dostoyevsky's *Notes from the Underground*, *The Diary of Anne Frank*, and Federico Fellini's cinematic triumph, *La Strada*.

Abbie and his friends—Mendy Samstein, James Goldman, Lynn Luria, Bernice Salomon, Gabrielle Rossmer, and Manny Schreiber— talked with a sense of great urgency and depth of feeling about apathy, alienation, anxiety, behavior modification, existential urges, and the pathology of society. All these ideas seemed new and exciting, and the precocious Brandeis students were often lost in lofty thought. "Abbie could not resist the demands made on himself by his own ideas," Lynn Luria remembered. "They would drive right through him."

Irving Howe noted that the Brandeis students of the 1950s "knew that education is not a matter of making oneself a receptacle into which a detached elder pours knowledge; it is an engagement in which sparring, conflicting, 'acting out' become a path to meaning." Abbie acted out his education both in the classroom and off campus; he tested ideas, overturned them, and gave himself permission to think the unthinkable. Brandeis didn't teach him what to think, but it taught him how to think and what to think about: eros and death, the personal and the political, sanity and insanity, civilization and dehumanization, capitalism and socialism, subjective perception and objective reality. At Brandeis Abbie learned to think dialectically, to look for contradictions, to link polar opposites, and to synthesize—to see the whole and all its parts. He discovered the giants of Western thought, from St. Augustine and Descartes to Marx and Freud, and he idolized the Brandeis intellectuals who were determined to fuse Marx and Freud, to connect class consciousness with the subconscious and the collective unconscious.

At college Abbie became introspective. He developed an awareness of himself, his past, and his place in the world, and he was able to size up and make sense of his experiences as pool-hall hustler and juvenile delinquent. He was not alone, he learned, but part of a larger wave of social change. Moreover, he lost his innocence and naïveté about contemporary history, and for the first time identified with the victims of the atomic blasts in Hiroshima and Nagasaki and with the Jews who died in the concentration camps at Auschwitz and Buchenwald.

Like many of his classmates, Abbie came to believe that the existence of the atom bomb inhibited the development of mankind, paralyzing progress and creativity. There could be no hope of social transformation and no optimism, he argued, until the threat of nuclear holocaust was abolished. Then, too, he accepted wholeheartedly contemporary academic critiques of postindustrial society, in which material abundance was accompanied by more divorce, drug addiction, suicide, and alcoholism than at any other time in history. Automation threatened to turn men and women into robots and to generate an insane society along the lines of Aldous Huxley's *Brave New World*—so he argued in class and in essays.

Brandeis provided an environment in which Abbie could shape himself and create his own identity. Bernice Salomon, a close college friend who went on to become a college professor, remembered Abbie as "protean" and "elusive." Even as an undergraduate, he "saw himself as a mythic hero on a journey," Salomon said. He "took on personas, created a symbolism of his own and made himself larger than life," she recalled. "He turned everything into a game, and when he played a game, the game was a game. He was in it and he was watching it at the same time. He was always consciously putting something over, and he knew that we knew it."

Abbie found intellectual nourishment for his heroic journey everywhere he could, from Homer to Joseph Campbell, but especially in the lectures and books of Abraham Maslow. "I loved Professor Abe Maslow," Abbie wrote. "There was something about his humanistic psychology . . . that I found exhilarating amidst the general pessimism that pervaded Western thought." Abbie delighted in Maslow's idea that every person had to find out "what one is *really* like inside, deep down." He was enthralled with Maslow's concept of "self-actualizing people" who found themselves in "peak experiences": the heightened moments when individuals transcend the "fear of death and insanity." Abbie was determined to become a self-actualizing individual, to have peak experiences, and to become, as Maslow put it in *Toward a Psychology of Being*, "simultaneously selfish and unselfish, Dionysian and Apollonian, individual and social, rational and irrational, fused with others and detached from others."

Abbie's other campus god was Herbert Marcuse, whose book *Eros and Civilization* was published in 1955 and was widely read and discussed by undergraduates. Marcuse's magnificent ideas were inspiring, especially when they appeared amidst the conservatism of the Eisenhower era. In *Eros and Civilization,* Marcuse offered the "vision of a non-repressive culture" in which there was no anxiety, but instead "freedom from guilt and fear." Abbie was especially taken with Marcuse's suggestion that the human body could "become an object of cathexis, a thing to be enjoyed—an instrument of pleasure," and he was encouraged to pursue physical pleasure without guilt or fear.

Abbie had entered Brandeis as a premedical student because his parents had wanted him to become a doctor, but he switched to psychology as he became fascinated with ESP, hypnosis, telepathic communication, and parapsychology. He took peyote, studied yoga, practiced meditation and self-hypnosis, and experimented with mysticism. Relentlessly, he followed the inner journey into his own psyche.

His journey also took him into the world. He loved to go to the movies, listen to folk music, hit the race track with the guys and gamble on the horses, and stay up late playing cards. Wherever he went, he was certain to go fast. He drove a golden bronze-colored Corvette, the only sports car on campus. Later he owned a Cadillac and finally a Volkswagen, always searching for the appropriate vehicle to express his personality. He went to the dances on big college weekends and played sports with a vengeance. On the basketball court he was aggressive, and on the tennis court, in his immaculate white shorts and shirt, he was tireless and full of good humor. During his senior year he was the captain of the unbeaten tennis team, and all season long he was locked in a battle of words and wits against Coach Bud Collins (later a TV sports commentator) for control of the team. "He didn't care for authority," Collins would write in *Sports Illustrated,* and added, "There was nothing revolutionary about Abbie's style. . . . He played like a cop . . . doggedly pursuing everything."

In the evenings Abbie sold submarine sandwiches in the dormitories. "Get your red-hot subs," he'd shout, and though he and his friends made ample pocket money, selling subs wasn't simply a business. "It was his *shtick,*" Bernice Salomon said. "It was an institution." And James Goldman added that Abbie "made a drama out of selling sandwiches. He came up with a new performance every night."

In high school Abbie had his first sexual encounters. In college, he took on the persona of the playboy and became a sexual role model for the younger, less experienced men on campus. "Abbie was almost always sexually charged and looking to make a sexual connection," Ira Landess recalled. Manny Schreiber remembered that "a lot of us wanted to have sex, but only Abbie had the 'balls' to make his lust known." Abbie tried his best to pass on his love lore, but he felt ambivalent about his status and reputation as a lover. "He didn't want women to fall in love with him because he didn't want the responsibility, and at the same time he didn't want them not to fall in love with him because he thrived on adoration," Bernice Salomon said.

At the end of his sophomore year he fell in love with and relentlessly pursued Sheila Karklin, a coed from a middle-class Jewish family. To outsiders they looked like a very romantic couple, but to many close friends there was something dark and even perverse about the relationship. Sheila was beautiful and a creative artist as well, but she seemed incapable of making decisions. Abbie obsessed about her and was determined not to lose her. His male friends thought that he was afraid of her, and felt that she exerted control over him. As they became more deeply involved, Abbie grew darker and more moody. According to Lynn Luria, the emotional tug-of-war between Abbie and Sheila led him "to learn what suffering was."

When he entered college in the fall of 1955, he wasn't sure why he was there or what he was doing. But he learned fast, and what he learned as an undergraduate he didn't forget. Brandeis taught him the lesson that it is not the environment that makes human beings, but human beings who make their own environment. He became a cultural relativist, an exponent of the social construction of reality, and a firm believer in Benjamin Whorf's thesis that "language shapes our environment." Again and again he came back to the idea that individuals are free agents, and to an image he found in the pages of Dostoyevsky's *Notes from the Underground:* that men are "not the keys of a piano." The darker side of Abbie identified with Dostoyevsky's antihero—especially with his notion that men will commit perverse acts if only to prove a point. "And if he does not find means he will contrive destruction and chaos, will contrive suffering of all sorts, only to gain his point!" the underground man explains. Abbie copied those words and remembered them for years, as he also remembered and copied the lines from Hemingway's *A Farewell to Arms:* "They . . . told you the rules and the first time they caught you off base they killed you."

Witness to an Awakening

At Brandeis the notion of breaking the rules and being killed was only a romantic flicker in his mind. A year later, as a graduate student at the University of California at Berkeley, Abbie found that notion had become a reality that dominated his thoughts. In the spring of 1960, death and the death penalty were on the minds of many students at Berkeley, as well as on the collective mind of America. On May 2, Caryl Chessman, one of the most notable inmates in the history of California, was executed in the gas chamber at San Quentin, despite a worldwide movement to eliminate capital punishment and save his life.

Abbie was among the hundred or so protesters, including students and a few celebrities such as Marlon Brando, who held a last-minute vigil outside the walls of the prison. Until early dawn there was hope that the Democratic governor would stay the execution. Chessman had allegedly kidnapped two women and forced them to engage in oral sex. By the laws of the State of California, he was guilty of a capital crime, and in the words of Governor Edmund Brown, he had shown a "lack of contrition" and a "steadfast arrogance." Still, punishment by death seemed unjust to millions of people around the world.

Abbie read Chessman's books, *Cell 2455* and *Death Row,* and like many others he was persuaded that capital punishment was barbaric. He'd come to feel that Chessman was, in Abbie's words, a "poor bloke" and the victim of an unjust system. Abbie had not joined the organized groups that rallied to save Chessman's life, and he had not taken part in the first round of protests outside the prison walls, but when he heard the news that Chessman's life was on the line, he piled into a car already packed with students headed for San Quentin.

It was his first participation in a political demonstration, and it was like nothing he had expected. "No one made a loud comment," he wrote. "No one threw a rock." There were signs that read "Thou Shalt Not Kill" and there was Marlon Brando's strong presence, but mostly the protesters stood silently. When word reached the crowd that Chessman was dead, there was a shared sense of devastation. "No! No!" someone moaned, and Marlon Brando exclaimed, "A vulgar, stupid, unutterably sad act has been perpetuated." Years later, in the essay "The First Time I Saw Berkeley" (reprinted in Lynda Rosen Obst's anthology *The Sixties*), Abbie would write that Chessman had lost his twelve-year battle with "Death's Stinking Seat." He would remember the sad car ride back to Berkeley. "How does that work?" someone had asked. "In a democracy, I mean, no one wants to see him die and the state kills him?"

In the spring of 1960 Abbie was a long way from home. He had left his family, his friends, and his girlfriend Sheila and had come to Berkeley to become a "shrink." Toward that goal he had enrolled in the master's program in the psychology department; he was also working as a teaching assistant in a class on child psychology and as a guidance counselor at a junior high school.

At Berkeley he was mostly a loner. He went to classes, played tennis, and sat in the coffeehouses on Telegraph Avenue and across the bay in North Beach, but he didn't have close friends, and he felt out of place. He picked up girls—sometimes two at a time—and told vivid tales about his sexual escapades to a freshman named Marty Kenner. He listened to Lenny Bruce records in his apartment, and introduced Lenny and his brand of biting humor to anyone who would listen. Religiously he went to the movies at the Cinema Guild; owned and operated by Pauline Kael, who would become the film reviewer for the

New Yorker, it showed mostly film classics. He dabbled in the art of shoplifting and ran small-time scams, such as using fake names to receive books and records at the addresses of friends and acquaintances, then selling the items for cash on Telegraph Avenue.

The campus felt overwhelming: in 1960 there were more than eighteen thousand students at Berkeley (compared with eight hundred at Brandeis), and many classes had enrollments of a thousand or more. Unlike Brandeis, Berkeley felt cold, impersonal, and impenetrable. And unlike Brandeis, Berkeley had left-wing political groups and demonstrations. This was, however, only 1960: only the beginning of the era of rebellion. By the middle of the decade, Berkeley had a reputation as a center of student radicalism, but when Abbie arrived it was just beginning to awaken from the sleep of conservatism. Fraternities still discriminated against blacks and Jews, participation in ROTC (Reserve Officers' Training Corps) was compulsory, and most students came from conservative backgrounds.

The paternalistic University of California enjoined its students from engaging in political debate and political activity on campus. In 1956 presidential candidate Adlai Stevenson had been refused permission to enter the campus to speak. The new president of the university, Clark Kerr, was confident that the rules limiting freedom of speech were not only fair and rational, but also in the best interests of the society. He was certain that students would appreciate his benevolence and that they would be a docile lot. "The employers will love this generation," he predicted. "They aren't going to press many grievances. They are going to be easy to handle. There aren't going to be any riots."

There *were* some grievances, though, and Abbie took note of them during his first semester, in the fall of 1959. Although the United States was not at war, a small number of students began to express their moral opposition to war. A freshman named Fred Moore, the son of a U.S. Air Force colonel, had registered as a conscientious objector and had gone on a hunger strike to protest the presence of ROTC on campus. Abbie watched him sitting on the steps of Sproul Hall with a sign and a statement that read, "I will neither participate in nor support any action whose purpose is killing. The purpose of military training is to train men for war—train men to kill. I therefore cannot comply with the ROTC requirement."

There were other signs of incipient rebellion. On campus a group called SLATE was running candidates for student government on a platform urging the establishment of a co-op bookstore, an end to compulsory ROTC, and an end to the death penalty. Harry Bridges, a radical trade union organizer, spoke on campus and received a warm reception from students. From the audience, Abbie introduced himself and asked Bridges about the prospects for radical change in America, only to be told that revolution seemed unlikely.

In Greensboro, North Carolina, on February 1, 1960, black students staged a sit-in at the local F. W. Woolworth store to protest the company's policy of segregated lunch-counter service. That spring, picket lines formed outside Woolworth and S. H. Kress stores in Berkeley (and across the United States) as students demonstrated their support for integration in the South. The Berkeley pickets were the first that Abbie ever saw, and he was astounded. Events moved quickly nationwide, and in April the Student Nonviolent Coordinating Committee (SNCC) was founded at a conference in Raleigh, North Carolina. The organization's statement of purpose elevated nonviolence into not only a political strategy but also a way of life and of spiritual redemption. "Non-violence . . . seeks a social order of justice permeated by love," the document read. "Through non-violence courage displaces fear. Love transcends hate."

That same spring, Northern white students formed Students for a Democratic Society (SDS), a liberal organization of undergraduates anxious to break out of the apathy paralyzing college campuses. By the fall of 1960 it seemed to many students—and to professors who were paying attention—that Clark Kerr was dead wrong: the new generation was born to riot, and they would be hell to handle. On September 22, 1960, in the pages of the *Michigan Daily,* student editor Tom Hayden wondered, "Why This Erupting Generation?" Professor C. Wright Mills, author of *The Power Elite,* noted in an essay entitled "Letter to the New Left" that "the Age of Complacency is ending. . . . We are beginning to move again."

The nationwide sit-in movement against segregation spelled out the shape of things to come. So did the protests that took place in San Francisco in May 1960, ten days after Caryl Chessman's execution at San Quentin. Abbie was there once again as a concerned observer rather than an active participant, yet even as an observer he was deeply af-

Abbott Hoffman, age five or six, at summer camp. Courtesy Jack Hoffman.

Abbott Hoffman in 1946 with his father, John; mother, Florence; brother, Jack; and sister, Phyllis. Courtesy Jack Hoffman.

(Top left) Shirtless Abbie Hoffman on the basketball court at Brandeis University in the late fifties. Courtesy Brandeis University.

(Bottom left) Wedding to Sheila Karklin at Temple Beth Am, Warwick, Rhode Island, July 1960. Brother, Jack; sister, Phyllis; mother, Florence; father, John; and grandmother, Anna. Courtesy Jack Hoffman.

(Above) Abbie with his wife Sheila and their two children, Andrew and Amy, in Worcester in 1965, soon after Abbie's first trip to the South as a civil rights activist and SNCC supporter. Reprinted with permission of the Worcester Telegram and Gazette.

(Above) Abbie in Lincoln Park, Chicago, during the 1968 Democratic Convention. Anita made the shirt. The hat was Abbie's trademark. One of his plans was to leave the hat with a friend, who would wave it about and claim that Abbie had been shot and killed by the police. Roz Payne.

(Top right) Under arrest in Chicago in September 1968, soon after the riots at the Democratic National Convention. "It's good to be back in Mississippi," Abbie said. Reuters/Bettmann

(Bottom right) At a press conference in Chicago in September 1968 with antiwar activists Tom Hayden and Rennie Davis. UPI/Bettmann

(Above) Under arrest in Washington, D.C., for wearing a shirt that resembled an American flag, October 1968. Abbie was to testify at hearings of the House Un-American Activities Committee investigating communist subversion at the Democratic National Convention in 1968. UPI/Bettmann

(Top right) Giving the finger to the Federal Courthouse in New York in March 1969 after indictment for conspiracy and incitement to riot at the 1968 Democratic National Convention in Chicago. With Black Panther David Brothers, attorney William Kunstler, and codefendants David Dellinger and Jerry Rubin. UPI/Bettmann

(Bottom right) At the Department of Justice in Washington, D.C., in October 1969, Abbie landed a right to the doors of the building and challenged Attorney General John Mitchell to "come down and fight." UPI/Bettmann

(Above) With Jefferson Airplane singer Grace Slick, who had been invited to a reception at the White House in April 1970 by President Nixon's daughter Tricia. Abbie was stopped at the gates. UPI/Bettmann

(Top right) With his wife Anita at Madison Square Garden in New York in July 1970 to protest a State Department–sponsored tour of Eastern Europe by the rock group Blood, Sweat and Tears. UPI/Bettmann

(Bottom right) The Chicago Seven and their lawyers, William Kunstler and Leonard Weinglass, at the Federal Building in Chicago in 1973. Abbie holds his two-and-a-half-year-old son, america. UPI/Bettmann

(Above) With his youngest son, america, in October 1973. UPI/Bettmann

(Top right) With New York senator Daniel Moynihan in August 1978. As the fugitive and environmental activist Barry Freed, he testified about the harmful impact of winter navigation on the St. Lawrence Seaway. UPI/Bettmann

(Bottom right) Abbie at 43, surrendering in New York in 1980 after six and a half years underground to face cocaine trafficking charges. "It was a media feeding frenzy," one observer noted. UPI/Bettmann

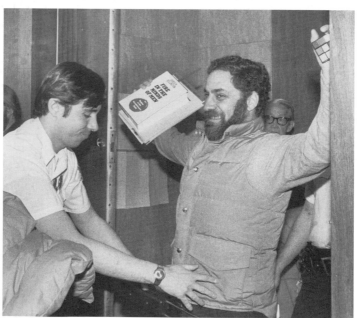

(Top left) In court in April 1981, with wife Johanna Lawrenson and attorney Gerald Lefcourt, for sentencing on charges of selling cocaine to undercover police agents. UPI/Bettmann

(Bottom left) Abbie being searched by an officer of the court before beginning prison term on cocaine charges in April 1981. The book Abbie is carrying contains a hacksaw blade. UPI/Bettmann

(Above) Soon after release from prison in January 1982, Abbie sings "I get high with a little help from my friends" with Carly Simon and actress Karen Black at a Studio 54 benefit to raise money for a heroin addiction program. UPI/ Bettmann

(Above) At a peace rally in New York's Central Park in June 1982, hugging Dr. Benjamin Spock. UPI/Bettmann

(Top right) At a Bucks County, Pennsylvania, sit-in in January 1983 with a new generation of activists trying to stop the construction of a nuclear power plant. UPI/Bettmann

(Bottom right) In front of the United States Embassy in Managua in January 1985 to denounce the Reagan administration's policy toward Nicaragua. UPI/Bettmann

In New York with Carly Simon and President Carter's daughter Amy at the "I Spy Ball" in March 1987. Abbie and Amy had been arrested protesting CIA recruitment at the University of Massachusetts. UPI/ Bettmann

On the set of Oliver Stone's movie Born on the Fourth of July, *in which he appeared in a cameo role, playing himself. Courtesy Jeff Nightbyrd.*

fected. "I was a witness to events that were to mold my consciousness forever," he would write.

The effect of Chessman's execution had been devastating. It had impressed upon Abbie the power of the state to take away an individual life, and it had made him feel that American democracy was a sham. The protests that took place subsequently at San Francisco City Hall reinforced the feeling of powerlessness against an inhumane system. The House Un-American Activities Committee (HUAC) had set up shop in San Francisco in 1960 to conduct investigations into communist subversion in the Bay Area. "It was one of the great anti-commie road shows designed to beef up the Cold War, get some teachers fired, and warn the nation about the ever-present *Red Menace*," Abbie wrote in "The First Time I Saw Berkeley." "People like J. Edgar Hoover wanted to keep their jobs. And his boys had nothing better to do, crime in America having been solved, I mean." Students circled San Francisco City Hall holding hand-lettered signs that read "Witch Hunters Go Home!" Inside, others waited in line to gain admittance to the hearings, but almost all of them were deliberately excluded.

Angrily they chanted "Open the door! Open the door!" then sat down and began to sing "We Shall Not Be Moved." The police department hooked up canvas hoses, opened the fire hydrants, and blasted the students with water at full pressure. The result was horrifying. "The rotunda seemed to erupt," KPFA reporter Fred Haines told his radio listeners. "The singing broke into one gigantic, horrified scream." Swinging their clubs wildly, police officers charged the demonstrators then dragged them down the steps feet first, their heads banging on the cold wet floor. The survivors stood together singing "The Star Spangled Banner" and with their fingers flashed the "V" for victory sign from World War II.

The media dubbed the event "Black Friday." David Horowitz, a Berkeley graduate student, wrote in *Student,* the first book about sixties protest, that "Black Friday was an education." Horowitz would soon become a New Leftist (and then, in the eighties, a Reagan Republican, much to Abbie's disgust). What he found educational in the protest against HUAC was the "direct experience of violence" from the police. That experience with police violence would be repeated over and over in the sixties as the New Left took shape.

Politically and culturally the decade of the sixties was born in many places, from the sit-ins in Greensboro, North Carolina, to the vigils at San Quentin and the protests against HUAC in San Francisco. Abbie liked to say that he had been there when the sixties were born, that he had seen the beginning of "the century's most turbulent decade," as he called it, and that he had witnessed the forging of a new generation as it "cast its spirit into the crucible of resistance." Indeed, the protest at San Francisco City Hall had many of the crucial elements that would eventually be found in sixties rebellion: the violence, of course, and the police riot, but also that sense that what was happening was unreal, unbelievable, surreal.

For Abbie, Black Friday was terrifying and nightmarish, much like a scene from Sergei Eisenstein's *Potemkin,* the classic film of the Russian Revolution, which had profoundly affected him. The police violence in San Francisco City Hall seemed un-American, indeed. Significantly, the students responded by singing the national anthem and the old spiritual "Down by the Riverside." Like the founders of the Student Nonviolent Coordinating Committee (SNCC), who held out the promise of a "redemptive community," the young white rebels in San Francisco and Berkeley had an almost religious sense of purpose and conviction.

"We were marching . . . for something much more important, tran-scending politics and laws," Michael Rossman wrote in the *Daily Californian* in an article about the protests at San Quentin. Abbie shared in this spiritual sense, in part because of his own religious upbringing—the Old Testament tradition he'd absorbed in temple—but also in part from his readings in existentialism and especially Camus. His own sense of spirituality would develop intensely in the years to come, both as he mixed with Catholic radicals and as he identified with SNCC and ech-oed SNCC's belief in the need for a "social order of justice permeated by love" and a "redemptive community."

He had come away from Brandeis with the idea that human beings shape their environment, and he had, in fact, left his mark on the school and on his schoolmates. No one who met him at Brandeis seems to have ever forgotten him. But at Berkeley, it was Abbie who was "molded"—to use his word—by the environment, rather than vice versa. Berkeley played him as though he was a guitar, and he reverber-ated accordingly. At Berkeley almost no one remembered him, because very few people met him. It was as though he allowed another side of himself to emerge in California: quieter and more withdrawn, a spectator not a performer, a secret sharer in a ritual of birth.

At the San Quentin vigil to protest Chessman's execution, according to Michael Rossman, one student urged his friends, "Look at this and remember it. Remember it and don't ever forget it." Abbie looked, remembered, and never forgot. He had been a witness to history—to one of the decisive events in the birth of the sixties. When he returned to Massachusetts and attended a showing of the Un-American Activities Committee's own film, *Operation Abolition*—which purported to document what had happened on Black Friday—he rose from his seat in the audience and addressed the crowd spontaneously. He was angry at the film's distortions and misrepresentations, he told the audience. He was no communist, and neither were the other students. The film was full of factual errors, he proclaimed. It was his first political speech, and he was swept away by his own rhetoric, as though possessed by his own words. "I saw myself as a Son of Liberty," he wrote in his autobiography, "riding through the night, sounding the alarm."

chapter three

CIVIL RIGHTS AND WRONGS

Master of Make-Believe

On July 14, 1960—two and a half months after he had witnessed the tumultuous protests against the House Un-American Activities Committee—Abbott Hoffman married Sheila Karklin, his long-time Brandeis girlfriend, at Temple Beth Am in Warwick, Rhode Island. In March, during spring break, Sheila had visited Abbie; now she was four months pregnant. Abbie was looking forward to becoming a husband and a father, but he also felt a sense of nostalgia for his freewheeling days with the guys in pool halls, bowling alleys, and fast cars. Getting married meant giving up his freedom and taking on responsibilities, and he felt anxious about the future. His mixed feelings are reflected in the tragicomic chapter of his autobiography "Faulty Rubber, Failed Marriage," which reads like an imitation of Philip Roth, Abbie's favorite Jewish novelist. In this chapter Abbie describes his own wedding ceremony in the third person, as an alienated spectator, not a key participant. "The groom wore a white tuxedo," he says of himself. "The bridesmaid cried. Manny, the best man, fumbled for the ring."

According to Abbie the ceremony was an embarrassment, and so was the gala reception: his father Johnnie got drunk; an uncle teased him about the size of his penis; a woman with blue hair squeezed him "between her enormous tits." Mr. and Mrs. Hoffman went on a honeymoon—a disaster by Abbie's description—then settled at 22 Trowbridge Road in Worcester. The Hoffmans tried to create a sense of togetherness. They were proud of their son Andrew, who was born in December 1960, and they were excited by their cottage industry, "The Trowbridge Candle Company." To friends and family members, the homemade candles seemed to signal that Abbie and Sheila were off to a good start. In fact the marriage was shaky from the start. By the spring of 1962, less than two years after they had been married, Sheila filed for legal separation in the Worcester Probate Court.

"We had fundamentally different approaches to life," Abbie observed matter-of-factly. "I was reckless. She was cautious. Be it movies, books, music, art, or drugs, we disagreed." He admitted that he "didn't know how to be married," but he was quick to add that Sheila "didn't know how to be married either." It was tit for tat. He accused her of physically assaulting him; "she threw a dish at me and chipped a bone in my elbow," he wrote, and added as if it was merely an afterthought, "I once got her head under a pillow and squeezed, squeezed, squeezed, squeezed." It's no wonder that Sheila wanted and was granted a separation by the Worcester Probate Court midway through 1962. But that wasn't the end of the relationship: by 1964 they were together again.

The marriage sputtered along, leaving deep pockets of resentment. Many of their closest friends believe that though the marriage was a failure, they never stopped loving one another, and though they were eventually divorced, they were never disentangled. Many of Abbie's college buddies portray him as the archetype of the hen-pecked husband, afraid of his wife and anxious to please her. Mutual friends remember Sheila as unrelenting in her criticism of Abbie. Outspoken and unconventional, she was often more shocking than her husband. An art teacher, she brought Modigliani nudes into the classroom to show to her young black students, only to be rebuked by their conservative Christian parents. At the Phoenix, a local group that sponsored public forums, she irked the largely Catholic audience when she defended the use of birth control and urged the legalization of abortion. In public, Sheila was always remarkably quiet about Abbie. It was only after his death that she emerged from her cocoon of silence, and even then she was enigmatic and evasive. "I never knew anyone who wanted to be a husband more than Abbie. But he didn't know how to do it," she told a reporter for *People*. To Amy Zuckerman, a Worcester native and writer for *Worcester Magazine,* she explained that her husband was "competitive" and easily "offended" by her success as a political organizer.

While he was married to Sheila, Abbie tried to hold a steady job, to be monogamous, and to put home and family at the heart of his world. Never again—not with Anita Kushner, his second wife, nor with Johanna Lawrenson, his third wife—would he define himself so thoroughly as a traditional husband and conventional provider. Never again would he be so tied down. In his autobiography, he claimed that the Worcester years were largely a failure, at least in personal terms. The marriage to Sheila felt like a series of unplanned pregnancies, abortions, and abortive abortions. His career as a psychologist floundered, and the various jobs he took for love or for money never amounted to much. He was continually borrowing time from one place and investing it in another, never fully present in any one place, and always at loose ends. As he put it, the Worcester experience was "schizophrenic."

Almost everyone who knew Abbie in Worcester in the mid-sixties describes him as both lovable and loony. Kathy Chaiklin, a student activist, remembered Abbie as "an incredible organizer but incredibly disorganized" and as a "leader who often undermined his own leadership." D'Army Bailey, a black student at Clark University and the leading civil rights organizer in town (who later became a judge), remembered Abbie as a "loose cannon." Still he played a useful role, Bailey felt, because he was "irreverent, bold, energetic."

Father Bernard Gilgun, a maverick Catholic priest who knew Abbie Hoffman as well as anyone in Worcester in the sixties, captured his identity in a poem entitled "A Song for Me and Abbie Hoffman," which was published in the *Worcester Punch.* In Gilgun's view, Abbie was a complex, Christ-like character with a hilarious sense of humor, a saint-cum-comedian:

> He's as crazy as heaven
> The cops ought to know it
> The Irish have called it
> A touch of the poet.
>
> He's hung up on Love
> You can't get him off it

So his books never balance
Showing both loss and *Prophet.*

But he dances like magic
Through walls made of words
And he laughs as he proves
That one half is two thirds.

It's one hell of a calling
I hope he doesn't blow it
What a wonderful thing
To be touched
Like a poet.

By the mid-sixties Abbie was already, at least in embryo, the zany character who would achieve fame and notoriety by the end of the decade. He was a mythical figure: magician, poet, prophet, comedian, would-be martyr, renegade son, gadfly. There was no major institution in Worcester that he left unscathed: not its newspapers, factories, schools, or churches. He was at war with his hometown and opposed to the status quo.

Several of his Worcester friends recall a memorable occasion when he delivered a talk on racial discrimination before the membership of the Probus Club, a liberal philanthropic organization of which his father was president. The audience was first impressed with his presentation, and then just as suddenly disappointed. When he stepped down from the podium to chat with his admirers, Abbie admitted that he hadn't conducted any research. So what if he'd made up his statistics on the spot? He'd told the essential truth, he insisted. But that explanation didn't wash. Making up facts, telling stories, and ad-libbing would become Abbie's trademarks in Worcester. According to Daniel Dick, a local Catholic radical, Abbie Hoffman was a "master of make-believe" and a "genius at giving impressions." The image was, if not everything, then certainly all-important. "Abbie knew that it wasn't what you did, but what people thought that you did, that counted," Dan Dick recalled.

On one occasion, when they were photographed at a demonstration by a man in a trench coat—an FBI agent, they assumed—Abbie urged Dan to take pictures with his home movie camera. That would be too much trouble, Dick argued; he'd have to buy film and load the camera. Abbie's idea was simpler. Why didn't Dan hold the camera, without film, and go through the motions of taking the FBI agent's picture? Pretending to film would be as good as really filming.

Still, Abbie's political life in Worcester wasn't all make-believe. A down-to-earth activist with practical goals, he emphasized "economic realities" such as "decent jobs" and "fair housing." In 1964, for example, as reported in the local radical newsletter *The Drum,* Abbie spoke on a panel with Father Gilgun and D'Army Bailey and argued that it was "time to bring all the alienated minority groups, the Puerto Ricans, the ex-miners in Kentucky, the migrant workers and even the so-called 'poor white trash' into the movement."

In 1963 the leaders of SDS, the newly formed left-wing student organization, were moving into the ghettoes of America and urging the creation of "an interracial movement of the poor." Abbie never joined SDS, but he echoed the sentiment and, in a spirit of brotherhood, made the Worcester ghetto his home, forging alliances—albeit tenuous— that cut across racial lines. In 1963 SDS called for "local insurgency" and for an outpouring of "local insurgents"; in his own way Abbie aspired to be the archetype of the local insurgent and to bring insurgency to the local level. He first marched and picketed then committed acts of civil disobedience in the struggle to integrate the workplace in Worcester. He was in favor of "obstructionism," as he called it, and he urged radicals to reject "passive demonstrations" and instead to embrace "more active, more aggressive tactics" that would attract media attention to political issues. All across the country, young radicals were turning their own bodies into weapons. In New York, civil rights groups blocked traffic on the Triborough Bridge, and in San Francisco young demonstrators like Mario Savio, a student at Berkeley, jammed the lobby of the Sheraton Palace Hotel. At Berkeley in 1964, in a historic speech, Savio told his fellow students, "There is a time when the operation of the machine becomes so odious, makes you so sick at heart, you can't take part. . . . You've got to put your bodies upon the gears. . . . You've got to make it stop." Abbie approved of these tactics and adapted them to Worcester. On one occasion, he, D'Army Bailey, and a group of Clark University students lay down in the middle of the street to prevent trucks from making deliveries to the Wyman-Gordon Company, a defense contractor that discriminated against blacks.

Abbie was involved in less spectacular efforts as well: gathering food and clothing for Southern blacks, writing letters to the editor of the *Worcester Telegram and Gazette,* circulating petitions, mimeographing and distributing leaflets, and bringing in speakers, including SNCC's Stokely Carmichael, the historian Howard Zinn, and novelist Jeremy Larner.

Movie Man

Political organizing didn't become a way of life for Abbie, however, until 1964. In the winter of 1960, as he settled down to married life in Worcester, he seemed apolitical. Most friends and acquaintances who remember him at the start of the decade say that he was more interested in fine art, good food, and his own career as a psychologist than in protesting. Abbie wasn't among the first movers and shakers in the Worcester movement, but Sheila was. A highly visible protester, she was politically active in the growing American movement against nuclear war and nuclear weapons that had been inspired by British philosopher Bertrand Russell and by the Campaign for Nuclear Disarmament (CND), which had staged powerful demonstrations in England against the atom bomb.

In the Worcester press it was Sheila, not Abbie, who received the lion's share of attention. When town residents gathered outside City Hall to demand a "peaceful solution . . . to the world's problems," the *Worcester Telegram and Gazette* reported that "Mrs. Abbott H. Hoffman brought along her son, Andrew, in his baby carriage" and that she carried a sign that read "O Sleepers Awake."

Sheila's notoriety irked Mr. Abbott Hoffman and contributed to the tension that had been brought on by the birth of their son, Andrew, on December 31, 1960. Abbie and Sheila wanted to share the joys and the responsibilities of child-rearing. Somehow, however, it fell to Sheila to feed and clothe Andrew, change his diapers, and put him to bed. Abbie played the part of the proud parent—he handed out cigars and shook hands at Andrew's bris—but when it came to his son's daily needs, more often than not he didn't lend a helping hand. Like his own father, he was often away from home, and even when home he was inattentive.

Abbie had dropped out of graduate school almost as soon as he had learned that Sheila was pregnant. He was disappointed that he hadn't earned an M.A., but he was able to find work as a psychologist at Worcester State Hospital, where he conducted research for two projects: one on "normal marriages" and another on schizophrenics. Here, too, Abbie's impulse to fictionalize brought him notoriety. Dr. Donald Broverman, who worked at Worcester State Hospital in the early 1960s, remembered that Abbie had a knack for finding huge numbers of both normal couples and schizophrenics and was able to collect far more data than anyone else connected with the project. It occurred to Dr. Broverman that Abbie was "fudging" his data or, worse, that he was "manufacturing" it. Obviously he was offbeat and eccentric; he boasted to the staff that he was a "mild psychopath," and rumor had it that he was introducing himself in town as "Doctor Hoffman." But there was no conclusive evidence against him, and the hospital staff clearly liked him. From Monday to Friday he kept the doctors entertained with jokes, quips, and one-liners.

Abbie still wanted a career as a psychologist, but in the meantime he was in the first phase of what would prove to be a lifelong love affair with the movies. At Berkeley he had discovered Pauline Kael's Cinema Guild, a theater that showed only classics and tried to educate audiences about movies as an art form. Inspired by Kael's example, and with a substantial loan from a local businessman, Abbie rented the downtown Park Theater and renamed it the Park Arts. After working at Worcester State Hospital all day, he moonlighted at night as the manager of his own highbrow movie house, thereby escaping from his humdrum reality. Like Pauline Kael, he showed classics (especially Charlie Chaplin) and contemporary European films. Like Kael, he provided audiences with program notes in which he discussed movie themes, movie directors, and outstanding actors. Like Kael, he refused to sell popcorn or show coming attractions because, as he put it, they "tend to play up the sensational parts of a movie."

Abbie's Park Arts opened its doors to the public on October 3, 1961, with two Ingmar Bergman classics: *Smiles of a Summer Night* (1955), a romantic comedy, and *The Seventh Seal* (1956), a dark and apocalyptic parable about modern life. Later the same month he showed Bert Stern's *Jazz on a Summer Day* (1959), Akira Kurosawa's *The Seven Samurai* (1954), and *The Crucible* (1957), a French cinematic adaptation of Arthur Miller's play about the seventeenth-century Salem witch trials, which offered insights into contemporary victims of persecution. Abbie's film selections certainly showed good taste.

In the late sixties he would embrace pop culture and rave about low-brow blockbuster movies like *Planet of the Apes* (1968), *Wild in the Streets* (1968), and *Rosemary's Baby* (1968). In the early sixties, however, he was a movie snob, a movie aesthete. In his guise as Park Arts manager he lambasted contemporary American films. To Margaret Lincoln, a reporter for the *Worcester Telegram and Gazette*, he explained that Hollywood movies were inferior to the European cinema because they were "geared to the emotions of a mass audience." He insisted that movies that ended happily were "obscene" and that Hollywood studios were reprehensible because they treated all audiences, regardless of age, as children. "In a way I may be idealistic, but I believe there's entertainment in a thought-provoking adult theme," he exclaimed. Federico Fellini's *La Dolce Vita* (1960), which had only recently come to American theaters, was his idea of a magnificent and intelligent movie. Granted, there was sex and violence in Fellini's epic about the decadent life of modern Rome—including an orgy, a striptease, and a suicide—but in his view *La Dolce Vita* was a work of art and anything but obscene.

Abbie wanted to upgrade Worcester's taste in movies. Still, he wasn't prepared to push the local Philistines too hard. After arranging a special screening with Jonas and Adolfas Mekas of their avant-garde film *Guns of the Trees,* he decided that it was too offbeat to show and that it would tarnish his reputation as an impresario of artistic films by famed European directors. Worcester, however, wasn't ready for the likes of Bergman or Fellini either. Audiences were enthusiastic but small, and after a short, memorable season, the Park Arts went dark.

Crisis at Home and Abroad

In 1962, prompted by the momentum that was gathering on college campuses across the state, Abbie shifted his attention from movies to politics. H. Stuart Hughes, a Harvard history professor, was running for the U.S. Senate on an antinuclear platform, and students formed the backbone of his campaign. In Worcester Abbie took charge of the petition drive to place Hughes's name on the ballot. Chester Hartman, Hughes's statewide manager, remembered that Abbie "worked very hard getting signatures and distributing leaflets." He also knocked on doors and informed voters about Hughes and his goal of unilateral nuclear disarmament. Moreover, in September 1962 he introduced Professor Hughes at an outdoor rally in Worcester. According to Hughes, no one showed up to hear him speak. "It was the most embarrassing event in the whole campaign," he remembered. "I could have been mad at Abbie for this humiliation, but he was so good-humored."

At San Quentin and at San Francisco City Hall Abbie had been a witness to rather than a participant in the protests. Hughes's campaign was his first direct involvement in politics, and though he found the experience "exhilarating," he didn't stick with it. Hal Gordon, who was in charge of Hughes's campaign in Worcester, remembered that Abbie was enthusiastic at first but soon "shifted his energy and attention." In fact he was caught up in a personal crisis.

Chester Hartman described Abbie as "sexually active" while he was organizing for H. Stuart Hughes. "He got a young campaign worker pregnant, and that caused a bit of a stir," Hartman remembered. Meanwhile Sheila was pregnant again, much to Abbie's annoyance. This time he insisted that she get an abortion. He helped to make an appointment with a doctor, but the plans fell through, and Sheila decided to have the child on her own. Now that she and Abbie were legally separated, she moved to Cambridge so that, as she put it, she "could enjoy the pregnancy." Abbie moved to New York and found a job as a theater manager at the newly opened Baronet-Coronet on Third Avenue.

On the surface Abbie enjoyed life in midtown Manhattan. "There were . . . acres and acres of movie theaters," he exclaimed in his autobiography. He watched new movies and raved about them, especially Tony Richardson's *The Loneliness of the Long Distance Runner* (1962), with its anarchistic hero. He felt good, too, that he could let in friends (like Marty Kenner, whom he'd met in Berkeley) for free, a gesture that made him popular. But he was also depressed by his separation from Sheila, and like many of his contemporaries he found his head spinning because of the Cuban missile crisis. On October 22, 1962, President

John F. Kennedy announced on TV that the Soviet Union had installed nuclear weapons in Cuba, and that the Soviet fleet was transporting still more weapons to the Castro regime. President Kennedy issued an ultimatum: the Russians had to remove their missiles and turn their ships around or risk nuclear war. To citizens around the world, and especially to young people, the situation exemplified the insanity of the cold war and the craziness of what President Eisenhower called the "military-industrial complex." For Todd Gitlin, a Harvard student active in H. Stuart Hughes's campaign—which fizzled in the wake of Soviet-American brinkmanship—life "was suddenly dwarfed and illuminated, as if by the glare of an explosion that had not yet taken place." For Tom Hayden and Richard Flacks, who were among the founders of Students for a Democratic Society, the missile crisis was "the week of madness."

Hal Gordon, who visited Abbie in New York in the fall of 1962, remembered that they stood in the projection room peering at the movie on the screen and "talked about the end of the world." In his autobiography, Abbie says nothing directly about the effect of the Cuban missile crisis on his state of mind. But his descriptions of New York that October offer clues about his inner landscape. "People crowded into bars," he wrote. "People emptied their savings accounts. Schools held daily air raid drills. The radio blared directions from civil defense officials. . . . Many people were convinced the end was at hand."

The Cuban missile crisis set the stage for a series of American showdowns, shoot-outs, and confrontations, from Dallas and Chicago to Washington, D.C., and Hanoi. This historical event imbued the sixties generation with an apocalyptic cast of mind, a sense of the absurdity of politics, and a suspicion of politicians. At the same time, it led to a social and psychic breakthrough. Oddly enough it introduced into radical politics the kind of madcap humor that would be reflected in Stanley Kubrick's brilliant 1964 film *Dr. Strangelove, or: How I Learned to Stop Worrying and Love the Bomb.*

Then, too, the Cuban missile crisis made the college readings in Albert Camus and the late-night conversations about existentialism suddenly relevant. Under the threat of universal death and destruction, it seemed imperative to give birth to something new *now,* to create a space right here in which life might thrive, love might grow, and people might come together in a kind of holy communion. The missile crisis encouraged a generation to take risks and to make history before it was too late.

Local Insurgent

Abbie's legal separation from Sheila proved to be emotionally painful; for all their conflicts, they still loved one another. Besides, Abbie quipped, it was cheaper for two to live together than to live apart. He moved back to Worcester and moved in with Sheila, Andrew, and Amy—who had been born in November 1962, while they were separated. The newly reconstituted family of four lived at 65 Hadwen Road, not far from his parents. With help from his father, he found a job as a detail man for a pharmaceutical supply company and began to make a modest salary: "bread for wifey and the kids," he sarcastically put it.

Working as a salesman was an honest attempt to make a living, but Abbie quickly turned the job into a scam and a hustle. By his own admission he spent as little time on the road as possible and gave as little of himself as he could get away with. Moreover, he later claimed that he had taken drugs from the company and from doctor's offices and sold them on the black market. His friend Hal Gordon remembered that when it came time to submit monthly reports to his supervisor, Abbie would make up "entertaining and voluminous" accounts of his life as a salesman. He explained: "To cover my tracks, every once in a while, I'd cover the complete territory, swiping gas station, motel and restaurant receipts by the handful . . . to prove I'd been traveling."

In 1963 and 1964, Abbie began to carve out a career for himself as a civil rights activist. How and why he became a radical isn't entirely clear because he obscured his own political evolution. Friends who knew him at Brandeis in the mid- to late fifties were surprised to discover that by the mid-sixties he had come to identify himself with the movement. Some of his college friends thought that it was an act—and indeed it was, but for Abbie there was nothing more authentic than acting. Again and again he promised to relate the true story of his conversion to the movement. In *Woodstock Nation,* for example, he told his readers, "I make up a lot of stories, but now for the first time I'm about to tell the TRUTH, the whole TRUTH and nothing but the TRUTH." He went on to say that it wasn't really the HUAC hearings in San Francisco that radicalized him, or Sheriff Bull Connor's use of force against civil rights demonstrators in Alabama in 1963, but rather Ed Sullivan's censorship of Elvis Presley. Abbie also offered half a dozen other explanations. For example, he claimed that working as a psychologist at Worcester State Hospital had radicalized him because he recognized that social solutions were needed in order to solve individual problems.

As Abbie took his first tentative steps into the movement, America was in the midst of the most dramatic social upheaval since the Civil War, a hundred years earlier. Across the South, African Americans were demanding the right to vote in local and national elections and the freedom to eat at downtown lunch counters, go to movies, take public transportation, and sit at the front of the bus. In Georgia, Alabama, and Mississippi, young and old marched, picketed, signed petitions, staged sit-ins, and gathered in black churches to listen to Dr. Martin Luther King, Jr., to sing "We Shall Overcome," and to pray for dignity and respect.

Almost everywhere in the South, law enforcement officials responded with cattle prods, fire hoses, attack dogs, and prison cells. The Ku Klux Klan and the white citizens' councils waged a campaign of terror against the black community, setting off bombs, lynching organizers, assassinating black leaders like Medgar Evers, and burning homes, offices, and churches. Like many others across the country, Abbie followed these events on television, and television played a part in radicalizing him (and others). He watched, too, as the civil rights movement spread to the North and white liberals became aware of racial inequalities in their own backyards. The civil rights movement came to Worcester in 1963, the year that would witness both the triumph of the March on Washington and the tragedy of the bombing in Birmingham, Alabama.

On September 15, 1963, Americans were shocked when a bomb exploded in Birmingham's Sixteenth Street Baptist Church, killing four young black girls. As Abbie observed at the time, that event prompted Worcester's white liberals "to open their eyes to the discrimination existing right in our city." Worcester, of course, wasn't the Deep South, though Abbie insisted that the North was merely "upsouth." Worcester voted by a wide margin for John Kennedy in 1960 and overwhelmingly for Lyndon Johnson in 1964. Joe Casdin and Paul Mullaney, Worcester's mayors in the early to mid-sixties, were liberal democrats who supported integration, established civil rights commissions, and donated money to activists like Abbie. Worcester had a chapter of the National Association for the Advancement of Colored People (NAACP), the largest, oldest, and most cautious of the major civil rights organizations in the mid-1960s. NAACP members in the Deep South were often at the forefront of the struggle and paid for their courage with their lives, but the national leadership of the NAACP was often more interested in fighting legal battles in the U.S. Supreme Court than in conducting civil disobedience in the streets. That cautious strategy didn't suit Abbie, who wanted nothing less than the transformation of the Worcester chapter from a moderate civil rights group that discussed issues and passed resolutions into a militant organization that took on the local establishment.

Nelson Ambush, the president and founder of the Worcester branch of the NAACP, had been born nearby in Cambridge, Massachusetts, in 1915, and had long since passed his days of militant protest. To Ambush, Abbie was an eager but misguided young man. "His hand always shot up," Ambush remembered. "Whenever I asked for someone to give a talk or attend a meeting in City Hall, he'd say, 'Send me. Let me go. I'll do it. Me. Me.'"

When blacks complained about garbage collection, Abbie suggested that he and his friends collect it themselves and dump it at City Hall. Nelson Ambush wasn't amused; under no circumstances was Abbie to deposit trash outside the mayor's office, and certainly not under NAACP auspices. Abbie escalated his attacks on the NAACP in the *Drum,* a monthly newsletter which he founded in 1964. Abbie edited, published, and distributed the newsletter free with help from Hal Gordon and Betty Price, a young black woman who had been born and raised in Worcester and, as she remembered later, determined to change its "lily-white face."

In the first issue of the *Drum,* Abbie—or rather Abbott, as his name appeared on the masthead—came on like a righteous crusader, issuing a "Statement of Policy" in which he announced that "discrimination does exist in Worcester. . . . It is *not* a minimal problem, as the Chamber of Commerce would have us believe. Serious injustices exist in education, housing and job opportunities." He explained that the purpose of the *Drum* was "to publicize the efforts of organizations and individuals working towards a solution of this problem." In capital letters, printed in bold, he proclaimed "JOIN THE NAACP." In fact, Abbie wanted to take over the organization. In the *Drum*'s second issue, he published an editorial entitled "The Do-Nothing NAACP," in which he complained that "the average Negro member is about 50 years old, middle-class, an old timer in Worcester and generally content with Worcester's racial situation." From Abbie's point of view, such members were so cowardly that they would "make the worst Uncle Tom blush." The NAACP was a part of the problem, not a part of the solution, he complained. "There is a total unawareness, on the part of the leadership, of what is going on in the country," he wrote. "None of the officers had heard of CORE [Congress of Racial Equality], the Urban League, SNCC, or knew the group that Martin Luther King represented. Only one had ever hear of W. E. B. DuBois (founder of the NAACP), none knew any freedom songs or had read a recent book on the Civil Rights movement."

In the same issue of the *Drum,* Abbie described SNCC as the organization which has "repeatedly done the most with the least amount of any group in the South." Indeed, ever since 1960, SNCC members had been at the forefront of the struggle against segregation. Casting themselves as existential warriors, many of them had risked their own lives in backwater towns when they tried to help disenfranchised black farmers register to vote. In its initial phase, SNCC was, as its name implied, nonviolent. But by 1964, after enduring violent attacks for years, many SNCC members were rethinking their commitment to nonviolence. In the *Drum,* Abbie reported that he'd heard one SNCC member say, "After you've been non-violent for six or seven years and are a bundle of scars and false teeth you begin to wonder." SNCC would soon divide around the issue of violence, and so would the New Left as a whole. Sociologist Kenneth Keniston observed in *Young Radicals* that "the issue of violence is to this generation what the issue of sex was to the Victorian world."

For Abbie, however, violence did not seem troubling or disturbing. By the spring of 1964, well before most SNCC militants were advocating the use of arms, he was arguing that civil rights activists should use weapons against white vigilantes. "Violence, in the South, might cause the bomb throwers and the snipers to think twice," he wrote in the *Drum.* "If they feared Negroes might retaliate with counter violence there might be a lessening of brutality." Malcolm X was by now openly ridiculing the nonviolent tactics of Martin Luther King, Jr., and urging his followers to consider revolution, rather than passive resistance, as the path to freedom. Abbie heard Malcolm X's message and began to think that violence could play an important part in the struggle to end segregation.

Like many young white radicals, Abbie regarded SNCC members as apostles. Not surprisingly, he wanted to join the "band of brothers standing in a circle of love," as James Forman, SNCC's National Secretary, called the organization. But SNCC was an odd organization; it didn't have a membership list, didn't give out membership cards, and didn't collect dues. To outsiders it often seemed on the verge of chaos and collapse. There were, of course, SNCC leaders—"field secretaries," they were called—and highly disciplined organizers, but according to Cleveland Sellers, SNCC had more than its share of "anarchists, floaters and freedom-high niggers" who felt that "every individual had the right and the responsibility to follow the dictates of his conscience, no matter what." To Mary King, a white activist who worked for years in SNCC's Communication Section in Georgia and Mississippi, the organization was "enigmatic" and "elusive." It was continually changing, continually reinventing its own political identity, and always difficult to pin down.

In many ways SNCC was the perfect political group for a character like Abbie, who thrived on the enigmatic and the elusive and was continually reinventing himself. Not surprisingly, he founded and appointed himself chairman of the Worcester Area chapter of the Friends of SNCC, an informal, nationwide organization that publicized and raised money for SNCC projects. In 1964, SNCC's one and only project was the Mississippi Freedom Summer Project. Designed to bring white students to Mississippi, the project was the brainchild of Robert Moses, a Harlem-born, Harvard-educated philosopher, and Allard Lowenstein, a liberal Democrat who was later elected to the U.S. Congress. SNCC organizers assumed that the presence of Northern students would be newsworthy and would attract media attention. In turn, the media would focus the attention of the nation on segregation in

Mississippi, and on the efforts of the white students who'd teach in "Freedom Schools," register black voters, and assist in the organization of the Mississippi Freedom Democratic Party, an alternative to the official, segregated Democratic Party. If all went according to SNCC plans, the Democratic National Convention, which would be meeting in Atlantic City in August, would recognize the Freedom Democrats and unseat the segregated Democratic Party delegation.

The project was risky. Southern bigots would regard the white students as "nigger lovers": Ku Klux Klansmen might lynch them, and redneck sheriffs and their deputies might harass them. Still, it was a risk that SNCC organizers were willing to take. After all, they'd risked their own lives for years. Moreover, hundreds of young whites were anxious to make the pilgrimage to Mississippi, join the struggle, and find their own personal freedom. Though they couldn't join SNCC or become SNCC members, they could volunteer to take part in the Freedom Summer Project. Mario Savio, who went to Mississippi and later became the leader of the Free Speech Movement in Berkeley, remembered it as "the most important political project in America since the Civil War. It was the moment of awakening." It's not surprising, then, that Abbie became obsessed with Mississippi and determined to go there.

In the winter and spring of 1964 he took time off from his route as a traveling salesman to visit the SNCC office in the basement of the Epworth Methodist Church at Harvard University. There he met Robert Zellner, a SNCC field secretary, and Dottie Miller, a Queens College graduate and veteran of the Southern civil rights struggle who was SNCC's only paid staff member in New England. Robert and Dottie were about to become husband and wife and to devote their energies to the Mississippi Freedom Summer Project. Robert Zellner later remembered Abbie as a "floater": an activist who moved in and out of struggles according to whim. Dottie Zellner remembered that in 1964, "Abbie Hoffman looked as straight as could be, but he had an unbelievably outrageous sense of humor, and he was eccentric." Listening to Abbie talk about his work with the NAACP in Worcester, Dottie had the distinct impression that "he was desperate to reach out to something outside his own little life."

In the chapter in his autobiography entitled "Going South," Abbie writes that "the Zellners had no trouble enlisting me as a SNCC worker early in 1964." He goes on to say that he "made a short trip to Jackson [Mississippi], the state capital, to confer on strategy" for the Mississippi Freedom Democratic Party in Atlantic City, and that he marched and was arrested in Jackson, along with three thousand other demonstrators. In the chapter's concluding paragraph he tells this story: "Once I had a noose dangled before my face by a redneck deputy who said I had run a red light in Yazoo City. Yazoo City had no traffic lights at the time. When I pointed this out, I was busted for insulting an officer."

The Zellners tell a different story. According to Dottie and Bob, they never tried to recruit Abbie for SNCC. Robert Zellner recalled that Abbie had volunteered for Mississippi Freedom Summer but was turned down because he was deemed "emotionally unstable" and "too far-out." According to SNCC organizers and field secretaries—including Bob Moses, John Lewis, and James Forman, as well as white organizers close to SNCC such as Staughton Lynd and Howard Zinn (all of whom were interviewed for this book)—Abbie didn't take part in Mississippi Freedom Summer.

Nor is there any other evidence that Abbie ever set foot in Mississippi in the summer of 1964. His name doesn't appear in SNCC records or in the papers of the Mississippi Freedom Democratic Party. Over the past three decades, nearly a dozen books have been published about Mississippi Freedom Summer and about the seven hundred volunteers who took part in the project, and Abbie doesn't show up anywhere. No one who wrote about SNCC or about Mississippi in 1964—including Sally Belfrage, Len Holt, Paul Good, Mary King, Tracy Sugarman, and Elizabeth Sutherland (again, all of whom were interviewed for this book)—ever encountered Abbie in their travels. It seems likely that he was disappointed by his "deselection" but didn't show it, at least not in public. He urged Worcester citizens to volunteer and, borrowing from one of Moses's speeches, promoted Mississippi Freedom Summer as "a massive Peace Corps–type operation." In the *Drum* he predicted that the summer of 1964 would be a "long hot summer" and "the summer of decision for the civil rights movement."

From the start the summer took a violent turn. Even before the bulk of Freedom Summer volunteers left the training session at the Western College for Women in Oxford, Ohio, the news media reported that three civil rights workers—Andrew Goodman, James Chaney, and

Michael Schwerner—had disappeared near Philadelphia, Mississippi. When their charred 1963 Chevy station wagon was discovered near a swamp, they were presumed dead. Five weeks later their bodies were unearthed in Neshoba County. Sheriff Laurence Rainey and Deputy Cecil Price had taken part in the lynching and were indicted by a federal grand jury.

After he became a media celebrity and an icon of the revolution, Abbie insisted that he had gone to Mississippi in 1964 and had almost been lynched there. "The terror was real," he told reporter Howard Goodman. "Mickey Schwerner could have been me. We were friends. He was in my generation of activists. It could have been me in that car, and you could have been interviewing him today." But Abbie Hoffman and Michael Schwerner were never friends. Moreover, in June 1964 Abbie was safely at home in Worcester, Massachusetts. On June 24, shortly after he heard the news that James Chaney, Michael Schwerner, and Andrew Goodman had disappeared, he issued a press release about the crisis. Abbie begged Worcester citizens to send telegrams to Congressman Harold Donohue "urging him to support federal protection of workers now in Mississippi." Moreover, he told the *Worcester Telegram and Gazette* that he was collecting money for a bail fund, and that it would be used if needed by the three Clark University students who were participating in the Mississippi Summer Project.

In his autobiography Abbie also claimed that he had played an important role at the 1964 Democratic National Convention. "I arrived early in Atlantic City," he wrote. "We lined up churches and camp fields for sleeping and local committees to do the cooking. . . . On the boardwalks we rallied around the clock. In hotel rooms we met with Democratic delegates from our home states. The mayor of Worcester pledged me his support for the Freedom Delegation. When we tabulated the votes we had more than enough. We were going to win! We had become the darlings of the convention." He went on to explain that the "freedom delegates were offered observer status and allowed to sit at the back of the hall but not to participate. It was called 'the back-of-the-bus compromise.' Only . . . the older NAACPers were happy. SNCC was furious. . . . Atlantic City had split our ranks."

The 1964 Democratic National Convention was a turning point for the movement, but again there's no evidence that Abbie took part in that decisive history. Worcester Mayor Paul Mullaney, who did attend the convention, does not remember meeting Abbie there, and no one in the Worcester delegation who participated in the vigil on the boardwalk in support of the Freedom Party delegates remembers him either.

When the Democratic Party regulars, including Senators Hubert Humphrey and Walter Mondale, refused to seat the delegates of the Mississippi Freedom Democratic Party, SNCC members were disillusioned. Bob Moses felt betrayed. Stokely Carmichael turned to black power and separatism. James Forman, SNCC's executive secretary, spoke for many when he noted that the lesson of Atlantic City was that "no longer was there any hope . . . that the federal government would change the situation in the Deep South." SDS's Tom Hayden observed that Atlantic City came down to "a bitter conflict between two generations of civil rights forces": older activists were prepared to accept compromise and work within the system, while younger activist chose to defy it and embrace confrontation.

A radical shift took place in the summer of 1964, but there's no evidence that Abbie shifted. After the convention he continued, as before, to support the Mississippi Freedom Democratic Party. In the pages of the *Drum* he wrote, "The Challenge goes on." And he added, "We are currently recruiting lawyers throughout the country to go to Mississippi for the purpose of taking testimony from Negroes who have been denied the right to vote." Though he had talked about trading the ballot for the bullet, he still hoped that the Democratic Party would clean its own house and that electoral reform would bring equality to the South. It was an old movie, and he replayed it in his own head long after other radicals were writing new scenarios for the revolution.

chapter four

WHITE MISCHIEF, BLACK POWER

Freedom High

Local insurgency was good, but activists didn't have much status until they left their campuses and communities and went to Mississippi to demonstrate their commitment to civil rights. Young activists, both black and white, had been going south ever since 1960; among the best-known and the bravest were the Freedom Riders, so called because they traveled by bus to challenge segregation in interstate travel. Brutally beaten by racist mobs—often while FBI agents stood by and watched—the Freedom Riders became symbols of movement courage in the wake of terror, violence, and all too often the indifference of the Kennedy administration. It wasn't long before almost everyone who went south was called a freedom rider—at least by black sharecroppers who were amazed that white people were willing to risk their lives for the cause of freedom.

Abbie took his freedom ride at the tail end of the freedom movement. He had missed the chance to be among the Freedom Riders of 1961 or the Freedom School teachers of 1964, and he was determined not to let the South slip through his fingers again. The summer of 1965 would be the last time that significant numbers of Northern whites would go to Mississippi for civil rights, and Abbie would be among them. Many of his closest friends at Brandeis, including Ira Landess and Mendy Samstein, had already been to the South, and Abbie wanted to follow in their footsteps. As Ira Landess remembered, "He told us that it meant a lot to him that we had gone down in 1964. He wanted to savor some of the experience for himself, and was resolute about going down in '65 after having missed the first summer." In fact, Abbie would continue to go south in 1966 and 1967, long after most Northern radicals had shifted political direction and had begun to look west, to Berkeley and San Francisco, for political and cultural models.

Abbie was also anxious to get out of Worcester. He was going to Mississippi, he told Father Gilgun in a letter that was full of ranting and raving, because he couldn't trust anyone anymore, perhaps not even Gilgun himself. There wasn't a genuine radical in the Worcester movement, he complained. The word "freedom" itself had been profaned, he claimed, by the phony activists who belonged to the Congress of Racial Equality (CORE), the NAACP, the Phoenix (an organization made up largely of Catholic radicals), and Prospect House, a community center. He was making his way to Mississippi for intensely personal rather than for ideological reasons, he explained to Gilgun. Moreover, he felt that he had no choice but to join other activists in the South. It was a matter of life or death. If he wasn't a part of the movement, in the thick of debate and struggle, creating a web of human connections, he would surely die. It seemed that clear to him.

On July 29, 1965, the *Worcester Telegram and Gazette* reported that Abbott Hoffman was going to Mississippi with Jan Selby, a minister of the Covenant Methodist Church. It was an auspicious moment in the history of the civil rights movement. In mid-June, more than eight hundred demonstrators had been arrested in Jackson, the state capitol of Mississippi, where they were protesting discrimination against blacks at the polls. On August 6, soon after Abbie arrived in Mississippi, President Johnson signed the Voting Rights Act of 1965, which led, over the next decade, to the electoral empowerment of two million African Americans all across the South. On August 11, when Abbie was midway through his Mississippi sojourn, African Americans in the Watts section of Los Angeles poured into the streets to express their rage. They smashed windows, stole merchandise, threw bottles at police cars, and talked about rebellion. The author Stanley Crouch, then an activist in a Los Angeles poverty program, described Watts as "a bloody carnival, a great celebration."

Abbie was headed south at a time when SNCC's forces in Mississippi were in disarray, when black power was displacing integration, and when many Northern liberals were retreating from the civil rights movement. In March 1965, hundreds of well-meaning liberals (including author James Baldwin and folksinger Joan Baez) joined Dr. Martin Luther King, Jr., in a historic march from Montgomery to Selma, Alabama. But as civil rights historian Clayborne Carson later observed, the Selma march would be "the last major racial protest of the 1960s to receive substantial white support." Abbie hoped that white support wouldn't dwindle altogether, and on the eve of his departure for Mississippi he told a reporter for the *Worcester Telegram and Gazette* that he was going south because he wanted to show blacks that "Northerners are still interested in their problems." He had not forsaken the cause.

Years later, Abbie would reframe his motives for going south. On one occasion, he told Allen Ginsberg that his civil rights experience was an extension of the Beat adventure, and that on the road to Mississippi he had read Jack Kerouac's *On the Road*. On another occasion, during a TV appearance in Chicago in the seventies, he explained that going south was an act of emancipation from his parents. "It wasn't until I headed for Mississippi that I finally discovered that freedom is essentially stopping the enactment of your parents' fantasies," he observed.

It made good sense for Abbie to choose McComb, Mississippi, as the site for his baptism in the civil rights movement. A rough-and-tumble blue-collar town in Pike County on the Louisiana border, McComb had been a center of SNCC activity the previous year and the scene of intense Klan violence. During Freedom Summer, from June to September 1964, there were seventeen bombings of black homes and offices. Abbie's college friend Mendy Samstein, one of the few whites who belonged to SNCC's inner circle, had nearly been killed in an explosion that ripped apart the Freedom House. Years later, Abbie would claim that he was "home in Massachusetts watching a TV news story on a bombing at some civil rights center and there was Mendy crawling out of the rubble." He would add, too, that "it was then I decided it was time to head South."

In 1964, television covered almost every move of the civil rights movement in Mississippi. It shed a piercing light on bigotry and brought Mississippi's backwardness to the attention of the nation. It conferred on the volunteers a sense of their own historical importance and drew young activists into the thick of the struggle. When Abbie arrived in McComb, almost a year after the bombing of the SNCC Freedom House, he found that "things were . . . falling apart." The Freedom House itself was in a state of disrepair, and the organization was collapsing. Many of SNCC's leading activists had regrouped in Lowndes County, Alabama, where the median income for blacks was $935 a year, and not a single black resident was registered to vote.

Disillusioned with the Democratic Party and unwilling to invest time and energy in the Mississippi Freedom Democrat Party, SNCC created the Lowndes County Freedom Organization, an independent political party whose symbol, the black panther, reflected the new militant ideology of black power. McComb wasn't on the front lines any longer, but it still had a Freedom School, and there were still dedicated teachers. Ira Landess, a close friend of Abbie's from Brandeis and a Freedom Summer volunteer in 1964, had returned to McComb, and he and Abbie conducted classes in a black church. With the exception of Ira Landess, no one in the McComb movement, and no one in SNCC or in the local NAACP chapter, has any memories of Abbie from the summer of 1965. According to Landess, Abbie spent about three weeks in McComb. "He was a veritable Pied Piper," Landess recalled. "During breaks he would bound out of the church with his kids and throw a ball around with them. He tirelessly gave everything he had to his students, and the result was a love affair between him and the kids."

On August 12, 1965, two weeks after his departure from Worcester, the *Telegram and Gazette* published a long letter from Abbie in which he described his arrival in Mississippi, his impressions of the South, and his attitudes toward its citizens. The letter, which was dispatched from 702 Wall Street—the address of the SNCC Freedom House in Mc-Comb—was obviously meant for publication. There's nothing of an intimate nature in Abbie's dispatch, yet it's similar to the personal letters that Freedom Summer volunteers had written to family members and friends in 1964 and that found their way into Elizabeth Sutherland's anthology *Letters from Mississippi.* Like the volunteers of 1964, Hoffman saw bleak poverty in black neighborhoods and smug prosperity in white neighborhoods. Like the activists who preceded him, he was profoundly moved by the show of affection from McComb's black citizens and deeply disturbed by the hostility that emanated from the town's white citizens.

Mississippi Rashomon

Mississippi struck Abbie, as it did many of the volunteers, as a dark mirror that reflected an America that seemed a Kafkaesque country. Jack Newfield reports that during the orientation session for Freedom Summer volunteers that took place in Oxford, Ohio, in June 1964, Bob Moses, the project's director, explained, "When you're in Mississippi, the rest of America doesn't seem real. And when you're in the rest of America, Mississippi doesn't seem real." Most of the volunteers would marvel at the accuracy of that observation as soon as their feet touched Mississippi soil. According to Nicolaus Mills, a volunteer named Clark Gardner recalled that "someone said at Oxford at the orientation session that once you are in Mississippi, everything outside seems unreal—there is a lot of truth in it." Abbie told readers of the *Worcester Telegram and Gazette:* "Entering Mississippi is a strange experience that affects you as soon as you cross the state line. Immediately you see a huge billboard that says 'Welcome to Mississippi—the Hospitality State.' Twenty yards down the road you see a second billboard that says, 'Martin Luther King is a Communist.' You know right away they didn't mean you in that welcome."

He went on to describe what his life was like in McComb: "In the mornings I teach at the Freedom School. This afternoon I marched with some local maids and civil rights workers. We picketed an inn. . . . It is the first strike ever to take place in McComb for anything and was completely the maid's idea. The picketing was tense, with a large crowd watching. There were no incidents. . . . We are working on a book composed of local Negroes relating their experiences in McComb. The stories are incredible: Lynchings, shootings in broad daylight, total economic bondage, superhuman bravery on the part of those who have protested. You almost feel they are all made up, that these things just never took place. But then you remember the intense hate you could read in the eyes of the whites, and you know it happened—all of it."

Most of all, he was excited about the "complete academic freedom" that he enjoyed at the Freedom School. "Teaching here is a real joy," he exclaimed. "Creative ability is the order of the day." Like a great many Freedom School teachers, he followed guidelines that had been set forth by SNCC organizer Mendy Samstein. For Samstein the key to reaching black students was the teacher's ability to make spontaneous performance an essential element of pedagogy. "The dramatic method can permit the expression of a wide range of feelings by the students, involve their total selves, stimulate creativity, provide the teacher with insights about the students, and, at the same time, get across content material," Samstein had written. Showing, not telling, appealed to Abbie's theatrical sensibility. To teach concepts of time, he persuaded his eight- and nine-year-old students to construct sundials. To convey ideas about justice, he persuaded the students to act out a courtroom drama: one student played the judge, while others took parts as the lawyers and members of the jury. "I was demonstrating the ideal of innocence until proven guilty," Abbie wrote to the *Worcester Telegram and Gazette.* "The real thing is a long way from the experience of Mc-Comb Negroes."

By writing from Mississippi, Abbie contributed to a growing body of civil rights history that activists were writing even as they were making it. Everyone in and around SNCC, or so it seemed, was a self-proclaimed historian. In accord with the organization's democratic ideals, each person was regarded as an expert witness to his or her own experience, and no one's experience was deemed more or less important than anyone else's experience. Mary King, who was twenty-four when she coordinated the SNCC Communications Office in Mississippi in the summer of 1964, observed in *Freedom Song,* her "personal story of the 1960s," that "everyone who participated has a different story," and that "no one can debate what I lived." Activists who were anxious for unimpeachable historical truths were often disturbed by SNCC's insistence on the integrity of the individual experience and the primacy of the personal story. Allard Lowenstein, for example, was troubled by the spectacle of so many conflicting accounts of the civil rights movement. "One of the great problems with dealing with history is that, as with 'Rashomon,' everybody's version of what happens differs," he complained in a speech entitled "Mississippi Freedom Summer Revisited."

Rashomon, Akira Kurosawa's Japanese classic, tells the story of a murder from several opposing points of view. The obvious point of the film is that there's no such thing as "the truth"; it all depends on who is telling the story. That was Abbie's perspective as well. What was essential, he believed, was to tell stories that would help transform the segregated South into an integrated community, and what better way than to make himself into a freedom rider. The South was Abbie's immense movie set, and the civil rights movement of the sixties provided an endless source of material for the ongoing fantasies he projected on the screen of history. He was producer, director, screenwriter, and star of the epic drama. He focused the camera on himself and cast himself as a beloved friend of the black community, a sworn enemy of white racist regimes, and a martyr to the cause.

The long, descriptive letter of August 12, 1965, that he sent to the *Worcester Telegram and Gazette* was hardly free of exaggerations and distortions. The picket line he joined was not the first of its kind in McComb as he claimed. And McComb itself was not, as he insisted, "the most dangerous spot in Mississippi, which means the South." For all the violence that took place in and around McComb, there were no lynchings there, as there had been in Neshoba County, the tragic burial ground for Goodman, Chaney, and Schwerner. Abbie's letter has its melodramatic moments: "The tension is always felt, especially at night when a car approaches or when you go into the white area," he wrote. There was also apprehension in broad daylight. "The picketing was tense, with a large crowd watching," he wrote. But Abbie didn't blatantly fabricate. He was level-headed enough to note that "there were no incidents." When he and several picketers had a meal at a recently integrated restaurant and there was no confrontation, he didn't make one up. "Most of the white people moved away or left, but the service was good," he wrote.

His August 1965 letter from McComb was the least fictionalized account that he ever wrote about McComb or the South. For the next twenty-five years he would go on retelling the story of his experiences in McComb in 1965. Each time he exaggerated, embellished, and elaborated until the story became a myth, and Abbott Hoffman, the young civil rights activist, was barely recognizable. "They were sophisticated fictions," Robbie Osman, a Freedom Summer volunteer, observed. "Abbie knew enough of the real history to create a believable world."

In his autobiography he retold the story about black maids in Mc-Comb who were on strike for higher wages. This time, however, he made himself the focal point, and this time there was the added element of violence and the added presence of a federal law enforcement official. "I was thrown to the curb and kicked repeatedly," he wrote. "An FBI agent leaned over and asked sarcastically if my civil rights had been violated." Needless to say, there exists no witness to this event, no FBI report, and no contemporaneous account. As late as the end of the 1980s, he was still reinventing the history of McComb and recreating his own experiences there. Shortly before he committed suicide, he told Jeff Kisseloff, an editor at the *Bill of Rights Journal* who was preparing a special issue on the sixties, that he had faced both the Ku Klux Klan and redneck prisoners while he was in McComb. Moreover, he claimed that he had been arrested several times, beaten in and out of jail, and nearly lynched.

"There were a lot of racial disturbances, as they were called," he explained to Kisseloff. "When the maids went on strike, we set up pickets, and every day the Klan came, beat us up, and then we were arrested. We would then be taken to the police station and beaten. That happened a few times. One time an actual noose was passed in front of my head." Abbie told Kisseloff that after one arrest, "I was fed to the prisoners in the tank. Along with giving them a bottle of liquor, they said to them, 'Here comes another Jew nigger lover from the north.'" He boasted that it was in the South that he "came to terms with death."

No one ever pointed out the exaggerations, distortions, and embellishments in Abbie's voluminous stories about the civil rights movement, and no one ever cross-examined him, either, not even when he appeared before the House Un-American Activities Committee in 1968 or on the witness stand at the Chicago Conspiracy trial in 1969. "I went South to work in civil rights, chiefly in Mississippi, during the summers of 1964, '65, and '66. Mostly my responsibilities were in voter registration," he told the congressional committee that investigated the riots at the 1968 Democratic National Convention. In federal court in Chicago, he testified that he was a SNCC "field secretary," and that he was "in charge of organizing Friends of SNCC groups." In *Woodstock Nation* he claimed that in Mississippi he had taken "a medical survey door-to-door." When friends questioned him, he'd often say that these experiences "might have happened to him," or that "they could have happened to him." For many activists, Abbie's stories were distressing, but for others they played an important part in building the movement. Len Holt, the official historian of the Mississippi Freedom Summer Project, might have resented Abbie's tales. Instead, he remembered that his "exaggerations and distortions spread a message of protest." By creating a mystique about the movement, Abbie contributed to its growth and its power, Holt insisted. Indeed, Abbie's stories made the civil rights cause sound like an incredible adventure.

The Evolution of the Revolution

In the summer of 1965, when Abbie returned to Worcester from the South, friends noticed that there was "a wilder look in his eye." There was also a stronger note of pessimism in his public pronouncements. In October 1965, for example, he wrote to the *Worcester Telegram and Gazette* to say that "small gains" had been made in the civil rights movement in the South, but that there had been "large losses" in the North. The American people looked at the movement and saw "great progress," Abbie explained, but in reality there was "great frustration and loss of ground." What was especially troubling to him, he said, was the white backlash in the North. However, he still had faith in ordinary people and in the democratic process.

In the fall of 1965, he started yet another organization—the Ad Hoc Committee on Poverty—and argued that poor people themselves, rather than civil servants or welfare bureaucrats, should be in charge of government poverty programs. "We trust the poor," he wrote. "We feel they should have the power to run their own programs because they know their own problems best." Abbie's language reflected his new political awareness. For the first time he used the word "revolutionary" as though he was perfectly comfortable with it. Bringing poor people into positions of leadership, he insisted, was "a revolutionary new approach to the poverty program in Worcester." And he warned that without the participation of the poor, the "democratic foundations" of the nation would crumble.

On January 6, 1966, after years of circling the issue, SNCC issued a direct condemnation of the war in Vietnam and U.S. imperialism. "We believe the United States government has been deceptive in its claims of concern for the Vietnamese people, just as the government has been deceptive in claiming concern for the freedom of colored people in such countries as the Dominican Republic, the Congo, South Africa, Rhodesia and the United States itself," the SNCC statement read. Two weeks later Abbie wrote to the *Worcester Telegram and Gazette* to affirm his identification with liberation struggles around the world.

Almost word for word his personal letter echoed SNCC's official pronouncement. "Our work, particularly in the South, has taught us that the government has never guaranteed the freedom of oppressed citizens and is not yet truly determined to end the rule of terror and oppression within its borders," he wrote. He went on to say, "We maintain that the government's cry of 'preserve freedom in the world' is a hypocritical mask behind which it squashes liberation movements which refuse to be bound by the expediencies of United States cold war policies." But he was slow to take an active part in the movement against the war in Vietnam. SDS staged its first major antiwar rally in Washington, D.C., in the spring of 1965, and Abbie did not attend. His loyalty was to black sharecroppers in Mississippi, not to peasants and workers in Vietnam. "One of the more unfortunate consequences of the war in Vietnam is that public attention is no longer focused on the civil rights movement in the South," he wrote in *Noww,* the Worcester newsletter he edited and published now that the *Drum* was defunct.

Gradually, however, he did become active in the peace movement, and in March 1966 he helped to organize a march in Worcester that coincided with antiwar rallies that took place in New York, Washington, Boston, and Berkeley. With local artists he made cardboard doves and distributed them, along with flowers and olive branches, to the 250 or so protesters who gathered at the courthouse in Lincoln Square and made their way through the hostile crowds that lined the streets.

Abbie could be intently serious about antiwar activities: he helped to bring Senator Wayne Morse, who opposed the bombing of Vietnam, to speak at Clark University. But he could also be playful, if not downright silly. On one occasion he suggested that everyone opposed to the war show up at Long Island's Jones Beach on a Sunday afternoon in July with nothing on but a bathing suit.

Tripping

In March 1966, the same month that he took part in his first antiwar demonstration, he open the SNICK Shop at 65 Main Street, where he sold elegant crafts handmade in Mississippi: candles, handbags, hats, quilts, dresses, and dolls, both black and white. The previous summer he'd met with representatives of the Poor People's Corporation, an umbrella organization that believed that blacks would achieve political and social equality with whites only if they had economic independence. The Poor People's Corporation provided blacks with jobs and skills, but it was more than just a moneymaking operation.

Jesse Morris, who founded the Poor People's Corporation in 1965 and who had a degree in economics from UCLA, envisioned the corporation as an all-purpose entity that would teach illiterate blacks how to read and write, and thereby enable them to lift themselves by their own bootstraps. Morris saw a place for Abbie in the grand design. Indeed, with his years of experience as a detail man for a pharmaceutical company and his dedication to civil rights, Abbie was a natural for the movement's corporation.

Right away he put himself to work: he read books and pamphlets on the history, theory, and nuts and bolts of the cooperative movement; collected catalogues from wholesalers; made contacts with producers and distributors of raw materials like cotton and leather; hustled funds from friends; and drew up elaborate plans for a network of stores in upper-class towns all across New England. In a letter to Ellen Maslow at Liberty House, the flagship store in Greenwich Village, he suggested that movement women should give parties in their own homes and sell the Mississippi-made crafts to their friends and neighbors. He offered to give a spiel about the Poor People's Corporation and let suburban women from Philadelphia to Boston know how much Northern support meant to Southern blacks.

Meanwhile he opened his own SNICK Shop in Worcester and launched a cute advertising campaign: there was "a little bit of soul in

each sale," he told customers. In addition to the crafts from the cooperatives in Mississippi, he stocked left-wing magazines like David Dellinger's *Liberation* and M. S. Arnoni's *Minority of One.* There were also
political buttons like "Make Love Not War," pop culture posters of
Humphrey Bogart, and (according to an article in *Noww*) "Greta
Garbo suede hats, fruitcakes from a peace co-op, [and] Negro history
books for children."

The SNICK Shop was no more of a financial success than the Park
Arts theater had been; Worcester wasn't ready for chic Mississippi crafts,
campy hats, or Hollywood nostalgia. But the SNICK Shop was significant as an early outpost of the "counterculture" that would blossom in
the late sixties and would include head shops, guerrilla theater groups,
underground newspapers, communes, collectives, food co-ops, and of
course the entire drug culture—the whole amorphous entity that was
connected mainly by a sense of opposition to the established culture of
middle-class, middle-aged, heartland Americans and everything they
consumed, from Campbell's Soup to Frank Sinatra records.

Abbie didn't realize it, but he was already riding the wave of the
hippie future that was emerging on the cultural horizon. In 1965, in an
article for the *Nation,* Hunter S. Thompson observed that within the
movement there was a clustering of "social radicals," as he called them.
They were "fervently committed to the civil rights movement," but
they were "arty," and according to Thompson their "real interests are
writing, painting, good sex, good sounds, and free marijuana." By 1965,
Abbie was straddling two worlds: the traditional world of civil rights
and the unorthodox world of cultural and sexual rebellion that Thompson described. At his and Sheila's home on Hadwen Road, he gave "love
feasts," as he called them, where he offered home-cooked food, music,
and wine to friends. He urged movement people to give "freedom parties": to "sing, dance, and drink" as well as discuss civil rights. "Abbie
liked to party—to get high, to drink wine, and to chase women," a
black friend in Worcester remembered. Slowly but surely he took up
marijuana and delved into the world of hallucinogenic drugs, but he
didn't publicize his new habits because the Worcester movement was
for the most part puritanical. Once, when the police interrupted a boisterous movement party, Abbie concealed a bag of marijuana by sitting

on it; he was later rebuked by colleagues for having jeopardized the cause.

In 1965, the year he took his first acid trip, hundreds or perhaps thousands of others were "turned on" by ex–Harvard professor Timothy Leary at his retreat in Millbrook, New York, and by novelist Ken Kesey and his crew of Merry Pranksters at San Francisco events called Acid Tests. Abbie's companions on his first voyage into the world of psychedelics were two college friends, Ira Landess and Manny Schreiber, and a local artist named Marty Carey, who offered his loft as the laboratory for their real-life experiment. It was fortunate the others were present because LSD (lysergic acid diethylamide), or "acid," intensified Abbie's natural speediness and magnified his innate sense of unreality.

Ira Landess, who had been a Freedom Summer volunteer in 1964 and had taught at the McComb Freedom School with Abbie in the summer of 1965, remembered that after taking LSD, Abbie was "out of control." Manny Schreiber, who'd scored the drug and brought it to Worcester, remembered that Abbie had "a hard time figuring out what was real and what wasn't real." A sense of unreality was to be expected, of course, on LSD. Albert Hofmann, the doctor who synthesized LSD in a Swiss laboratory in the late 1930s, explained that acid produced a "not unpleasant state of intoxication." When he took the drug, he experienced what he described as "an intense stimulation of the imagination and an altered state of awareness of the world." But Abbie's imagination ran wild without benefit of LSD, and *with* acid it went berserk. According to his friends he thought that Marty Carey's loft was exerting a strange power that prevented them from coming or going. "It was like the [Luis] Buñuel movie *Exterminating Angel,* in which the guests are trapped inside the dining room," Manny Schreiber remembered.

Abbie was determined to escape from Carey's loft and to free his old friends. He "broke" out, roamed the streets, and stopped at a diner for hearty provisions. Returning to the loft, he gave out sandwiches and then, imagining himself as liberator, guided his friends to Father Gilgun's church, where he was scheduled to deliver a speech. It was here, while on acid, that Abbie discovered that he could give a talk without following a prepared text. Years later, Abbie would insist that it was LSD that had led him to become a full-time political activist. It probably wasn't *the* cause, but his first experiments with LSD did coincide with intensified movement activity. For a great many sixties radicals, taking LSD was indeed a decisive experience. Carl Oglesby, SDS President in 1965–66, explained that acid gave a sense of "powerful and explicit transformation," and that it was the psychic equivalent of "bursting through the barricades."

Abbie's LSD trips coincided with the end of his abortive career as a pharmaceutical salesman and the final break-up of his stormy marriage. Sheila refused to take acid or to smoke marijuana, and for Abbie her refusal was decisive. "Taking acid created a feeling of definite separation from those who had not," he explained in his autobiography. "To this day, on some level, I still don't trust people who have not opened themselves enough for the experience. On some anal-retentive level they are saying they fear looking inside." Sheila upbraided Abbie for taking LSD; friends remember that she reminded him that he was the father of two children and ought to be more responsible. Now, however, Abbie felt less guilty than ever before if he disappointed Sheila and much less hurt by her anger. She could disapprove all she wanted; she could try to browbeat him, but he would not stop smoking marijuana or "dropping" acid, and so the rift between them intensified.

Politically as well as personally, Abbie took on an angry and defiant identity that mirrored SNCC's new phase as a militant black power organization. In July 1966, he attended the Newport Folk Festival and, as a representative of the Poor People's Corporation, shared space with SNCC's field secretaries, who showed up en masse to publicize the organization. While Abbie was selling crafts made in Mississippi, SNCC members, including Stokely Carmichael (later Kwame Turé) and Julius Lester, sold books and pamphlets and talked about the philosophy and the strategy of black power, which he wholeheartedly endorsed.

For years, blacks and whites in SNCC had worked side-by-side—albeit uneasily—to show the rest of America that racial equality was possible and that integration could work. Inside the organization itself, however, an unequal relationship of power existed between blacks and whites. As early as 1963, according to Nicolaus Mills, some SNCC field secretaries had expressed serious doubts about the effect on the organization of the Northern white students pouring into Mississippi. "I came to SNCC, and I saw Negroes running the movement, and I felt good," Ivanhoe Donaldson said. But then whites began to exert more influence in SNCC, and Donaldson didn't feel good anymore. "I get the feeling the way students are going, in two or three years the movement will be run by white students," he complained. Mendy Samstein, Abbie's Brandeis friend, expressed similar feelings in 1964, on the eve of Mississippi Freedom Summer. "If thousands of whites come down, there is the problem of relationships between blacks and whites," he said. "Whites convincing blacks of their rights—this entrenches the concept of white supremacy."

By 1965 white lawyers and fund-raisers were wielding great power in SNCC, and many blacks didn't like it. Moreover, SNCC's new leadership identified with African countries that had recently thrown off white colonial rule. The African paradigm of liberation ought to apply to African Americans, they argued: it was time for whites to leave the civil rights movement and organize in the "mother country"—in their own communities. Abbie echoed these ideas in a passionate letter he dispatched to the *Worcester Telegram and Gazette* in the summer of 1966. "We say integration is irrelevant," he proclaimed. He went on to explain, "One of the things that cannot be done is for whites to organize all-black communities. It's like trying to organize a Puerto Rican community without being able to speak Spanish." He was disturbed, he said, by attacks on SNCC and on black power that had appeared in the press, and he warned that if these attacks continued they would "lead to more black and more white violence."

SNCC's new leaders—Stokely Carmichael and H. Rap Brown—were influenced by Malcolm X, who had been assassinated in New York in February 1965. Abbie looked to Malcolm X, too, and had borrowed from his speech "The Ballot or the Bullet?": "If Negroes cannot gain power through the ballot, they will resort to bullets," Abbie had predicted in the *Drum* in 1964. For the most part he was optimistic about the prospects for social change. In Lowndes County, Alabama, SNCC was running black candidates for public office, and Abbie endorsed the strategy. "Lowndes County is a key to the definition of black power and to the direction of the racial struggle in this country," he wrote. He was hopeful, too, about the new role for white radicals. In his view they ought to publicize black power, raise money for SNCC, and organize poor whites. At some point in the future, he predicted, there would be a "black-and-white coalition in a politics for the alienated."

At the 1966 Newport Folk Festival, Abbie felt at one with SNCC and its black power advocates. He smoked marijuana until he was "stoned out of his mind," and he went backstage with SNCC members to meet some of the folksingers. At last he felt that he belonged to the inner circle. He was also proud of his bravery when members of the Newport Police Department attacked SNCC members late one night. Stokely Carmichael remembered that "Abbie could have side-lined, but he instinctively threw himself in the front. This was one of his strongest point[s]. Abbie would put his body on the line at any moment for any cause he was involved in."

Immediately after the incident he appeared at a panel discussion in Worcester on black power, where he told the audience that he could identify the police officer who hit him. "I have his badge number," he proclaimed. With all the indignation he could muster, he accused the police officers of public intoxication and of using profanity. Moreover, he announced that he and SNCC would file a lawsuit against the Newport Police Department for its abuse of "blue power." Nothing ever came of the suit. According to files obtained under the Freedom of Information Act, the FBI investigated the charges and concluded that Abbie and the SNCC activists were at fault—not the Newport Police. According to the FBI report, the officers had "prodded and pushed" Abbie and his associates, but only because they had refused "to leave the grounds after the evening performance."

Six months earlier, in the winter of 1966, he had tried to break out of Worcester and into big-time movement activity. He had written to Saul Alinsky in Chicago and applied for a job with the Industrial Areas Foundation. Alinsky, who called himself a "professional radical," had a national reputation as a rambunctious organizer who got results. Born in Chicago in 1909 and raised in a family of Orthodox Jews, he had followed an unconventional path through the working-class battles of the 1930s. Neither a Communist nor a Trotskyite, but rather a Midwestern populist with an abiding faith in "the people," he believed that the poor would succeed in political struggle only if they formed their own pressure groups. Unlike the staid old leftists, he wasn't afraid to use obscenity or to be irreverent, if not downright crude. Among his legendary tactics were the "piss-in" and the "fart-in." At "piss-ins" thousand of demonstrators would invade bathrooms to urinate and flush toilets simultaneously. At "fart-ins" demonstrators would eat massive amounts of beans and later break wind together at corporate headquarters, forcing executives to evacuate offices. By merely threatening to use these tactics, Alinsky often won his demands, making himself highly in demand as a community organizer.

Abbie couldn't have created a more perfect role model if he'd wanted to. In his book *Reveille for Radicals,* Alinsky explained that he aimed for what he called "cool anger"; his political actions and his theatrical demonstrations were "calculated" rather than spontaneous and were "designed primarily to induce certain reactions based on an analysis of circumstances." For Alinsky "truth" was "relative and changing," and life was "an adventure of passion, risk, danger, laughter, beauty, love." Then, too, he envisioned the organizer as a "free man" without ideology or party, "a creative person" unconcerned with "reputation." Alinsky was impressed with Abbie's credentials, and would have liked to hire him—so he said—but unfortunately didn't have a position for a white activist. Abbie was not easily put off. In the spring of 1966, he and Father Gilgun, Worcester's radical priest, drove to Boston to hear Alinsky speak, and then to drink Scotch together in his hotel room.

Once again Abbie asked for a job, and once again Alinsky turned him down. Father Gilgun remembered that Alinsky said, "You're just what I want, but you're the wrong color. I don't need another Jew. I need a black." Years later Abbie would boast that he "picked Alinsky's brain clean that night." Alinsky's advice, he recalled, was "Never respond to criticism or else you'll be doing everybody's thing but your own." What he learned from Alinsky—whom he called a "fantastically great artist"—was that "artists never 'need' love." In *Revolution for the Hell of It,* Abbie explained that "when you're an artist, your art is the point as well as the reason you keep going. Applause, boos, analysts, critics are all irrelevant."

Throughout the early to mid-sixties, Abbie zigzagged from art to politics and from politics to art: from the Park Arts movie theatre to H. Stuart Hughes's campaign for the U.S. Senate; from the *Drum* to the SNICK Shop; from the McComb Freedom School to the Newport Folk Festival. Though he never managed to merge these worlds, he was attracted to the idea of a grand synthesis. It wasn't surprising, then, that in the summer of 1966 he had jumped at the offer to become the National Sales Director for the Poor People's Corporation, and to manage a shop where Mississippi crafts would be sold in a low-key, noncommercial atmosphere. Working for the Poor People's Corporation would enable him—he argued, with some justification—to make the grand synthesis. As Sales Director of the corporation, he could serve as a vital link between poor blacks in the South and affluent whites in the North. There were practical advantages of the job, as well: he could get out of Worcester, away from Sheila, and make a living while working for the movement. To Abbie the Poor People's Corporation seemed like the answer to all his problems, and he began preparing to relocate in New York.

Ironically, just as he was leaving home, the *Worcester Telegram and Gazette* finally ran a glowing account of Abbott H. and Sheila Hoffman. Reporter Julian Grow described them as "atypical SNCC workers: married, parents of two children, long out of school." Abbie repeated what he'd been saying for years: "Learn something of the Negro culture," he told readers of the *Telegram and Gazette.* "Recognize, above all, that a Negro culture does exist." Moreover, he told Julian Grow that "by doing nothing either for or against civil rights," Worcester citizens would only "help perpetuate a racist society." As far he was concerned, there was no such thing as an "innocent bystander." In the pages of the *Telegram and Gazette,* Abbie and Sheila looked like a happy movement couple, the proud parents of two happy children. The black-and-white photograph showed Andrew nestled against his father and Amy, holding a baby bottle, in her mother's arms. The SNCC poster on the wall behind the Hoffman family depicted an old black man holding a young black girl on his lap.

Surely Abbie was delighted to see himself in the paper, yet the upbeat story and the idyllic photo must have troubled him, too. Sheila had filed for divorce on grounds of "cruel and abusive treatment," and he was waiting for a court ruling that would order him to make alimony payments of $72.00 a month, $22.50 of which was to go for child support. On November 4, 1966, just three weeks after Julian Grow's glowing story was published in the *Telegram and Gazette,* Sheila and Abbie were no longer husband and wife. Looking back at the divorce from the vantage point of 1980, he tried to sound flip about it, and yet there was an underlying tone of bitterness in his voice. "Sheila got the house, the kids, the books, and the lawn mower," he wrote, as though he'd been martyred. "I got two suitcases filled with clothes and my candle-pin bowling balls." The Worcester Probate Court granted him the right to "receive reasonable visitation" from Amy and Andrew, but that was small consolation. Now at last he was a free man, yet his newfound freedom was bittersweet. Suddenly he felt that he had nothing to show for his life: no career, no real home, no great accomplishments as a movement activist. He didn't even have his youth anymore.

On November 30, 1966, he turned 30. To celebrate the occasion, as well as to mark his departure from Worcester, his friends threw a party that turned into a roast. Johnnie Hoffman was in rare form and addressed the gathering with characteristic wit. "My son Abbott—" he began, then paused for a moment before adding, "I don't know him well enough to call him Abbie."

Margery and Daniel Dick remembered that they presented Abbie with a going-away gift: a homemade crown of thorns. It acknowledged the Christ-like persona he'd adopted and seemed to say that, like Christ at 30, his apprenticeship was over. It was time to make his place in the world. Going to New York felt like a momentous occasion, and he envisioned the journey from Worcester to Manhattan in highly symbolic terms, as a rite of passage. Entering the city by bridge, he saw himself as an initiate crossing from one realm into another. At last he had ascended from the provinces to the metropolitan center.

In Manhattan he found an apartment on the Lower East Side and a new location for Liberty House at 343 Bleecker Street in Greenwich Village. Abbie was suddenly a landlord with tenants—the building had several rent-controlled apartments—as well as a shopkeeper, with an inventory to maintain and customers to serve. But first he had to clean the floors and windows and plaster and paint the walls. He applied himself to all the details, but his mind was on a lot more than the store. Abbie had a practical solution to the political impasse in the movement, and he presented it in an article entitled "The Craft of Freedom," which was published in the October–November 1966 issue of *Catholic Worker,* the radical newspaper edited and published by Dorothy Day. "The Crafts of Freedom" was undoubtedly the best single article that Abbie Hoffman ever wrote under the name of Abbott Hoffman. It was also his last article published with that byline. A month later, he would appear in print, for the first time, as Abbie Hoffman. Never again would he use Abbott Hoffman in print, and never again would he use the serious intellectual style that he had used as editor of the *Drum*.

"The Crafts of Freedom" remains a glowing testament to his identity as a moderate movement organizer and a reasonable radical in a sea of heated ideological debate. In the pages of the *Catholic Worker,* he presented himself as a financial wizard who knew the ins and outs of the business world. And he cast himself as a political craftsman who could weave together a sense of wholeness from opposing factions. It was far too late in the game to put the old civil rights movement back together again, but that was precisely what he set out to do. On one side, he pointed out, there were the integrationists; on the other side, the advocates of black separatism. It was still possible, he insisted, to create an economic program that would "find acceptance by almost all theoretical positions." Moreover, the Poor People's Corporation was the vehicle in which all factions and parties might ride together.

Marxist terminology doesn't crop up in the article—indeed, it's remarkably free of left-wing jargon—but the article is informed by Marxist ideas about labor and about alienation. What emerges, however, is a utopian socialist view. Abbie argues for "worker-owned cooperatives," which he describes as a natural outgrowth of "rural, Negro communities." He admits that there will be major problems ahead for the cooperatives. "The project is plagued by a variety of difficulties which revolve around the lack of financial support," he writes. "In order to produce the goods at competitive prices, raw materials have to be purchased in large quantities, and this cannot be done at the present time." But he feels reasonably sure that the project will be a success, and that it may "provide the model for more ambitious economic programs." In a not-too-distant future, there might be a whole network of worker-controlled banks, factories, supermarkets and even investment houses. The article is upbeat and concludes with the image of the Poor People's Corporation as a beacon that will "light the way."

Here Comes Abbie

In a matter of weeks, however, Abbie's mood changed radically—ostensibly as a result of momentous changes inside SNCC. Almost six months earlier, in May 1966, Stokely Carmichael had replaced John Lewis as the chairman of SNCC, and black power had became the official ideology of the organization. Then, at a staff meeting in Kerhonkson, New York, that lasted from December 1 to December 8, 1966, SNCC voted 19–18, with 24 abstentions, to exclude all whites from the organization. It was the single most important meeting that SNCC ever held, and political reverberations were felt throughout the movement.

Abbie did not attend the staff meeting, but he heard about it immediately and was instantly offended. Setting aside his immediate responsibilities at Liberty House, he drafted a long article which he showed to friends like Jeremy Larner, a Brandeis graduate who'd published a first novel, *Drive, He Said,* about a crazy college radical who resembled Abbie. Larner remembered that Abbie was "conflicted about what to write, that he held back some of his criticisms and that he toned down others." In the first draft he accused blacks in SNCC of raping white women and robbing white men under threat of violence. But those remarks seemed too explosive, and he took them out.

The final version of the article, which was entitled "SNCC: The Desecration of a Delayed Dream," was published in the *Village Voice* on December 15, 1966. It caused "a shit storm" in the movement, according to one SNCC organizer. The byline identified the author as "Abbie Hoffman"; it was the first time that "Abbie" had appeared in print. Moreover, it was the first time that Abbie had used the writing style which would become his trademark. He was cool and he was hip in a New York kind of way, and he made sure that his readers knew it. Abbott Hoffman of Worcester rarely wrote in the first person and rarely if ever referred to his own immediate experiences. Granted, in the letter he'd written from McComb to the *Worcester Telegram and Gazette,* he had described his daily activities, but that was unusual. For the most part, Abbott Hoffman appeared in print as an impersonal spokesman for the movement at large. Now, as Abbie Hoffman, he used the first-person pronoun "I" and discussed personal experiences.

He had a long history of movement activity, he explained in the *Voice,* "generally as head of a Friends of SNCC group, but also as an organizer in the South." He mythologized his radical past, insisting that he'd been "connected with SNCC from its beginning in 1960." Nowhere in the article did he mention Worcester, and nowhere did he indicate where he'd organized in the South or precisely what he'd done.

Leaving large areas of his life blank, he left it to readers to imagine what he might have done. He had been at the 1966 Newport Folk Festival, he explained, and claimed that he and a Boston activist named Martha Kocol "had the unique distinction of being the last whites beaten in SNCC." After the festival, he wrote, he'd served as the chairman for a panel discussion on the war in Vietnam. Stokely Carmichael had embraced him, he claimed, and had said, "Abbie's in SNCC, he's white and he's beautiful."

Perhaps what was most significant about the *Village Voice* article was that Abbie talked candidly about his sense of anger and betrayal. The opening sentence of the article read, "One thing that has always been present in the Movement has been the attitude that if you feel something is wrong you say so regardless of the consequences. I feel SNCC is wrong and now is the time to say what has been bothering me for the past few weeks." He went on to say, "Now I'm mad. Emotionally and intellectually I'm mad." His anger toward SNCC, he explained, was "the kind of anger one might feel in, say, a love relationship, when after entering honestly you find that your loved one's been balling with someone else, and what's worse, enjoying it." The expulsion of whites from SNCC made him feel naked and ashamed; indeed, he felt "like a schmuck." Abbie had grown up listening to his relatives speak Yiddish, and among friends he would toss out Yiddish expressions, but this was the first time he had used Yiddish in print. In years to come he would introduce Yiddish expressions into the movement at large, injecting a Jewish identity into radical politics.

As Abbott Hoffman, he'd written about race and class. As Abbie Hoffman, he showed an awareness of gender, as well, and consciousness of the conflict that existed between black men and white women in the civil rights movement itself—an issue that had become of great concern to women. In the fall of 1965 Casey Hayden and Mary King, two white SNCC activists, had written a manifesto entitled "A Kind of Memo" in which they'd argued that a "sexual-caste system" existed in the ranks of SNCC, and that women were treated as second-class citizens and were systematically exploited. Whenever they raised the issue of "personal relations" in movement circles, they had found, men felt threatened. Abbie borrowed their ideas and wove them into his own personal account of his relationship with SNCC. He made *feelings* a crucial part of his politics, and he made *subjectivity* his rallying cry.

For Todd Gitlin, one of the old guard of SDS, "an 'analysis' was a ticket to the elite world of movement cadres." For Abbie, analysis was obsolete. "SNCC: The Desecration of a Delayed Dream" shows that what was important for him was to communicate feelings. In this crucial respect he was outside the movement elite, but closer to everyday movement experiences.

For years there had been rumors about the intense sexual activity that had taken place in SNCC's Freedom Houses throughout the South. Mississippi politicians like McComb mayor Gordon Burt had dismissed the Freedom Summer project as nothing more than a "damn screwin' orgy." To forestall those kinds of attacks, SNCC leaders had insisted on strict codes of behavior between blacks and whites. Ivanhoe Donaldson, the SNCC field secretary in Holly Springs, Mississippi, explicitly warned white women not to become involved with black men. "Interracial relationships will provide local whites with the initiative they need to come in here and kill all of us," he said. "Even if the whites don't find out about them, the people will, and we won't be able to do anything afterwards to convince them that our primary interest here is political."

Despite all the rules and regulations, black men and white women did engage in sexual relationships. Now, in the pages of the *Village Voice*, Abbie turned the organization's private affairs into a matter of public concern. For years, he had remained silent on the subject, he said; he had been a loyal "revolutionary" whose main concern had been "the over-riding injustice that exists in this society." In the past, he had "accepted a lot of crap," but that was no longer possible, he claimed. Not to speak out would be a betrayal of the movement's ideals. It wasn't only what Abbie said about SNCC that created a stir, but also the way he said it. His language was frank, and it conveyed his personal anger and resentment. "I feel for the other whites in SNCC, especially the white females," he wrote. "I identify with all those Bronx chippies that are getting conned out of their bodies and bread by some darkskinned sharpie." As the writer Abbott Hoffman, he had never used words or phrases like "chippies" or "darkskinned sharpie." And as Abbott Hoffman, he had idolized black men in the civil rights movement. Now he was accusing them of taking advantage of white women, both sexually and financially.

He was profoundly disturbed by SNCC's fund-raising activities and strategies—probably because he'd been a SNCC fund-raiser, and now felt that he'd been used. Black power would be fine if it was financed by black money, but SNCC used guilt to go after liberal white money, he complained. That was "sick money"; he wanted no part of it, and he hoped no other white radicals wanted a part of it either. Indirectly, Abbie was calling for an economic boycott of SNCC.

Abbie's harshest attack was leveled against Stokely Carmichael, SNCC's new chairman, whom he had gotten to know and admire at the Newport Folk Festival. Now he accused Carmichael of perverting the organization and betraying its ideals and goals. It took courage to criticize Carmichael, who was then at the height of his fame. For years SNCC had been run democratically, Abbie argued. Now, with Carmichael at the helm, SNCC had become a "one-man show." He insisted that as long as Stokely Carmichael "says he doesn't trust any white people I personally can't trust him."

"SNCC: The Desecration of a Delayed Dream" was one of the very first published articles by a movement activist that criticized SNCC. Following the December SNCC meeting at which whites were expelled, there was a great deal of anger and resentment, but with the exception of Abbie's article little of it was openly expressed. After the article appeared in print Abbie talked with Mendy Samstein, who had worked for SNCC throughout the sixties and had attended the heated meeting in Kerhonkson, New York. Though they'd been friends for a decade, their friendship was now over. "We left each other, each convinced that he was right, knowing that we could never speak to each other again," Abbie wrote. Black power had come between them, as it would come between a great many movement friendships and relationships, ending marriages between blacks and whites.

In SNCC and in civil rights circles generally, those who read the *Voice* article viewed Hoffman for the most part as a crybaby. Jerome Washington, a black activist, remembered feeling that Abbie had taken SNCC's decision to expel whites too personally. "He just felt that they kicked *him* out," Washington said. Bob Zellner remembered that the article was "self-serving." Dottie Zellner remembered that Abbie Hoffman "exaggerated his participation in SNCC" and "took it upon himself to speak for many of us when he had no right to do that." She also suggested that writing the article may have expressed "a kind of resentment" for his rejection from the Mississippi Freedom Summer Project two and a half years earlier. It seems likely that Abbie's anger toward SNCC was also fueled by his anger toward Sheila. Sex and money—his issues with Sheila—were also his issues with SNCC. Sheila had divorced him; SNCC had expelled him. He felt wounded and betrayed, knocked down and kicked out, both by his ex-wife and by the organization to which he'd been emotionally and psychologically linked. When both blacks and Sheila took power into their own hands, he had neither a marriage nor a political life.

After the article was published, Abbie was afraid that he would be killed—or so he claimed. He phoned Howard Zinn, who had been a trusted SNCC adviser and whom he had met in Worcester in 1965, and claimed that Ivanhoe Donaldson had threatened him. Howard Zinn later remembered telling Abbie that he didn't think Abbie was in physical danger, "but if he *felt* insecure, he should let things cool off for a while." So Abbie went into hiding on the Lower East Side with Marty and Susan Carey, who'd recently moved from Worcester. Marty remembered that Abbie was afraid that "SNCC members were hunting him down." From his hiding place at the Careys' apartment he dispatched a follow-up article, which was published in the *Village Voice* on December 22 under the title "Another Look at the Movement." In it he told readers that he was "in exile" and had "a fear of dying." Clearly, he enjoyed the irony of the situation. In Mississippi he had been afraid that whites would kill him on "some dark road" because he was a civil rights worker. Now he had "a "fear of dying" for all the wrong reasons, "at the hands of one of my black brothers," he said. He had been prepared to give his life for the movement, and now the movement was unjustly preparing to take his life. In his scenario, he was the white martyr on the cross of black power.

For at least a year Abbie continued to express a fear of blacks and of black power. In a short essay for a colloquium on black power that was published in the *Partisan Review* in 1968, he told a story—highly exaggerated no doubt, and perhaps completely untrue—about a "black militant" who was "bringing a truckload of guns" to Roxbury, Massachusetts. "What about me . . . are you going to shoot me?" Abbie wanted to know. "Yes, even you," he was told. "Maybe if I saw your SNCC button I wouldn't but when the shit hits the fan it's hard to see buttons. I'd just shoot anything white." The moral of the story, Abbie explained, was that it had convinced him to become a hippie, or, as he put it, a "new nigger." Indeed, a year after the *Village Voice* article appeared in print, Abbie shed his skin as a civil rights activist and SNCC supporter and emerged as a marijuana-smoking dropout on the Lower East Side. If only other white radicals would become hippies, too, there might be a real movement, he believed.

chapter five

DEATH OF A SALESMAN, BIRTH OF A HIPPIE

Angry Artist

From his perch at Liberty House Abbie watched the New York scene unfold, but he felt unable to decide where he belonged. He had spurts of tremendous energy followed by periods of intense paralysis. At times he was not only incapable of acting but incapable of making up his mind. From all the available evidence—including letters he wrote and the testimony of friends—it appears that in the winter of 1966–67 he was in the middle of his first prolonged manic-depressive episode, though at the time no one used that term to define the intense mood swings he was experiencing. He was up; he was down; he was unable to move and unable to stop moving.

He raced about the city tasting all that life had to offer, as he explained in a letter to Father Gilgun. Though he was smoking marijuana and taking LSD, he didn't need drugs, he insisted. He was high on life itself, exhilarated by New York art and architecture, New York people and pop music. The city itself seemed like a nonstop circus of wonderful sideshows and strange acts, and he didn't want to miss anything on the program. He had just discovered Lao-tzu's classic *The Way of Life*, he told Gilgun, and it was now his all-time favorite book, surpassing even *The Diary of Anne Frank,* which had inspired him since his heady days as an impressionable college undergraduate.

At the same time he experienced a puzzling sense that he was without willpower, unable to choose, and unable to come to a resolution about anything. He felt that he was falling apart, that everything and everyone was falling away from him: his family and all his possessions, his sexuality, and his rationality. Perhaps he was even on the brink of madness, he wrote. The only thing that he was dead certain about was the war in Vietnam. "The fuckin' War poisons everything," he told Father Gilgun, and then added, "I can't work right." When a group of antiwar activists proposed sending a brigade to Vietnam to rebuild the damage caused by U.S. bombs, he was among the first to announce he was ready to go.

In 1964, during the first year with Lyndon Johnson as president and Robert S. McNamara as secretary of defense, there were twenty-three thousand U.S. troops in Vietnam and 147 dead Americans. By 1967, there were nearly half a million U.S. soldiers in Vietnam, and nearly fifteen thousand dead Americans. That year the air force flew two thousand sorties a week and dropped more than a million and a half tons of bombs on Vietnam. The aerial bombardment surpassed the total tonnage dropped on Germany, Italy, and Japan in World War II. Thousands of U.S. aircraft were shot down, sometimes by sophisticated Soviet-made missiles and sometimes by peasants armed with rifles. At home there was rapid polarization about the war, with "hawks" urging total military victory on the battlefield and "doves" calling for a ceasefire and a negotiated settlement. Black Americans—who made up 10 percent of the total U.S. population, 12 percent of the army, and 14.6 percent of the battlefield dead—pointed out the racism implicit in the war. In April 1967, World Heavyweight Boxing Champion Muhammad Ali refused his induction into the U.S. Army and became a symbol of the mounting resistance to the military draft. "Black men are being cut up by white men," Ali exclaimed. Stripped of his boxing title, barred from fighting in his own country, and sentenced to five years in prison, he was celebrated as "The People's Champ."

Polarization—between hawks and doves, blacks and whites, parents and children—was the name of the game. The generation gap swept across the nation, and thousands of young people left their middle-class suburban homes and settled in the Haight-Ashbury District in San Francisco ("The Hashbury") and in the East Village in Manhattan. Unlike the beatniks of the 1950s, the "hippies" (as the media dubbed them) belonged not to a shadowy subculture that gathered in coffeehouses and isolated apartments, but to a visible counterculture that colonized whole neighborhoods and congregated in public parks to smoke marijuana, trip on LSD, listen to rock 'n' roll, and have sex and call it "fucking."

The hippie sexual revolution eroded old codes of courtship, undermined the nuclear family, and mocked the ideal of monogamy. Ed Sanders, a classics scholar from Kansas, moved to New York and founded the Fugs, a rock group that celebrated the new forms of dalliance in songs like "What Are You Doing after the Orgy?" and "Slum Goddess of the Lower East Side." He later remembered the era as the "Golden Age of Fucking." Young Americans were having sex earlier than ever before and enjoying it more, or so they claimed. Never before in American history—not even during the bohemian heydays of the 1920s—had there been such a dramatic break with Puritan morality and the Protestant work ethic. That the extravagant hippie protest and quest for pleasure was occurring at the same time as the war in Vietnam was escalating made it all the more spectacular.

Abbie had never been more promiscuous. In his own imagination he was a sixties version of Rudolph Valentino, star of *The Sheik* and of other silent films, who always played the dark, mysterious lover. The Lower East Side was his tent; the women of the neighborhood belonged to his harem. Every night, he boasted, he could "bed down" with another new beauty.

Professor Maslow's daughter Ellen, who worked with Abbie at Liberty House during this period, remembered that he "had great bursts of energy," and that he "kept molting" at an "accelerated" pace. "He turned a crank in his mind and he was no longer doing what he was doing," she remembered. Abbie bounced from identity to identity, from persona to persona, and from one cultural milieu to another in rapid succession: from Hare Krishna gatherings to the offices of the *Catholic Worker,* from meetings of Timothy Leary and Richard Alpert's psychedelic League for Spiritual Discovery to the office of the Cuban Mission to the United Nations.

Whenever he had a spare moment, he'd dash off a letter to Danny Schechter, an SDS member who was studying at the London School of Economics. Abbie boasted that he and Schechter were going to revive the Committees of Correspondence, the organization which had kept the American revolutionaries of 1776 in communication with one another. Their letters would eventually, he hoped, become a book about the revolution of 1967, which was taking place at that very moment in New York and in London.

At the end of January, Abbie took time off from work at Liberty House to attend the lectures, readings, and performances that were part of Angry Arts Week: an occasion for poets, painters, and writers to express their opposition to the war in Vietnam. He looked forward to the event with great anticipation, but when it was over he was highly disappointed. "The panel shows were like vaudeville acts," he complained in a letter to the *Village Voice.* What disturbed him about Angry Arts Week was the left-wing audience, which insisted, repeatedly and dogmatically, that the panelists—who included poet Robert Bly and critic Susan Sontag—make art that was clearly and directly aimed at stopping the war right then and there. To Abbie, that attitude was absurd. "Demanding that artists do antiwar art is like demanding that chefs cook antiwar food," he wrote. It was wrong to condemn entirely artists who ignored Vietnam, he insisted. Moreover, he disagreed with the whole idea of Angry Arts Week. Leave anger, "hate and violence" to the "Johnson-napalm-McNamara clique," he advised in the *Voice.* Leave artists alone, and let them "transcend anger" in their work. From Abbie's perspective, "art should be an affirmation of life": it should inspire, uplift, give a sense of collective purpose.

Of all the arts, it was music that stirred him most; music broke down the barriers between audience and performer and between performance and improvisation, and it opened a window to the spiritual world that he was now taking seriously for the first time in his life. He read Lao-tzu's *Tao-te Ching,* or "The Way of Life," a text central to the variety of Zen Buddhism that was becoming popular in the new youth culture. Abbie like the book so much he recommended it to Father Gilgun; he was enthralled with the idea that "the way to do is to be." He wanted to be in the moment and to transcend concerns about performance, ego, and recognition, and in that sense he shared common ground with the Zen-minded hippies.

He saw this philosophy in practice at Carnegie Hall, where he watched the Indian musician Ali Akbar Khan play the sitar, an event he described in the *Voice.* The evening turned out to be pure revelation. At the start of the concert, however, Abbie was annoyed; he couldn't tell when Khan was tuning up his instrument and when he was playing it. He had the uncanny feeling that Khan was "putting on" an audience that was unfamiliar with the forms of Eastern music, and he was resentful. But his attitude changed during "the driving finale" of the piece, when a string broke and Khan abruptly stopped playing. The hall was stunned into silence. Along with everyone else, Abbie watched in amazement as Khan added a new string "with a delicacy I had never seen before and then continued at breakneck speed just where he left off." To Abbie the "message" was that "whether he was tuning up or playing was irrelevant." Ali Akbar Khan "began when he woke up in the morning, perhaps when he was born, perhaps when the world was born." If only Abbie could rise to that level of creativity!

At the Dom on the Lower East Side, he watched—or rather took part in—the performances of Andy Warhol's *Exploding Plastic Inevitable*. He loved the multimedia environment: the strobe lights that roamed the room; the male and female go-go dancers, who were in perpetual motion; Warhol's experimental films, which were projected on a screen in the background; the singing of Nico; and the rock 'n' roll of Lou Reed and the Velvet Underground. The *Exploding Plastic Inevitable* offered a total assault on the senses; Abbie reveled in it, and he came to appreciate Andy Warhol as a master of "modern media."

He went regularly to the theatre and enjoyed Barbara Garson's *MacBird,* which reworked Shakespeare's *Macbeth* to tell a tale about the Kennedy assassination, power politics in Washington, and guilt in high places. A piece he found more unsettling than entertaining was Peter Weiss's avant-garde political drama *The Persecution and Assassination of Jean-Paul Marat as Performed by the Inmates of the Asylum at Charenton under the Direction of the Marquis de Sade*—better known as *Marat/Sade.* For Abbie, *Marat/Sade,* which opened in New York in December 1965, provided a near-perfect mirror in which to see the conflicts of his own era. Like eighteenth-century Charenton, twentieth-century America was a madhouse, he told friends. Like the inmates at Charenton, the inmates of America were in rebellion. The play also affected him personally; he found himself identifying not only with Marat, the passionate, despairing revolutionary, but also with the Marquis de Sade, the cool, satanic pleasure-seeker.

Abbie's own dualities—of hope and despair, faith and disbelief, collectivity and individuality—are apparent in the poems that he wrote that winter. These are neo-Beat works that capture the depressing reality of his own neighborhood in New York, but also express a sense of revolutionary optimism. They're imitative rather than original works, but they indicate his desire to break into new forms of expression. In "View from Canal 11th," which was published in *Punch,* Worcester's first underground newspaper, he describes a grotesque and surrealist wasteland:

> The air chokes of gas from the patriot palls of death
> in the sky
> Family feet scratch the bloodless curb searching
> for hand-me-
> down
>   down
>   down

The poet is surrounded by the nauseating smells of urine, beer, gas fumes, and "junkie puke"; he's jarred by the sounds of police sirens, pulsating Latin music, and poor families as they search noisily through the garbage. The people in this landscape are muggers and their unfortunate victims: the sick, the diseased, and even the leprous. Indeed, Abbie's New York is a fiery hell. In the closing lines, he writes that "there is so much to do / To change the way the wheels spin / So far to go before we win." The task seems overwhelming, and the poet himself appears too exhausted to even make the effort.

"Venceremos!" which was also published in *Punch,* begins on an upbeat note. The one-word Spanish title translates as "We will win," and there's a resounding battle cry that echoes throughout the poem, but it, too, is infused with a sense of despair:

> In older days they used to talk 'bout
> Angels and things
> and how gossamer they were
> But now the Pentagon Power plans to see
> Just how many pins fit in an angel's head,
> How many pins before he's dead.

"Venceremos!" takes readers through the political battles of the sixties, from Freedom Summer in Mississippi to the Free Speech movement in

Berkeley. It celebrates sixties radicals and their heroes: Bob Moses, Joan Baez, Dorothy Day, and Fidel Castro. The poem's most powerful descriptions, however, are of "Pillage & Rape & Plunder & War."

Abbie told Father Gilgun that everything around him in New York had the intensity of poetry, and that he couldn't help but think in poetic terms. In fact, his letters to Gilgun and to Terri Priest, a Worcester artist and peace movement organizer with whom he had become romantically involved, are like prose poems. There are vivid images, lyrical passages, and conscious echoes from other poets, including Robert Frost, William Blake, Allen Ginsberg, and folksinger Bob Dylan, in whose music Abbie heard the sounds of his own surreal state of mind, especially in songs like "Rainy Day Women #12 & 35" and "Desolation Row."

His handwritten letters are like maps of his inner turbulence. They're almost psychedelic. Words are capitalized and repeated, as though they had magical powers. Diagrammatic arrows run across the page, and there are drawings of spinning wheels as well as elliptical dots and long dashes that suggest the fragmentary quality of his own thoughts. In the letters Abbie is introspective, moody, insecure, and full of sadness about the loss of his family. Despite the whirlwind of activity that he described, he was desperate for intimacy and acceptance. To Terri Priest, he explained that he felt painfully cut off from everyone and had no one to turn to. Loneliness was inescapable, and the present moment seemed limitless. Saddled with insomnia, he'd sit at the front window in the middle of the night and watch the poorest of the city's poor shiver in the cold and dig through the garbage for scraps to eat. On his own street there were heroin dealers and addicts, he wrote to Priest, and though he wasn't using heroin, he could identify with the strung out junkies. Like them, he was down and out, or so he liked to think. And he was getting high on marijuana.

Shopkeeper

Though Abbie was drawn to off-Broadway theatre, hip happenings, Indian music, and Buddhist philosophy, it was economics, not culture, that he emphasized in his political pronouncements, and it was money, not art, that he worried about day-in and day-out. Liberty House provided him with an income, but it wasn't enough to live on as well as make alimony and child-support payments to Sheila, whom he resented deeply. She was so angry and hostile, he complained, that she was certain to report him to the police if he failed to send her the seventy-two dollars per month to which she was legally entitled.

There were also financial woes in Mississippi—at least one cooperative had gone belly-up—and the Poor People's Corporation showed signs of instability. In letters to Gilgun, Abbie agonized about the collapse of the whole enterprise; in public, however, he put on a smiling face. As the corporation's public relations man, he wrote an article in April 1967 for *Liberation* magazine in which he boasted that the enterprise had started "from nothing" and had "grown into a network of fifteen worker-owned manufacturing cooperatives, employing close to two hundred former sharecroppers." The future was rosy, he insisted.

In fact, Liberty House provided the only anchor in his otherwise frenetic existence, and he kept coming back to it. Running it efficiently, he wrote, would require that he begin a project of "total self-education." No longer could he and his colleagues remain "free-floating movement activists"; they would have "to become versed in a variety of production, purchasing, warehousing, distributing and marketing skills, most of which were alien to their character." It was a challenge, and he rose to the practical tasks at hand, soliciting sales, wrapping packages, chatting with customers. Liberty House provided him with a rare opportunity to meet radicals from around the country and swap experiences. Indeed, the Bleecker Street shop was a movement institution and a cultural center. SDS members, civil rights organizers, pacifists, anarchists, and lawyers stopped by Liberty House to browse, chat, and make the acquaintance of Abbie Hoffman, who began to acquire a reputation as an eccentric radical.

With his passion, his imagination, and his verbal pyrotechnics, he was clearly someone to watch. John Lewis, SNCC's former chairman, sought him out at Liberty House and was impressed with his dedication. Another SNCC veteran who dropped by was Julius Lester, a columnist for the *National Guardian,* the leading left-wing newspaper of the day. Lester, a recent convert to Cuban socialism, regaled Abbie with tales of his experiences in Havana. Abbie had never been an admirer of the Soviet Union; he told friends, such as Stew Albert, that it seemed "dull, bureaucratic-sterile-puritanical," and that the countries of the Eastern block seemed even worse. He was enamored, however, of Fidel Castro, who was toying with utopian ideas and talking about abolishing money in Cuba.

As a way to generate practical solutions to economic troubles at home, Abbie arranged a miniconference at Liberty House at the end of March, 1967. Earlier, SNCC's H. Rap Brown had given a talk about black power, and civil rights attorney William Kunstler had read his poetry. Now, to discuss economic equality, Abbie brought together a group of intellectuals and activists whom he felt were "capable of love and revolution simultaneously." It was a remarkable gathering: Jesse Morris, founder and executive director of the Poor People's Corporation; César Chavez, founder and mainstay of the United Farm Workers of America; Oscar Lewis, anthropologist and celebrated author of two controversial works, *The Children of Sánchez* (1961) and *La Vida: A Puerto Rican Family in the Culture of Poverty* (1966); and Paul Goodman, who as an anarchist philosopher and author of *Growing Up Absurd* (1960), as well as coauthor, with Fritz Perls, of *Gestalt Therapy* (1951), was one of the New Left's intellectual heroes.

Not surprisingly, one of the hottest topics of the forum turned out to be the "culture of poverty," a concept originated by Oscar Lewis. In *La Vida*, Lewis had observed that "the poverty of culture is one of the crucial aspects of the culture of poverty." Poor people, he argued, were deprived culturally as well as materially; they lived in isolation from one another and helped to create the conditions of their own "helplessness" and dehumanization. In radical circles, Lewis was accused of blaming the victims and of failing to see the cultural values that were embedded in poor communities. But his defenders, like Puerto Rican scholar Manuel Maldonado-Denis, insisted that he was revealing "the true nature" of society. Abbie argued in an April 1967 article for *Liberation* that a "culture of poverty" existed, but that Lewis had painted too grim a picture. The Poor People's Corporation, he wrote, was an effective weapon in the war to undo the "psycho-social qualities" of ghetto life. Moreover, the corporation destroyed "the myth about the poorest of the poor being untrainable" and undermined the notion that poor people were inherently lazy. Abbie insisted that the poor, at least in Mississippi's black communities, had "political savvy" and that in the poor white communities of Appalachia they had "a natural creativity in crafts." In America there was "no poverty of ideas" but a "poverty of will," he concluded. If people only made the effort, the war on poverty would be won.

Abbie admired Paul Goodman as a maverick intellectual and adopted him as a father figure. In the summer of 1967, when Goodman's eighteen-year-old son, Matthew, died mountain climbing in New Hampshire, Abbie wrote a poem in which he expressed his grief and compassion. Abbie could also agree with Paul Goodman on the importance of cooperatives, but they clashed over the idea for a guaranteed annual income. Abbie saw it as a form of "repressive tolerance"—a way to contain and co-opt dissent. For Goodman, the guaranteed annual income was "not a welfare device but a citizenly right." It would provide poor people with a little capital of their own so they might become enterprising and attain a better standard of living.

Be-Ins, Put-ons, Wed-Ins

All around him on the Lower East Side Abbie saw a generation of young people who were deliberately rejecting work and middle-class possessions. To him, it was so much nonsense. The hippies thought that the ghetto offered "soul," but ghetto life was a life of poverty, he insisted. The hippies were apolitical and unreliable, and he let everyone know it in a snide letter published in the *Village Voice* on May 11, 1967. He explained that he had recently been disturbed by a television commercial for Levi's white denim jeans that featured the Jefferson Airplane, San Francisco's premier psychedelic rock group. The ad, Abbie explained, "summarized for me all the doubts I have about the hippie philosophy." The Jefferson Airplane was "just doing their 'thing,'" he wrote, as though the notion of "doing your own thing" was sinful. "While the Jefferson Airplane grooves with its thing," he added, "over 100 workers in the Levi Strauss plant on the Tennessee-Georgia border are doing their thing, which consists of being on strike to protest deplorable working conditions that characterize most Southern textile factories." He was all for the workers and their trade-union struggle, he exclaimed, but all against the "mind-expanding" hippies, who simply gave him "a headache." The unsuspecting reader of the *Village Voice* might have envisioned Abbie as a square or as "straight"—as the hippies called their button-down counterparts. In fact, Abbie had been a lively participant at the Be-In that had taken place in Central Park on Easter Sunday in March 1967, and anyone who'd seen him there might have mistaken him for a hippie.

Two months earlier, on January 14, the first Be-In had taken place in San Francisco's Golden Gate Park. The San Francisco Be-In, or "Gathering of the Tribes," was meant to link the drug culture with the political movement, and to connect the aging Beats with the younger hippies. The "cause" wasn't peace, justice, or freedom, but "being" itself. Poet Gary Snyder signaled the start of festivities by blowing on a conch shell. Allen Ginsberg chanted Indian mantras. LSD apostle Timothy Leary urged the crowd to "turn on, tune in, drop out," though few seemed to need any urging. The Jefferson Airplane sang "Let's Get Together," and most of the crowd, estimated at twenty thousand people, accompanied them. There was music from the Grateful Dead, Big Brother and the Holding Company, and Quicksilver Messenger Service, and—in the words of *Rolling Stone* editor Charles Perry—there was "flopping, formless, freak-freely dancing."

The New York Be-In boasted no long list of political celebrities and no big-name rock groups, but there was much the same sense of wonder and joy as there had been in San Francisco. Reporter Sidney Bernard observed that there was a new breed of "beautiful people, not out of *Vogue*, but out of that New York tempo and tone that spells fun, neighborliness, love." In *Revolution for the Hell of It*, Abbie described his own experiences at the Be-In, or "Was-In," as he called it. He dropped acid that day and was "totally zonked." He painted his face with Day-Glo Gold and wore flowers in his hair. "I had a ball," he exclaimed. He was high and so was everyone else—if not on acid, then on "bananas, kids, sky, flowers, dancing, kissing." He was delighted that "people kept giving things away for free—fruit, jelly beans, clothes, flowers, chicken, Easter eggs, poems." He felt that he was at "an emotional United Nations." But he wasn't so stoned that he couldn't think straight enough to engage in his own street theatre, involving a minor confrontation with the police. "Draft Cardinal Spellman," he chanted outside St. Patrick's Cathedral; the Roman Catholic cardinal had called Vietnam a "war for civilization," and Abbie was prepared to hurl verbal barbs his way. When he tried to enter the cathedral, however, the police stopped him. "You can't go in with that uniform," an officer shouted. Hoffman quipped, "It's my Easter suit," but he backed down, and later on berated himself because he'd "chickened out."

For months he'd avoided romantic entanglements, but now he was beginning to spend most of his time with Anita Kushner, a twenty-five-year-old drug counselor at Manhattan's Beth Israel Hospital. Anita had become, literally overnight, the new love of his life. He and Anita went everywhere together. They'd been to the Be-In in Central Park, but Anita was no hard-core hippie, at least not yet. Born in 1942 to a middle-class Jewish family from Baltimore, Maryland, she had graduated from Goucher—then an all-women's college—and had then obtained an M.A. in psychology from Yeshiva University. When she met Abbie at Liberty House in the spring of 1967, she was beginning to think of herself as culturally hip and politically daring. For years she'd been, as she remembered, a "huge Henry James nut"; now she was listening to the Motown sound of the Supremes and volunteering at the American Civil Liberties Union, which she regarded as *the* ultra-radical organization in New York. Soon after they met, Abbie began taking her to places she'd only read about: artists' lofts, head shops, soul food restaurants where blacks and whites mingled, and meetings where she could hear the likes of Allen Ginsberg or Ed Sanders hold forth.

Unlike Sheila, Anita wasn't judgmental about drugs, though she had very little drug experience and had never tried LSD. On the day they met, Abbie tossed her a tab of acid. "She juggled it the way you would a lighted firecracker," he wrote. Almost immediately they tripped together and smoked marijuana together, and before long they were living together—"without conflict," Abbie claimed in *Revolution for the Hell of It*—in a small apartment at 10 St. Marks Place, or as he put it, at "the exact center of the busiest street (Saint Marx Place) on the Lower East Side."

The rent, Anita remembered, was $104 a month: much higher than they were prepared to pay. But she had just inherited a thousand dollars, which enabled them to move into the apartment of their dreams and buy a twenty-one-inch color TV. The TV surprised their friends, but Abbie explained that it was an essential tool for every revolutionary. Abbie built a loft bed that was seven feet high and covered with an immense American flag, and soon he was boasting that he and Anita spent most of their time there making love. Together they painted the apartment red, white, and blue—"it was like a work of art," Anita remembered—then decorated it with posters and photographs, including one of them naked that scandalized Abbie's aunt and uncle when they visited from Worcester.

"There was a huge sexual attraction between us," Anita later remembered. "It was just an incredible thing." Their friends and acquaintances said that they cast themselves as mythological lovers. Kate Coleman, for example, a recent graduate from Berkeley who was working at *Newsweek* and covering the hippie scene, remembered that "there was a braggadocio about their sexual prowess." Abbie made no secret of his sexuality: he was always on the make, and women were continually trying to make him. According to the rules of the counterculture, which they adopted as their own, Abbie and Anita were "free people," unfettered by the bonds of monogamy. "In that brave new hippie world, you weren't supposed to have property ownership or a sense of possessiveness," Anita remembered. "We could fuck around and have other lovers."

It was Abbie, however, not Anita, who acted according to the rules of sexual liberation and, according to Anita, "There was really a double standard operating." Anita was hurt by Abbie's sexual encounters with other women, though she tried not to show it. "I did have a property sense," she recalled. "I thought, 'he's my mate.' I felt that women who wanted to fuck him had no respect for my ownership. I can still picture certain hippie women whom I hated for no other reason than that they wanted to fuck Abbie." Unlike Sheila, Anita was prepared to play Abbie's sexual game and to accept his "head trip" as well, which meant mythologizing him and allowing him to mythologize her. To her, he was Pan and Dionysus: orgiastic, irrational, and tremendously creative. In *Trashing,* Anita's fictionalized account of their relationship published in 1970 under the pseudonym Ann Fettamen, Abbie is Danny, a drug dealer, anarchist, and inspired genius who makes Ann's "previous life irrelevant." On their first date, he rolls a marijuana cigarette, gets stoned, and mischievously exclaims, "Don't tell anybody, but I'm God."

Anita wasn't Abbie in drag, but that's the way he often cast her. She was his twin, his soul mate, his mirror image. "If I had been born a woman I would have been Anita," he exclaimed in the chapter of his autobiography entitled "Love and Utopia on the Lower East Side." Years later, in 1980, he told reporter Charlotte Cohen that he and Anita "look the same . . . use the same gestures . . . come from the same racial background . . . use the same system for arguing." Marrying her was like marrying his other self and making himself one, and indeed it was in the spirit of oneness that the silk-screened invitations to their wedding read "1 + 1 = 1."

On June 8, three weeks after the *Village Voice* had published his anti-hippie diatribe, Abbie married Anita in a sumptuous hippie wedding ceremony that took place on the lawn outside the Metropolitan Museum of Art in New York's Central Park. Abbie called it "the most famous marriage in hippiedom history," but it was also a crucial event in his own personal mythology: as dramatic a turnaround as any in his protean and metamorphic career. It was only three months after he had met Anita and only seven months after his divorce from Sheila, yet he showed no signs of caution or apprehension. Getting married—and in hippie garb, no less—was Abbie's way of saying that he was no longer in a state of doubt and uncertainty, that he was prepared to make the biggest of personal and political commitments. He'd broken out of his depressive cycle. At last he'd regained the ability to make a decision.

The person Abbie asked to perform the ceremony was Freeman House, who was a member of the San Francisco Diggers, a boldly imaginative countercultural group. House was also a Boo Hoo, or priest, in the ersatz Neo-American Church. He was the perfect man for the job, even though he'd never performed a wedding ceremony before. An English and drama major at Berkeley and the editor of *Interspace, a Journal of Psychedelics,* he was proud to be a hippie and delighted that Abbie, whom he had met at Liberty House, was finally ready to embrace the counterculture he'd resisted for so long. "At first Abbie couldn't understand the hippies," House remembered. "He thought that they were flakes, but at the same time he was fascinated by them. He was consciously looking for the next step in his own political development beyond civil-rights and the peace movement, and he studied the hippies the way an anthropologist would study another culture."

House's only request of Abbie was that he not invite representatives of the media to attend the wedding ceremony and "not make it a media event." But that was asking too much. Abbie was already far too dependent on media coverage—both of himself and of his causes—to give it up. "He thought that he could command media attention, and yet remain outside media control," House remembered. "He thought that he could make himself into a mythic figure, and yet at the same time not lose his own personal identity. He made a kind of Mephistophelian deal with the media devil."

For more than a year Abbie had been watching mass media coverage of both the hippie scene and the antiwar movement. He'd concluded that mass media coverage was essential if the movement was to grow. Moreover, if the movement was to capture media attention, it would have to stretch its own provincial boundaries and stage highly visual events that were made for TV. At antiwar demonstrations, for example, he'd observed that crowds were energized by raucous marchers who chanted "Hell no, we won't go!" as though they really meant it. Even more effective were the "eye-catching" street performances of Peter Schumann's Bread and Puppet Theatre, a troupe of actors who impressed even the most cynical of television reporters. "The point is," Abbie wrote in *WIN,* a pacifist magazine, "nobody gives a shit anymore about troop strength, escalation, crying over napalm. A peace rally speech to me is like watching the TV reports of Highway Fatalities which is like praying for riots to end which is like BULLSHIT!"

Ever since October 1965, members of the Bread and Puppet Theatre had appeared at antiwar demonstrations in costumes such as black robes and death masks. They'd also used props—most noticeably a large, black coffin that was meant to symbolize the Americans and Vietnamese who had been killed in the war. "That was drama, not explanation," Abbie exclaimed after he watched members of the Bread and Puppet Theatre carry the black coffin through the streets. Network television crews agreed, and on the evening news there was extensive footage of the Bread and Puppet Theatre. For Keith Lampe, a Korean War veteran who'd become a pacifist organizer and a friend of Abbie's, the lesson was obvious. "The peace movement cannot grow much more unless it scores more points on the television tube," he asserted. "From now on, any action that fails to get broad press coverage must be regarded as incestuous."

Abbie took that message to heart, and at the start of May 1967 he organized the "Flower Brigade," a small contingent of antiwar activists who carried flowers and dressed up as hippies then marched down Fifth Avenue in the annual "Support Our Boys in Vietnam" Parade. Abbie wore a brightly colored cape emblazoned with the word "Freedom." Along with the other members of the Flower Brigade, he waved an American flag to show that the antiwar movement was patriotic—that doves had as much right as hawks to the Stars and Stripes. Predictably, members of the Flower Brigade were attacked by pro-war demonstrators. Abbie had assumed that they would be; before the march had begun, he had rallied his troops and had delivered what he called his "we're gonna-get-the-shit-kicked-out-of-us" speech. Then he'd shown the members of the Flower Brigade how to protect themselves by kneeling and crouching, a defensive posture he'd learned during his days in the civil rights movement.

Anita was terrified by the sudden violence: "I was pelted with vegetables and ran away because they were threatening to beat us up," she remembered. "I was scared shitless." Abbie reveled in the attack, as his humorous and colorful description of it attests: "Zonk! fists, red paint, kicks, beer cans, spitting—the whole American Welcome Wagon treatment," he wrote in *Revolution for the Hell of It.* It was precisely the kind of drama that TV and print journalists needed and that he had hoped for. From his vantage point as media strategist, the most effective street scenes were those of pro-war demonstrators grabbing American flags from the peace demonstrators and ripping them up.

Village Voice reporter Joe Flaherty described the event with great gusto. "Grown men lustily punched and kicked girls no older than their daughters," he wrote. "American flags were ripped from their hands and torn into bits seemingly because they were contaminated." It was that picture and others like it that prompted Abbie to boast, in June 1967, that "the press eats it up. . . . They print it, not aware of the disruption they cause." From his point of view the picture was easily worth a thousand words in the war for the hearts and minds of the American public.

Overnight, Abbie's ad-hoc peace group was the talk of the movement. "The Flower Brigade lost its first battle, but watch out America," he wrote in *WIN* in an article entitled "Love and Hate on 5th Avenue."

"We were poorly equipped with flowers from uptown florists. Already there is talk of growing our own. Plans are being made to mine the East River with daffodils. Dandelion chains are being wrapped around induction centers. Holes are being dug in street pavements and seeds dropped in and covered." The march of the Flower Brigade and its media aftermath taught him the power of the "put-on" and encouraged him to perfect its use. Jacob Brackman, the foremost authority on the subject, defined the put-on as a "destructive device born out of desperation—a weapon to force people out, through confusion and loss of confidence toward honesty." For Brackman, put-ons were the expression of a generation "that doesn't take the news straight, that doesn't take the utterances of public figures straight, that doesn't take social games straight." He concluded that "the *news itself* is a put-on." Abbie had been watching the TV news and had come to the same conclusion on his own.

When he married Anita in a hippie wedding ceremony in Central Park, it was pure put-on: part spoof, part hoax, but also a deadly serious performance for the representatives of the mass media whom Abbie had invited. Abbie was no garden-variety hippie, though that was the image that he meant to convey. Clearly there was a subtext to this hippie wedding. According to Jim Fouratt, a Harvard dropout who had helped to organize the New York Be-In, "when you scraped away Abbie's hippie surface, you found an intellectual who read Marx, Lenin, Mao Tse-tung, [and] talked about alienation in postindustrial society and about Herbert Marcuse's theories."

Abbie liked being a hippie; he enjoyed the costumes, the sex, the drugs, the hedonistic lifestyle. But becoming a hippie, in name if not in reality, was also a part of his grand political design. If the Flower Brigade was meant to transform the media image and the popular conception of hippies from long-haired wimps to macho patriots, then the Central Park wedding was meant to transform Abbie's own image from hard-core politico to gentle soul. In the wake of black power, SNCC had urged white people to organize their own communities. Taking on the hippie identity would allow him to claim the hippies as his people and the Lower East Side as his territory. Becoming a hippie himself would give him an edge, he felt, in the battle to convert hippies—the "glassy-eyed zombies," as he called them—to the cause of revolution.

Finally, it would allow him to put one over on everyone and to have fun doing it.

The *Village Voice* publicized the June 8 "Wed-in" and urged everyone, even if they didn't know Abbie or Anita, to attend the ceremony. "Bring flowers, friends, food, fun, costumes, painted faces," Howard Smith urged readers of his weekly "scenes" column. Abbie and Anita were going to be united "in holy mind blow," he wrote, and, in the style of the put-on, he added, "It's for real." On June 15, 1967, the *Voice* ran a photo by Fred W. McDarrah that showed Abbie, Anita, Freeman House, and invited guests. "It was a simple ceremony, despite a score of cameras," Howard Smith wrote. "The bride and groom, both dressed in white with daisies in their hair, sat on the grass in a small grove of trees amid the smell of incense, and the sounds of recorders, bells, and tambourines." Afraid that her parents would see the event on the evening news and rebuke her, Anita wore dark glasses to conceal her identity.

During the ceremony, House read from the *I Ching, or Book of Changes*—the three-thousand-year-old Chinese text that the hippies had adopted as their bible. Freeman also led the couple in a chant of "Om Mane Padme Om." Abbie grinned, giggled, smirked, and laughed out loud, in part because he was high on marijuana and on MDA (methylene dioxyamphetamine), a drug known as "speed for lovers," which he thought would provide him with added sexual power. The wedding couple exchanged rings and received garlands of flowers. The crowd applauded and photographers—from the *Voice* and from *Time*—snapped dozens of pictures. Abbie and Anita handed out silkscreened wedding announcements to the guests and flowers to the children in the crowd. They even offered flowers to the police officers, who draped them around their jeep.

Several weeks later, on July 7, 1967, in an issue devoted to "The Hippies," *Time* ran a photo that showed Abbie and Anita with heads bowed, which made them look like a solemn couple and made the ceremony seem a serious affair. Neither Abbie's nor Anita's name appeared in the article in *Time;* they were identified only as a "beflowered couple." Still, it was their first appearance in a national publication, and it provided notoriety and a new status in movement and countercultural circles.

In the caption to the photo, *Time* informed its readers that in addition to their "hippie wedding," the couple had applied for and received a civil wedding license "just to play safe." Still later, on July 2, 1967, Abbie and Anita were married by Rabbi Nathan A. Perilman at Temple Emanuel on East Sixty-fifth Street in Manhattan. Though Abbie didn't publicize that ceremony, which would have undermined his hippie image, it was as much his idea as Anita's or that of her parents, who regarded their new son-in-law with trepidation. There was also yet another ceremony at Marty and Susan Carey's apartment, where they listened to sitar music and tripped on LSD. For Anita, the "hopeless romantic," it was their "real marriage" and the "final rite of passage into the new consciousness."

For Abbie, becoming a hippie made a lot of sense from a political and a cultural point of view. The dropouts, the pot-heads, and the flower children were not only colorful characters on the American landscape, but controversial as well. California governor Ronald Reagan defined the hippie as a creature who "dresses like Tarzan, has hair like Jane, and smells like Cheetah." Herbert Marcuse, one of the grand old men of twentieth-century Marxism, stunned students at the Institute for Policy Studies in Washington, D.C., when he insisted that the hippies presented the "only viable social revolution" in advanced societies because they rejected war, material possessions, and the spirit of competition. Moreover, in *Eros and Civilization,* which Abbie had read when he was an undergraduate at Brandeis and which was reissued in paperback with a new preface in 1966, Marcuse celebrated the whole rebellion of youth "against the false fathers, teachers, and heroes." This was the kind of language that Abbie understood and knew how to translate into theatre and mythology. He assumed that he could make the hippies into almost anything and everything that he wanted them to be. What was appealing about the scene on the Lower East Side, he explained in his autobiography, was that "The reality and the vision could be created from scratch." So in his scenario the hippies became the "new niggers," the "white niggers," the "runaway" slaves of the twentieth century. They were the new oppressed minority, he claimed.

Becoming one of them—letting his hair grow, putting on hippie garb, and peppering his conversation with words like "chick," "groovy," and "spade"—meant joining the underclass, he insisted. In his guise as hippie, he boasted that he was "getting to understand what a black person goes through on a level not even reached by getting kicked around in the civil rights movement for years." When he passed another hippie on the street, he would smile and say hello; he was able to connect, he wrote in *Revolution for the Hell of It,* in a "kind of comradeship that I've seen black people show when they are alone in the white world."

George Metesky, the Diggers, and SDS

In the summer of 1967, Abbie threw himself into the hippie scene on the Lower East Side, but without losing himself in it. He turned himself into a larger-than-life hippie role model, a kind of super-hippie, and that meant presenting himself as a Digger. A Digger was not exactly the same as a hippie, but "both are myths," he wrote in an essay entitled "Diggery is Niggery." "Both are in one sense a huge put-on," he explained, but while the hippies were "created by media" and were "forced to play media-orientated roles," the Diggers had "learned to manipulate media." They were also, Abbie insisted, "more politically oriented." As a Digger, Abbie assumed he could master the media, not be mastered by it.

In San Francisco, where they'd emerged, the Diggers—Emmett Grogan, Peter Berg, Peter Coyote, and Freeman House—fed and clothed the hippies. But they also tried to teach the hippies by example how to create a culture without leaders or followers. Most of the Diggers had been actors with the San Francisco Mime Troupe, and they thought that theatre could teach the young about revolution. The San Francisco Diggers had taken their name from the Diggers of seventeenth-century England, a group of utopian revolutionaries who believed in the right to cultivate public lands and share the bounty of the harvest without paying taxes to the crown. Translated into twentieth-century terms, that meant not paying for things whenever possible. It meant that everything was, or at least should be, "free." Freeman House recalled later that it had meant "cutting through the acquisitive part of self" and learning how to "live in the material excesses of the sixties." So the Diggers managed to find, hustle, borrow, or sometimes steal—

or "liberate," as they would say—food and clothing from the haves and, in the spirit of Robin Hood, make it available to the hippie have-nots.

Richard Goldstein, who introduced the Diggers to New Yorkers, wrote in a March 1967 *Village Voice* article that the Digger rebellion was "centered around rejecting money." Moreover, he explained, the Diggers encouraged a cult of anonymity. Many of the Diggers were discarding their own given names and taking the name George Metesky. "We're all Meteskys," a young woman told Goldstein. "We're a generation of schizophrenic mutants." Sharing the name Metesky was a key ingredient in the communal experience of rebellion and defiance. No one was supposed to become a leader or a media celebrity. Everyone was supposed to share equal billing.

In fact, George Metesky was the real name of a disgruntled employee for Con Edison, New York City's public utilities company, who'd expressed his hostility in the fifties by detonating a series of bombs, attracting media attention. To the Diggers, as well as to many hippies, George Metesky was a hero: the little man fighting for a just cause against a giant corporation. Only after a failed letter-writing campaign had he turned to sabotage. As Steve Pelletiere explained in the pages of *WIN,* "George's bombs were ideal happenings for television, as they took place in movie theatres, subways, public telephone booths." Pelletiere went on to insist that the hippies were following in Metesky's footsteps. "They have shown genius in handling the media," he wrote. "Yellow submarines, Love-ins and Gentle Thursdays are sure attention-getting devices. Also . . . they grab headlines and screentime to advertise a cause—Peace—which the newsmen as lief would overlook." What Pelletiere didn't acknowledge was the very real difference between George Metesky's bombs and the metaphorical explosions that the hippies set off. But that blurring of distinctions suited Abbie. If figurative bombs could attraction the same attention as Metesky's actual explosives had, so much the better.

Taking George Metesky as his own pseudonym and adopting Digger ideas, Abbie wrote in *WIN* magazine that "the free thing . . . is the most revolutionary thing in America today. Free dance, free food, free theatre (constantly), free stores, free bus rides, free dope, free housing, and most important free money." He urged readers to "really fuck with money": "burn it, smoke it to get high, trade with it, set up boxes of it in the street marked 'Free Money,' panhandle it, steal it, throw it away." As one might expect, this philosophy ran counter to almost everything that he was doing at Liberty House for the Poor People's Corporation. Suddenly buying and selling crafts was counterrevolutionary—at least by the Digger rules of the game, which Abbie adopted. Much to the annoyance of Ellen Maslow, who had ultimate authority at the store, Abbie began to give the crafts away. It was his final act at Liberty House: the free distribution of dolls, hats, handbags, dresses, quilts, and candles. From then on Liberty House was off-limits to him, but he didn't care anymore. There was so much else to do. At last he was free of the cash register, the rents, the banking, and the shopkeeper's hours.

Now he spent most of his time in the street or preparing to perform street theatre. He hustled, played games, pursued women, smoked pot, gave out leaflets, went to the movies, visited the Peace Eye Bookstore, and talked with hippies and Puerto Ricans in Tompkins Square Park. In the spring and summer of 1967 he staged a series of guerrilla theatre skits with social significance. One Saturday afternoon, Abbie and company arrived on Third Street in the Village with brooms, mops, rags, and sponges and staged a "sweep-in." "It was a goof," Don McNeill reported in the *Village Voice* (in an article later reprinted in his book *Moving through Here*). "The cops were bewildered"—especially when an officer walked up to a hippie and the "hippie began to scrub his badge." Fortunately, the cop smiled. On another occasion Abbie and the New York Diggers planted a tree in the middle of St. Mark's Place. The Ninth Precinct's deputy inspector, Joseph Fink—whom Mayor John Lindsay called his "favorite hippie"—made the event possible by closing down the street and rerouting traffic. Wavy Gravy—a kind of impresario of the counterculture who later had a flavor of Ben and Jerry's ice cream named after him—remembered that Abbie arrived in a flatbed truck with a tree, a sign that read "Only God Can Make a Tree," and several hundred containers of purloined yogurt which he of course distributed for free.

Another time he and the Diggers showed up at the headquarters of Con Edison, where they threw soot in the air and on employees in jackets and ties. They sprayed mist from aerosol cans to make a point about the pollution of the atmosphere, danced on a carpet while tossing flower petals, laughed, and clowned. Don McNeill thought that Abbie and his company were "weird," but he gave them a rave review. "It was classic street theatre," he wrote, "a Digger drama improvised with the idea that a handful of soot down an executive's neck might be more effective than a pile of petitions begging for cleaner air."

In June 1967 Abbie attended his first SDS Conference in Denton, Michigan. The organizers, most of whom were SDS's founding fathers and were known as "the superintellectuals," called the gathering "Back to the Drawing Boards." Their idea, they said, was to begin a dialogue among SDS's long-standing members to rethink basic strategies. The younger, more freewheeling members accused the Old Guard of trying to maintain control of the organization in order to keep it on an intellectual level preoccupied with refined analysis.

In the seven years since it had been founded in 1960, SDS had grown into a powerful political organization that unequivocally opposed the war in Vietnam. SDS urged students to burn their draft cards and to refuse military induction. By the summer of 1967, there were thirty thousand members and 247 chapters, from Ivy League schools in the East to community colleges in the West. Moreover, SDS's ranks were rapidly swelling. Greg Calvert, the national secretary, articulated the new direction of the organization as embracing "revolutionary consciousness," a position that wasn't far from Abbie's own. Kirkpatrick Sale reports that Calvert urged members to think of themselves as the oppressed and to struggle for their "own freedom in unity with others who share the burden of oppressions." Still, that was a minority opinion. SDS was an umbrella organization that included a wide range of political persuasions. Carl Davidson, vice-president in 1966–67, noted, "We have within our ranks Communists . . . socialists of all sorts, 3 or 4 different kinds of anarchists, . . . social democrats, humanist liberals . . . libertarian laissez-faire capitalists, and, of course, the articulate vanguard of the psychedelic liberation front."

SDS's Old Guard disliked the upstarts with their marijuana, beads, Bob Dylan records, long hair, and bad manners. They didn't want their organization taken over. The Old Guard staked out its territory, but a great many SDS members were unsure what political direction to take. As Dotson Rader, a Columbia SDS member, observed, "The Civil Rights Movement was dead. Pacifism was dead. Some Leftists . . . knew it early. . . . It took the rest of us a while to get it." The San Francisco Diggers knew that civil rights and pacifism had died, and they were going to Denton, Michigan, to tell SDS the news. Why didn't Abbie meet them at the conference, they suggested? So Abbie and his friends Jim Fouratt, Keith Lampe, and Paul Krassner, editor of the *Realist,* flew to Kalamazoo. They dressed as hippies, with "Jim in his beautiful Goldilocks hair and purple pants, I in beads, boots, bellbottoms, and a cocky Mexican cowboy hat," Abbie wrote in *Revolution for the Hell of It.* They knew full well that their fashion statement would be read as a militant call-to-arms.

On the first night at Denton, the Diggers burst into the camp dining hall and disrupted SDS leader Tom Hayden, who was delivering the keynote speech about difficulties he was having as an organizer in Newark. One of the Diggers, Billy Fritsch—otherwise known as Billy Tumbleweed—beat a tambourine in time. Peter Berg, who identified himself as Emmett Grogan, told the SDSers, "Get out of the system, do your thing. Don't organize students, teachers, Negroes, organize your head. Find out where you are, what you want to do and go out and do it." The real Emmett Grogan, playing himself, called the audience "Faggots!" and shouted, "You haven't got the balls to go mad. You're going to make a revolution?—you'll piss in your pants when the violence erupts."

Bob Ross, a member of SDS's Old Guard, told Grogan, "If the CIA wanted to disrupt this meeting they couldn't have done it any better than by sending you." Todd Gitlin, another member of the Old Guard, felt that the Diggers not only derailed the conference but also drove a permanent wedge "between political and cultural radicals." Years later, in *The Sixties: Years of Hope, Days of Rage,* he would write that the conference had been a failure: "no organization was founded, no further plans sketched." Moreover, in the wake of the Digger disruption, the New Left failed to ever "outgrow the student movement."

For Abbie, however, it was "a monumental meeting, probably never to be repeated." From his perspective, Billy Tumbleweed was a "beautiful cat," and Peter Berg was "a white Snick Nigger." Berg's "scatological" speech was inspired and inspiring, a model of rhetorical power. "Holy shit," Abbie exclaimed. "Excitement, Drama, Revolution." The

Digger performance at Denton gave him hope. If organizers like the Diggers could give the hippie dropouts "a new, positive, authentic frame of reference," they might never return to their middle-class values and institutions, he predicted.

By the next morning the Diggers had departed, but not Abbie. Conference participants remember that he stayed up smoking marijuana, flirting, and rapping. Over the weekend he attended workshops and panel discussions, representing himself as a former community organizer and local insurgent who understood SDS history and experience. Participatory democracy had long been his philosophy, he explained. Only now it meant "do your own thing." It was obvious that SDS's future was with hippies, not with students, he insisted.

At a workshop on the New Left and the hippies, Abbie defended the use of marijuana; getting stoned never stopped him from organizing the revolution, he insisted. As usual, he couldn't resist clowning. When Tom Hayden asked SDS members at a workshop he was leading "How do you prevent cooptation?" Abbie grinned and said "*Copulation*," much to the amusement of the crowd. For many SDS members, he was a welcome addition to the family of radicals. Indeed, Ann Forer, an SDS member, recalled Abbie as "the first person in the new left who seemed like a likable guy and had a face full of fun and a mind full of sense."

In the summer of 1967, he organized a successful "Smoke-In" in Tompkins Square Park. Hippies got stoned together in the sun, and no one was arrested. That September, he waved a marijuana cigarette while serving on a panel about "the relationship between radicals and hippies" at the Socialist Scholars Conference in New York. Wearing an army-surplus jacket and carrying a toy cap pistol in a holster on his hip, he "rambled on in the manner of a stand-up comic," Gerald Long wrote in the *National Guardian,* the movement's leading newspaper. SDS's Greg Calvert explained to the standing-room-only audience "how hip the people in SDS were," and Abbie told them "how political 'dropping out' was." If nothing else, Abbie had opened a dialogue with the New Left and had narrowed the gap between the movement and the counterculture. "A hip radical and a radical hippie have a lot in common," Gerald Long observed. Indeed, from Abbie's perspective, the "Back to the Drawing Boards" conference had been the start of a long, productive collaboration between students and hippies, dropouts and protesters.

Herbert Marcuse, who was in the audience at the Socialist Scholars Conference and who'd recently made public his use of hashish, expressed his appreciation for Abbie's cultural strategy. But he had a warning, as well. "Flowers have no power," he said, "other than the power of the men and women who let them grow and protect them." Abbie had no immediate rejoinder for Marcuse, but he seems later to have thought about the comment. "I want the flower and the fist," he would say, and on other occasions he noted, "I always held my flower in a clenched fist."

chapter six

THE MYTHIC
REVOLUTIONARY

Burning Issues

The media called them "long, hot summers," and year after year they defined the American political climate. In Harlem in 1964, Watts in 1965, and Chicago in 1966, African Americans set fire to ghettoes and looted stores, and many were shot and killed by police officers and National Guardsmen. Now it was the summer of 1967, and across the country there were major riots ("rebellions" and "insurrections," New Leftists called them) expressing anger toward "honky" America as well as scorn for the nonviolent protest espoused by Dr. Martin Luther King, Jr.

In Newark, New Jersey, a city rife with corruption, poverty, and racism, there were six days of rioting: 26 blacks were killed, 1,200 injured, and over 1,000 arrested. In Detroit, the fury lasted eight days: 43 people were killed, 2,000 injured, and 7,000 arrested. There was no room for compromise now, no hope for reform through civil rights bills. "Violence is as American as cherry pie," SNCC chairman H. Rap Brown proclaimed. A riot, he claimed, was "a dress rehearsal for revolution."

SDS members watched the burning ghettos with a sense both of elation and of apprehension. For Todd Gitlin, who was living in Chicago, it was a terrifying summer. "All of us are on the brink of madness," he wrote to a friend. For Tom Hayden, who was living and organizing in Newark, the riots pointed toward an "American form of guerrilla warfare based in the slums." As for Abbie, he was elated by the news from Newark and from Detroit, where hippies had joined blacks to burn and loot. To him the participation of young whites in the riot showed that the flower children were transforming themselves into tough rebels. While sociologists and media pundits were busy trying to define the causes for Newark and Detroit, Abbie urged his contemporaries to analyze less and act more. "Riots—environmental and psychological—are Holy, so don't screw around with explanations," he insisted in the article "Diggery is Niggery."

Shortly after the riots he formed an ad hoc group called "The Committee of Concerned Honkies"—a name meant to provoke laughter—and drove to Newark with a truckload of "stuff" that he delivered to Tom Hayden. Wearing a bead necklace and a black hat over his long hair, he strolled through grim neighborhoods, stopping to play touch football with black teenagers. Along with Hugh Romney, who would soon rename himself Wavy Gravy and become known for his role in the Hog Farm and Woodstock, Abbie performed a street theatre skit that was meant to parody the slave auction of the pre–Civil War South. As Romney recalled it, Abbie flexed his muscles and opened his mouth wide, revealing his teeth, as Romney invited members of the crowd to place bids. "How much do I have for this Digger?" Romney shouted. Abbie clowned around with young black kids, but he also wanted to convey a serious message of solidarity. "Spades and Diggers are one," he wrote in "Diggery Is Niggery." "Diggersareniggers. Both stand for the destruction of property."

Other white radicals did not call themselves "honkies" and certainly did not dare to call blacks "spades" or "niggers." Abbie was brazen; he violated all the linguistic taboos. At the same time he seemed to keep one eye on the dictionary as he returned over and over to the essential definitions of words. A "riot," he reminded readers of *WIN* magazine, meant an outbreak of laughter as well as an outburst of violence; a riot was therefore successful if "everyone has a good time." The point, as far as he was concerned, wasn't to burn down buildings or shoot police officers, but to detonate brain cells and create a revolution in consciousness. When Bobby G. Seale and Huey P. Newton of the Black Panther Party of Oakland, California, posed with weapons at the state capitol in Sacramento to dramatize their Constitutional right to bear arms, Abbie saw their demonstration as guerrilla theatre, not a literal call to insurrection. "Guns alone will never change this System," he wrote in *Revolution for the Hell of It.* "You don't use a gun on an IBM computer. You pull the plug out." It was "silly-putty sabotage" that he had in mind, and he advised the left that "our job is to line the streets of the country with banana peels."

In Worcester in 1964 he had called his brand of rebellion "obstructionism." Now he was uncomfortable with almost all "isms," including communism as well as capitalism, and distrustful of all "ists" except for artists, whose role he had adopted for himself. Not surprisingly he began to call his approach "creative disruption." Social protest, he felt, ought to be based on a sense of aesthetics as much as ideology. "People fight from where they are," he explained to David Katz, editor of *A Rebirth of Wonder,* an independent high school newspaper in New York. "Like we can't say, 'Yankee, Go Home.' We're in Yankee Stadium. . . . We can't say, 'Get Whitey.' We're white. So we have to evolve a whole different strategy from who we are." Since America was made up of freewheeling individualists, the revolution would not be created by party leaders or by collective fiat. Americans, Abbie explained, were "faced with a very existential kind of revolution where the individual has to decide from his base how he can best serve the revolution." In Latin America and Asia, real guerrillas were fighting in real jungles; in the United States, "existential warriors" were fighting in a media jungle. He later expanded on this idea in his autobiography: "A modern revolutionary group headed for the television station, not for the factory," he wrote in the chapter entitled "Here Come the Hippies." "It concentrated its energy on infiltrating and changing the image system."

In the summer of 1967 Abbie was extraordinarily proud of hippies. He was beginning to evolve an identity for himself as a hippie nationalist: the countercultural counterpart to black nationalists, who had sprung up all across American ghettoes and who espoused the gospel of separatism. If blacks had their own nation, so too did young whites, Abbie insisted. Two years later he would call it "Woodstock Nation," a cultural and political entity composed of hippies and dropouts who smoked marijuana, listened to rock 'n' roll, and rejected the Protestant work ethic. When black militants like SNCC's Rap Brown sneered at "flower power," Abbie accused them of breaking the rules of the political game. It was none of Rap's business putting down the hippies, he insisted. Rap ought to direct his comments to ghetto youth and leave the white dropouts and longhairs to white organizers like himself.

Hippies and blacks were never more separate, either culturally or politically, than in June, July, and August of 1967. While young blacks were rioting, a great many young whites were drifting through the Summer of Love. There was a "love-in" in L.A. and a pop music festival in Monterey with the hippie theme of "Music, Love, and Flowers." Abbie's own musical tastes were changing with the times, and the changes reflected his newfound hippie identity. In *Revolution for the Hell of It* he explained that every revolution has its own unique "rhythm": the antifascists of the 1930s had found it expressed in the songs of the Abraham Lincoln Brigade, whereas the hippies found it embodied in "white psychedelic rock." During the winter of 1967 he was mostly listening to protest music: to Bob Dylan's "Blowin' in the Wind" and to Phil Ochs's "I Ain't A-Marching Anymore," which served as the anthem of the antiwar movement. By the summer of 1967 he was a convert to psychedelic rock and the San Francisco sound: Janis Joplin, Country Joe and the Fish, and the Jefferson Airplane, all of whom had played at the Monterey Pop Festival.

In the mid-sixties, Abbie enjoyed the Beatles, especially their film *A Hard Day's Night* (1964), but when *Sgt. Pepper's Lonely Hearts Club Band* was released in June of 1967, he suddenly became an avid Beatles fan. During the Summer of Love he listened to *Sgt. Pepper* again and again, often in the company of friends. Keith Lampe remembered that when he and Abbie heard the final chords to "A Day in the Life," the last song on the album, "it was as though the millennium was at hand." What Abbie and Keith, as well as many others, heard on the album was a utopian message of endless joy and eternal youth. "You can dance forever. That's the Beatles message," he wrote in *Revolution for the Hell of It.*

In 1987, on the twentieth anniversary of the release of *Sgt. Pepper,* Abbie observed that the album had "summed up so much of what we were saying politically, culturally, artistically, expressing our inner feelings and our view of the world in a way that was so revolutionary. It was Beethoven coming to the supermarket. It allowed someone like myself to see the vehicle, the style, the modality in which we could put across counterculture politics." In the Beatles themselves Abbie saw the preeminent heroes of his era. The "Fab Four," along with their wives and girlfriends, formed a "new family group," he insisted. They were "the perfect model" for hippies to emulate—a small circle of friends who rejected hierarchical structures. John Lennon, Paul McCartney, George Harrison, and Ringo Starr had "unlimited creativity," he insisted. They were "a continual process, always changing, always burning the old Beatles, always dropping out." Indeed, the band had reinvented itself and recreated its image over and over again, much as Abbie wanted to do himself.

The Anti-Christ

Ever since 1965, activists had been burning draft cards to protest the war in Vietnam. At antiwar rallies, demonstrators carried signs that read "BURN DRAFT CARDS, NOT CHILDREN" and "WOULD CHRIST CARRY A DRAFT CARD?" In an article entitled "Draft Cards Are for Burning," pacifist Tom Cornell explained that the Selective Service cards and the American flag were "secular symbols" that had replaced the religious symbols of Christianity and Judaism. From Cornell's point of view, a draft card was "a sacrament"; burning it was "a defilement, a real blasphemy against the state." Moreover, he suggested, burning a draft card was "a kind of castration symbol and an Oedipal thing." The movement as a whole was thinking in much the same terms.

For Abbie, draft card burning was never a crucial act, perhaps because his own card classified him as "4-F": unfit for duty due to bronchial asthma. He burned his own card without fanfare in the spring of 1967, and he supported the call from members of the Cornell SDS chapter for a mass public burning of draft cards. On April 15, 1967, he was present at a demonstration in New York when about 175 young men, many of them from Cornell, burned their cards. That date was, in fact, a landmark occasion for the antiwar movement. Abbie's pacifist friend Marty Jezer, who set fire to his card that day, explained that "not to have burned a draft card on April 15 would have been tantamount to living in Boston in 1773 and not to have dropped tea in Boston Harbor." Columbia SDS member Dotson Rader described the protest that day as "a kind of theatre, with banners and songs and ritualistic language." It was exhilarating, he explained, because there was a sense that "your side invades the center of the city and holds captive the physical symbols of power."

Like Tom Cornell, Dotson Rader, and many others in the movement—that all-encompassing political and cultural entity that included almost everyone who was protesting anything—Abbie had a profound appreciation for symbolic theatre. Dollar bills, not draft cards, however, were his primary props. Soon after his hippie wedding in June, he began setting fire to ones and fives, and he quickly gained a reputation in the movement as a maverick who thought it was "more important to burn dollar bills than draft cards." Burning draft cards undermined the military; burning money sabotaged the whole system, or so he argued.

Abbie practically begged to be prosecuted. Dressed as a pauper, his hair deliberately unkempt, he would stand outside a bank and turn the sidewalk into a stage. When an audience had gathered, he would ceremoniously burn a small portion of a dollar bill (a federal offense). Witnesses to the crime were essential, as was the evidence, which he deliberately preserved. He even made sure that a photographer was on hand to capture his performance on color film. There was plenty of provocation, but no one bothered to arrest him or even to investigate, and he began to dream of bigger, bolder actions.

Jim Fouratt, who was his closest movement collaborator, was trying "to figure out an action that would focus public attention on corporate America's role in Vietnam," he remembered. For much of the summer Abbie and Jim brainstormed until they came up with a scenario. Once again, money would be the prop, but this time the New York Stock Exchange would serve as the stage for their performance. Dressed as hippies—to distinguish themselves from the suit-and-tie stockbrokers—they would make their way to the visitors' gallery on the third floor, then scatter dollar bills, thereby disrupting the day's trading.

It is unclear who deserves principal credit for the idea; Fouratt and Hoffman both claimed authorship. For Jim Fouratt, who was preoccupied with the war in Vietnam, the stock exchange symbolized the military-industrial complex. For Abbie it was the epitome of the capitalist empire. But his brand of guerrilla theatre on Wall Street was as much Freudian and Jungian as it was Marxist. It was a ritual of defilement as well as a piece of daring child's play in the working adult world. Abbie also hoped to send a message to the traditional Left about the very nature of messages and meanings, à la Marshall McLuhan. Linear thoughts were out; icons and images were in. Guerrilla theatre was far more powerful than a manifesto, he insisted; mythic events were more effective as agents of social change than were clearly defined demonstrations.

Reporter Richard Goldstein also deserves acknowledgment for the idea of invading the stock exchange. In his March 1967 *Village Voice* article "In Search of George Metesky," which had inspired Abbie, Goldstein had suggested that it would be "interesting to watch the crucifixion when Diggers drive money changers from the temple." Abbie was, of course, familiar with the New Testament passage that describes how Jesus "poured out the coins of the money-changers and overturned their tables" (John 2:15). When he wrote about the stock exchange incident in *Revolution for the Hell of It,* Abbie called the chapter "Driving the Money Changers from the Temple," and in his autobiography he wrote that it was "the TV-age version of driving the money changers from the temple." For Abbie, who consciously aimed to recycle traditional myths and symbols, going to the stock exchange served as a way of updating Jesus's antimaterialist gesture.

The stock exchange incident also enabled Abbie to act out the ultimate put-on. As Richard Goldstein later observed, Abbie had performed a parody of Christ and in doing so had become "an anti-Christ." Abbie's implicit identification with Jesus was grandiose, but it was also very much in keeping with movement mythology. For sixties radicals, Jesus was the prototype of all radicals: an outlaw persecuted by the authorities, as well as the self-effacing leader of an underground movement. It's no wonder that Bob Moses, Director of the Mississippi Freedom Summer, had been known as "the Jesus of the project."

Demonstrating in New York's financial district wasn't a new idea. In 1965, for example, SDS members, including Tom Hayden and Todd Gitlin, had staged a sit-in in front of the headquarters of the Chase Manhattan Bank. Their protest had had a specific purpose: to persuade banks to divest in holdings in South Africa. Abbie's assault on the stock exchange was different: there was no list of demands and no specific goal. The form was as important as the content. Moreover, the participants weren't members of any group or organization. Indeed, many of them didn't even know one another. As director and producer of the event, Abbie alone had the whole picture in mind. He raised the cash, wrote the script, and recruited most of the cast. His list of apostles numbered a dozen or so: a young woman who called herself Morning Dove; Keith Lampe, a Korean War veteran turned pacifist; Marty Jezer, the editor of *WIN* magazine who admired Abbie's ability to inject humor into the "hopelessly dull . . . peace movement"; two Berkeley peace activists, Jerry Rubin and Stewart ("Stew") Albert, who had just moved to New York; and several members of an antiwar group called the Mobilization for Direct Action, which had recently staged a sit-in on the U. S. Navy destroyer *Newman K. Perry.*

On the morning of August 24, 1967, they met for the first time at the visitors' entrance to the New York Stock Exchange at 20 Broad Street. Nearly a dozen photographers and reporters, including John Kifner of the *New York Times,* had been informed of the plan and were waiting at the scene. In *Revolution for the Hell of It,* Abbie insisted that he "didn't even bother to call the press," and in his autobiography he wrote that "at that time we really had no notion of anything called a media event." Most of the other participants, however, distinctly remember that Abbie had alerted the media. Moreover, by his own admission, he planned the event knowing that there would be media coverage. "Every newscast has the stock market reports, so you know it's going to make every news show in the country," he said in 1969 when interviewed by Tom Forcade, founder of the Underground Press Syndicate, the counterculture's version of the Associated Press and United Press International. "It's a natural," Abbie continued. "Right after the news report . . . comes the human interest story—crazy hippies throwing money."

Over the years, the event at the stock exchange achieved mythical proportions, in large part deriving from Abbie's own accounts. There was "pandemonium" on the floor, he boasted in his autobiography. "The sacred electronic ticker tape, the heartbeat of the Western world, stopped cold. . . . The system cracked a little. Not a drop of blood had been spilled, not a bone broken, but on that day, with that gesture, an image war had begun. In the minds of millions of teenagers the stock market had just crashed." Descriptions of the event differ, and to this day it's uncertain exactly how much money was dropped and precisely how many people took part in the event. After more than a quarter of a century many of the participants themselves are unsure of who was there. But a reliable if not definitive account of the day's events can be pieced together. Abbie handed out money to the assembled cast of characters, many of whom stuffed it into their pockets. The group filed inside the building, then waited on line with the tourists as though they intended to take the official tour. Jim Fouratt approached John Whighton, the captain of the security force, and identified himself as George Metesky. He and his friends were members of ESSO, the East Side Service Organization, he said. Whighton called them hippies and accused them of planning to disrupt the stock exchange. "No demonstrations of any form are allowed," he warned. Abbie replied, "Who's a hippie? I'm Jewish and besides we don't do demonstrations, see we have no picket signs."

Whighton winced at the word "Jewish." Unwilling to create a scene or to be accused of anti-Semitism, he ushered George Metesky and friends into the gallery, where they immediately began to float dollar bills to the floor. Abbie had argued that guerrilla theatre should be performed as quickly as "slapstick movies," and indeed the performance was over in a matter of minutes. Stew Albert, who was a veteran of Berkeley street demonstrations, remembered that the stock exchange action was like "a wild comic book," unlike any protest he'd ever experienced. Bruce Dancis, a pacifist who'd organized draft card burnings, recalled that "at first people on the floor were stunned. They didn't know what was happening. They looked up and when they saw money was being thrown they started to cheer, and there was a big scramble for the dollars." As they were ushered out of the gallery, the demonstrators continued their performance, mugging for the cameras and sparring with reporters. "It's the death of money," Jim Fouratt explained. When a reporter asked where he'd gotten the cash, he explained that "it was from General William Westmoreland's mother who disapproved of her son's military policy in Vietnam." Abbie set fire to a five-dollar bill, then held it in the air and posed for photographers with Jerry Rubin and Stew Albert.

When reporters asked him his name, he replied, "I'm Cardinal Spellman." When they wanted to know "How many of you are there?" he told them, "We don't even exist." That night he watched TV; the next day he read the New York newspapers. Much to his delight, "every news report differed." The guerrilla theatre at the Stock Exchange was "a perfectly mythical event," he concluded in *Revolution for the Hell of It.* No journalist described what had actually happened; rather, each one created "his own fantasy." To Abbie it was yet more evidence that reality was made up and that news was a fiction.

The account he liked best appeared in the *Daily News,* which unabashedly embraced the spirit of guerrilla theatre. "A shower of green power descended on the heads of the startled capitalists," the *News* reported. "The youngsters . . . seemed to be demonstrating their scorn for the almighty bucks." Not surprisingly, the *Times* exercised restraint. "Dollar bills thrown by a band of hippies fluttered down on the floor of the New York Stock Exchange . . . disrupting the normal hectic trading pace," John Kifner's article began. Over the course of the next year, Abbie would defend the *Daily News* and condemn the *New York Times.* "The *Daily News* responds on a gut level," he wrote. "The *New York Times* has no guts." He didn't love the tabloid *Daily News,* but it was "more honest than the *New York Times,*" and its front page was "the closest thing to TV."

The stock exchange incident made New York and the whole nation sit up and take notice of Abbie Hoffman. As far as Mayor Lindsay's administration was concerned, burning money gave the city a "bad image"; accordingly, Hoffman and Fouratt were fired from the hundred-dollar-a-week jobs they held on the city's Youth Board Council. A representative of the Treasury Department in Washington, D.C., agreed that burning money was a crime, but told reporters that charges would probably not be filed, and they never were. There seemed to be a place within the system itself for Abbie's brand of theatre. One stockbroker liked the act at the stock exchange so much that he invited the Diggers to do a repeat performance.

In the *Village Voice* Don McNeill raved about the "Digger dollars" piece, as he called it, and noted that "Manhattan is becoming a certified stage." Kate Coleman remembered that her editors at *Newsweek* thought that Abbie "was like Huck Finn—a bad boy whom they could like" and that they wanted more coverage of him. At last he had the kind of attention he wanted. Indeed, if he never did another thing, the stock exchange incident would ensure Abbie Hoffman a place in the history of the sixties.

Guerrillas at the Pentagon

For all the publicity that it received, however, the stock exchange event was still a side show to the main theatre of movement activity, which was antiwar organizing. The National Mobilization Committee to End the War in Vietnam—known as "the Mobe" to movement people—called for a week of protests in October 1967 that would culminate in Washington, D.C. The moderates in the Mobe wanted a well-behaved, law-abiding "peace-in"; the radicals insisted on a freewheeling action that would raise the political stakes.

David Dellinger, who shaped the event as much as any other single individual, envisioned a multilevel protest that would allow for both "Gandhi and Guerrilla": nonviolent resistance and direct confrontation. On Saturday, October 21, there would be something for almost everyone: a rally with speakers at the Lincoln memorial; a peaceful march from the Capitol across the Potomac River to Virginia; a rally in the Pentagon's parking lot; and, finally, civil disobedience on the grounds of the Pentagon itself. To add the guerrilla ingredient and to recruit the younger antiwar activists, Dellinger brought in Jerry Rubin, who had proved himself as a skillful organizer and popular activist. Shortly before moving to the East Coast, Rubin had run for Mayor of Berkeley and had received twenty-two percent of the vote. Unlike many movement activists, who were content to be spoilers and to make defiant gestures from the sidelines, Rubin wanted to grab and hold political power. But he wasn't afraid to confront established power, either. It was his bold idea to stage the protest at the Pentagon, the seat of military power, rather than at the U.S. Capitol, as the Mobe had originally planned. After all, Rubin argued, it was the generals, not the members of Congress, who were primarily responsible for the War in Vietnam.

Born in 1938 to a Jewish working-class family in Cincinnati, Rubin grew up an all-American kid. Whereas Abbie presented himself as a symbolic "orphan of America," Jerry Rubin was a real, live orphan: his mother had died in 1960 and his father in 1961. And whereas Abbie took on different personas while remaining essentially the same perennial troublemaker, Jerry Rubin really did undergo a series of profound metamorphoses. In the fifties he was a sports reporter and a keen supporter of Democratic presidential candidate Adlai E. Stevenson. In the sixties, after a brief stay in Israel, he had traveled to Cuba with a leftwing group and had returned home a supporter of Castro. In Berkeley he'd helped organize one of the first teach-ins against the war in Vietnam, and in Oakland he'd taken part in demonstrations to block trains that were carrying troops. When the House Un-American Activities Committee subpoenaed him in 1966, he appeared in the uniform of a 1776 American revolutionary. "I felt that to take the committee seriously would be devastating," Jerry wrote in "A Yippie Goes to Washington." "We had to attack its very legitimacy. My action was addressed to a specific audience . . . young people across the nation, and I knew my uniform would communicate to them that you didn't have to be scared, that you could turn your fear into courage."

As soon as Rubin heard that a man named Abbie Hoffman had been burning money, he was intrigued. "What an imagination, what weird and absurd ways of looking at things," he exclaimed. "I knew I had to meet this guy." The chemistry between the two was instant, at least from Jerry's point of view. "Abbie has this incredible effect on me," he told J. Anthony Lukas, who was writing an article about Rubin and the Yippies for *Esquire*. "Just revolutionized me." Jerry let his hair grow, exchanged his white shirts and slacks for "the more freaky garb of the East Village and started dropping acid regularly." Eventually, after frolicking with Abbie, Jim Fouratt, Keith Lampe, and Ed Sanders, he came to find the Mobe much too sedate and sought a new, wilder venture.

Abbie had heard about Jerry long before he met him. He was impressed with Rubin's appearance at HUAC in 1966, and he admired his rhetorical skills so much so that he called him "the white Rap Brown." Jerry didn't alter Abbie as intensely as Abbie altered Jerry, but Abbie needed him nonetheless as a comrade, business partner, and costar. Almost all his life, Abbie was more effective when he worked in tandem than when he worked on his own. Jim Fouratt had served him well, but Jerry Rubin—with his Jewish identity, his Berkeley background, and his hunger for fame—would serve him even better.

Abbie and Jerry were as fiercely competitive as two siblings, as egotistical as two anointed celebrities. But as attorney William Kunstler and others noted, the clash of their egos and the spur of competition drove them to be more creative and more daring. In the late summer and early fall of 1967, they joined forces to assault the war makers in the Pentagon—"the evil hulk that sits like a cancerous death-trap on the Potomac," Abbie called it in *Revolution for the Hell of It*—and to outwit the pacifists in the Mobe, whom Abbie dismissed at movement gatherings and demonstrations as "fucking prudes."

The strategy that Abbie had in mind was to mount a crazy kind of protest that would embody the ideas of Antonin Artaud, the twentieth-century French theater director, actor, theoretician, and madman who insisted on theatre that was "total spectacle." Artaud had committed suicide in 1948, but his ideas continued to influence the plays of Samuel Beckett and Eugène Ionesco as well as the performances of the Living Theatre. For Artaud, a written text was unnecessary, and so was a conventional stage. In *The Theatre and Its Double* (1938), his most important work, Artaud argued that performances should be "like renewed exorcisms," and that the "only value" of theatre "lies in its excruciating, magical connections with reality and with danger." Abbie found in Artaud's writings the intellectual framework to support his own theatrical experiments in the streets and at institutions like the New York Stock Exchange. "No need to build a stage, it was all around us," he wrote in the chapter of his autobiography entitled "Museum of the Streets." "Our whole experience was theatre—playing the flute on the street corner, panhandling, walking, living protest signs."

At the end of August Abbie appeared at a press conference with Jerry Rubin, comedian Dick Gregory, and H. Rap Brown to announce plans for an "exorcism to cast out the evil spirits" at the Pentagon. The "flower power contingent" would encircle the building, chant incantations, and make it "rise in the air," Abbie promised. His press conference performance was well rehearsed and carefully paced. He had his props in hand: a stick of burning incense and something that looked like a bowling ball, which he called a "psychedelic bomb." With mock solemnity, he tilted his head back and rolled his eyes, as though watching the Pentagon leave the ground and hover above Washington, D.C.

Exorcising the Pentagon was a colossal put-on, of course, and Abbie played it to the hilt. Like military scouts on a mission, Abbie and Martin Carey surveyed the impending battleground. They were arrested outside the Pentagon by a General Services Office administrator and charged with littering. Hippies were planning to link arms and perform a magic ritual, Abbie explained. Could they have a permit to raise the building three hundred feet? According to *Time* magazine, "the administrator graciously gave his permission . . . to raise the building a maximum of 10 feet, and dismissed the charges against the hippies."

When the government threatened to use Mace against protesters, Abbie announced that the Diggers had their own secret weapon, "a high potency sex juice" called Lace. When reporters showed up at his apartment, two couples volunteered to demonstrate the power of the chemical. They sprayed one another with the purple liquid, then undressed and began to make love while reporters watched with glee. Making love would triumph over making war.

There would be more sex at the Pentagon itself, Abbie proclaimed in a letter that appeared in the *East Village Other* under the George Metesky byline. "We will fuck on the grass and beat ourselves against the doors," he wrote. The letter painted a colorful portrait of a fantastic demonstration that would turn Washington, D.C., upside down and humiliate the President himself. "We will dye the Potomac red, burn the cherry trees, panhandle diplomats and try to kidnap LBJ while wrestling him to the ground and pulling his pants off," he wrote. In the poetic style of Allen Ginsberg, he described the apocalypse that would follow the Pentagon protest: "Schoolchildren will rip out their desks and throw ink at stunned instructors, office secretaries will disrobe and run into the streets, newsboys will rip up their newspapers and sit on the curbstones masturbating, storekeepers will throw open their doors making everything free, accountants will all collapse in one mighty heart attack, soldiers will throw down their guns," he wrote in an article published in *Revolution for the Hell of It* as "TWA Never Gets You There on Time."

When the big day arrived, he and Anita dressed in costume: she wore a Sergeant Pepper jacket; he wore beads and a linen shirt embroidered with an Egyptian snake, which Anita had made especially for the occasion. Both of them wore tall Uncle Sam hats. Abbie took several hits of LSD and experienced a "super" trip that was helped along, he explained, "by large doses of revolution, [and] no food or water."

At the Lincoln Memorial Benjamin Spock, the world-famous "baby doctor" turned antiwar activist, told a crowd estimated at a hundred thousand people that "the enemy is Lyndon Johnson." John Lewis, the former chairman of SNCC, led the chant "Hell, no, we won't go," and David Dellinger announced that the Pentagon protest marked "the beginning of a new stage in the American peace movement in which the cutting edge becomes active resistance." As for Abbie, although in the months before the Pentagon demonstration he had attracted national media attention, at the Pentagon itself he faded for the most part into the anonymity of the immense crowd. Indeed, nothing he did that day—including urinating ("pissing," he said) on the walls of the Pentagon—made him a memorable figure. He and Anita attended the rally then joined the march from the heart of Washington, D.C., to the Pentagon in Virginia.

American and Vietcong flags fluttered in the breeze, and there were placards with provocative comments like "LBJ, PULL OUT NOW, LIKE YOUR FATHER SHOULD HAVE DONE" and "NO VIETNAMESE CALLED ME NIGGER." SDS members, including Tom Hayden and Rennie Davis— who had just returned from a meeting with the Vietnamese—turned out en masse and provided a sense of discipline. Among the tens of thousands of college students, hippies, and middle-class suburbanites there were also intellectuals, writers, and celebrities, including Paul Goodman, Noam Chomsky, Dwight Macdonald, Robert Lowell, and Norman Mailer, who would celebrate the day's historic events as a revolutionary rite of passage in the Pulitzer Prize–winning book *The Armies of the Night* (1968).

In the north parking lot at the Pentagon, Ed Sanders and the Fugs began their ritual atop the flatbed truck that served as their open-air stage. A strip of canvas decorated with a Day-Glo dollar bill served as the backdrop for the performers. Drums beat, a trumpet wailed, and voices chanted, "Burn the money, burn the money, burn it, burn it." Then Ed Sanders, who had made a careful study of ancient exorcisms, began his incantation (as recorded by Mailer): "In the name of the generative power of Priapus, in the name of totality, we call upon the demons of the Pentagon to rid themselves of the cancerous tumors of the war generals." A small group of demonstrators, many of whom belonged to the "Revolutionary Contingent," rushed the Pentagon as Secretary of Defense Robert S. McNamara and several assistants watched from an office window. To Norman Mailer, who was soon arrested, the assault on the Pentagon was like a scene from the American Civil War. To Abbie it "looked a lot like the storming of the Bastille in the French Revolution." Two dozen protesters managed to enter the building and were immediately beaten and arrested. Others staged a nonviolent sit-in: they were clubbed and their heads bloodied; then they were arrested and carted away.

In the plaza outside the main entrance, 5,000 people were confronted by federal marshals wielding clubs and by soldiers armed with bayonet-tipped M-14 rifles. By nightfall, 3,000 troops and 1,800 National Guardsmen were defending the building. Some of the protesters hurled eggs, shouted obscenities at the troops, and wrote graffiti on the walls, including "Pentagon Sucks." Others, including a 23-year-old former Green Beret named Gary Rader, took part in an impromptu teach-in about Vietnam that went on for hours.

Anita remembered that while their friends Martin and Susan Carey "had a picnic in the grass, listened to music, and got stoned, Abbie was looking for barriers to break and insisted on confronting the troops." He and Anita jumped a fence and planted an American flag in the ground. When military police (MPs) surrounded them, Abbie proclaimed, "'We're Mr. and Mrs. America, and we claim this land in the name of Free America." They sat down, hugged, kissed, and offered to shake hands with the MPs, who finally let them go. In front of the Pentagon Abbie and Anita watched a Berkeley radical named "Super Joel" come within inches of a young soldier and, in what seemed to them a "gesture of courage and love," place a flower in his gun barrel. Soon flowers poked from gun barrels everywhere; the media captured the image, and it went around the world as a symbol of the power of flowers over weapons.

"Those were the greatest moments of togetherness with human beings that I've ever experienced," Anita remembered. "It was spiritual. We faced danger; we knew that others faced it, too, and that we all believed in something worthwhile." Demonstrators invited the troops, many of whom were barely twenty, "Join us! Join us!" Abbie was exhilarated when a few soldiers threw down their guns and helmets and broke ranks. When darkness fell, the troops used tear gas to dispel the mostly young protesters who still huddled around bonfires, singing hymns, smoking marijuana, burning draft cards, and sharing sandwiches. At about midnight Saturday, when "the TV camera-eye could no longer see," as Abbie put it, the marshals clubbed and then arrested more demonstrators, but veteran pacifist Sidney Peck grabbed a bullhorn and persuaded them to stop. After all, the protesters had a weekend permit that had not yet expired. Just before dawn, SDS leaders called upon the demonstrators to withdraw in a dignified manner.

On Saturday night Abbie and Anita celebrated in Washington, D.C., but on Sunday they returned to the Pentagon, where the teach-in was once again in progress. "Ex-soldiers talk to MPs," Abbie wrote in *Revolution for the Hell of It.* "So do girls, college kids and priests, for twelve long hours. Talking, singing, sharing and contrasting Free America vs. the Uniformed Machine." At midnight on Sunday the forty-eight-hour permit expired, and Abbie and Anita, along with a core of demonstrators, were arrested and incarcerated at the federal prison in Occoquan, Virginia. A total of 683 people were arrested at the Pentagon that weekend, more than had ever been arrested at an antiwar demonstration. On the way to Occoquan, Abbie sang "Carry Me Back to Old Virginny." In jail, where he identified himself as "Abbie Digger," he played the clown. "Jail is a goof," he exclaimed. The matron didn't believe him when he proclaimed, "I'm a girl," but he insisted: "No, honey, I'm just flatchested, honest." In a cell with other demonstrators, he recalled the movie *Stalag 17* (1953) and promptly demanded to be treated like a prisoner of war. Marty Jezer, who was also incarcerated, noted that Abbie "put a sheet over his head" and screamed at the police, "I'm in here with Jews and Commies. Let me out!" The next day, when he and Anita appeared in court to pay a ten-dollar fine each and receive five-day suspended sentences, he told the judge, "The family that disobeys together stays together."

In *Coming Apart: An Informal History of America in the 1960s,* historian William L. O'Neill observed that despite the huge turnout, the October 21 protest had no visible effect on the men in the Pentagon and in the White House who were running the Vietnam War. In public, at least, they remained intransigent. President Lyndon B. Johnson ("LBJ") accused the antiwar protesters of dividing the nation and delaying an end to the hostilities. General Maxwell Taylor, one of the principal architects of the war, authored a *New York Times Magazine* article entitled "The Cause in Vietnam Is Being Won," which was published just six days before the March on the Pentagon. In it General Taylor claimed that the problem was "the illusion that the United States is deeply divided over Vietnam."

It was soon apparent, however, that the national division was no illusion. Polls showed that more Americans than ever before favored an immediate cease-fire and withdrawal of troops. The March on the Pentagon intensified the debate about the war. On military bases across the country and in Vietnam, too, soldiers began to identify with the protesters and to regard their own officers as the enemy. Even inside the Pentagon itself there was dissension. Daniel Ellsberg, who was drafting plans with Secretary of Defense McNamara for an invasion of North Vietnam, watched the protest on October 21 and began to revise his own thinking. The sight of marshals brutally clubbing pacifists, as well as the rumors about the levitation, played a part in Ellsberg's monumental decision to release the Pentagon Papers, a top-secret study of U. S. involvement in Vietnam. The publishing of the Pentagon Papers in 1971 unmasked the inconsistencies of the country's Vietnam policy and thereby helped to end the war. The Pentagon Papers also showed that the protest on October 21, 1967, had restrained the hawks in the administration from more vigorous pursuit of the war, because the Johnson administration began to fear that "domestic crisis" would mount and there would not be "sufficient forces . . . available for civil disorder control."

The protest at the Pentagon rejuvenated the peace movement and brought together almost all its factions. Cynics pointed out that the Flower Brigade had failed to make the Pentagon rise above the ground, but they missed the point. As Allen Ginsberg would explain years later to Derek Taylor, "the authority of the Pentagon" had been "demystified" and that "in that sense we *did* levitate it." It was "a poetic metaphor . . . a triumph of the human imagination over heavy metal materialism." For Abbie the demonstration was an absolute triumph on all fronts. Part-time protesters had been transformed into "total political animals," he insisted, and protest itself had been qualitatively changed. "The peace movement has gone crazy and it's about time," he gushed in *Revolution for the Hell of It.* "The Pentagon happening transcended the issue of the War." From now on, he predicted, protest would be "directed to the entire fabric of a restrictive, dull, brutal society." Paul Krassner remembered that after the Pentagon "Abbie believed that, like people in positions of authority, he could manipulate the media, and that realization gave him a tremendous sense of his own power." He was increasingly on his own and accountable to no one but himself.

Before the end of November he was already planning "a big event" for the Democratic National Convention in Chicago the following August. In his madcap scenario, disorder would be the order of the day. Little by little Abbie's ideas took shape: there would be a counterconvention, a pop festival, and an all-encompassing week of protest. "Chicago" itself would become synonymous with the megaevent. Long before their plans became finalized, Abbie and Jerry—now an inseparable movement duo—were publicizing Chicago as well as promoting themselves. Folksinger Phil Ochs interrupted a Carnegie Hall performance to invite them on stage to announce the demonstration. "Fuck Lyndon Johnson, fuck Robert Kennedy, and fuck you if you don't like it," Abbie shouted. The Carnegie Hall management cut the power, leaving the hall in darkness.

Abbie, Jerry, and their friends also took part in Phil Ochs's "War Is Over" demonstration in New York on November 25. Allen Ginsberg, America's poet-legislator, had urged that peace activists should "simply declare the war over." He inspired Phil Ochs, who'd been singing protest songs for most of the decade, to write the song "The War Is Over," with its refrain: "I declare the war is over / It's over." On November 25 Ochs met with demonstrators in Washington Square Park, sang his song, and then led a march up Fifth Avenue to Times Square. The war in Vietnam, he explained, was "only a figment of our propagandized imagination, a psychodrama out of *1984*." George Orwell's fantasy had become a reality. If enough people saw the war as an illusion and refused to believe it, then the war would really end, Ochs suggested.

For the most part, however, playful demonstrations now belonged to the past, along with the Summer of Love and flower power. In November Abbie and several thousand activists, including many SDS members, tried to disrupt the arrival of Secretary of State Dean Rusk, under heavy police protection, at the Hilton Hotel in New York, where he was scheduled to give a speech. By Abbie's vivid account in *Revolution for the Hell of It,* it was a "bloodbath": the demonstrators tossed plastic bags filled with "symbolic blood," as well as real cow's blood, and in turn they were bloodied by the police.

A month earlier, during Stop the Draft Week in Oakland, California, radical demonstrators had created havoc in the ten square blocks around the induction center. They'd commandeered a city bus, built barricades, blocked traffic, defied police orders, and created what they called "liberated territory." The movement's new militant strategy, as articulated by Oakland organizer Frank Bardacke (who would soon be indicted for conspiracy) was to convince the establishment that radicals could "cause chaos in this country as long as the war continues."Abbie liked the concept of creating havoc as a strategy to end the war, and he promptly became a street-fighting man at the Rusk demonstration, which replayed in the heart of Manhattan the "mobile street tactics" of Oakland.

In *Revolution for the Hell of It,* Abbie described the minibattle that unfolded in New York the night Rusk spoke at the Hilton Hotel: "Suddenly the intersection erupts. Cars jam up. Horns beep. Smoke bombs go off. Flares are lit. A straight couple ask me what's going on? I shout, 'There's a WAR on! Can't you see?' A long black limousine has blood splattered on its windows and Peace in Day-Glo letters sprayed on its trunk lid. 'Let's get out of here,' someone yells and everyone runs toward Sixth Avenue. It's a wild scene. Cops charging people, demonstrators, Christmas shoppers, people going to hear Dean Rusk. Cops in formation wading into crowds, clubbing away." Abbie found himself in a fistfight with a man he assumed was a "right-wing heckler," but who turned out to be a plainclothes policeman. Arrested and taken to the sixteenth precinct in Manhattan, he and some of his old friends sang Beatles tunes, swapped movement war stories, and nursed their wounds.

In the Florida Keys that December, Abbie and Paul Krassner took acid, snorkeled, swam naked, and began to conspire about the Democratic Convention in Chicago the following August. Ellen Sander, Krassner's companion, listened apprehensively while the two men "rapped about revolution" and "guns and warfare." Even before the plans had been worked out, Abbie spread the word. On Christmas Day he outlined his scenario in a letter to Father Gilgun: "We plan to bring 250,000 people to the Democratic Convention. We expect about 100,000 of them to be committed to disruption or sabotage. Both are worthwhile."

The Yippie Myth

When Abbie returned to New York from Florida, he devoted his energy to the protests at the Democratic National Convention, which he assumed would be "the most significant event of the year." In public, of course, he didn't emphasize sabotage and disruption. His main objective, he explained, was to bring about a "cross-fertilization of the hippie and New Left philosophies" and thus to create "a potlitical grass leaves movement." Abbie had chosen his words carefully: the new movement would embody the uninhibited freedom that Walt Whitman had espoused in *Leaves of Grass*. It would make room for both marijuana smokers and SDS members and rewrite the stuffy textbook of revolution. In addition, Abbie wrote in Krassner's magazine *The Realist,* he and his friends wanted "to make some statement, especially in revolutionary action—theatre terms, about LBJ, the Democratic Party, electoral politics, and the state of the nation."

From Abbie's point of view, the Democratic Party was illegitimate and unrepresentative. At the 1964 convention in Atlantic City, he reminded friends, the Party had refused to seat the legally elected delegates from the Mississippi Freedom Democratic Party. President Johnson and Vice President Humphrey were both down-and-dirty, wheeler-dealer politicians, he insisted, and both were to blame for the egregious exclusion of blacks. Moreover, there wasn't a single Democratic Party politician whom he respected. "There's not one fucking congressman, not one fucking senator, for immediate withdrawal of all U.S. troops from Vietnam," he complained. Not for a moment was he tempted to support Wisconsin Senator Eugene McCarthy, who had announced his candidacy for president in November 1967 and who had attracted a strong following on college campuses because of his antiwar stance. Students were urged to remain "Clean for Gene": to shave beards, cut long hair, and present wholesome images that wouldn't alienate middle-class voters. Jeremy Larner, Abbie's college friend, became McCarthy's main speech writer, but Abbie was so disgusted with the "Clean for Gene" approach that he even disrupted one of Mc-Carthy's speeches in Washington, D.C.

By 1968 he had given up entirely on electoral politics. It made more sense to run a real, live pig than a third-party candidate, Abbie believed, because all the candidates were pigs anyway. In Chicago, he claimed, the demonstrators would roast the presidential pig, then "eat him as a symbol of our direct participation in politics." The immediate task, he argued, was to persuade "huge numbers of people to come to Chicago." Masses of people in the streets were essential, and that would be no small feat because Abbie and his small circle of friends had "no organization, no money, no nothing," as recalled by Stew Albert, though they had ample talent and an instinct for publicity. For almost a year, Abbie had called himself a Digger; now the Digger identity would no longer do. As far as Abbie was concerned, the Diggers had taken a wrong turn by denouncing the hippies as mere consumers and dismissing the counterculture as a gimmick to sell commodities. Even the gun-toting Black Panthers had accepted the hippies as their natural allies; in *Soul on Ice,* which appeared in the winter of 1968 and quickly became a bestseller, Panther minister of information Eldridge Cleaver wrote, "The characteristics of the white rebels which must alarm their elders—the long hair, the new dances, their love for Negro music, their use of marijuana, their mystical attitudes toward sex—are all tools of their rebellion."

Abbie and the Diggers were divided not only by issues but also by personal animosity. Emmett Grogan accused Abbie of stealing Digger ideas and exploiting the Digger mystique to aggrandize himself. Abbie felt that the ideas weren't anyone's private property, and he argued that he wasn't using the Diggers to build his own fortune or power in the movement. Grogan became even more hostile and vindictive, and to make his point about theft of property he entered Abbie's apartment and stole something. Abbie, of course, was enraged. He knew that it was time to cut his ties to Emmett and the Diggers. The political solution that he and his friends arrived at collectively was to create a new organization that would be both mythical and mysterious, a paper party with make-believe leaders and an imaginary membership. It was a put-on and a prank, a colossal fiction that soon became a disturbing reality to police chiefs, mayors, and military officers. At the time, Abbie believed that everything should be free—free money, free love, free sex, and of course a free society—so he argued at first that the organization should be called "Freemen." Freemen even sponsored a few guerrilla theatre events in New York. But the founding mothers and fathers of the organization decided instead to call it "Yippie!" (with a fat exclamation point at the end to convey enthusiasm) or "YIP," which suggested Walt Whitman's "barbaric yap." Only later was it called the Youth International Party.

To explain what he meant by myth and how it connected to the Yippie concept, Abbie turned in part to Albert Camus, who had written in his *Notebooks* that "the revolution as myth is the definitive revolution," and in part to George Sorel, a French anarchist who had written in *Reflections on Violence* that "as long as there are no myths accepted by the masses, one may go on talking of revolts indefinitely, without even provoking any revolutionary movement." For the most part, however, Abbie relied on Marshall McLuhan, who had explained that "myth means putting on the audience, putting on one's environment" and that "young people are looking for a formula for putting on the universe—*participation mystique*." The Beatles had done it, McLuhan claimed. They had used "musical effects" to put on "a whole vesture, a whole time, a *Zeit*." Abbie added ingredients of his own. In *Revolution for the Hell of It,* he asserted that myth had to have "a high element of risk, drama, excitement and bullshit."

The founders of Yippie took it upon themselves to act as though they belonged to a real party: they held press conferences; announced demonstrations; printed and distributed leaflets, posters, and buttons; and encouraged the youthful inmates of the madhouse of American society to run amok. In January they turned practical and rented space at 32 Union Square in Manhattan. Wasn't that inconsistent with Yippie anarchist ideals? *National Observer* reporter Daniel Greene wanted to know. "We did open an office," Abbie admitted, but he went on to explain that "we left the door unlocked so that anybody could wander in and answer the phone and be a Yippie spokesman." To *Village Voice* reporter Sally Kempton, whose article was aptly entitled "Yippies Anti-Organize a Groovy Revolution," Abbie explained, "we're not leaders, we're cheerleaders." Like real organizers, the Yippies held meetings, but as Kempton observed, "People laugh a lot . . . and there is nearly always someone in the back of the room blowing up balloons."

Almost all of the founding Yippies, including Jerry Rubin, Abbie Hoffman, Ed Sanders, Keith Lampe, Paul Krassner, and Stew Albert, were veteran radicals, but they'd managed to operate outside movement organizations like SDS and the Mobe. They were mavericks, and they were cocky, courageous, and egotistical. The Yippies were writers and performers, and they were comfortable with the media. Half a dozen women, including Anita Hoffman, Nancy Kurshan, Judy Gumbo, and Robin Morgan, helped to create Yippie and to run the organization day to day, but they worked in the shadow of the male elite. Later, as they became involved in the growing women's liberation movement, they dissociated themselves and even denounced their male comrades for their elitism, egotism, and more. "Yippie is involved in removing repression," a leaflet for Yippie women began. "Yet within YIP women are deh umanized *[sic]*."

The Yippie men were over thirty, but they envisioned their followers as high school and college students, dropouts in their teens, kids rebelling against their parents. To recruit them for Chicago, the Yippies created an icon. "We realized that we couldn't build things around just a youth festival," Jerry Rubin told J. Anthony Lukas in November 1969. "We had to build it around a new person. Let's create a new figure, we said, a longhaired, crazy revolutionary. I said it had to have youth because we definitely believed it was a generational thing. And it had to be international because we envisioned youth festivals in Russia, in Latin America."

When Abbie helped to shape Yippie, he drew on his experience of SNCC. The Student Nonviolent Coordinating Committee that he had known and loved had no formal organization, not even a coordinating committee. It allowed for floaters and drifters who never filled out membership forms or paid dues but adhered to SNCC ideals and participated in SNCC projects. Abbie wanted to recreate that freedom and individuality in Yippie and wanted Yippie to take on the mantle of myth that SNCC had accepted after years of struggle. Myth had helped to elevate SNCC's stature and to create a mystique about the civil rights movement. Myth would skyrocket Yippie. Already, only a few months after its creation, it was the talk of the nation. Abbie explained to Sally

Kempton,"We have two alternatives in Chicago, both of them ok. The opposition determines what will happen, they're living actors in our theatre. Suppose they choose to tolerate us. Then we'll . . . present a vision of a new life-style that will be projected across the country. Suppose they don't tolerate us? Then they'll face a bloody scene. We'll have to adopt guerrilla techniques for dealing with them. And we'll take home their message of a brutal society and deal with it in the communities."

At the start of 1968, the newly hatched Yippies emphasized the cultural aspects of their "potlitical grass leaves movement." As an alternative to the Democrats' "Convention of Death," the Yippies were sponsoring a "Festival of Life," featuring Allen Ginsberg, Tim Leary, the Bread and Puppet Theatre, and a long list of singers, including Arlo Guthrie, Judy Collins, Phil Ochs, the Fugs, and Country Joe and the Fish. The first Yippie leaflet, entitled "People, Get Ready," announced that "agents of the Potheads Benevolent Association have planted hundreds of thousands of pot seeds" in Chicago and informed readers that "the long hot summer of 1968 is expected to produce ideal weather for marijuana growing, and most of the crop should be ready for smoking by the end of August." An unsigned Yippie manifesto urged people to "bring blankets, tents, draft cards, body paint, Mr. Leary's cow, food to share, music, eager skin and happiness." The authors insisted that "the threats of LBJ, Mayor Daley and J. Edgar Freako will not stop us. We are coming. We are coming from all over the world!"

Almost all the Yippie advertisements for Chicago contained both covert and overt messages. As usual, Abbie reveled in ambiguity and innuendo. He scattered words and images and assumed that they'd take root, consciously or unconsciously, in young minds, and that each and every demonstrator would dream up his or her own scenario. The text for one of his posters about Chicago offered a list of deliberately chosen words, though it looked like a stream-of-consciousness poem: "Spree— woweee — Arlo Guthrie — color — giggle — pleasure — happening— dancing—joy—the politics of ecstasy—Country Joe and the Fish— blankets — poetry — slapstick — venceremos — lights — challenge — yes — Allen Ginsberg — free — tribes — experience — zig-zag." The words and the names all had rich reverberations for Abbie personally as well as communicating a complex range of countercultural experiences.

"Zig-zag," for example, was the brand name for the popular cigarette papers that hippies used to roll marijuana joints. "Spree" suggested an innocent shopping expedition as well as an outburst of violence. Nothing against the law was explicitly encouraged, but illegal activities, like smoking marijuana, were implicit.

Abbie assumed that the Yippie ads would provoke the powers-that-be. Years after the demonstrations, he explained some of his thinking in the days before Chicago to Abe Peck (alias Abraham Yippie), who had been a leading Chicago Yippie as well as the editor-in-chief of the city's underground newspaper, the *Seed.* He told Peck that "an activist seeks out the moments, like the situation in Chicago, when authority looks like a blind, raging, brutal, ignorant bull." He also explained to Peck, who had become a professor at Northwestern University, that there was a "lot of truth in the psychoanalytical view of life." Unfortunately, the media often used Freudian psychology to discredit radicals while ignoring their nobler social motives, Abbie said. The movement had been hurt, as he had been, by Freudian interpretations. Still, he couldn't deny Freud's truths. "If your father beat you up, you'd hate your father," he told Peck. And he added that "the government had behaved like a father, a cruel father." The trick, according to Abbie, was to bring the rage of the fathers out of the closet and into the streets, where everyone could see it. Indeed, Abbie's revolutionary genius lay in his ability to antagonize the fathers and the father figures while aiding and abetting the younger generation as it transformed personal animosity toward parents into political anger at the system. Abbie used Freud to fuel the rebellion against authority.

The Yippies spent a lot of time, both in private and in public, talking about what would happen at Chicago. Along with Paul Krassner and Jerry Rubin, Abbie gave John Wilcox an interview for the first issue of New York's new underground newspaper, *Other Scenes.* In it, he declined to predict what would happen in Chicago in August. "Revolution's a lot like a river, you know, it sort of seeks its own level," he explained. What he felt most confident discussing was the power of TV. If images of "kids running through the streets yelling and screaming . . . flashed across the television screens of America," he asserted, "there'd be blood, violence, boom."

In private, the Yippies engaged in no-holds-barred debate with one another about Chicago. Curiously, when they sat down to talk to one another without the presence of the media, the topics of conversations were not drugs, sex, and rock 'n' roll, but party politics and political strategy. One of their rap sessions was even taped and transcribed; reading it years later provides a fascinating behind-the-scenes look at the Yippies as they prepared to make their mark on history. It was an early March meeting attended by Abbie, Jerry Rubin, Phil Ochs, Keith Lampe, Martin Carey, and Paul Krassner. Jerry Rubin suggested that the Yippies ought to "force a confrontation in which the establishment hits down hard, thereby placing large numbers of people in a state of crisis and tension." Abbie snickered: "On that theory the only way that Chicago would be a success is if 20 of us got shot to death," he said. He was "against disruption until it's clear who the Democrats are going to nominate in Chicago." If Johnson was to run for reelection, then he would be prepared "to take risks at demonstrations and pull fire alarms and throw fire bombs."

Why couldn't the Chicago demonstration be like the guerrilla theatre at the Stock Exchange? Abbie wanted to know. "If you can't come away from a demonstration and tell a funny little story about it, it's not going to work," he said. Still, he wasn't in the mood to humor or be humored. "I hate America enough to run the risk of getting killed," he insisted. Jerry Rubin replied, "No, no, no, no, no, no. You don't hate America the way that any black you can point to does. America has been in large part good to you." When Abbie argued that dissent didn't threaten the political system, Jerry insisted that dissent "encourages revolution." And when Jerry insisted that there was "no base for fascism" in America, Abbie disagreed vehemently and pointed to the growing power of the military.

For the most part, Abbie was in despair. It didn't matter, he concluded, whether Johnson or Bobby Kennedy became president. "Johnson is the dirty old man," he said. "Kennedy is like an IBM machine." It didn't matter, either, what the United States did in Vietnam. "Whether it withdraws, whether it makes a compromise, whether it goes for negotiations, whether it escalates—it's all lost," he predicted. Without much difficulty he could even imagine fascism coming to New York and the Port Authority bus terminal transformed into a concentration camp. But his mood also swung toward exuberant optimism.

There was greater tolerance than at any other time in American history, he reminded his friends. "We couldn't have pulled this shit during the Korean War, during the Second World War," he said. "I mean there are people going to Hanoi, collaborating with the enemy, people carrying the Viet Cong flag."

One of the ideas that the Yippies toyed with was a demonstration to be held on March 15, the Ides of March: the day that Julius Caesar had been assassinated in 44 B.C.E. Paul Krassner liked the date because it "implies assassination without ever saying it." Abbie was intrigued because the Ides of March had a "unifying, mystical" appeal. But it was life, not death, that the Yippies most wanted to emphasize, so they decided instead to hold a demonstration in New York's Grand Central Station on March 22. The idea was to hold a tribal ritual to celebrate the spring equinox and to encourage "spring mating." It was called a "Yip-in," and it would start at midnight and continue until dawn, when the revelers would "Yip up the sun."

The leaflet for the Yip-in advised people to bring "Bells, Flowers, Beads, Kazoos, Music . . . Pillows, Eats, Love and Peace." Although that description sounded mellow, six thousand boisterous, angry people crammed into Grand Central, and the terminal turned into "a sea of heads." At 1 A.M., firecrackers and cherry bombs exploded, and the sound echoed in the vaulted room. One young man climbed above the information booth, raised a fist in the air, and unfurled a banner that read, "Up Against the Wall, Motherfucker." Others led the crowd in chanting "Yippie," "Long Hot Summer," and "Burn, Baby, Burn." Still others began to spin the hands on the big clocks and then to break them off; the urge to "rape time" was "irresistible," *Village Voice* reporter Don McNeill observed. Finally, someone spray-painted "Peace Now" on the face of one of the clocks, and that was going too far.

Suddenly the Tactical Patrol Force (TPF) entered the terminal, surrounded the information booth, and without warning began clubbing demonstrators to the floor. Don McNeill was tossed into a glass door then hurled into the street, his face and his press card covered with blood. Abbie would call the event "Grand Central Massacre." He noted, too, that the demonstrators had been able to "trigger" the police attack, and that was valuable information he filed away for Chicago. Even as the beatings went on, hundreds of people raised their arms in the Nazi salute and shouted "Sieg Heil!" Abbie watched the attack with a sense of horror; he wanted to act but was uncertain what to do. In a matter of moments, he reached what he called "a difficult decision": he approached Mayor Lindsay's aide, Barry Gottehrer, and asked if he could use the terminal's public address system to calm the situation.

It was a "conscious, deliberate attempt to assert leadership," he explained in *Revolution for the Hell of It,* and hardly his style. When Gottehrer refused, Abbie demanded that the police be withdrawn. The request was denied, and again the TPF attacked with clubs, forcing people to run a gauntlet of club-wielding policemen in order to reach the street. Abbie himself was viciously attacked. Anita tried to protect him, and so did several friends, including Bradley Fox, but the police pummeled him until he was unconscious. The next day Alan Levine, a lawyer for the New York Civil Liberties Union, told *New York Post* reporter Arthur Greenspan that Grand Central had been "The worst display of police brutality I've ever seen outside of Mississippi." The Yippies called it a "police riot" and announced they were following the path of the Black Panther Party for Self Defense and forming the Youth International Party for Self Defense. Like the Panthers, the Yippies now referred to police officers as "pigs" and were determined to fight them with rocks and bottles. "We did not choose this direction," the Yippies insisted. "It was forced upon us by the pigs."

Don McNeill described the Yip-in as "a pointless confrontation in a box canyon" and "a prophecy of Chicago." For Abbie it was indeed, as he later told the Walker Study Team, a "preview of what was gonna happen in Chicago," and what's more, he was delighted. The police assault was vicious, but it made the Yippies big news; indeed, Michael Stern's dramatic story appeared, with photos, on page one of the Sunday *New York Times,* under the headline "Political Activism New Hippie 'Thing.'" That was precisely the message that Abbie himself wanted to communicate. Granted, people had been injured by the police. He seemed to feel guilty about that, but was unwilling to accept any blame. "I was the only one who tried to cool out the scene," he boasted. He had taken the same risk everyone else had taken. He had deceived no one about Grand Central, and "no one was under orders to come." His attitude toward violence might sound "cold-blooded," he wrote in *Revolution for the Hell of It,* but, he pointed out, "revolutionists are cold-blooded bastards."

The day after the Yip-in, Abbie, Jerry, and Paul Krassner attended a meeting in Lake Villa, Illinois, called by the Mobe, which was still debating what sort of protest, if any, to mount during the Democratic National Convention. Abbie and Jerry met with Tom Hayden and Rennie Davis, who suggested a "funeral march" to O'Hare Airport as President Johnson was renominated, a demonstration that would clog the streets of Chicago, and an "attack on the Democratic convention." Abbie was his outrageous self. He smoked marijuana, giggled in the midst of serious discussions, called for "an end to pay toilets," and urged the Mobe to support Polish students who were rebelling against communism. To Abbie, Mobe leaders appeared to be cut from the same cloth as officials in the Johnson administration. "They understand each other," he would complain in his testimony to the Walker Study Team (which investigated events in Chicago). "They all wear suits and ties, they sit down, they talk rationally, they use the same kinds of words." He spoke another language altogether, he claimed. "I'm into emotion," he insisted. "I'm into symbols and gestures and I don't have a program and I don't have an ideology and I'm not a part of the Left." Indeed, the Yippie poster for Chicago, which he distributed free to Mobe members, didn't look anything like left-wing propaganda. There was a jigsaw puzzle map of the United States, and an arrow aimed at the heart of Chicago. The text read: "Music Lights   Free Theatre   Magic."

From Lake Villa, Abbie and Jerry moved on to Chicago, where they joined the local Yippies in asking the city for a permit to hold a "music festival" in Grant Park in August. Mayor Richard Daley was out when the Yippie crew arrived at his office to present their innocuous-sounding application, and they had to settle for Deputy Mayor David Stahl. The Yippies wanted to seduce, not sabotage, the city, or so it seemed. A young, scantily clad Yippie woman, who called herself Helen Running Water, handed Stahl the application form rolled up in a *Playboy* magazine centerfold with the inscription "To Dick With Love, the Yippies." Then she pinned a Yippie button to his jacket and kissed him on the cheek. Abbie predicted that Mayor Daley would "use scare techniques for the next few months to try to stop everyone from coming," but that in the end he'd grant a permit.

Then on Sunday evening, March 31, President Johnson announced, at the tail end of a televised address about Vietnam, "I shall not seek, and will not accept, the nomination of my party for another term as your president." The nation was shocked. The Texas wheeler-dealer president suddenly appeared in the guise of a self-sacrificing saint. There is "division in the American house," Johnson said. "This country's ultimate strength lies in the unity of our people." Supporters of Senator Eugene McCarthy could almost smell victory, especially when their candidate swept the Wisconsin primary on April 2. In the antiwar movement there was joy as well as apprehension. Berkeley radicals were euphoric, but Dr. Benjamin Spock and the Reverend William Sloane Coffin, both of whom had been indicted in January on charges of conspiracy to "counsel, aid, and abet young men to violate the draft laws," expressed suspicion. Bombings might begin anew; there was no time to rest. David Dellinger argued, "It's important to keep up the kind of pressure that brought the Administration to the point of making gestures, whether sincere or not."

Abbie felt a sense of admiration for President Johnson. "He was so predictable when Yippie! began," he wrote with great gusto in Krassner's *Realist*. "And then *pow!* He really fucked us. He did the one thing no one had counted on. He dropped out. 'My God,' we exclaimed. 'Lyndon is out-flanking us on our hippie side.'" With the nation's number one authority figure in flight from the White House, the protest in Chicago didn't have a clear target, and the Yippie raison d'être was now in doubt. "Yippie stock went down quicker than the money we dumped on the Stock Exchange floor," Abbie quipped. "The United States political system was proving more insane than Yippie! Reality and unreality had in six months switched sides. It was *America* that was on a trip; we were just standing still. How could we pull our pants down? America was already naked. What could we disrupt? America was falling apart at the seams."

The nation was, in fact, caught up in an unprecedented crisis. In Vietnam, U.S. forces had been on the defensive ever since January, when communist forces had invaded the U.S. embassy in Saigon, demonstrating that the Americans weren't invincible. At home, protests were increasing both on campuses and in the ghettoes. America, Abbie wrote in a Yippie leaflet, was "being torn asunder by the forces of violence, decay and the napalm cancer fiend." Then on April 4, 1968, Dr. Martin Luther King, Jr., was assassinated in Memphis, and African Americans rioted in eighty cities across the country, including the nation's capitol. In Chicago, which had managed to squeak through the previous summer without a major disturbance, the ghetto exploded. Fires were set and stores were ransacked, and President Johnson sent in National Guardsmen. Mayor Daley imposed a curfew and issued an order "to shoot to kill any arsonists or anyone with a Molotov cocktail in his hand . . . and . . . to shoot to maim or cripple anyone looting any stores in our city." Nine blacks were shot and killed, and 2,150 were arrested. To Chicago columnist Mike Royko, the ghetto looked like "a devastated, looted, bleeding place."

Like most movement activists, Abbie Hoffman was shocked by King's assassination. And like most activists, he read King's death as a sign that the old civil rights struggle, which had been in decline for years, had finally passed away. When a priest phoned him from Worcester and suggested that they honor King by going to Memphis and marching in protest "like the old days," Abbie insisted, "I ain't marching anymore." It was time to start fires, not to sing "We Shall Overcome," he believed.

chapter seven

THE APOTHEOSIS OF
ABBIE HOFFMAN

1968: Annus Mirabilis

Except for 1936, the year that he was born, and 1989, the year that he died, 1968 was the single most decisive year in Abbie's life. There would be other dramatic occasions in the decades ahead, but none would be as exhilarating or as fulfilling for him as that traumatic moment when American society seemed to come unhinged at the strife-torn Democratic National Convention in Chicago in August of that year. Then and there, the arc of his biography intersected with the trajectory of history. The conjunction seemed so dazzling that many of his friends would say that the time had been created expressly for the man. Paul McIssac, for example, who was in the streets of Chicago with Abbie in the summer of 1968, remembered, "That moment was really made for him. He was an opportunist in the best sense of the word; he had the arrogance to think beyond the limitations of the situation, to just leap past all the barriers. He operated in an absolutely sanctified space."

There were others who argued that Abbie and the rebels of 1968 were opportunists in the worst sense of the word, and that the historical moment brought out the psychopaths, not the prophets, of the protest movement. The turbulent events of the year prompted Professor Abraham Maslow to note in his journal that "*any* social upheaval, revolution, war, riots . . . will bring into the open and into acting out" many people who were "violent, vengeful, deeply hostile, the unconscious killers and suicidals." In December 1968, four months after the protests at the Democratic National Convention, Professor Maslow wrote that American radicals like his former student Abbie Hoffman had "turned into publicity seekers." Their chief goal, Maslow complained, was "to get TV and newspaper publicity." There was a whole cast of these shameless characters, but Abbie seemed to be, from Maslow's point of view, the quintessential "revolutionary clown, the advertiser and public relations expert."

Maslow complained further that "all sorts of clownishness (à la Abbie Hoffman) and psychopathic personality seeking of the limelight has developed as never before." Abbie himself probably wouldn't have taken issue with Maslow. After all, he boasted that the Yippies were "living TV ads," providing "an advertisement for revolution." Moreover, he thought of himself as a comedian, and from time to time he had even labeled himself a "mild psychopath." Maslow was so busy denouncing the publicity-seeking sixties rebels that he didn't recognize how much Abbie had in common with his own model of the "healthy fully-grown" person who "actualized" his potential and achieved "peak experiences." For Maslow, human wellness was largely defined by the courage to rise above one's society. In the essay "Health as Transcendence of Environment," he wrote that it was essential to resist the social environment, "to stand against it, to fight it." Healthy individuals, he insisted, refused to adjust to society, or to social opinion. According to this definition, no one was healthier than Abbie, especially in Chicago in 1968.

Before going to Chicago, Abbie envisioned the "Festival of Life" that would take place there as a kind of "psychological utopia," in Maslow's terms. He borrowed directly from Maslow when he argued that the week-long series of events would be a therapeutic experience "so intense that you actualize your full potential." In the winter and spring of '68, however, he felt a long way from psychological utopia and personal fulfillment. Though he took part in a protest at Columbia University in April and celebrated that event as a "liberating experience," he didn't feel at home on the campus or among students, especially among SDS types, who were suspicious of utopian dreamers and the countercultural community. He also felt out of sync with the movement. "Right now I feel like Dwight Eisenhower on an acid trip," he wrote in "Talking in

My Sleep," a candid interview with himself that was subtitled "An Exercise in Self-Criticism" (included in *Revolution for the Hell of It*). His dilemma, he explained, was that he was uncertain about the proper political and cultural course of action to follow. "On the one hand this—on the other hand that" was how he described his own ambivalent state of mind. He went on to explain, "I think it's a case of information overload."

Not since Brandeis in the fifties had he been so profoundly introspective. Moreover, for the first time in his life, he noted a connection between the fluctuating state of the movement and his own alternating states of mind—his "summer" and "winter" moods, as he called them. When the movement was down, he was often depressed. When it was running at full speed, he was elated. To be really alive, he concluded, he had to be in the midst of intense political activity and social turmoil. "I am conditioned to perform well in chaos—actual chaos," he wrote in "Talking in My Sleep." "Say a riot. In a riot I know exactly what to do. . . . I have to live in total summer if I am to survive."

Nineteen sixty-eight was, of course, the archetypal year of riots and chaos—the year in which everything appeared to be falling apart, as the world-famous intellectual Hannah Arendt observed that July. In a letter to the German existentialist Karl Jaspers, Arendt lamented "the disintegration of the major cities, the collapse of public services, all of it very concrete: the failure of the schools, the police, the postal service, public transportation." It was the kind of social collapse and failure that delighted Abbie but alarmed Arendt. "Things are in an extremely dangerous state here," she explained to Jaspers just two months before the protests in Chicago. And she added apprehensively, "No one knows how the two big party conventions will end." To Arendt all the signs indicated that massive social unrest lay ahead, and she predicted "that children in the next century will learn about the year 1968 the way we learned about the year 1848."

"The Miracle of Television"

For more than a quarter of a century, historians, sociologists, and political scientists have offered various, often conflicting interpretations of the events that took place in Chicago in 1968. No one has understood them as well or described them as clearly and as concisely as has *New York Times* reporter Tom Wicker. "Chicago, I think, is the place where all America was radicalized," Wicker wrote a year after the riots, on August 24, 1969. "The miracle of television made it visible to all— pierced, at last, the isolation of one America from the other, exposed to each the power it faced. Everything since Chicago has had a new intensity—that of polarization, of confrontation, of antagonism, and fear."

Movement activists reached conclusions almost identical to Wicker's. "The important thing about Chicago . . . was that it was televised," SDS member James O'Brien wrote in *A History of the New Left, 1960– 1968,* a pamphlet published in 1969 that was one of the earliest assessments of the political turmoil of the sixties. Of course, it was obvious to almost everyone who protested in the streets of Chicago that the decisive event of the week was not Hubert Humphrey's nomination for president inside the convention but rather the television coverage of the police riots in the streets. On August 30, 1968, for example, the *New York Times* ran John Kifner's article "Chicago Protesters Say Police Action on Television Will 'Radicalize' Many Viewers," the title of which says it all, or nearly so.

It seemed obvious, too, that the televised riots would cost Humphrey the election in November. "The whole world is watching," demonstrators chanted on the night of August 28 as the Chicago cops attacked them outside the Hilton Hotel—or the "Conrad Hitler," as Abbie called it. From his point of view the battle for the hearts and minds of the nation was fought on television, and the Democrats lost it long before election day. David Farber, historian and author of *Chicago: 1968,* was only a boy growing up in Chicago when the riots took place, but like many of his peers he watched them on TV, and like them he was stunned. "When they showed the violence in the streets," he wrote, "I thought it was incredible." The nation at large watched as the cops clobbered the unarmed kids, and while many citizens blamed the kids for being in the streets in the first place, most of them agreed that the scene was unbelievable. In the words of Mike Royko, the celebrated columnist for the *Chicago Tribune,* it was "one of the most dramatic moments in the history of the medium." On TV, America looked like a nation in which the conflicts between the generations had erupted in civil war. The truth was terrifying.

Of course television coverage of the protests in Chicago was the linchpin in Abbie's strategy for cultural revolution. "We want to fuck up their image on TV," he explained to the Walker Study Team. "It's all in terms of disrupting the image, the image of a democratic society being run very peacefully and orderly and everything according to business." If TV showed images of protesters, then more young people would join their ranks, he insisted. Young viewers would imitate the political gestures and cultural styles they saw on TV screens, he argued. Though there was no evidence to support his contention, he insisted, in a 1978 interview for the underground newspaper *Yipster Times*, that "there were people watching on television, and they ran away from their dinner; they had fights with their parents and ran out of the house and got on a plane, and came to Chicago."

From Abbie's point of view, television was the Yippie secret weapon that invaded living rooms, divided families, and set parents and children against one another. When Jerry Rubin told John Wilcox, editor of the underground newspaper *Other Scenes,* that most of the violence in Chicago would "come from the law and order representatives in uniforms, licensed to carry guns and carry clubs," Abbie begged to differ. "There's a kind of symbolic violence that comes from our side," he insisted. "Psychic violence. You know, just the vision of a TV screen with kids running through the streets yelling and screaming."

In the months before Chicago Abbie consciously crafted the Festival of Life as a colossal event that was made for TV: a revolutionary opera for the masses of young people who were alienated from their parents and teachers and from American society as a whole. To attract the youth of the nation, Abbie promised rock 'n' roll, guerrilla theatre, violent confrontations, and, of course, bloodshed in the streets. Marshall Mc-Luhan, who spoke of "hot" and "cool" media, provided inspiration. "Projecting cool images is not our goal," Abbie wrote in *Revolution for the Hell of It.* "We do not wish to project a calm, secure future. We are disruption. We are hot. . . . We are cannibals, cowboys, Indians, witches, warlocks. Weird-looking freaks that crawl out of the cracks in America's nightmare."

At the outset, the Festival of Life looked like it would be a sell-out event, but by the end of April the whole enterprise threatened to go belly-up. For starters, the Chicago Yippies were terrified of bloodshed in their own neighborhoods—and rightly so. Mayor Daley's police had been clubbing and arresting radicals, whether they belonged to SDS or the Black Panthers, Yippie or the Mobe. Anxious to protect themselves as well as their sisters and brothers across the country, the local Yippies warned the movement about the perils of protesting in Mayor Daley's armed camp. "Don't come to Chicago if you expect a five-day festival of life, music and love," they proclaimed in the *Seed,* the Midwest's leading underground newspaper. "The word is out. Chicago may host a festival of blood."

Abbie felt betrayed. The Chicago Yippies "got paranoid" and "chickened out," he charged in an angry article entitled "A Non-Response to the Doubting Thomases" (reprinted in *Revolution for the Hell of It*). Just in case anyone wanted to know, he explained that "Paranoia is when you look in the future, see gloom, then run and hide in the past." There was no legitimate reason to be paranoid. "Those that act peacefully will be treated peacefully," he insisted, as though he meant to reassure the Chicago contingent and to lure them back into the Yippie fold. The city was large enough to contain every variety of protest, peaceful as well as violent, he insisted. "There'll be everything happening here," he proclaimed. "All kinds of politics. People will visit the Zoo, people will sell newspapers, and others will debate your ideology and march on the Amphitheater and dance in the park and give out food, and swim, and smoke dope, and fuck, and fight cops and give cops flowers and get pregnant and laugh and cry and live and die."

Of course, Abbie, Jerry, and company had far greater problems with Mayor Richard Daley and Deputy Mayor David Stahl—"shoot-to-kill Daley" and "the liberal schmuck," as Hoffman called them, respectively. Both Daley and Stahl were adept at manipulating the media. At press conferences Daley insisted that city officials were "talking to the hippies, the Yippies, and the flippies," and that the city of Chicago would welcome every kind of protest, "hippie and square." For the TV cameras Daley smiled broadly and sounded like a paragon of tolerance. But weeks and then months went by, and still no permit for the Festival of Life was issued. Providing the Yippies with a permit so that they could sleep in the park would be like letting them sleep in "the city's living room," Mayor Daley declared.

Abbie enjoyed the complex process of negotiation for a permit to hold the Festival of Life. He called it a "cat and mouse game". As the rambunctious Yippie mouse, he went about breaking all the rules, then turned around and with great delight insisted that the bureaucratic cats adhere to them. Then when they broke the rules, too, he adopted a more-responsible-than-thou attitude and scolded them. Yet for all the fun of negotiating, the failure to obtain a permit proved frustrating, though he was unwilling to admit it.

There was no getting around the permit problem. As Tom Hayden explained, "the crucial thing was the permits, because without the permits you couldn't get the musicians, [and] without the musicians you couldn't get the youth base." Without a permit, folk singers like Judy Collins and Arlo Guthrie, who were in contact with Abbie, wouldn't perform in Chicago, and without them, or stars like them, there wouldn't be much festivity in the Festival of Life. It began to seem certain that hundreds of thousands of young people would never show up, and that the carefully constructed myth of Chicago would never become a reality. But the really bad news was still to come.

From Abbie's point of view, the biggest blow to the Yippies came in May as Senator Robert Kennedy slowly but steadily gained ground in the race for the Democratic Party nomination for president. "Hollywood Bobby," as he called him with envy, "was the real threat. A direct challenge to our theatre-in-the-streets, a challenge to the charisma of Yippie!" Hoffman watched Senator Kennedy on television and marveled at his mastery of the medium. It seemed as though Kennedy had studied Marshall McLuhan: he knew how to involve the viewing audience and how to come across as a vulnerable human being. On TV, Bobby Kennedy reached out to the public as though he genuinely wanted help. At the same time, he had the immense clout of the Kennedy clan. "Bobby had the money and power to build the stage," Abbie wrote in the *Realist* article "The Yippies Are Going to Chicago" (also included in *Revolution for the Hell of It*). "We had to steal ours. It was no contest. . . . Every night we would turn on the TV set and there was the young knight with long hair, holding out his hand. . . . When young longhairs told you how they'd heard that Bobby turned on, you knew Yippie! was *really* in trouble." Even Phil Ochs, one of the original Yippies, was ready to jump on board the Bobby Kennedy bandwagon.

It was harder for Abbie than for anyone else to let go of the scenario for the Festival of Life. "When you bite the tail of the tiger you don't let go," he explained in 1980, when he sat down with journalist Abe Peck to reminisce about 1968. "From my point of view there was no calling off the demonstrations in Chicago. I mean it would be like calling off the idea that young people should go to Mississippi and fight for civil rights." Little by little the Yippie plans for Chicago receded on the political horizon, and grassroots organizing on college campuses and in hippie neighborhoods loomed larger and larger. "National action seemed meaningless," Abbie noted in "The Yippies Are Going to Chicago." "Local action became the focus and by the end of May we had decided to disband Yippie! and cancel the Chicago festival."

To many radicals as well as most liberals it seemed that the system would finally reform itself. On June 4, Robert Kennedy won the California primary and emerged as the front-runner in the race for the presidency. SDS leaders like Carl Oglesby were prepared to lead the movement into the Kennedy camp and to oppose any violent demonstrations in the streets of Chicago that might embarrass the Democrats and lose them the election. But then everyone's plans changed drastically when Robert Kennedy was shot by Sirhan Sirhan in Los Angeles on June 5. To many longtime liberals, Robert Kennedy's death felt like the tragic finale to a decade of reform. "The sixties came to an end in a Los Angeles hospital on June 6, 1968," Richard Goodwin would later observe in his memoir *Remembering America*. In the wake of Kennedy's assassination, Carl Oglesby implored the movement to abandon Chicago altogether. "I thought we should evacuate the place, declare it a dead city and nobody go near it," he said.

Abbie and the Yippies weren't immediately sure what to do. At the end of May they drafted a statement announcing the cancellation of the Festival of Life, but at the last minute the announcement was held back. "We postponed calling off Chicago and tried to make some sense out of what the hell had just happened," he wrote in "The Yippies Are Going to Chicago." "It was not easy to think clearly. Yippie!, still in a state of critical shock because of LBJ's pullout, hovered close to death somewhere between the 50/50 state of Andy Warhol [who had been shot and critically wounded by Valerie Solanis] and the 0/0 state of Bobby Kennedy."

"The Lenin of the Flower Children"

After a great deal of discussion, Abbie concluded that radical protest was "more relevant than ever" because the Democratic Party was "more closed than ever before." It was a "chaotic moment in history," he explained to the Yippies. "There had been a couple of assassinations . . . that threw people into states of unsettledness." The time was right, he believed, for the Yippies to "jolt history."

To Abbie, the Democratic Party leadership looked inept at best, insidious at worst. Senator McCarthy had withdrawn from the fray, and many of his young, idealistic followers felt abandoned. Vice President Hubert Humphrey hadn't entered a single primary yet had, as Hoffman observed, "a lock on the convention." Years of political struggle to make the Democratic Party more democratic had failed, at least for the moment, and the failure was disillusioning. "We were back to power politics, the politics of big-city machines and back-room deals," he observed. His anger at Humphrey and at the party was genuine, and he let everyone know it. "The Democrats had finally got their thing together by hook or crook and there it was for all to see—fat, ugly, and full of shit," he exclaimed in "The Yippies Are Going to Chicago." Now that Bobby Kennedy had been assassinated, Abbie called for "a reality in the face of the American political myth." It was essential to "bring huge numbers to Chicago," he wrote, so that there might be "a huge march across town to haunt the Democrats." Now that the Festival of Life was on again, Abbie was upbeat and energetic. He didn't feel like "Dwight Eisenhower on an acid trip" anymore but instead like "the Lenin of the Flower Children," as he called himself, half-seriously and half-mockingly. As he saw it, his job was not to order people about, but to "stimulate actions," and he did it better than anyone else.

Abbie never had the "bourgeois qualities" of thrift, strict discipline, and absolute fidelity to the law that Lenin had insisted were necessary when revolutionaries like the Bolsheviks succeeded in seizing state power. But he did possess the rabble-rousing qualities of "fiery eloquence, dashing courage, [and] fearless iconoclasm" that Lenin claimed were essential during the initial period of revolutionary turmoil. In the weeks immediately preceding the start of the Democratic National Convention, Hoffman was eloquent, courageous, and iconoclastic; even Lenin might have been pleased by his performance.

When Abbie flew to Chicago at the start of August, he was accompanied by fellow Yippie Paul Krassner and by Richard Goldstein, a reporter for the *Village Voice* who had covered the Diggers and now was covering the Yippies for *New York Magazine.* Goldstein's September 1968 article, "Chicago—Wild in the Streets," is one of the most insightful pieces ever written about Abbie; it suggests that to understand him it's essential to map his pathology, not his ideology. "Abbie Hoffman is psyche over substance," Goldstein wrote. "Abbie's approach to protest, like his entire lifestyle, is only as predictable as his instincts." Goldstein knew nothing about Abbie's childhood or his relationship to his father, but he had observed him at rallies and in confrontations with the police, and he sensed that Sigmund Freud rather than Karl Marx offered the key to understanding his personality.

Goldstein offered a vivid portrait of Abbie on the ramparts of rebellion: "He appears at demonstrations wrapped in a nickel bag of charisma. His eyes dart toward the barricades, his hands gesture at the immobile wall of cops. His whole body seems to be directed toward the immediate goal of impact. . . . The moment of Abbie's arrest is often charged with the sexuality of resistance and retribution. He is led away between burly blue shoulders, hands behind his back, eyes flashing fulfillment." Twenty-one times Abbie had been arrested; "you could conclude that Abbie Hoffman has a thing about authority," Goldstein wrote. "In fact, if you like your heroes wrapped in Freudian cellophane, you could say he's positively hung up on authority." For Goldstein, Anita Hoffman was the responsible mother figure in Abbie's stormy life. "She is a cool asset, strong and hovering," he wrote. "In emergencies, she's the one who gets Abbie home anonymous and alive." At home with Anita, Abbie was charming, indeed. Put him in front of a television set, and he was "like a kid looking at a starry sky," Goldstein observed.

On the flight to Chicago, Abbie was in rare form. "We're the Yippies," he told another passenger. And he went on to say, "Whatever you think I am, I'll be the opposite." In Chicago, he was in constant verbal eruption, and Goldstein was on hand to record his comments. When Deputy Mayor David Stahl asked him not to smoke pot in his office, he quipped, "We don't smoke pot. . . . That's a myth." When Stahl asked him what the Yippies had in mind for the week of the convention, Abbie acted dumb. "I dunno, but whatever it is, it'll be designed to, uh, bring down the Democratic Party," he replied. Stahl assumed that Abbie and his cohorts were serious about dismantling the party in power. "The Yippies . . . will try to involve their supporters in a revolution along the lines of the recent Berkeley and Paris incidents," he wrote in a memo immediately after meeting with Abbie and Jerry. "They propose to block the streets, send men into the Negro sections of the city to breed disorder. . . . One of their objectives is to get someone killed to serve as a martyr."

"Reality Is a Subjective Experience"

On August 4 Abbie took the nom de guerre "Frankie Abbott" and held a sidewalk press conference to announce that the Yippies would hold the Festival of Life with or without a permit from the city of Chicago. During negotiating sessions with Deputy Mayor David Stahl, Abbie had insisted that the Yippies never made plans. Now, however, he disclosed an elaborate schedule of events that would begin on Tuesday, August 20, and end on Wednesday, August 28. Most of the events would take place in Lincoln Park, which the Yippies renamed "Che Guevara National Park." Abbie envisioned the park as "liberated territory"; the longhaired, pot-smoking troops in the army of youth were supposed to regard the park as the cradle of their own new culture and defend it against the "pigs." Yippie maps, which Abbie helped to design, showed the park divided into sections: "Future City," "Drop City," "Free City," and "Century City." On paper, at least, there was something for everyone in the counterculture, including a "Free Store" for the needy and a "Church of the Free Spirit" for the reverential. For Abbie, the crucial areas were the communications center and the military headquarters, or "Yippie Pentagon" as he called it, where, presumably, he would set up his command post. Of course, there was nothing real about any of it, but if anyone complained that there was no organization, no structure, and no social services, Abbie scoffed at them. After all, as he explained in the opening chapter of *Revolution for the Hell of It*, "reality is a subjective experience. It exists in my head." There was nothing clandestine about the Yippie schedule of events, either. In fact, everything was in the open for anyone to see. But across the top of the mimeographed flyers, Hoffman wrote "Top Secret Yippie Plans," hoping that they would fall into the "enemy hands" of city officials and contribute to "heightening the tension."

On Sunday, August 25, the opening day of the convention, there would be a "Welcoming of the Democratic Delegates" at the downtown hotels, though the point, of course, was to put them on the spot and make them feel unpopular and uncomfortable. On Monday, August 26, the Yippies would offer free workshops for the hippie community on "drug problems, underground communications, how to live free, guerrilla theatre, self-defense, draft resistance, [and] communes." On almost every day there would be cultural as well as political events, and from the very start there was widespread sexual activity. Paul McIssac remembered that though Anita was in Chicago with Abbie, her presence didn't inhibit him from becoming sexually engaged with women at almost any time of the day or night, whether indoors or outdoors, even in the middle of Lincoln Park.

McIssac also remembered that the Yippies brought several large bottles of hash oil (a distillate of cannabis) to Chicago. Some of it was sprayed on hand-rolled cigarettes, which were distributed for free as "hippie tobacco." And some of it was cooked up with honey in a "secret laboratory." It was "quite a potent substance," McIssac said, and it was distributed widely. "There was a moment when it felt like the Yippies had got everybody in Chicago high," he remembered. For some demonstrators, however, the hash oil was a real downer. Tuli Kupferberg of the Fugs devoured the mixture of honey and hash oil and promptly passed out. Paul Krassner took a large dose and was "zonked" out of his mind. "I was on my knees, holding onto the grass very tightly so that I wouldn't fall *up*," he wrote in his autobiography, *Confessions of a Raving Unconfined Nut.*

In the original plans a music festival was scheduled for Sunday afternoon, and on Monday night there was to be a party on the shores of Lake Michigan with "folksinging, barbecues, swimming, lovemaking." It sounded like summer camp and a hippie orgy all rolled up in one. To respectable citizens the prospect was terrifying. At dawn on August 27 there would be "poetry, mantras, religious ceremony," Abbie promised. Allen Ginsberg was angry (as angry as a Beat poet could get) at Abbie in particular and at the Yippies in general for offering "bloody visions of the apocalypse" in Chicago. Still, he couldn't stay away from the festivities and couldn't resist putting himself in the thick of things: chanting, "om"-ing, and reciting William Blake's visionary poetry.

On the afternoon of August 27, the Yippies would nominate their own candidate for president: a farm-raised hog named Pigasus. And, along with their allies in the Mobe, including Tom Hayden and Rennie Davis, they would hold a festive "Un-birthday Party" for LBJ, who would turn sixty that day. Wednesday, August 28, would start with fun and games: the "Yippie Olympics" and the "Miss Yippie Contest." It would culminate in a "March on the Convention." To "spook" Mayor Daley and the Democrats, Abbie intentionally left that evening's events unspecified. "Plans to be announced at a later date," he wrote, hoping "the enemy" would assume that he had a secret plan to disrupt the convention. In his estimation, which wasn't far off the mark, city officials were "so paranoid" that the Yippies could "say anything, and they'll automatically accept it as the truth."

Indeed, the Yippies were saying just about anything and everything to spook or haunt Mayor Daley, David Stahl, and the police. (For Abbie, to "spook" was to stage a put-on, but with menace. The term itself derived from the *Communist Manifesto:* "A specter is haunting Europe—the specter of Communism," Marx and Engels wrote in 1848.) One of the Yippies' most provocative leaflets called for a "generation of people who are freaky, crazy, irrational, sexy, angry, irreligious, childish and mad." In a deliberate parody of the *Communist Manifesto,* which had been addressed to the workers of the world who had "nothing to lose but their chains," the Yippie leaflet was directed at young people who had "nothing to lose but their flesh." The Yippies encouraged these young people to defy all authority figures, create chaos, and become what Abbie called "life-actors": "Fuck nuns: laugh at professors: disobey your parents: burn your money: . . . break down the family, church, nation, city, economy: turn your life into an art form, a theatre of the soul and a theatre of the future."

Yippie rumors, which flew fast and furious, played on Middle America's fear of sex, drugs, and disorder as well as the delegates' fear of public ridicule and embarrassment. The Walker Study Team, which investigated the disorders in Chicago and published its report in the fall of 1968, concluded that it was the police, not the protesters, who rioted that summer, but it compiled more than a dozen provocative Yippie scenarios that had been deliberately leaked to the media before the start of the convention. Probably the most alarming rumor was that the Yippies were going to contaminate the city's reservoirs with LSD, turning Chicago's citizens into drug-crazed freaks.

The idea was, of course, preposterous. Moreover, according to David Farber's authoritative study *Chicago: 1968*, even the Deputy Superintendent of Police, James Rochford, knew that the Yippie threats were put-ons. Still, it was Rochford's job to take them seriously and to take what he thought were appropriate measures, including the placement of law enforcement officers around Chicago's reservoirs. Abbie kept up a steady barrage of rumors, threats, and innuendoes, many of which seem both hilariously funny and totally absurd in hindsight, but which kept the police busy twenty-four hours a day. According to the Walker Study Team report, the Yippies planned "to paint cars like independent taxi-cabs and forcibly take delegates to Wisconsin; . . . to engage Yippie girls as 'hookers' to attract delegates and dose their drinks with LSD; to bombard the Amphitheater with mortars from several miles away; to jam communication lines; . . . to assemble 100,000 people to burn draft cards; . . . to dress Yippies like Viet Cong and walk the streets shaking hands or passing out rice; . . . to have ten thousand nude bodies floating on Lake Michigan."

In *Boss,* his trenchant biography of Mayor Richard Daley, Chicago columnist Mike Royko traced the fascinating relationship between Yippie rumor, the right-wing press, and police behavior. According to Royko, who followed the events as closely as anyone in Chicago, the "Red Squad" of the police department gathered "every silly rumor" and passed it on to reporters as unimpeachable fact. More than any other paper, the *Chicago American* "went on an almost daily binge of eye-popping headlines and stories about the plans to disrupt the convention," Royko wrote. Abbie himself was delighted that *Chicago American* reporter Jack Mabley quoted from his article "The Yippies Are Going to Chicago," and he loved the headline: "Yippie Leader a Put-On But Underneath Dead Serious." Royko pointed out that even weeks before the convention, Chicago policemen were predisposed to think of the Yippies as drug-crazed, bomb-throwing sex maniacs. After they read the sensational stories in the press, they "became even more fearful." With a great deal of help from the media, the Yippies had created a Frankenstein monster who would go on to attack them.

Royko noted that the "only weapons" in the Yippie arsenal were "words and the stunts devised for the TV cameras." In his view Hoffman, Rubin, and company were a "piddling" lot with "divergent politics" and no leadership abilities. They posed no threat whatsoever to the established order. Attorney General Ramsey Clark agreed wholeheartedly. The Yippies didn't frighten him in the least, and accordingly he opposed Mayor Daley's requests for additional manpower. But President Johnson gave the city all the troops it wanted. "By the time the convention began," Royko pointed out, "the most massive security arrangements in the history of America politics had been completed."

All the groups on the American Left—the Yippies, the Mobe, and SDS—had managed altogether to bring at best a few thousand demonstrators to Chicago. Most of them were young men between the ages of eighteen and twenty-five; many were from Chicago itself, or from nearby cities and towns. A substantial portion of them were unemployed. Most were unaffiliated with any organization; they were new to political demonstrations and to street protests. If they belonged under anyone's aegis, it was Abbie's.

Confronting this ragtag army of hippies, freaks, "McCarthy kids," antiwar activists, and hard-core SDS members, were 12,000 Chicago policemen, 5,000 members of the National Guard, and 6,000 army soldiers, all of whom were prepared for hand-to-hand, building-by-building combat all across the city. "Never before had so many feared so much from so few," Royko concluded. It was indeed, as Abbie hoped it would be, a clear case of overkill.

As the city of Chicago relied increasingly on police power and military might, Abbie and the Yippies shifted tactics and began to cast themselves as reasonable men seeking legal remedies. Their First Amendment right to assemble peaceably and "to petition the government for a redress of grievances" had been abridged, they charged. At the last minute, they asked Democratic Party Chairman John M. Bailey to meet with Mayor Daley and present their case for a permit. Bailey declined, but Abbie refused to give up the idea that the Yippies had a Constitutional right to be in the parks, and that, as American citizens, the city owed them a permit.

It was only when he took a drive to see Daley's house just "two days before the shit hit the fan," as he put it, that he finally gave up. "It was a simple, sturdy bungalow no different from the others on the block, except for the guards," he wrote in *Revolution for the Hell of It.* "On the corner of the block, not fifty feet from Daley's house, was a huge, dull building with a sign over the door that said POLICE HEADQUAR-TERS. After seeing the rugged way he lived, there was no doubt in my mind that we would ever get a permit for anything." Abbie told the Walker Study Team that when he looked at Daley's bungalow, he ex-claimed, "This guy is a tough Irish cop. He wants to show the world that. He wants to show that he doesn't want to budge an inch." He admitted that he'd "kinda suspected" it, and that he'd "had a hunch" that Daley's city was "just another dumb Southern town."

All of his hunches and suspicions were confirmed on Thursday, Au-gust 22, when a Chicago police officer named Manley shot and killed Dean Johnson, a seventeen-year-old Native American from Sioux Falls, South Dakota. According to Canadian journalist David Lewis Stein, Abbie was profoundly distressed by Dean Johnson's death. "He flung himself around the *Seed* office, banging tables and smashing his fist into walls and pillars," Stein wrote in *Living the Revolution: The Yippies in Chicago.* Moreover, Hoffman exclaimed, "Don't let them kill no more people. We've got to stop them killing our people." Abbie was genu-inely distressed by Johnson's death, but there were other occasions when his theatrics seemed deliberately staged. One day in the *Seed* office, for example, he took a dollar bill from his wallet and burned it ceremoni-ally. "Now I am ready for battle," he intoned, as though he were a warrior primed for deadly combat.

Demanding the Impossible

August 22 was also significant because it was the day that Hoffman stood outside the Federal Building and, with TV cameras rolling, gave a dramatic reading of an eighteen-point "list of demands," which he entitled "Revolution towards a Free Society: Yippie" (included in *Revo-lution for the Hell of It*). Though Abbie had written the document with-out help from his friends, he was unwilling to take credit for it; on page one, the author was identified simply as "A. Yippie." However, he ex-plained that the "list of demands" was personal and didn't necessarily express the official views of any group or party. If reporters wanted to know what the Youth International Party stood for, he insisted, they would have to "ask each and every Yippie in Lincoln Park why they have come to Chicago."

No one could have written a document quite like Abbie's. Characteristically, the eighteenth point was left blank so that each individual could add his or her own demand. Yet for all its individuality, the document captured the collective consciousness of many sixties people. "We demand a society . . . based on humanitarian cooperation and equality," he wrote, "a society which allows and promotes the creativity present in all people and especially our youth." Shortly after Yippie was founded in the winter of 1968, Abbie had explained that "there is no program. Program would make our movement sterile. We are living contradictions. I cannot really explain it. I do not even understand it myself." Now he was offering a concrete program and making specific demands because he wanted Yippie to become a real rather than a mythic entity. A program would make the organization seem less crazy and far more rational, at least in movement circles.

The language and the style were uniquely American, but many of the ideas were the common property of the international revolutionary movement of the late sixties. In May Abbie followed the protests by students and workers that were shaking the very foundations of the French government. "A national general strike à la France" could never happen in the United States, he concluded. But American Yippies would do well to imitate the bold and irreverent style of their striking comrades in Paris, he believed. Indeed, Abbie borrowed one of the key slogans of the French movement and put it at the very top of his own practical yet visionary list of demands: "BE REALISTIC. DEMAND THE IMPOSSIBLE."

Predictably, his first demand was for "an immediate end to the War in Vietnam and a restructuring of our foreign policy." He also called for the abolition of the draft and for the withdrawal of all U.S. troops from foreign soil. No one in the movement was likely to argue with him on any of these scores. The second demand, which called for "immediate freedom for Huey Newton of the Black Panthers and all other black people," was more controversial, especially for pacifists, because the Panthers carried guns and advocated armed self-defense.

In his third point, Abbie spoke for the drug culture in demanding the legalization of marijuana as well as the release from prison of all inmates incarcerated on narcotics charges. Points 9 and 10 called for an ecology program: clean air and water; the preservation of natural resources; encouragement of rural living; and "decentralization of our crowded cities." Points 13, 14, 16, and 17 focused on the mass media, art, and culture. Abbie demanded the development of cable TV, viewer access to channels, and the use of TV in national referenda on crucial issues. In addition, he called for the "end to all censorship" and "a society in which every man would be an artist."

Point 15 may have been the most controversial since Abbie insisted that "people should fuck all the time, anytime, whomever they wish," though he added that it wasn't really a demand, but a "simple recognition of the reality around us."

"Truer than Reality"

His demands received little media attention—not surprisingly, since they weren't accompanied by guerrilla theater. But Pigasus, the Youth International Party's candidate for president, was perfect for the media, and predictably the media pounced on the animal in their extensive coverage of preconvention events. The idea of campaigning for a pig had been a part of the original plan for the Festival of Life, but Abbie wasn't terribly excited about it until the middle of August. Suddenly he became preoccupied, if not obsessed, with pigs of the figurative variety as well as those on nearby farms, which the Yippies began to visit.

"The concept of the Pig as our leader was truer than reality," he wrote in the essay "Creating A Perfect Mess," which was published in *Other Scenes.* He went on to explain that in Chicago "everything is Pig," and that the "concept of the pig as our leader . . . was the perfect symbol." Abbie insisted, in his writings and his speeches, that the city's police officers physically resembled pigs. "With their big beer bellies, triple chins, red faces, and little squinty eyes they really did look a lot like pigs," he said. Moreover, the politicians, especially Mayor Daley and Vice President Humphrey, were "Pig as all hell." With so many Chicago police on the streets, Abbie was reminded of George Orwell's satire on totalitarianism. "It was shades of *Animal Farm,*" he insisted. "You couldn't tell the pigs from the farmers or the farmers from the pigs." The search for the presidential pig turned farcical when Jerry and

Abbie began to feud about whose pig made the better candidate. Abbie's was cute; Jerry's was ugly. The two Yippie leaders engaged in one long shouting match, and Stew Albert remembered that they would have come to blows had he not come between them.

The fight had a lot to do with their clashing egos. Jerry accused Abbie of turning Yippie into his own "personality cult." Abbie maintained that Jerry was "posing for the media more than organizing on the street and in the park." But there were genuine political and cultural differences as well. "Jerry wants to show the clenched fist," Abbie explained to the Yippies in Chicago. "I want to show the clenched fist and the smile. He wants the gun. I want the gun and the flower." For Abbie, smoking marijuana, listening to rock 'n' roll, and watching guerrilla theatre were essential activities that would build the counterculture. For Jerry, the street battles between police and protesters were what really counted.

After a great deal of bickering, Jerry's pig was chosen to lead the Yippies. "Today is a historic day for America," he announced at a press conference outside the Chicago Civic Center, with Pigasus and Abbie at his side. "We are proud to announce the declaration of candidacy for the President of the United States by a pig." No sooner was Pigasus nominated than he was taken into police custody. Phil Ochs, Stew Albert, Jerry Rubin, and several other Yippies were arrested and charged with disorderly conduct, though they were soon released for twenty-five dollars in bail.

The battle with Jerry infuriated Abbie, but he had more violent foes to contend with, and not just on the police force. Late one night the landlord of the building in which he was staying waved a loaded pistol and screamed, "Where's Abbie Hoffman? I'm going to kill him." The police arrested the man, but the next day he was back on the street, much to Abbie's annoyance. A martyr's death on the barricades was one thing, but to be shot and killed in a dingy apartment by a lone nut was unenviable.

The threat on Abbie's life made the newspapers, albeit on the back pages, while the political and military events that were taking place in Czechoslovakia dominated the front pages. On August 20, Soviet troops poured across the Czech border to crush the fragile experiment in democracy that had provided a glimmer of hope to all of Eastern Europe.

Except for members of the American Communist Party, who defended Moscow, radicals all across the country were outraged by the Soviet invasion. Abbie used the situation in Eastern Europe to mount a media campaign against the domestic forces of law and order. At a press conference he announced that Chicago (which he pronounced "Czecago") was a "police state." Moreover, he warned that "the cops want to turn our parks into graveyards." To the assembled TV cameramen and newspaper photographers, Abbie issued an open invitation to "come around and take pictures of today's Czechoslovakian demonstration."

So far he liked the pictures he'd been watching on TV. The networks aired footage of the amphitheater (where the convention would take place) ringed with barbed wire, and that image, more than any other, prompted him to claim that the Yippies had won a "propaganda victory." Chicago really was an armed camp, as everyone could see. The Yippies themselves couldn't have arranged for more favorable coverage, or for more tension in the air.

Crazy Conspiracy

By the time the Festival of Life began on Sunday, August 25, the atmosphere in Chicago was spooky indeed. Abbie was cracking jokes and laughing, but gallows humor had replaced slapstick comedy. His own martyrdom in Chicago would be funnier than anything, he insisted. "When I'm shot, I'm gonna laugh like a son of a bitch," he said. Getting shot wasn't outside the realm of possibility. The battle lines were drawn, the ultimatums delivered. The city imposed a curfew stating that demonstrators had to be out of Lincoln Park and off the streets by 11:00 P.M. or risk arrest and jail. The Yippies insisted they had a right to sleep in the park; some of them, including Abbie, insisted that they would die defending their right to be in the park. When the police posted notices urging that protesters "Please cooperate," the Yippies replied with a leaflet that proclaimed "Beware: local cops are armed and considered dangerous."

On Sunday, the Yippies joined with Mobe protesters, including Tom Hayden and Rennie Davis, for a march to the hotels where many of the Democratic Party delegates were staying. No violence took place there, but when the Yippies returned to Lincoln Park, which was out of the media spotlight, the police freely assaulted the demonstrators. From Abbie's perspective, a blood ritual had begun. The Yippies were now tribal brothers, and there was no turning back from violent revolution.

That evening, a thousand or so protesters gathered in Lincoln Park. They raised the red flag of revolution and the black flag of anarchy, built bonfires, burned draft cards, and set fires in trash cans. At about sunset the police reminded everyone of the 11:00 P.M. curfew, but they were met with jeers and verbal assaults. "Motherfuckers," "shitheads," and "pigs," the crowd roared. Allen Ginsberg tried to defuse the volatile situation by chanting "Om, ommm, ommm," but Abbie was in no mood for a relaxation of tensions. "We're gonna stay here till eleven o'clock at night," he told one police commander. "And at eleven o'clock at night, we're going to test our legal right to be in this park and sleep here." The commander replied that if demonstrators remained in the park after curfew, they would be arrested. "Groovy," Abbie replied, as though fun and games were about to begin.

When the police began to attack the demonstrators at about nine o'clock, he scolded them for jumping the gun. "Can't you wait two hours?" he asked facetiously. For days he'd been the provocateur and the troublemaker. Now, when "police anarchy really broke loose," as he put it, he delighted in switching sides and playing the part of the sheriff. "Where the hell's the law and order in this town?" he demanded. His strategy worked, albeit briefly. For a short while there was an uneasy truce in Lincoln Park. Then at 11:00 P.M. a message was broadcast over the loudspeaker system: "This park is closed. All persons now in the park, including representatives of the news media, are in violation of the law and subject to arrest." The Mobe "marshals," as they were called, urged protesters to evacuate the park. "This is suicide, suicide," one marshal shouted. The Yippies promptly denounced him as an authoritarian and insisted that leaving or staying was a matter for each individual to decide on his or her own.

When the Yippies stood their ground, the police clubbed them with their nightsticks. The police smashed the Free Store, confiscated bull-horns and walkie-talkies, and drove the Yippies into the streets. One contingent poured into Old Town, Chicago's version of Greenwich Village, while another headed for the downtown hotels where delegates were staying, chanting slogans like "Ho, Ho, Ho Chi Minh, NLF [the

Vietnamese National Liberation Front] is gonna win" and "The streets belong to the people." On the Michigan Avenue Bridge, demonstrators clashed with the police, scattered, then coalesced and clashed again.

One eyewitness later told the Walker Study Team that the Chicago demonstrators had constituted a new kind of crowd: a crowd that "thrived on confrontation." During the ghetto riots in Newark and Detroit, "the police would break up the crowd and the crowd would stay broken up," the observer noted. But in Chicago in the summer of 1968, "the crowd would not run away; . . . it would regroup and surge back to the police." Abbie made much the same comment. "We never retreated," he claimed. "We persisted in fighting for our right to stay in the park the total time we were in Chicago."

On Sunday night the police also attacked representatives of the mass media. "It was clear that police were looking for reporters, that they were the prime target," Mike Royko wrote. That, too, was a new and startling development. For most of the decade of the sixties, law enforcement officials, especially in the Deep South, had felt unfairly treated by liberal reporters from the North, but they had refrained from deliberate, premeditated attacks. All of that changed in Chicago, in large measure because Mayor Daley publicly blamed the media for the social unrest in America. "The television industry is part of the violence and creating it all over the country," Daley insisted. His solution was brutal punishment; accordingly, the Chicago police beat dozens of reporters and photographers.

From Norman Mailer's perspective (in *Miami and the Siege of Chicago*), the attack on the media in Chicago was the start of "the counterrevolution" that would return Richard M. Nixon to power in Washington, D.C., and revive political conservatism across the nation. But Abbie thought that the police riot advanced the cause of the revolution. "It made Chicago a moral as well as strategic victory for us," he wrote. The Yippies were the victims of state terror, and they deserved international assistance, he claimed.

On Monday, August 26, he and the Yippies wired a telegram to U Thant, Secretary-General of the United Nations, "charging that law and order had broken down in Chicago" and requesting that the U.N. dispatch an "impartial observer" to the city. Then they held a press conference to publicize their plea. That afternoon the action shifted from Lincoln Park to the Loop. The Democratic National Convention had begun, but the amphitheater was ringed by the police, and there was no opportunity to get inside. The Yippies marched to police headquarters and then to Grant Park, where demonstrators climbed the equestrian statue of Civil War general John Logan and waved red flags, black flags, and the flag of the Vietnamese National Liberation Front. There was no destruction of property and no graffiti, but it looked like a scene from the revolution, and the police dragged the demonstrators from the statue and arrested them.

That night the Yippies tried to march to the Loop, but they were stopped by a wall of police. In Lincoln Park the demonstrators built barricades and prepared to defend themselves. "Isn't it fantastic?" Tom Hayden exclaimed. "Kids fighting for a park they hadn't even heard of two days ago? It means we can stage confrontations any time, anywhere, just by challenging them for a piece of land." At about 12:30 A.M., the police attacked the demonstrators with clubs and chanted "Kill! Kill! Kill" and "Kill the motherfuckers." Tear gas was fired at the crowd, and once again reporters were attacked, cameras damaged, and film confiscated. This time, twenty reporters needed hospital treatment. When Mayor Daley was questioned about the violence directed at the media, he replied, "How can policemen tell the difference between a demonstrator and a newsman?" The national news media were beginning to show pictures of rioting police, and the American public was beginning to realize that something bizarre was taking place in Mayor Daley's city. "To a nation and a world, his Chicago was beginning to look like a madhouse," Royko observed.

To Abbie and to many others, the Mayor appeared to be a bit mad. Abbie himself was on the edge and was taking a great deal of amusement from playing the part of the dark wizard. On Monday night, for example, he came up with the crazy idea of spreading the rumor that he had been assassinated. That information, he thought, would rally the Yippie troops and encourage a new wave of insurrection. As he explained in *Revolution for the Hell of It,* "At midnight . . . a girl with a brown cowboy hat covered with blood was supposed to have run into the Lincoln Park area, screaming that I had been killed. It would have worked too. Lincoln Park at midnight just before the tear gas hit was the best place in the country to begin that sort of spook story. It was the hour of Paranoid's delight." Lincoln Park was "absolutely eerie," as Tom Hayden noted, and paranoia was rampant; the story of Abbie's death might very well have been believed, but the young woman chose not to play her part, and he soon came out of hiding.

On Tuesday, August 27, Abbie delivered an hour-long speech in Lincoln Park that captured much of the craziness of the Chicago protests. Taped by Charles Harbutt, it was published first in the *Tulane Drama Review* under the title "Media Freaking" and later in Mitchell Goodman's anthology *The Movement toward a New America*. A quarter of a century later, the speech seems to have little if any sense of direction or of coherence, but to many of those who heard it in 1968, it made perfect sense. After hearing the speech, Daniel Lewis Stein observed, "I began to really understand what Yippie! was and to see clearly what Abbie and Jerry and all the rest of us were trying to do in Chicago."

In Abbie's own estimation, the speech was a masterpiece of rhetoric. "I was really flying," he wrote in *Revolution for the Hell of It.* "I was the best." In a disjointed way, he took his audience through his own experiences in the sixties, and at times it seemed as though he was reliving the high points of his own movement history: the protest against HUAC in San Francisco, the money-tossing at the New York Stock Exchange, the exorcism at the Pentagon, and the protest against Secretary of State Dean Rusk in November 1967.

Much of the Lincoln Park speech was about the Chicago police; it was also directed at them. Abbie assumed that undercover agents were in the crowd and that he could have a great deal of fun by taunting them. "Cops are like Yippies," he joked. "You can never find the leaders." The cops were also like the Yippies, he insisted, in their tendency to operate under a "system of anarchy." They didn't want to work; they just wanted to "beat the shit out of people," he said.

Abbie wanted to allay fears and boost confidence in the youthful crowd. The Yippies didn't have guns, but they did have advantages over the police, he insisted. "You're physically stronger than they are," he said. "You came here for nothin' and they're holdin' on to their fuckin' pig jobs. . . . We've got them by the balls." The more outrageous the protesters behaved, the safer they'd be, he claimed, but that notion gave many of the young demonstrators a false sense of security. "If you convince 'em you're crazy enough, they won't hurt ya," he said. Unfortunately, in most cases the police thought the kids were crazy and hurt them anyway. But Abbie told them that a protester ought to be able to overpower a police officer simply by looking him "right in the eye." If they were pursued by the police, he said, they might evade an arrest by jumping into Lake Michigan and swimming for freedom. It didn't take long before pacifists in the movement were calling Abbie irresponsible and blaming him for the violence that took its toll on many demonstrators.

Abbie also boasted that he wasn't going to tell the crowd what political action to take. "Only SDS tells you what to do," he said scornfully. But he didn't hesitate to make predictions about what people would do or what would happen. On the night of Wednesday, August 28, "the shit is really going to hit the fan," he said. The Yippies would "bust out of the park" and perform "some mighty strange theatrical events" which were bound to attract media attention. No one would give the command, he said, but "by magic" there would be "200,000 fuckin' people marchin' on the amphitheater." Protesters might undress and run naked through the streets, he suggested. "Forget about your clothes, your money," he said. "Just worry about your ass."

At the end of his Lincoln Park speech, he encouraged everyone to head to the International Amphitheater, where the Democratic National Convention was taking place. "Just ask the guy next to you how to get there," he said. "Put your arm around his shoulder and go with him." After about ten blocks the demonstrators were stopped not only by a line of troops but also by an armored vehicle ringed with barbed wire and equipped with rotating searchlights. Even Abbie was amazed by the show of military force. "It was unbelievable," he wrote. The armored vehicle was "the biggest fuckin' tank" that he had ever seen. Abbie turned to a young black man named Frankie, whom he described as a "spade cat," and suggested, "Let's go up and fuck around." One Mobe marshal tried to restrain them, but it was no use. Others might be frightened, but not Abbie. He was "not afraid to die," he proclaimed. Berkeley radical Art Goldberg remembered that he lay down in the street in front of the tank and extended his middle finger in a gesture of defiance. In one of the very few footnotes in *Revolution for the Hell of It*, he scolded himself for what he felt was a feeble performance. "Better theater would have been to punch the tank or at least stand up roaring with laughter," he wrote. "I got co-opted by the pacifists."

Abbie next took a bullhorn and shouted at the line of policemen, "You cops out there cool it." He explained to comedian Dick Gregory, who was one of the protesters in the street, that he had a secret plan. His "rap to the cops was a bluff," he said. His real "strategy was to get the head cop down here, grab him, and get us through." In short, Abbie wanted to take Deputy Superintendent of Police James Rochford hostage. What was he going to do if the police touched him, Dick Gregory asked. Abbie replied, "I would kill the Top Pig." It was no empty threat, he insisted. "I meant it," he wrote in *Revolution for the Hell of It*.

Abbie Hoffman may have had these incidents in mind when he later told Dr. Oscar Janiger, a Los Angeles psychiatrist, that his behavior in Chicago in the summer of 1968 had been "irrational." In 1979, shortly before he surfaced from the underground, he told Dr. Janiger, whose care he had entered, that his first "overexcited" episodes had coincided with the riots at the Democratic National Convention. "I was so involved I was wound up like a yo-yo string," he said. Moreover, he'd been unable, he said, to "stop my mental processes." On the basis of nearly a dozen consultations with Abbie, Dr. Janiger diagnosed him as manic-depressive. His psychological report (which was included with Abbie's petition for a pardon from the governor of New York in the eighties) concluded that in Chicago in 1968, Abbie's "behavior was out of control and was no longer calculated, or for deliberate effect, but . . . deteriorated into fragmented, irrational and at times delusional proportions entirely inappropriate with and without obvious direction—even to the point of placing himself purposefully in great jeopardy or physical harm." Abbie certainly placed himself in great danger and was often out of control. Still, it's difficult to say when his craziness was "calculated," to borrow Dr. Janiger's word, and when it wasn't.

When he appeared at a Mobe meeting on Tuesday, August 27, for example, was he "acting" or was he really crazy? Carrying a club, which he waved menacingly, he insisted that the Yippies were arming themselves. "Whatever the pigs dish into the park, we'll dish out," he said. In the afternoon, when he spoke at the "Un-birthday Party" for President Johnson, he sounded his utopian rather than his nihilistic note. "We're going to build a beautiful free city in Lincoln Park," he proclaimed. "We're gonna hold Lincoln Park tonight."

To the protesters it seemed as though the revolutionary moment had finally arrived in Chicago, and nothing and no one could stop it: not Mayor Daley, not the police, and not the National Guard, who were in full battle gear. At a Mobe rally in Grant Park on Wednesday, August 28, an eighteen-year-old named Angus MacKenzie, who worked for a radical newspaper in Birmingham, Alabama, lowered the American flag to half-mast because, as he later explained, the police had "killed democracy." Someone else raised the red flag, as though to signal the start of the insurrection. The police interpreted the lowering and raising of the flags as an affront to the established order and attacked the demonstrators with clubs and tear gas. But this crowd wasn't passive, and it retaliated with rocks and bottles. A bloody battle raged, and a great many protesters were injured and arrested.

By mid-afternoon there was a Mobe march to the amphitheater where the Democrats were meeting. Though they were turned back with tear gas, the demonstrators maintained a strong sense of dignity by singing "The Battle Hymn of the Republic" and "America the Beautiful." By nightfall the entire "revolutionary army," as Norman Mailer called it—composed of SDS members, Yippies, and "McCarthy kids"—had gathered in front of the Hilton Hotel, where the television networks were ready for the apocalyptic drama to unfold.

Journalist David Lewis Stein, who witnessed the scene, wrote that "the lights from the TV cameras played over the huge, dancing mob that filled Michigan Avenue and spilled out into Grant Park." Without warning, and "for no reason that could be immediately determined," according to *New York Times* reporter J. Anthony Lukas, the blue-helmeted policemen and the National Guardsmen began using clubs, rifle butts, tear gas, and Mace against demonstrators, reporters, and even innocent bystanders.

Years later, Tom Hayden would say that the massacre of student protesters in Beijing, China, in 1989 made Chicago in 1968 look like "a Pacifist Teaparty." But that analogy is hardly fair; twentieth-century Chinese history has been far more violent and far more turbulent than twentieth-century American history. Moreover, China is by no means a democratic nation. The Chinese army has a long record of resolving conflicts with armed force. In the United States, military intervention at a political convention was extraordinary.

What took place in the streets of Chicago was hardly a "Pacifist Teaparty," at least by American standards. The police assaulted anyone and anything that moved. A thousand people were injured; 178 people were arrested. Young women were dragged through the streets, and the police even entered the Haymarket Inn, a restaurant inside the Hilton Hotel, and assaulted people who had fled there to safety. The police dragnet began in front of the Hilton but spread throughout downtown Chicago, until no one was safe on the streets. Many demonstrators dispersed, but hundreds of others, including McCarthy supporters and Yippies, stood their ground and chanted "The streets belong to the people" and "Hell, no, we won't go."

All this was unusual, to say the least. What made it even more so was that it was all recorded by television cameras, as though a violent TV movie had been in the making. David Lewis Stein noted that the police arrested people and beat them up "in a white Hollywood glare." The day after the riot, *New York Times* television critic Jack Gould noted that "untold millions of viewers" had watched the "chilling TV tape recordings of Chicago policemen clearing the streets" and that "the pictures alone were enough to send a shudder down a viewer's spine." Moreover, Gould predicted that "television's influence" on the convention "is likely to be a subject of study for years." The delegates at the Democratic Convention watched the scenes on TV and were profoundly alarmed.

On the floor of the convention, Connecticut senator Abraham Ribicoff lashed out at Mayor Daley and the Democratic Party establishment. "With George McGovern, we wouldn't have Gestapo tactics on the streets of Chicago," Senator Ribicoff proclaimed. The Mayor shot back, "Fuck you, you Jew son of a bitch, you lousy motherfucker, go home." He would later deny ever saying these words, of course, but his speech had been filmed; lip-readers watched it carefully over and over again, and concluded that he had indeed called Ribicoff a "motherfucker" and a "Jew son of a bitch."

The "police riot" prompted Keith Lampe, one of the original Yippies, to exclaim, "We have ripped the smiling mask from the face of the man." In *Woodstock Nation,* which appeared in 1969, Abbie defined Chicago in apocalyptic language as the place "where the facade of a democratically run convention was washed down the streets with the blood of young people. The Whole World Was Watching and what it saw was . . . a 'police riot.'" Todd Gitlin, who was also on the scene, made much the same observation when he wrote in *The Sixties*, "I remember an eerie satisfaction: *At last we're shown they can only rule at gunpoint. The world is going to see.*"

Allen Katzman, the editor of the *East Village Other*, asserted in an article entitled "Bandages and Stitches Tell the Story," which was written in the heat of the moment, that "the battle for Chicago will be remembered in the heavy years to come as the beginning of a Revolution." In impassioned prose, Katzman added, "As I write this, protesters, thousands strong, are being slugged, kicked, gassed, and martyred before the Conrad Hilton hotel, the site of Hubert Humphrey's Death Headquarters. It is a scene not to be believed. It is Viet Nam. It is Prague. It is Chicago." Norman Mailer watched from the nineteenth floor of the Hilton and described what he saw in language that implied Armageddon was at hand: "It was as if the war had finally begun, and this was therefore a great and solemn moment, as if indeed even the gods of history had come together from each side to choose the very front of the Hilton Hotel before the television cameras of the world. . . . The Democratic Party had here broken in two before the eyes of a nation like Melville's whale charging right out of the sea."

"My Own Private Movie"

Ironically, Abbie did not appear at the Hilton Hotel until hours after the "police riot." When he finally showed up, he told the assembled Yippies that he'd been arrested on charges of obscenity and had spent most of the day in jail. That morning, while he was getting dressed, he had borrowed Anita's red lipstick and "painted" the word "FUCK" on his forehead. While he was eating breakfast in a restaurant, the Chicago police had arrested him. By writing "FUCK" on his forehead, he seemed to be saying "Fuck You" to the world. The four-letter word was certainly an attention-grabber. It expressed Abbie's defiance, his confrontational style, and his desire to polarize. It also implied that the Democratic National Convention, the police violence, and Mayor Daley's obstruction of the democratic process were far more obscene than any four-letter word could possibly be.

In *Revolution for the Hell of It,* Abbie offered a detailed account of the arrest for obscenity, which he called "a bust written by a Hollywood screenwriter." While he was having breakfast with Anita and Paul Krassner, he said, two policemen politely asked him to remove the hat he was wearing. At first he refused to obey the order, but when the officers drew their guns and demanded, "Take off your hat," he complied. Abbie insisted that "the cops beat the shit out" of him and that "throughout the beatings I kept laughing hysterically." When one police officer showed him a gold bullet and said that Abbie's name was written on it, Abbie claims to have replied, "I have your name on a silver bullet and I'm the Lone Ranger. . . . We whipped you fuckin pigs, we whipped your asses. You cocksuckers are afraid to lose your jobs and we ain't afraid to die."

In *Revolution for the Hell of It*, he presented his jail experience in the form of a one-act play. The main character, of course, was a revolutionary named Abbie Hoffman. Other characters included a police officer named "One Fat Pig," a naked hippie called "Iron Mike," and two dozen or so pacifists. As the play opens, "One Fat Pig" appears on stage, and Abbie immediately begins his performance: "I dash across the cell, throw myself at his feet, clutch his pants. 'Sir! Sir!' I plead, 'We have no food! We have no water! Please, sir!' . . . He's three times my size. But that doesn't matter, I can kick the shit out of him any time I want 'cause I ain't afraid to die and he's afraid of losing his job." How much of this account is fact and how much of it is fiction isn't entirely clear. Abbie himself noted in his autobiography that he "played" his arrest "like I was in my own private movie," a statement that suggests fictionalization. Staughton Lynd, a pacifist and professor of history who had worked with SNCC in the early 1960s, and who shared a jail cell with Abbie on August 28, 1968, has no recollection of any unusual or dramatic behavior on his part. "As I remember, Abbie was lying face down on a cot," Lynd said. "He was not weeping and he was not distressed."

In 1979 and 1980, during his therapy sessions with Dr. Oscar Janiger, Abbie claimed that while he was in jail in Chicago, he had "climbed all over the bars of the cell . . . like a monkey and never stopped yelling at the guards." He also insisted that when a naked hippie was placed in the cell with him, he had "hypnotized him" and that the hippie "fell down, crawled across the floor and kissed my feet." In *Revolution for the Hell of It*, Abbie claims that when he was finally brought into court, he dismissed his lawyer, then tore up the legal documents in the case. "It was all *Catch-22* bullshit anyway," he wrote. "I was really mad though because they had succeeded in keeping me out of the battle of Michigan Avenue."

It was ironic, indeed, that Abbie wasn't on the scene when TV finally shattered the image of America as a peaceful, law-abiding society. Mayor Daley blamed television directly for the violence: "Everyone knows television forced it," the Mayor said. Not long afterward, on September 12, Abbie told the *Worcester Telegram and Gazette*, "I think Daley was right when he said it was the newsmen and TV that brought many of the demonstrators there." He went on to explain, "Many of us understand the use of mass media as both weapon and a battleground. In this country, it's what's news that's going to determine the future and what's news is violence."

It seemed perfectly fitting that he and Mayor Daley would agree on the role of television. Hoffman and Daley were both masters of media manipulation, and both were quick to claim victory and to defend their own actions. When CBS's Walter Cronkite asked the mayor about the use of violence against the demonstrators, he explained that he'd had no choice. "Certain people planned to assassinate the three candidates for the Presidency," he insisted, though he never named names. He went on to explain that "With all of these talks of assassination and it happening in our city I didn't want what happened in California to happen in Chicago." Daley was bluffing. There was no conspiracy to assassinate any candidate in Chicago. Granted, Abbie had threatened to "pull down LBJ's pants" as well as Humphrey's at the Democratic National Convention, but that could hardly be taken as a threat on the president's or vice president's life. Daley had no evidence of a conspiracy, no testimony from police informers, and no wiretapped conversations. Unfortunately, Walter Cronkite never pressed the mayor for details, and a great many Americans assumed that Daley had been in possession of classified information about the security of the nation and had acted accordingly. His strong-arm tactics had worked to his advantage. As Mike Royko noted, "Daley came out of the convention even more popular than before because 'bust their heads' was the mood of the land and Daley had swung the biggest club."

Abbie claimed that he wasn't at all surprised by the "reaction of middle-class America to the police brutality." People simply believe what they see, he explained. "From their position police brutality isn't true. . . . They watch Mod Squad [on television] and all the information that reaches them makes the cop a good guy. . . . So when they saw cops beating up kids who were seen on some psychic level as their own, their reaction was disbelief."

Abbie watched Hubert Humphrey's acceptance of the Democratic Party nomination for president on television and became ecstatic. "We had smashed the Democrats' chance [to win the election]," he concluded. He believed that the Yippies had "destroyed the two-party system in this country and perhaps with it electoral politics." Hubert Humphrey offered much the same thought when he later noted that "the whole environment of politics had come apart" during the convention. Abbie was proud of the fact that "a small number of people" had been able to hurt "a huge and powerful political party." Moreover, Chicago was a "great victory," he would explain later in *Woodstock Nation,* because it "clearly established" the lines between "us" and "them," between "the people in the streets" and "the people in authority." Undoubtedly, the Yippie strategy in Chicago contributed in part to the defeat of Hubert Humphrey and the Democrats at the polls in November. In their book *Who Spoke Up?*—a thorough and compelling study of the movement against the war in Vietnam—Nancy Zaroulis and Gerald Sullivan concluded that the TV broadcast of the chaos in the streets of Chicago was "ultimately more significant and more crucial to the outcome of the election than what it watched of the Democrats' deliberations in the Amphitheater."

Abbie and the Yippies had indeed rocked the foundations of American power, but they did not deserve all the credit that Abbie took. "Because of our actions in Chicago, Richard Nixon will be elected President," he predicted in September 1968. Granted, the election would turn out to be amazingly close; Nixon defeated Humphrey by seventenths of a percentage point. But surely Humphrey played a part in his own defeat, just as surely as Nixon contributed to his victory. Moreover, Mayor Daley and the Chicago police also deserve credit for the chaos, violence, and disruption. Abbie regarded himself as a great puppet master who had manipulated the police. "Another week and we could have gotten the cops to assassinate Humphrey," he boasted in "Creating the

Perfect Mess." But the police were not simply the unwitting agents of the Yippies.

In the fall of 1968, Abbie was optimistic about Nixon's imminent victory at the polls. He insisted that Nixon, unlike Humphrey or Mc-Carthy, would be able to reach a negotiated settlement with the National Liberation Front and would "end the war in Vietnam." Other radicals came to much the same conclusion; an anti-Communist like Nixon would be able to sign a peace accord with Hanoi, they argued, because no one could accuse him of being "soft" on communism.

Unfortunately, movement optimists would be disillusioned: the war would go on for years. Thomas Aquinas Foran, the U.S. Attorney for the Northern District of Illinois and the prosecutor of the Chicago Conspiracy trial, would blame Hoffman, Hayden, and company for Humphrey's defeat. With Nixon in the White House, the war in Vietnam was prolonged, Foran insisted in a 1988 interview with *Chicago Tribune* writer Jeff Lyon. Tom Hayden also looked back at Chicago, but he told Lyon that the demonstrators had not been "responsible for the coming of Richard Nixon." What took place was "tragedy," Hayden said, and "in a tragedy everyone shares responsibility for what happened."

During the Democratic National Convention, it seemed that Abbie had little, if any, private life. But in fact his emotional landscape was in upheaval. From time to time he would phone home to tell John and Florence that he was fine and they shouldn't worry about him. The senior Hoffmans weren't doing well at all. While watching the demonstrations on television, John was suddenly stricken with acute pain and was admitted to the emergency room of Worcester Memorial Hospital, where he spent the next twenty-nine days. The editor of the *Worcester Telegram and Gazette* sensed that John Hoffman's heart attack was news, and reporter James A. Gourgouras was assigned to do a story that was subsequently published under the title "Heartache Real for Hoffmans." The story succeeded in making Abbie feel guilty.

"Look, I don't feel that I have any interest in what he's doing," John Hoffman told Gourgouras. "Our entire family is against it. Maybe some people are able to say I should be more understanding about his 'new way of life,' but how can I?" The only reason that his son was involved in political causes, John argued, was because he liked to be in "the spotlight," and that instinct for attention was an embarrassment for the whole family. Abbie had been given the best of everything, John claimed. And he'd willfully rejected all of it. "Don't you think I'd like to point to his picture on the mantel and tell you my son is doing this—or that—in his chosen field?" he asked the reporter. "Instead, I have to turn to the tabloids, and the long, detailed stories in papers throughout the country, to discover what my Abbie has been up to the day before." However, the whole family wasn't against Abbie, as John claimed. Younger brother Jack admitted that Abbie had done some "strange things"; still, many of them made a lot of sense. "What he's trying to prove is that this isn't a free society," Jack told *Worcester Telegram and Gazette* reporter Raymond Girard. "Abbie believes we have to rebel completely against the hypocrisy of our present society."

According to FBI agents, Abbie took personal credit for his father's near-fatal heart failure. In their report to J. Edgar Hoover, agents claimed that when Abbie's "father saw him on television during the Democratic Convention disorders from Chicago, Illinois, he suffered a heart attack and is still in the hospital." In *Revolution for the Hell of It,* Abbie provided a different account of his encounter with the FBI, which took place at his apartment in New York in early September 1968. He offered the agents "an analysis of J. Edgar Hoover's latent homosexuality," he wrote. To the FBI agents Abbie seemed strange. His hair "was fully grown, like a female," and he spoke "in the jargon of the 'beatnik,'" they noted in their report. Like almost everyone who observed him, the agents concluded that Abbie "appears to enjoy being the center of attention."

No one was more acutely aware of his love of attention than his wife, Anita. No one was more worried about him, either, especially in the days and weeks after the protests in Chicago. Like the FBI, Anita tried to keep tabs on her husband, and like them she wrote a report about him. Hers was in the form of a personal letter to Susan Carey, her closest friend. Years later, she insisted that she had not intended for Abbie to read her letter, but he read it nonetheless and then urged her to publish it because it was about him. In January 1969 the letter appeared in *Eye* magazine under the title "Diary of a Revolutionary's Wife." Anita was greatly alarmed by her husband's state of mind and body. Ever since childhood he had suffered from asthma, she explained.

Now he was having terrible fits of coughing. He was often unable to sleep at night, or to relax and have fun. Occasionally he would "come down" from his high, but for the most part he was manic for days on end.

Anita explained that her life with Abbie had always swung back and forth between two extremes. On the one hand, there was the "dangerous, dynamic play of Abbie's revolution"; on the other hand, there was "the more static, homelike play of good times." But now there was something new and disturbing about Abbie's extremes. "It is much like he is 'possessed,'" Anita wrote. "I don't know whether it is truly a 'high' or a state of being full of tension and being 'driven.'" What bothered her most was Abbie's "driven quality." In Chicago, she insisted, his energy had been both necessary and understandable. It enabled him, she believed, to "perform very heroic, brave and imaginative feats." For example, he had urged "a crowd on Michigan Avenue in Chicago that they all kidnap the police chief." But now that energy had no creative outlet.

Before Chicago, Anita wrote, Abbie was able to "remain free" of the adulation and the hero worship that he received. After Chicago, he was truly "egotistical"; at the same time, his ideas had taken on "more of a paranoid" quality than ever before. Abbie had begun to believe "the myth more than he usually does," she wrote with alarm. What obsessed Abbie as much as anything else, Anita explained, was his relationship to Jerry Rubin. Sometimes he even talked about Jerry in his sleep, Anita wrote, which concerned her but also gave her "something to laugh about." With a sense of irony, she wrote, "Here he and Jerry are fighting like crazy and both facing probable conspiracy charges for their activities in Chicago."

Public Enemy Number One

Abbie had been working on *Revolution for the Hell of It* for nearly a year, and parts of it had already appeared in print in the *Realist, Other Scenes, Seed,* and *WIN.* Moreover, he had dozens of bits and pieces— including poems, letters, and theatrical skits—that needed to be reworked and rearranged. In the wake of Chicago and with a great burst of creativity, he was finally able to give the book a modicum of the sustained attention that it deserved. As soon as he returned to New York, he promised Joyce Johnson, his editor at Dial Press (who had some fame as Jack Kerouac's lover in the mid-fifties), that he would finish the book in a few days. He began to write in longhand on a pad of yellow paper with manic energy. As soon as an essay was complete, he'd hand it to Anita, who typed it up.

Joyce Johnson remembered sitting on the floor of her office with Abbie trying to make a book out of the disparate parts. "It was like putting together a collage," she said. In *Woodstock Nation,* Abbie described *Revolution for the Hell of It* as a "non-book" that was written in a "non-way." Indeed, *Revolution for the Hell of It* exuded a sense of chaos and craziness, and those very qualities made it one of the quintessential American texts of the era. No other book—including Norman Mailer's *The Armies of the Night* and Eldridge Cleaver's *Soul on Ice,* which were also published in 1968—captured as successfully the frenetic energy and the disjointed character of the times in which it was written. For all its messiness, however, *Revolution for the Hell of It* offered several repeated themes: objective truth doesn't exist; reality is a subjective experience; and generational, not class, conflict drives the engine of history.

Near the end of the book, Abbie offered a critique of nineteenth-century Marxism and the idea of class struggle. "It makes sense to join the workers together, establish a concept of national trade unionism, and fight the tyrannical bosses if the economics of the system fit," he explained. But the economics no longer fit, he insisted. Unions and strikes were obsolete concepts, he argued, as was the idea of economic scarcity. "The truth of the matter is that most workers in America have a good deal materialistically," he wrote. Twentieth-century revolutionary theory, he insisted, would have to be built on the "premise of abundance." With the advent of automation and computers, the whole political and economic map would have to be redrawn. Moreover, Abbie suggested that middle-class Americans—such as salesman, secretaries, and college students—should drop out of the system rather than confront it and should instead reincarnate themselves as hippies. In Abbie's utopian society of eternal youth, cooperation would replace competition, play would supplant work, and "instant gratification" would be more important than "postponement of pleasure."

At the start of September Abbie put what he thought were the finishing touches to *Revolution for the Hell of It* and then set off for Provincetown, Massachusetts, to meet his literary idol and rival, Norman Mailer. "I've got a bigger ego than Mailer's," he told Jimmy Breslin of the *New York Post*. Mailer wasn't at home, but that didn't stop Abbie from making up stories about him or using Mailer's name to promote himself and advertise his own book. To Frank Dudock, the editor of *Punch,* Worcester's underground newspaper, Abbie explained that *Revolution for the Hell of It* was "a bigger ego trip than anything Mailer's ever done, and he's very jealous of it."

In fact, as it turned out, Abbie's book wasn't really finished. Almost every day occurred another dramatic episode in his life which begged to be included in the pages of the book. So *Revolution of the Hell of It* was expanded to include an "Epilogue" in which the author described his ongoing adventures.

On September 17, when he returned to Chicago "to stand trial for the infamous four-letter WORD," as he put it, he was arrested not once but three times, in rapid succession. Fortunately, he was represented by Gerald Lefcourt, a young, combative New York attorney. Lefcourt had been a conservative in college but had been radicalized by the civil rights movement and by his work for the Legal Aid Society in Manhattan. Lefcourt's first major political case had been for the Black Panther Party, though he was later to admit that at the time "I didn't even know what the Black Panther Party was." Soon thereafter he received a phone call from Abbie. "He said that he had a doctor and a dentist, but what he really needed most in the world was a *lawyer,*" Lefcourt said in an interview with Claudia Dreifus for the *East Village Other* (later included in Allen Katzman's anthology *Our Time*). It would take four or five lawyers scattered all over the country "to handle Abbie," Lefcourt observed, and he was proud to be one of them.

"We never thought of ourselves in terms of the lawyer-client relationship," Lefcourt later remembered. "We were close friends and political allies. We had a pact. He was going to make the revolution, and I was going to keep him out of jail for as long as possible, though in those days we feared that it wouldn't be for long." No sooner had they made their pact than it was put to the test, on September 17, which Lefcourt was to call "one of the most unusual and hilarious days of my life."

Abbie's first arrest that day took place at O'Hare Airport. As soon as he and Lefcourt stepped off the plane, Abbie was handcuffed and charged with jumping bail. Lefcourt remembered that Abbie's first words were "It's great to be back in Mississippi." He noted, too, that "Abbie could laugh through one arrest after another."

Though Abbie had made no deliberate attempt to avoid prosecution, he had inadvertently missed a scheduled court appearance, and the judge in the case had issued a bench warrant for his arrest. According to Lefcourt, Abbie had been afraid of returning to Chicago. "In the eyes of law enforcement he was Public Enemy Number One," Lefcourt said. Abbie and his lawyer dashed from courtroom to courtroom. They persuaded Magistrate Louis Gilberto to drop the bail-jumping charges and to reschedule a trial date. Abbie was free, but no sooner was he out of the courtroom than the Chicago police arrested him all over again, for illegal possession of a weapon: a penknife.

Placed in handcuffs and driven to the Federal Building, he was asked if he had ever used an alias. He responded with a long list of names, including Casey Stengel, George Metesky, Spiro Agnew, Muriel Humphrey, Marilyn Monroe, and Joe DiMaggio. Photographed and fingerprinted, he spent the night in jail, complained about the food, and the next morning appeared before a Federal Commissioner. "Thanks to the Chicago police, I've just become a very successful writer," he announced. "I've just finished a book about Chicago . . . and I'm working on a movie. I made $10,000 this week, but I plan to burn it." When he was asked if he'd ever jumped bail, he claimed that he had, on one occasion in Mississippi. "The Ku Klux Klan was organizing a lynching party, and my attorney thought it was wise if I blew town," he said. The judge took him seriously and imposed severe restrictions on his travel.

Abbie returned to O'Hare, collected his belongings, and boarded a plane for New York. "The plane taxied on the runway and suddenly stopped," Lefcourt remembered. "The doors opened and in walked these three gentlemen in business suits: 'You're Abbie Hoffman? We're from the House Committee on Un-American Activities and we have a subpoena for you to appear in Washington.'" After smugly serving him, they went their merry way. Dozens of other activists, including Tom Hayden, David Dellinger, and Jerry Rubin, were also being subpoenaed. Democratic Congressman Richard H. Ichord told *New York Times* reporter Marjorie Hunter and others that the purpose of the hearing was to determine "the extent to which and the means by which" the demonstrations in Chicago "were planned, instigated, incited and supported by Communist and other subversive organizations."

Abbie had long admired Jerry Rubin for his theatrical performance at the 1966 HUAC hearings; now he, too, could create a circus atmosphere before the committee. As soon as he returned to New York he began to publicize his upcoming appearance. "I plan to turn state's evidence," he told Liberation News Service, which published his remarks in an article entitled "My Life to Live" in October 1968. "I plan to squeal on everybody. . . . I'm going to indict my friend Peter Rabbit." His strategy, he explained, was to "get crazy. Craziest motherfuckers they ever seen in this country. 'Cause that's the only way we're gonna beat them. So fucking crazy that they can't understand it at ALL."

Abbie printed and distributed his own subpoenas, which were addressed to "Yippies, Motherfuckers, Commies, Narcos, Saboteurs, Conspirators, Sons of Liberty, Freaks, Guerrillas." His subpoenas urged everyone to come to the hearings with "pot, incense, yoyos, molotov cocktails, flowers, energy, black widow spiders, balloons, flags, gold balls, PIGS, music, banners, LSD, flaming crosses, hats, fruit, battleships, life, rice, licorice, slogans, flesh, rocks, lights, noise makers, buttons, cameras, gorillas."

On October 1, the opening day, the subpoenaed radicals and their lawyers, including William Kunstler and Michael Kennedy, staged a "stand-in" to protest the investigations. "The Constitution is being raped, and we as lawyers are being emasculated in an armed camp," Michael Kennedy shouted. Jerry Rubin wore a bandolier of live cartridges and carried a toy M-16 rifle. Abbie appeared in a tie-dyed T-shirt with two feathers in his long hair. A group of women who had recently formed the Women's International Terrorist Conspiracy from Hell (WITCH) carried brooms and wore black dresses and black hats. Forming a circle around Jerry, they burned incense, danced, and chanted. These Yippie theatrics at the HUAC hearings were a dress rehearsal for the performances that were to take place in the courtroom at the Chicago Conspiracy trial.

The HUAC hearings also, however, enabled the government to try out its conspiracy case against Hoffman and Rubin and the other defendants in the Chicago Conspiracy Trial. Undercover agent Robert L. Pierson, for example, who would appear on the witness stand in Chicago in 1969, testified before HUAC that the Yippies, the Mobe, and the Black Panthers were intent on "overthrowing the United States Government by force."

Gerald Lefcourt later remembered that Abbie did not want to let HUAC steal the media spotlight. "He wanted what *he* was about to be on the evening news, and not what *they* were about," Lefcourt said. He explained that Abbie "had the idea of wearing a flag shirt and saying 'I'm more American than you.' He was certain that he would be arrested, and that the arrest would make the news and steal the show from the committee. Moreover, he had a hunch that the police would rip off the American flag shirt from his back. Then, *they'd* be guilty of desecration."

On the morning of October 4, everything went more or less as Abbie had planned. Anita painted the flag of the Vietnamese National Liberation Front (NLF) on his back. Then Abbie put on a commercially made American flag shirt and pinned on two of his favorite buttons: one that read "Wallace for President: Stand Up for America" and another that said "Vote Pig in Sixty-Eight, Yippie." He also wore dark glasses that made him look mysterious and a bit menacing as well. Sure enough, on the sidewalk outside the Cannon Office Building, law enforcement officers stopped him, tore up his shirt, and arrested him for desecration of the flag. Abbie spent the night in jail. It was a dreadful experience that only added to his sense of outrage about the whole affair. "The law I was arrested under would make everyone who dresses in an Uncle Sam costume and most drum majorettes criminals," he wrote in the Epilogue to *Revolution for the Hell of It.* And he added that he had recently watched Phyllis Diller on TV wearing "a miniskirt that looked more like an American flag than the shirt I wore," but no one had arrested her.

He was the first person to be prosecuted under the new federal statute that made it a crime to deface or defile the flag. U.S. Attorney Benton Becker argued that the flag was "symbolically the United States of America," and that the government had "a legitimate interest in maintaining the sanctity of its symbols." Gerald Lefcourt defended Abbie on First Amendment grounds: wearing the flag was a form of symbolic speech, Lefcourt argued. His client had never intended to dishonor the flag. Moreover, there was no physical violence, no personal injury, and no provocation to the public. "The communication of ideas is what this country is all about," Lefcourt told the court. "If we don't protect the communication of ideas, then we're leading ourselves down the path of serious trouble to a repressive society."

On the witness stand, Abbie explained that he wore the American flag shirt because "I was going before the Un-American Activities Committee of the House of Representatives, and I don't particularly consider that committee American, and I don't consider that House of Representatives particularly representative; and I wore the shirt to show that we were in the tradition of the founding fathers of this country." He was found guilty of desecrating the flag and was sentenced to a thirty-day prison term, although an appeals court would subsequently reverse the lower court's decision. "Your honor, I regret that I have but one shirt to give for my country," he said after he was sentenced.

Abbie refused to testify before HUAC. Moreover, he raised too much hell for the Committee to compel him to testify. But he willingly cooperated with the Walker Study Team. Headed by liberal Chicago lawyer Daniel Walker, the group was the investigative arm of the National Commission on the Causes and Prevention of Violence, which had been appointed by President Johnson and given the task of explaining the recent rise of disorder and lawlessness in the United States. This group eventually published a report concluding that Chicago had been a "police riot." Abbie told *New York Times* reporter Max Frankel that the Walker report would not prevent future police misconduct. But he praised the study team "for finally seeing the same reality we saw in Chicago."

However, Abbie's own testimony (much of which was published in a 1969 paperback entitled *The Conspiracy*, with an introduction by Noam Chomsky) suggested that he and the demonstrators bore some responsibility for the violence. "Do you know of anyone that participated in activities in one way or another in Chicago during convention week who espouses the violent overthrow of the government?" Abbie was asked. "Me," he replied, teasingly. When he was asked if he knew any other protesters who advocated violent revolution, he refused to name names. "I don't care about anybody else," he said. "I espoused the overthrow by any means necessary. I'd like to see it done with bubble gum, but I'm having some doubts." When pressed further for names, he responded, "Yes. [Georgia governor] Lester Maddox. He was in town and making some pretty violent statements."

In the weeks before the November election, Abbie did everything he could to foment rebellion and to make as much trouble as possible for Hubert Humphrey, whom he and other activists now called "The Hump." "We're going to follow Humphrey around the country with the slogan 'Dump the Hump,'" he told the *Worcester Telegram and Gazette,* which ran his comments in an article entitled "Yippie Leader Outlines Anarchy." In mid-September he began to urge citizens to boycott the elections altogether. In his view all the candidates were "pigs." No matter who was elected, the Yippies were planning to hold an "In-hog-uration" in January, he told crowds on college campuses. They would lead Pigasus triumphantly through the streets of the nation's capitol.

At the end of October, Abbie, Jerry, and Stew Albert issued a "Yippie Call" for election day that was published in the *New York Free Press,* among other places. "Every man a revolution! Every small group a revolutionary center!" they declared. The Yippie triumvirate urged citizens to "come into the streets and to 'vote with your feet.'" They proposed a national strike, as well: "Nobody goes to work. Nobody goes to school. Nobody votes." At the start of November Abbie urged citizens to sabotage the elections by staging sit-ins inside voting booths and by gluing voting machines shut. There were minor protests in the streets and isolated acts of disruption, but for the most part the election took place without movement sabotage.

By the end of 1968, Abbie was depressed once again, in part because he had contracted hepatitis. In his own words, he "almost died." But at Albert Einstein Hospital, where he was confined for twenty-one days, he saw "cracks . . . in the bastion of medicine," and his spirits began to lift. Now he was ready to take on the world all over again.

chapter eight

BUSY BEING BORN, BUSY DYING

Kafkaesque

Immediately after the Democratic National Convention came to a bloody conclusion and the smell of tear gas cleared, Abbie had no doubt he would be indicted on conspiracy charges for his role during the disturbances. FBI agents had knocked on his door to ask him about Chicago, and rumors were flying about the official investigation. As early as September 9, 1968, less than two weeks after the last day of protest, a grand jury under the tutelage of Federal Judge William Campbell, a Democrat and a good friend of Mayor Daley's, began to focus on the role of the radicals, rather than the police, in the Chicago riots. The testimony of witnesses was secret, of course, but word spread quickly through the movement that indictments were imminent. Radicals looked forward, albeit apprehensively, to a new round of confrontation, this time in court.

Before the end of October, 1968, FBI director J. Edgar Hoover announced that the government was going to prosecute twenty leaders of radical groups and organizations. In his view, "a successful prosecution . . . would be a unique achievement for the Bureau." Moreover, Hoover argued that a big conspiracy trial would "seriously disrupt and curtail the activities of the New Left." It was not until March 1969, however, that Judge Campbell's grand jury finally announced its indictments against Abbie and his seven codefendants: Jerry Rubin, Tom Hayden, Dave Dellinger, Bobby Seale, Rennie Davis, John Froines, and

Lee Weiner. The Chicago Eight would become the best known of all the sixties radicals who went on trial, including the Boston Five, the Oakland Seven, and the New York Panther Twenty-One.

The long delay was largely the doing of U.S. Attorney General Ramsey Clark, who was uncomfortable with the anti-riot provisions of the Civil Rights Act of 1968, under which the Chicago Eight were prosecuted, and intolerant of the idea of a big "conspiracy" trial of sixties activists. Clark had engineered the prosecution of the Boston Five, including Dr. Benjamin Spock and William Sloane Coffin, the Yale University chaplain, on charges of conspiracy to "counsel, aid, and abet young men to violate the draft laws." But soon thereafter he had experienced a profound change of heart. Not only had he opposed sending federal troops to Chicago in August of '68, but he'd also turned down FBI requests to wiretap the telephones of known radicals, including many of the Chicago Eight. He openly disapproved of Judge Campbell's blatantly vindictive grand jury. For months he stalled the investigative process, until President Johnson complained about his "hemming and hawing." As soon as Clark was no longer at the helm in the Department of Justice, having been replaced by John Mitchell, President Nixon's law-and-order appointee, the domestic war against the movement intensified, and the political climate darkened. There had been government attempts to chill activists under Kennedy and Johnson, of course, but they took on a new and more menacing direction under Nixon.

In the fall of 1968, Abbie had naively suggested that Richard Nixon would make a better president than Hubert Humphrey, but soon after Nixon took office, he did an about-face. "Nixon is no improvement over Humphrey," he told Jaakov Kohn, editor of the *East Village Other*. Like many others in the movement, he was afraid that fascism American-style was in the offing, and that California governor Ronald Reagan—"the fascist gun in the west," Abbie called him—and President Richard Nixon were its smiling emissaries. Early in 1969 the White House proposed two pieces of legislation, both of which Abbie took to be ominous: the "no knock" provision, which would allow police officers to enter private homes without warning; and "preventive detention," which would deny bail to anyone who had been charged with (but not convicted of) a crime if law enforcement agents thought the person was likely to commit another crime. North Carolina Democratic senator Sam Ervin, later of Watergate fame, complained that preventive detention "smacks of a police state" and appeared to denote a "Gestapo mentality in the White House."

To Abbie, the wiretapping of activists, the appointment of conservative judges to the Supreme Court, and the Chicago conspiracy indictments themselves were "all part of a wave of repression." As he put it, "Richard Nixon wants to put an end to demonstrations." In fact the new administration in Washington, D.C., didn't disguise its vendetta against the movement. In the winter of 1969, six weeks after being installed as attorney general, John Mitchell told representatives of the media that he was ready to prosecute "hard-line militants" who "crossed state lines to incite riots." Richard Kleindienst, the deputy attorney general, told a group of Harvard Law School alumni, "You've got to crack down." As *New York Times* reporter Tom Wicker observed, Kleindienst's words "could have been the motto of Nixon's White House." So the crackdown came as little, if any, surprise to Abbie and the Chicago Eight, all of whom had long histories of activism.

Jerry Rubin had been on the barricades and had run for mayor of Berkeley as a peace candidate. Tom Hayden had been at the forefront of the civil rights movement in Mississippi and had been working as a community organizer in Newark, New Jersey, when the riots took place in 1967. Dave Dellinger had spent most of his adult life in the pacifist and antinuclear movements. Rennie Davis had helped to shape SDS. Abbie Hoffman had taken a firm hand in pushing the apolitical hippies into the cauldron of political rebellion. Moreover, the defendants had all been at the Pentagon, at Columbia, and, of course, in Chicago in 1968. They were all effective public speakers and persuasive pamphleteers, and they each had a significant following, whether in the movement or in the counterculture.

The only real surprise among the defendants was Bobby Seale. Granted, he'd made two militant speeches in Chicago and had suggested that armed self-defense was an appropriate response to police harassment. But he'd only been in Chicago for a couple of days, and he'd had no substantial contact with the organizers of the protest other than Jerry Rubin. Seale's presence made perfect sense from the government's point of view, however: he was the charismatic chairman of the

Black Panther Party, the largest and the most militant African American political organization in the country. Seale had been indicted because he represented the black liberation struggle. Indicting him was, in J. Edgar Hoover's eyes, an effective way to crack down on a generation of black men who were proud of their rebelliousness.

One of the earliest strategy meetings of the Chicago Eight took place at the Black Panther Party office in Oakland, California. "It was an opportunity for the defendants to get to know Bobby Seale," Stew Albert remembered. Abbie was there, along with Tom Hayden and Jerry Rubin. "The main thing that we agreed on was that Charles Garry would be their number one attorney and that the white defendants would do nothing to embarrass Seale or the Panthers," Albert recalled. Garry had successfully defended Huey P. Newton, Minister of Defense of the Black Panther Party, whom Eldridge Cleaver, the Panther minister of information, had described as "the baddest motherfucker ever to step inside of history." Newton had shot and killed an Oakland police officer, and though he was charged with murder, Charles Garry persuaded a jury to return a guilty verdict on the lesser charge of voluntary manslaughter. After three years in jail and two more trials, Newton's conviction was reversed and he was released, and both he and Garry were touted as heroes of the revolution. Garry had also successfully defended the Oakland Seven, a group of militant antiwar activists who had been arrested during Stop the Draft week in October 1967, but who didn't go on trial until January 1969. As Frank Bardacke, probably the most articulate of the defendants, pointed out in his essay "The Oakland 7," Charles Garry had turned the trial "into a teach-in on free speech, police brutality, and the war in Vietnam."

Abbie and Jerry couldn't help but admire "Charlie," as they called him, but they also had strong reservations about him. After all, Charlie had insisted that the Oakland Seven wear jackets and ties whenever possible, behave themselves in the courtroom, and refrain from calling liberal judge George W. Phillips a "pig." As Yippies, Abbie and Jerry didn't want a boring courtroom teach-in, and they didn't want to take back seats at the defense table while Charlie strutted his stuff. Moreover, they didn't want a repeat of the inglorious trial of the Boston Five, though they admired the venerable Dr. Spock, who'd wanted to use the "Nuremberg defense" and argue in court that U.S. government officials were guilty of "war crimes," "crimes against peace," and "crimes against humanity." If Spock had had his way, the crucial issue in the case would have been the illegality of the war in Vietnam, not his own violation of the draft laws. But federal judge Francis Ford, who was eighty-five years old and bound by an ironclad sense of the law, refused to allow the Nuremberg defense. Spock and his codefendants accepted Ford's ruling without much of a fight, and for the most part the trial bogged down in technical details. As the Reverend William Sloane Coffin had observed, it became "dismal, dreary, and above all demeaning to all concerned," which was precisely what Abbie and Jerry wanted to avoid at their trial.

In hindsight, Spock argued that the Boston Five had erred in not using the mass media to appeal to the hearts and minds of the American people. "Since we had been denied every single day in court any opportunity to say why we were in it or where we thought we were right, we should have had a press conference every day at the end of court to explain our point of view." Spock's words encouraged Abbie and Jerry to turn to the media, especially TV, and take their case to the people. Long before the Chicago trial began, it became clear that the Yippie defendants weren't going to act like the Boston Five or the Oakland Seven; they were going to be "cut-ups," whether Charlie liked it or not. "This is the greatest honor of my life," Rubin proclaimed in "I Accept! I Accept! I Accept!" an article that appeared in the *New York Rat* immediately after the indictments came down. To serious members of the New Left, Rubin was preposterous. No one was supposed to be happy to be indicted by the government, yet Rubin was ecstatic. "I join the list of outstanding world figures who have crossed state lines to create disturbances: The Beatles, Elvis Presley, the late Marilyn Monroe, rock bands, the President of the United States and Joe Namath," he exclaimed.

Abbie was no less irreverent than Jerry, and in no way willing to lower his impious profile. On March 21, the day after the conspiracy indictments were announced, he took part in a lively demonstration outside the hallowed offices of the *New York Times*. For years he'd railed against the institution for being fuddy-duddy; it didn't even have the comics, he complained. Now he ridiculed the *Times* as America's "Security Blanket," the newspaper that gave the nation a false sense of comfort. What's more, he exclaimed, it was just another part of the military-industrial complex, just another multinational corporation that didn't care about its own workers. To show his disdain for the *Times,* he offered pedestrians sheets of toilet paper made from newsprint.

A few weeks later—on April 9, 1969—Abbie performed his own special antics when he appeared in Federal Court before Julius Jennings Hoffman, the presiding judge in the Chicago Conspiracy Trial, a seventy-three-year-old former corporate lawyer who had a reputation as a liberal. When Abbie arrived in Judge Hoffman's courtroom on the twenty-third floor of the Federal Building, he wore a Chicago policeman's shirt and a mischievous grin on his face. Listening to the "mumbo jumbo" indictment on charges of conspiracy and intent to cause a riot was like entering the world of surrealist fiction, he explained to friends and colleagues in the movement. It was like being in Franz Kafka's *The Trial.*

When Abbie, Jerry, and Lee Weiner entered pleas of "not guilty," they clenched their fists and raised them above their heads, thereby serving notice that they were not going to act "like good little boys," as Dr. Spock had described his own behavior and that of his codefendants at their trial. Despite his resolute "not guilty" plea in open court, Abbie felt profoundly ambiguous about his relationship to the law before, during, and after the trial. As reported by John Schultz in *The Chicago Conspiracy Trial,* Abbie remarked, "I don't know whether I'm innocent or guilty." Sometimes he felt like changing his plea and blurting out "I am Guilty," or "Guilty due to sanity." Then, too, he couldn't make up his mind if a conspiracy did or didn't exist and who the real conspirators were. "When you get down to it, we are guilty of being members of a vast conspiracy," he wrote just before the trial began. But soon after the trial was over, he noted emphatically, "I think the chief aspect of our case was that we didn't have a conspiracy." On still other occasions he played radical psychologist and said that the conspiracy charges were psychological projections of the guilt felt by the real criminals, who lurked in Washington, D.C., and in Mayor Daley's office. "If there was a conspiracy on the part of the government and the city officials . . . to form violence, they would have to project that on someone else," he explained. "They would have to call the victims the conspiracy that fostered the violence."

At the preliminary hearing in April, Judge Hoffman made it clear that he intended to control his courtroom and make the defense lawyers toe the line. Garry was unable to make his scheduled appearance, so arguments for the defense were left to William Kunstler, who had made his mark as a lawyer for Dr. Martin Luther King, Jr., and to Michael Kennedy, a young, brilliant San Francisco attorney. "Many of us consider this one of the most important trials in the history of the United States," Kunstler said. "It is the right of free speech and dissent in this country that is on trial here." From the start, Kunstler made it clear the First Amendment was *the* crucial issue.

Marijuana, Mao Tse-tung, and Lenny Bruce

Shortly after his court appearance in Chicago, Abbie set off for Austin, Texas, to attend a regional SDS conference. He hoped to drum up support for "The Conspiracy," as the defendants proudly called themselves, and to make it clear that cultural revolution was going to be on trial. He immediately discovered that SDS had no intention of making the Chicago trial a cause célèbre or of adopting cultural revolution as its rallying cry, which sent him into one of his intermittent rages against left-wing activists. When he returned to New York he wrote a furious attack on SDS that was published in the *East Village Other* under the title "Fuck the Vanguard, Power to the People." Instead of "Fuck the System," his new rallying cry was "Fuck SDS."

The Chicago Eight were facing "an extremely vicious attack by the power structure," Abbie wrote, whereas SDS hadn't even been scratched by the powers that be. By his calculation, SDS's decision not to rally behind The Conspiracy was evidence that it was racist, elitist, reformist, and just plain "chicken shit." Whenever the organization had been faced with a confrontation, such as at the Pentagon or at the Democratic National Convention in Chicago, it had collapsed "in the protective arms of the establishment," Abbie insisted. SDS theoreticians spent too much time analyzing the "why" of revolution and not enough time on the nuts and bolts of "how" to make it, he charged. As far as Abbie was concerned, SDS's biggest problem was that it failed to appreciate the significance of the "new cultural revolution [that was] taking place among young whites." The hippie movement wasn't "a rebellion of rich white kids," he proclaimed, but "classless" and "international in character." It was the only genuine movement around.

SDS's Jeff Shero, a young activist from Texas, rallied to the organization's defense and lashed out at Abbie in an article entitled "Echoes in the Asylum." Shero was still bitter about Abbie's troublesome role during the Democratic National Convention and accused him of whipping up hysteria in the streets, thereby guaranteeing that hundreds of "naive souls" would be "trapped and beaten" by the police. Moreover, Abbie had ignored SDS's radicalizing role, Shero insisted; for most of the sixties, the organization had been "the principal force in mobilizing white Americans." Abbie's politics were deeply flawed, Shero claimed, because he was a "showman" and "an individual spokesman" isolated from the people. Moreover, he was "an egocentric media freak without responsibilities." That attack seemed to sting Abbie; soon afterward he insisted that "like almost everyone in the left I have a genuine suspicion of the mass media and especially television." Yet he couldn't resist the allure of TV.

In the spring of 1969 Abbie came under sharp criticism from other quarters besides SDS. Feminists charged him with being a male chauvinist pig; he promptly replied, rather pathetically, that he "helped paint the apartment," "cooked a lot," and took out the garbage. He admitted that he still referred to women as "chicks," but what the hell did it matter? He really did regard them as equals, he asserted in movement groups and in his writings. Abbie took women's liberation seriously and genuinely tried to alter his sexism, but his habits were deeply ingrained. While he sometimes took the feminist side, often he cast himself as a victim of feminism and felt sorry for himself. After all, he was "white and male and over thirty," he pointed out, and practically a has-been in a movement that increasingly valued youth, the Third World, and women.

Unfortunately, his fellow white men were also raking him over their own ideological coals. In the March/April issue of *Liberation,* Dave Dellinger, one of the Chicago Eight, complained that Yippie culture was "distressingly like the mirror-image of the culture" it claimed to reject. Abbie and Jerry had "creative insights," Dellinger allowed, but they also exhibited large doses of "ego-tripping," "fantasies," and "bullshit—which in the end get in the way of making a revolution." In the same issue Marty Jezer, a long-time pacifist, noted that the Yippies "suffered from schizophrenia" and that their strategy in Chicago had deteriorated into an "inevitable confrontation with the police." With friends like these, who needed enemies? Abbie moaned.

If anyone wanted evidence of his showmanship, egomania, or creativity, it could easily be found on television in the spring of 1969. The conspiracy indictment had turned him into an instant mass media celebrity, and he accepted an invitation to appear on the *Merv Griffin Show*, a popular TV talk show. From Abbie's point of view, his appearance on Griffin's show was a textbook case of how to manipulate the media. But his appearance also suggests some pitfalls in his strategy of revolution by TV. Abbie represented no group, organization, or cause. *He* became the focal point, and *his* battle with the network became more important to him than anything else. When he testified before the Walker Study Team in the fall of 1968, he explained that "the thing that fucks up a movement right off is the thing that the press and the establishment try to do, which is to constantly focus on leaders, create leaders." Now he was going against his own better judgment by allowing the media to focus on him.

When he walked onto the set of the Merv Griffin show, Abbie wore a fashionable suede jacket, and with his curly hair piled high above his head, he looked as hip as could be. In one hand he carried a copy of Mao Tse-tung's *Little Red Book* (then all the rage in SDS); in the other hand, a marijuana joint. What he aimed to do symbolically was to marry the New Left advocates of Asian communism to the American drug culture (a marriage that neither the apolitical hippies nor the puritanical Maoists were eager to enter into). After reading passages from Mao and offering the marijuana to Arthur Treacher, Griffin's cohost, he took off his jacket, revealing underneath a shirt made from an American flag. Not surprisingly, the Stars and Stripes turned out to be far more controversial than either Mao or the marijuana, at least to CBS executives. During the show itself, Abbie predicted that his appearance would be carefully "edited," and sure enough, censorship was exercised. When the show was broadcast, a blue screen blocked his image whenever he was on camera.

From CBS's point of view, broadcasting Abbie in an American flag shirt would have been blatantly unpatriotic, and executives wanted no part of it. So TV viewers could hear Abbie, but they couldn't see him, much to his delight. Even better, from his point of view, was the appearance of the American flag in an advertisement that was aired during an intermission. The hypocrisy was there for everyone to see: the flag could be used to sell products, but not to make a political statement.

"Electronic masking" was the term CBS used to describe the process of concealing Abbie's image. He called it "electronic fascism," and he insisted that it proved how much power he possessed. "With a simple shirt I brought the Columbia Broadcasting System to its knees," he boasted. His sudden appearance and swift disappearance on the Merv Griffin show made him feel that he inhabited the best of all possible worlds. He was far too popular to be ignored by the media, yet too dangerous to be allowed to reach the American public unadulterated.

The night the show aired, Abbie invited a group of friends to join him and Anita in their new rooftop apartment at 114 East Thirteenth Street for a party that included marijuana and color television. Watching his own image vanish from the screen was like "watching his own death," he insisted, and though "it was scary," he seemed to enjoy the spectacle of his own martyrdom on the cross of television. His image gave him life, he seemed to be saying. To take away the image would be to kill him.

In the summer of 1969 he was in fact preoccupied with his own death and dying. "It was a depressing summer of sitting in courtrooms and waiting for the Big Trial to begin in Chicago," he wrote in *Woodstock Nation,* which was published on the eve of the trial and which offered an accurate reflection of his suicidal state of mind. "I spent a lot of time discussing my arrests and wondering if I would end up like Lenny Bruce," he explained. As usual, it was the sitting and the waiting—not the chaos or the manic intensity—that threatened to kill his spirit. For years Abbie had celebrated Lenny's comic genius and irreverent creativity, but now all he could think of was his "anguish" and his "tragic death" of a drug overdose. "The picture of him lying naked on the bathroom floor . . . flashed through my mind each day," Abbie wrote. A few years later, when he learned that Bob Fosse was directing a movie about Lenny, Abbie tried to land the part, convinced that no one else could play the final bathroom scene as well as he could.

Pilgrims or Lemmings?

In the summer of 1969, what also played over and over in Abbie's mind was Bob Dylan's line "He not busy being born / Is busy dying" from the song "It's Alright, Ma (I'm Only Bleeding)." Abbie was afraid that he was becoming obsolete, that history had left him high and dry. For most of his life—from high school and college to the Lower East Side and Chicago—he had continually given rebirth to himself, taking on new identities as quickly as the zeitgeist changed. Now he was stuck in old routines and old poses that felt like a living death. What also distressed him were the ways that "the Big Boys" at the Bank of America, Dow Chemical, and AT&T appeared to be adapting to the cultural revolution. Corporate executives weren't "schmucks like J. Edgar Hoover and his pack of dumb dinosaurs," Abbie wrote in *Woodstock Nation*. "They were prepared to do anything to stay in business, even grow their hair a little longer and put on some beads."

As he noted, the word "revolution" itself was no longer un-American. In fact, it appeared in prime-time advertisements for products like underarm deodorant and toothpaste. He argued proudly that his own book, *Revolution for the Hell of It,* had helped to Americanize and popularize the word and concept of "revolution," and he was probably right. But now he was afraid that the transformation had gone too far and had lost its punch. Everyone was appropriating the word. By the early 1970s, he would find it even more difficult to tell hip capitalists from hippie revolutionaries since they both wore the same brands of faded jeans, uttered the same countercultural phrases ". . . man," bought the same long-playing albums, smoked the same marijuana, and enjoyed the same liberated sexuality. Just what kind of Pandora's box had the hippie rebellion opened? he asked himself. And what had his role been?

Like many others in the movement, Abbie had banked on the incorruptibility—the purity—of the sixties revolution, and like many others he was shocked to see that the "revolution was becoming a saleable commodity," as he put it in *Woodstock Nation*. The whole counterculture was in danger of being gobbled up by big business. Rock 'n' roll *had been* subversive: it had introduced young whites to the music of black America. It was still wonderful, Abbie allowed. He loved Janis Joplin, who sang with the "sadness of Billie Holliday and Bessie Smith," and he had to admit that the Doors had expressed his own political views better than any left-wing organization had done. "We want the world and we want it NOW!" the Doors sang; those words, he said, summed up his own sentiments.

But rock 'n' roll was now an empire within the American empire;

rock stars belonged to the "hipoisie" and lived in a "za-za" world far removed from their adoring fans. For Abbie, the bottom line was that rock 'n' roll no longer rocked the boat. Cultural co-optation—which he defined as "being lured to your doom by the power structure"— gave him a "headache," he complained. But so did those New Left purists who accused *him* of selling his radical soul to Random House and MGM.

Abbie wasn't sure where he stood anymore. "During the past few years," he wrote in *Woodstock Nation,* "I have straddled the line between 'the movement' and 'the community,' between 'the left' and 'the hip,' between the world of 'the street' and the world of 'media.'" He was still straddling the line, still perched on the fence, he said, but he felt increasingly lonely and fragile. "I have doubts that I can go on balancing these forces in my head," he added. He was coming apart at the seams, and so was everything around him, or so it appeared to him. The movement was imploding, and SDS was in the throes of fierce factional fighting. At the SDS national convention in Chicago in June, 1969, which he described as "a bummer," rival ideological camps shouted hostile slogans at one another, each claiming to be more revolutionary than the next.

Abbie enjoyed the SDS crack-up. "We have come to praise SDS, not to bury it," he exclaimed on his arrival at the convention, in a parody of Mark Antony's speech from Shakespeare's *Julius Caesar.* His not-so-hidden message was that SDS ought to be buried. But the disintegration of the counterculture was much more distressing to Abbie. The hippies who had pioneered the Summer of Love had moved to the countryside and abandoned the political struggle, he lamented. The Lower East Side, where he still lived and which he still loved, was now a wasteland. The hippie dream had turned to ashes.

It was a summer of depression for Abbie, but it was also a summer of anger. His anger exploded everywhere. After watching the Beatles movie *Yellow Submarine,* which he called "pure cotton candy bullshit," he launched a tirade against "love" and against the Beatles, too, whom he'd adored during the Summer of Love. "They say all you need is love," he sneered in an interview published in the *East Village Other* in May 1969. "I think they put a definition on love which is not my definition of love. I think killing a cop can be an act of love."

At the end of July, when Neil Armstrong, the commander of the Apollo 11 mission, became the first man to set foot on the moon, Abbie fumed. Armstrong was "a number one all-Amerikan cracker," he exclaimed in *Woodstock Nation*. He watched the historic moon landing on TV, in the company of Anita and friends. Though he liked the "special effects," which he thought would have made Walt Disney envious, he complained about the way the landing was commercialized and politicized. Planting the "fuckin' flag" on the moon sent him over the edge. That Norman Mailer was writing about the space program (in a book that would be called *Of a Fire on the Moon*) struck him as an evasion of moral responsibility.

Abbie's cycles of anger and depression culminated at the Woodstock Festival of Peace and Music, which he celebrated in *Woodstock Nation* as "the first attempt to land a man on the earth." For the most part, Woodstock is now remembered as a majestic event, a triumph of the human spirit, and a glorious open-air concert. For three days hundreds of thousands of people lived side by side, shared food and marijuana, and listened to Jimi Hendrix, Janis Joplin, Richie Havens, The Who, Sly and the Family Stone, and Grace Slick, to name just a few of the outstanding lineup of performers.

In the eighties, Abbie would celebrate Woodstock as the musical event of the century, but at the time he felt profoundly ambivalent about it. When he left Woodstock to return to New York, he would be unsure what had happened there and how he felt about it. Though he didn't have clear answers, he would ask all the right questions—much the same questions that radicals were asking all that summer. "Were we pilgrims or lemmings?" Abbie would wonder. "Was this really the beginning of a new civilization or the symptom of a dying one? Were we establishing a liberated zone or entering a detention camp?" Part of him believed that Woodstock was a dead end, that the thousands of people who flocked there were self-destructive, and that festivals like Woodstock would fetter rather than free a whole generation. "You could sure come away pessimistic about the future," he would write after the event was over.

One of his most paranoid fears was that rock festivals were the sixties equivalent of German concentration camps. "When the Jews entered the ovens at Dachau, the Nazi played hip Wagner music, passed out flowers, and handed out free bars of soap," he would write in *Woodstock Nation*. Now that America, or "Amerika" in his spelling, was turning fascist, weren't music festivals a beautiful way to tranquilize the hippies? he wondered. It seemed likely that if they were given rock 'n' roll, flowers, and a little freedom in a big outdoor compound, they'd be unlikely to protest anything, even their own paisley cages. Despite his doubts, Abbie persuaded himself that "smoke-ins, fuck-ins, [and] liberated zones" simply could not be absorbed into American society. In the end he decided Woodstock was subversive. It was "functional anarchy [and] primitive tribalism"; it was the start of the "Aquarian Age." "I vote THUMBS UP!" he would write near the end of *Woodstock Nation*. "Right on! . . . I'm happy and smilin. Cocksure of the future."

Woodstock was the event that would spur him on to define himself as an outlaw and cultural revolutionary. It would also help to prepare him and his lawyers (especially Lenny Weinglass, a friend of Hayden's from Newark, New Jersey, who accepted Abbie's invitation to attend the Woodstock Festival) for the upcoming Chicago Trial. As Abbie would explained in the single most important passage in *Woodstock Nation*, "When I appear in the Chicago courtroom, I want to be tried not because I support the National Liberation Front—which I do—but because I have long hair. Not because I support the Black Liberation Movement, but because I smoke dope. Not because I am against a capitalist system, but because I think property eats shit. Not because I believe in student power, but that the schools should be destroyed. Not because I'm against corporate liberalism, but because I think people should do whatever the fuck they want, and not because I am trying to organize the working class, but because I think kids should kill their parents. Finally, I want to be tried for having a good time and not for being serious."

After a confrontation with the promoters of the Woodstock Festival, Abbie received space to publish an insightful article in the official program, entitled "The Hard Rain's Already Fallin'," which made the point that "the authorities want to destroy our cultural revolution in the same way they want to destroy our political revolution." Irked by the notion that masses of young people were going to get together to hear music, get high, and have fun in the sun, Abbie saw it as his mission to wake them up and convert them. "The revolution is more than digging rock

or turning on," he sermonized. "The revolution is about coming together in a struggle for change. It is about the destruction of a system
based on bosses and competition and the building of a new community
based on people and cooperation." Abbie sounded like a Marxist. Indeed, he claimed that he was for "soulful socialism," as Stew Albert
called it: for a classless society that provided for the spiritual as well as
the economic needs of its citizens. At Woodstock, however, no one
would have recognized him as a socialist of any stripe. For the entire
festival he was high on marijuana, hashish, Darvon, and bad acid. The
drugs colored his perception of the event and affected his behavior,
which was bizarre to say the least. At Woodstock he felt oddly alienated
from everyone and experienced a devastating sense of "loneliness . . . in
a crowd of 300,000." The acid also seemed to bring out his latent racism, sexism, and preoccupation with violence.

At one point he thought that he saw an "African," as he put it,
"throw a spear at me like in the movie 'Bwana Devil.'" It was an odd
and disturbing image. Then, while wandering aimlessly under the
stage, he thought that someone came at him with a gun. There was also
the "naked dude" he saw "humping" a "weird-looking blond chick"
from behind; he looked back at them and thought that the "dude" was
Elvis Presley and the "chick" was Sharon Tate, the actress who had
just been brutally murdered by Charles Manson and his "family" in
Southern California. At yet another point Abbie had a pornographic
vision of a beautiful but deadly-looking young woman who appeared,
he said, as though she had stepped out of the *New York Times Magazine.*
She was, Abbie wrote in *Woodstock Nation,* "a long wisp of a creamy
thing with straight black hair down to her ass and long eyelashes that
fluttered when she perked her thin ghost-like lips." When he suggested
"let's . . . . . . f. . . . u. . . . c. . . . k," she replied, "you've come a long
way, baby . . . but you've still got a long way to go."

Given the fact that he was high on drugs for three days, it's a wonder
that he was able to achieve as much as he did at Woodstock. With Wavy
Gravy and other members of the Hog Farm, he set up a makeshift
hospital staffed with doctors and nurses that helped dozens of people
who took bad acid and were trapped in nightmarish psychedelic trips.
From a hunk of brown canvas he fashioned his own military uniform
and appointed himself "Commander" of the "John Sinclair Hospital,"

as he called it. Later he would say that he reminded himself of "General George Patton inspecting the troops in Normandy" during World War II. In a more tender vein, he also envisioned himself as "Mr. Florence Nightingale of the Flower Children." Abbie also boasted that he was following in his father's footsteps, and that "John would sure be proud of me now." It was a strange but revealing comment and implied that despite all his anger and hostility, he wanted John's approval.

Helping people on bad acid gave Abbie a sense of achievement, but he wasn't content to remain inside the medical tent. He wanted to be on the stage along with the performers whom he adored: Abbie Hoffman wanted to be a star. Little by little he moved closer to the center of activity. For a while he lurked backstage talking to performers. Then for a long time he lingered at the edge of the stage talking to Michael Lang, one of the producers of the event, while muttering to himself and working himself into a frenzy. He was itching to make a speech and to remind the audience that John Sinclair, the leader of the White Panther Party—the Ann Arbor, Michigan, group that had prescribed marijuana and rock 'n' roll as the solution to America's ills—was in jail for doing nothing more than smoking marijuana, as they were doing that very moment. While the British rock group The Who were performing, Abbie finally leapt to his feet and grabbed the microphone. In a voice that he later described as "black-leather acid," he began his speech, but didn't get very far before lead guitarist Peter Townshend attacked him and drove him from the stage.

Almost no one heard his rap about John Sinclair, and no one wanted to hear it. The crowd had come for rock 'n' roll, not speeches—a reality that Abbie didn't want to accept. Still, there were a few people who appreciated his effort to inject a sense of social awareness into the party atmosphere. Music critic Paul Williams insisted in 1993 on National Public Radio's "Talk of the Nation" that "the high point of Woodstock was when Abbie Hoffman grabbed the microphone and gave a spiel about John Sinclair." In *Woodstock Nation,* Abbie described in detail what he called his "battle" with The Who. It was the culminating experience of the entire event, he said, and it symbolized his "amity-enmity attitude toward that particular rock group and the whole rock world in general." Peter Townshend had "clonked" him on the "head with his electric guitar," he wrote. Briefly he'd collapsed on the stage, then he'd risen to his feet in defiance. "There we were shaking fists at each other and yelling," he explained. Townshend shouted "Get the fuck outta here," and Abbie shot back "Fascist pig." Moments later he told producer Michael Lang that Peter Townshend had "tried to kill me."

Years later Abbie insisted that the incident with Townshend had never occurred. He told Joel Makower, who compiled an oral history of Woodstock, that he and Townshend had accidentally "bumped" into one another, and that was all. It was no big deal. But Townshend said, in an interview with *Rolling Stone* reporter Jonathan Cott, that he'd hit Abbie so hard that "he must have felt it for a couple of months." Henry Diltz, the official photographer for Woodstock Ventures, said that he saw Townshend use his guitar "like a bayonet" to jab Abbie in the back, and John Morris, the production coordinator for Woodstock, said that Townshend had "laid him one upside the head with a guitar." In the seventies and eighties Abbie wanted to be remembered as a founding father of the era of sex, drugs, and rock 'n' roll. Making war on Peter Townshend, one of the icons of rock, at the sixties decade's quintessential festival of peace and music, was bad for the image he wanted, so he denied it. Once again, Abbie the spin doctor recast his own history.

With Woodstock behind him, Abbie's mood improved dramatically; now he saw humor almost everywhere, even in suicide. He dedicated *Woodstock Nation* to Lenny Bruce, explaining that suicides always wore a "shit-eatin grin" and that they "fight like hell" even though they're dead.

In preparation for the conspiracy trial, Chris Cerf and Michael O'Donoghue, who would later start the *National Lampoon,* helped Abbie write and design a twenty-four-page color program, which they called "The Official Pogrom." It purported to be a program for a baseball game in which the two opposing teams were the Chicago Conspiracy, who wore red uniforms, and the Washington Kangaroos, who wore red, white, and blue. The cover of the program showed cartoon versions of Hoffman, Rubin, and Hayden standing on the pitcher's mound ready to hurl bombs at Vice President Spiro Agnew, who stood at the plate holding a policeman's truncheon in place of a bat. An umpire wearing a mask and aiming a revolver at the defendants shouted "Play Ball."

Just before the trial began, Abbie and Jerry arrived at O'Hare Airport waving pennants and wearing Chicago Cubs baseball caps as well as buttons that read "Screw Magoo" ("Magoo" was their pet name for Judge Hoffman, who bore an uncanny resemblance to the blind cartoon curmudgeon Mr. Magoo). They belonged to the home team, they said, and they were in town for the "World Series of Injustice." In case that name didn't make the trial sound exciting enough, Abbie explained that it was "going to be a combination Scopes trial, revolution in the streets, Woodstock Festival and Peoples Park, all rolled into one." As it turned out, he wasn't far off the mark.

Indeed, the Chicago Conspiracy Trial would be a *kulturkampf* (culture war), as Dwight Macdonald, one of the grand old men of the American left, called it: "a head on collision, a public confrontation between the extremes of American politics and lifestyle." In that sense it was, as Abbie hoped it would be, very much like the Scopes trial of 1925—the circuslike "monkey trial" in which the advocates of Darwinian theory had confronted the advocates of the Biblical story of creation. In the Scopes trial state's attorney William Jennings Bryan had clashed with Clarence Darrow, the lawyer for John T. Scopes, a high school biology instructor who had been arrested for teaching evolution. Much as the Scopes trial reflected the cultural and intellectual issues of the twenties, the Chicago trial mirrored the lifestyles and values of the sixties.

The Chicago trial was the "crescendo" of 1969, according to Abbie. In many respects it marked the crescendo of the sixties as well, since it brought to a head the ongoing clash between the government, on one hand, and the movement and counterculture, on the other. As defense attorney Leonard Weinglass noted, "The proceedings in Chicago dealt not only with the disturbances at the time of the Democratic National Convention, but focused on and exposed what the United States had actually become by the close of the Decade of Protest."

chapter nine

FIRE IN A CROWDED COURTROOM

The Personal Is Political

Judge Hoffman's Chicago courtroom provided Abbie with the perfect stage and all the ingredients he needed to act out his brand of guerrilla theatre. There was the cantankerous judge himself, who became the symbol of all authority and who played right into Abbie's hands by overreacting to the Yippies, much as the police had done in the streets and parks of Chicago. There were the twelve members of the jury, mostly suburban housewives and widows, who were stand-ins for the American people and whom Abbie tried to seduce into the counter-culture.

There were the friends, relatives, and supporters of the defendants, who packed the gallery and served as a microcosm of the movement and counterculture, which were continuing to grow even as the trial unfolded. There were the representatives of the mass media who reported the proceedings and willy-nilly helped to transform them into a mythic event. There was the ritual of the trial itself, which Abbie, Jerry, and their codefendants mocked from beginning to end, much as they had mocked the Democratic National Convention. There was the testimony of witnesses, most of which focused on the language and gestures of the Chicago Eight during the convention; their testimony provided Abbie with information that allowed him to hone the verbal weapons, body language, and expressions he'd used at the stock exchange, at the Pentagon, and in the streets and parks of Chicago in the summer of 1968.

The Chicago trial allowed Abbie to give one last, enduring performance after years of dress rehearsals. Though he always aimed to make the personal political, he never did so with more panache than at the conspiracy trial. The public and the private selves were as one. There were fathers and sons, sons and fathers, and the trial often seemed to be about those relationships, which was largely Abbie's doing. On the eve of the trial he received a letter from his father, who urged him to behave himself. The senior Hoffman explained to his unruly son that he knew what was best for him. He had "lived through two atrocities of man's inhumanity to man," Johnnie wrote. He had seen the worst of twentieth-century history, but he'd also seen the best because he'd come to America as an immigrant and had reaped the benefits of democracy and capitalism. The United States was "a God-given land," Johnnie told Abbie.

Annoyed by his father's Polonius-like words of caution, he wrote back to say that the atrocities would never have happened if ordinary people had not been intimidated by irrational leaders. The Nazis had *legally* executed six million Jews, Abbie reminded his father. His responsibility, he felt, was not to his own father or to the Hoffmans, but to the family of humanity. If Johnnie thought that resisting illegitimate authority was bad manners, then so be it. Abbie would rather be found guilty of bad manners than be complicit in atrocities, whether in the jungles of Vietnam or the streets of Chicago.

The text and subtext of his correspondence with his father provided him with most of the verbal ammunition he needed to wage cultural war against Judge Hoffman and U.S. attorneys Thomas Aquinas Foran and Richard Schultz. Indeed, he transformed his personal argument with Johnnie into a public debate about good manners and moral integrity, collaboration and confrontation, fascism and democracy. Abbie's dispute with his father inspired him to stage the trial as Jewish theatre, and in fact almost all of the principal characters were Jewish: defense attorneys Weinglass and Kunstler, U.S. attorney Schultz, defendants Rubin and Weiner, and, of course, the two Hoffmans.

Abbie cast himself and his codefendants as the "good Jews" and Julius Hoffman and Richard Schultz as the "bad Jews," who were betraying their own people to the men of German ancestry in power in the White House: Henry Kissinger, Richard Kleindienst, H. R. Haldeman, and John Ehrlichman. Before long the whole country was aware of the Jewish presence in the courtroom. David Duke, a pro-Nazi college student who would later run for office as a right-wing Louisiana politician, picketed the trial with a swastika on his arm and a sign demanding the gas chamber for the defendants. The trial also elicited President Nixon's anti-Semitism, as revealed in transcripts of the White House tapes. "Aren't the Chicago Seven all Jews?" Nixon asked his chief of staff, H. R. (Bob) Haldeman, as though he assumed that Jews and radicals were one and the same. "Davis is a Jew, you know," the president continued. When Haldeman explained that Rennie Davis was definitely not a Jew, Nixon retorted, "Hoffman, Hoffman's a Jew." There was no dispute there. "Abbie Hoffman is and that's so," Haldeman agreed.

Abbie turned his personal conflict with Johnnie into a wider generational conflict between fathers and sons. He cast himself as the archetypal son and Judge Hoffman as the archetypal father. To needle the judge, he boasted that he was "Julius's son," and Judge Hoffman was his "illegitimate father." The fact that defendant and judge shared the same last name was fortuitous, indeed, and Abbie exploited it for all it was worth. Thus, he explained that he was going to change his first name to "Fuck" so that when he took the witness stand to testify, he could swear under oath that he was, in fact, "Fuck Hoffman." Moreover, the younger of the two Hoffmans made much of the forty-odd years separating them in age. Judge Hoffman—or "Julie," as Abbie called him—was so ancient, Abbie explained, that he was from the nineteenth century and thus "beyond the generation gap." He said he felt sorry for the aristocratic judge with the "tired blood" and promised to send him a case of Geritol so that he might regain his youth and vigor.

Opening Skirmishes

When the trial began in September 1969, it wasn't clear what tone would dominate the proceedings. The prosecution had a careful strategy to nail the defendants, and Judge Hoffman and the U.S. attorneys saw eye to eye on almost every point. The defense, however, was in a state of disarray, in part because at the eleventh hour it became apparent that Charles Garry would be unable to appear in court, leaving William Kunstler and Leonard Weinglass holding the legal reins for the Chicago Eight. The defendants themselves were also in a state of disarray because they represented "various kind of politics or life-styles," as Abbie put it, and wanted to make different though not mutually exclusive points. In time Abbie would come to see this diversity as a strength. "The defense became like the building of a huge temple," he would explain shortly after the end of the trial in an interview published in Jonathan Black's *Radical Lawyers*. "Everybody just threw on their pile of garbage. . . . In that situation you get a highly militant defense, a highly complex and varied defense. . . . You get a mess. Everybody can identify with it. Everybody can find that somewhere in the mess is what they like."

But at the start of the trial, the mess seemed overwhelming. Bobby Seale wanted the trial to focus on black issues and the repression of the Black Panther Party. Dave Dellinger, Rennie Davis, Tom Hayden, and John Froines wanted it to be about the war in Vietnam. The Yippies saw the trial as an opportunity to dramatize the cultural divisions in America and to ridicule the judicial system. The defendants all wanted to recreate Chicago 1968 in the courtroom, but they had different ideas about how to do so. Abbie wanted to restage the Festival of Life, while Tom Hayden wanted to repeat the political protest. "There was clearly going to be a conflict," Leonard Weinglass remembered years later. "On the eve of the trial there was a major debate among the defendants about what was going to be the tone that would be taken on the opening day."

On the first day of the trial, Richard Schultz announced that the government would prove the defendants had "conspired together to use state commerce to incite and to further a riot in Chicago." Kunstler countered "that what actually happened in the streets of Chicago was not a riot caused by demonstrators but a riot engineered by the police of this city" and that the "real attack was on the rights of everybody, all of us American citizens, all, to protest under the First Amendment of the Constitution." Weinglass later remembered that Abbie and Jerry were shaken by Kunstler's remarks. "They were furious because Bill gave a First Amendment opening," he recalled. "There was no mention of the counterculture. At lunch they ordered me to give the Yippie opening."

Unlike Kunstler, Weinglass had been to Woodstock, as one of Abbie's guests. He'd listened to the music and heard the cultural vibrations. Though he was closer to SDS than to the Yippies, he was well qualified to present the Yippie point of view. "I became involved with the Chicago Conspiracy case through Tom Hayden," Weinglass recalled. "But I drew closer to Abbie and eventually became more sympathetic to the counterculture." Thus, on the opening day of the trial, Weinglass told the jury, "There was [a] group of people who came here not for the purpose of protest, and not even for the purpose of demonstrating, in fact, but for the purpose of showing the public, and the leaders, and the rulers of this country that were was emerging within the country a new culture, and this group was generally called the Yippies. Now the Yippies came here for a conclave very similar to the one which was widely publicized last month at Woodstock, New York, a conclave which was then to be known as Festival of Life."

In *The Barnyard Epithet and Other Obscenities, New York Times* reporter J. Anthony Lukas divided the trial into five phases. Phase I was "Jelly Beans"; Phase II, "Gags and Shackles"; Phase III, "The Government's Day in Court"; Phase IV, "Sing Along with Phil and Judy"; and Phase V, "The Barnyard Epithet." Lukas's terms capture the dramatic shifts that took place in the courtroom, but they also make the trial seem too much like musical comedy. Granted, there was a great deal that was entertaining at the conspiracy trial. For example, Lukas pointed out that after Mayor Daley took the witness stand, Abbie approached him during a break in his testimony and "in his best Gary Cooper–High Noon drawl said, 'Why don't we settle this here and now—just you and me? The hell with all these lawyers.'" Daley couldn't help but smile. Furthermore, when Dr. Spock showed up in the courtroom to watch bad boys Abbie and Jerry in action, Kunstler suggested that he approach the bench for an introduction. But Judge Hoffman wasn't interested in meeting the celebrated doctor. "My children are already grown," he said.

But beneath the comic one-liners and the continuous spate of cute remarks, there was deep-seated anger and hostility on both sides. The trial might more accurately be broken into three phases: "Opening

Skirmishes," "Scattered Battles," and "Total Warfare." In the first phase from late September until early December, as the government presented its case, a series of police officers, undercover agents, and city officials filed in and out of the courtroom.

Raymond Simon, Corporation Counsel for the City of Chicago and the first prosecution witness, explained to the court that Abbie and Jerry had wanted a permit so that Lincoln Park would be "under their control for what they wanted to use it for." Richard L. Thompson, a Chicago policeman, said that on August 29, 1968, he saw Abbie Hoffman point to Deputy Superintendent of Police James Rochford and heard him say, "'Well you see that cat? When we get up to the top of the hill, if the cat don't talk right, we're going to hold him there and then we can do whatever we want to and the police won't bother us.'" Chicago policeman Frank Riggio testified that Hayden had spat at another police officer and called him a "motherfucker." Riggio said that "all hell broke loose" in Chicago and that the defendants, not the police, were responsible. On November 7, a newsman for Chicago radio station WIND played a tape recording of a speech that Abbie made in Lincoln Park on August 27. "We're never going to retreat," he exclaimed. "We're consistently going to fight for our right to be in that park."

Scattered Battles

During much of the government's presentation of its case the defendants disrupted the proceedings and presented their own agenda. On October 14 Abbie and his codefendants petitioned the court for an adjournment to participate in the Vietnam Moratorium, a national protest against the war. When Judge Hoffman denied the motion, Kunstler argued that the trial was like convention week in August 1968 all over again. Time and time again his clients asked for permission to exercise their Constitutional rights and were rebuffed. On October 15 Kunstler, Weinglass, and the Chicago Eight wore black armbands and displayed the flags of the United States and the National Liberation Front on the defense table. This was the start of the second phase of the trial: "Scattered Battles." Judge Hoffman ordered both flags removed, but Abbie argued that they had a right to display the flags. He grabbed one end of the NLF flag as a marshal grabbed another end, and soon they were in a fierce tug-of-war. The marshal prevailed, and the flag was removed from the courtroom, but as Random House editor Jason Epstein pointed out, Abbie had succeeded in transforming the trial into "a political confrontation between the defendants and the government."

During the first weeks of the trial, Seale was more often engrossed in Frantz Fanon's *Wretched of the Earth* and *The Autobiography of Malcolm X* than in the proceedings at hand. But from October 20 to the end of the month he made repeated motions to be allowed to defend himself since Charles Garry had been unable to appear in court. Judge Hoffman refused his requests, and finally Seale could no longer contain himself. On October 27 he denounced "this racist government with its Superman notions and comic book politics" and added, "we're hip to the fact that Superman saved no black people." Abbie and Jerry upped their antics, too. On Seale's birthday they brought a cake with the inscription, "Free Huey. Free Bobby," but a marshal seized it. "That's a cakenapping," Abbie quipped. The judge escalated the already volatile situation by adding more marshals to the courtroom; their presence gave the distinct feeling of an armed camp. "There's twenty-five marshals in here and they all got guns," Abbie observed. "Two of them are practically in the jury box."

On October 29, when Seale once again demanded the right to defend himself, the marshals forced him to take his seat. Judge Hoffman ordered his hands and feet chained to a metal chair. Moreover, a piece of muslin was crammed into his mouth. When he continued to speak, his mouth was covered with adhesive tape, and his shackles were tightened. Seale struggled with the marshals and was struck in the testicles. "You may as well kill him if you are going to gag him," Abbie said. Judge Hoffman replied, "You are not permitted to address this court, Mr. Hoffman, you have a lawyer," whereupon Abbie said, "This, man, isn't a court. This is a *neon oven*." Kunstler got into the act. "This is no longer a court of order," he exclaimed. "This is a medieval torture chamber."

At the end of the day Seale was carried out of the courtroom, but not before he managed to yell "Cruel and unusual punishment" and "You're a fascist dog, Judge." Abbie noted in his autobiography that

Seale's struggle "was the most remarkable testimony to the human spirit I've been privileged to witness." In a spirit of humility he also said that "what happened to Seale was far and away the most significant episode of the trial" and that it was "Seale's willingness to push things to the limits that broke the trial wide open."

Judge Hoffman severed Seale's case on November 5, and the Chicago Eight became the Chicago Seven. Judge Hoffman also sentenced Seale to four years in prison for contempt of court. When one of Seale's lawyers requested bail, the judge refused. "He is a dangerous man," he said. He "seeks to destroy and overturn the American judicial system."

On November 15, Hoffman, Rubin, Dellinger, and Froines went to Washington, D.C.—with the court's permission—to attend an antiwar rally sponsored by the National Mobilization Committee to End the War in Vietnam. The crowd numbered at least half a million people, which made it the largest political march and rally to take place in the United States. Abbie wasn't impressed by the size of the demonstration, the speeches, or the music, which was provided by folksingers Peter, Paul, and Mary as well as Pete Seeger, who persuaded the crowd to join him in singing "Give Peace a Chance." For Abbie the event was a colossal dud because the speakers were mostly liberal and the crowd was tranquil. Woodstock had been a better peace demonstration, he exclaimed, and the Rolling Stones concert he'd recently attended in Chicago had been more lively. The Mobe demonstration indicated to him that the peace movement had been co-opted, diluted, and defused.

"The system in power can not only deal with such mobilizations, it can actually thrive on them," he wrote in an article entitled "Commuter Protest." What Abbie wanted was more violence. "You cannot express outrage at the policies of the American Government by raising a V sign," he insisted. "Outrage takes on a meaning when you see someone throwing a rock through a window." When several thousand demonstrators attacked the Justice Department with rocks and bottles, he was delighted. Even the tear gas didn't dampen his enthusiasm.

In the fall and winter of 1969–1970 there was more movement violence, especially at an event in Chicago sponsored by the Weathermen called the Days of Rage (Abbie supplied the name). But government violence was far more prevalent and far more outrageous than any violence by protesters. On December 4, 1969, fourteen Chicago police officers, on orders from the Illinois attorney general, broke into a Black Panther apartment and killed two members of the party, Fred Hampton and Mark Clark, while they were asleep. Seven Panthers were arrested and charged with attempted murder, but there were no indictments against the police. Law enforcement officials claimed that the Panthers had shot first, but all of the nearly one hundred bullets, except for one stray, were later proven to be fired from police weapons. As Abbie pointed out, the attack was part of a "nation-wide crack-down on the Panthers."

Along with several thousand citizens, he attended the memorial service for Hampton and Clark. He also visited the murder scene. "There were bullet holes all over the place [and] blood on the mattresses," he said. Now fascism was no longer just a word to be tossed about for effect. "It's an absolute total police state in the black community," he noted in an interview with Lincoln Bergman on radio station KPFA in Berkeley. The deaths of Hampton and Clark sent shock waves across the movement and gave the courtroom proceedings a new sense of urgency. "We want to use the trial to organize around the political repression that's going on, and in particular what's happening to the Black Panther Party," Abbie explained. The deaths of Clark and Hampton, which coincided with the end of the prosecution's case, also raised profound questions among the defendants and their lawyers. "There was a debate about whether we should go on with our case," Weinglass later remembered. "I was in favor of resting. I thought that we could rest and win the case. Moreover, we weren't ready to go forward with our case. We had exhausted ourselves fighting the government. Then Tom Hayden stepped in, and he put the defense case together."

Orphan of America

In December 1969 and January 1970, the cultural revolution of the sixties unfolded at the Chicago Conspiracy Trial. Allen Ginsberg initiated the theme when he took the witness stand. He testified about the police attack on the Yippies in Lincoln Park, read from *Howl* (he pointed a finger at Judge Hoffman as he chanted "Moloch the heavy judger of men!"), talked about the power of yoga, and chanted "Hare Krishna, Hare Krishna, Krishna . . . Hare, Rama, Rama, Rama, Hare, Hare."

For Abbie, Ginsberg's presence was decisive because it depicted "the clash in culture" that existed in America—the world of machinery, death, war, and government versus the world of love, sex, drugs, and rebellion. When Ginsberg read from *Howl,* Abbie broke into tears. It was his all-time favorite poem, he said. It celebrated "holy laughter," the spiritual as well as the comic. Moreover, it was "*the* poem of the Sixties," Abbie exclaimed, though it had been written in the fifties and portrayed a "generation destroyed by madness."

In the aftermath of the Democratic National Convention, there were uneasy feelings between the Yippies and Ginsberg. "Yippie . . . was a poetic creation but it wasn't on a high order of poetry because it was artificial," Ginsberg had explained in an interview with Jaakov Kohn published in the *East Village Other.* "Take the military imagery the Yippies employed. I don't like the toy guns. This is silly yet pathetic." Ginsberg said that the high point of convention week in Chicago had been a mellow gathering of Yippies, McCarthy people, and blacks in Grant Park. "There was an almost psychedelic sense of liberation of consciousness. It was like being high on yoga," he said. Ginsberg brought much the same peaceful perspective to the trial. One morning while he was on the stand, Kunstler and Judge Hoffman began to argue about the length of the lunch recess, and others joined in the noisy debate. Immediately Ginsberg began to chant "O-m-m-m-m-m-m-m-m, O-m-m-m-m," and, as Kunstler observed, "the Babel of voices miraculously fell silent."

That afternoon, U.S. attorney Thomas Foran cross-examined Ginsberg and made sure the jury knew that he was a homosexual. Foran asked him if he had kissed Abbie when they had met one another during the Democratic National Convention. "Yes," Ginsberg replied. Next Foran asked, "Is he an intimate friend of yours?" Ginsberg replied, "I felt very intimate with him. I saw he was struggling to manifest a beautiful thing, and I felt very good towards him." Foran asked him to read his short poem "The Night-Apple," which includes the lines "faces urine sperm / saliva all one / odor and moral taste," and to say what it meant. "It is a description of a wet dream," Ginsberg explained. In open court, Foran couldn't directly condemn homosexuals and homosexuality, but when the trial was over, he no longer held back. "We've lost our kids to the freaking fag revolution," he told the Loyola Academy Booster Club.

At the end of Ginsberg's testimony, Abbie felt that he and his codefendants had crossed a great divide. "The eight of us are already feeling our way into the Seventies with different attitudes," he said during his interview on radio station KPFA in Berkeley. Now, more than ever before, he was convinced of the need for "revolutionary violence and . . . cultural revolution," he said, and he emphasized both when he took the witness stand and became the star of the show. As Dwight Macdonald noted, Abbie's testimony was "the crux of the trial, the most extensive and intense expression of the new-radical style. It's also extremely amusing and penetrating; Abbie combines wit, imagination and shrewdness."

Weinglass later recalled some of the problems Abbie faced during testimony. "In *Revolution for the Hell of It,* he had written about snatching Deputy Superintendent of Police James Rochford. I told him 'they are going to come at you and say that you were attempting to incite a kidnapping or an assault on the police.'" Abbie wasn't worried. As far as he was concerned, his comments about Rochford—whose name he pronounced "Roquefort" and whom he described as the "big cheese"—were "within the bounds of American humor." Abbie suggested that Groucho Marx testify on his behalf, and he persuaded Weinglass to try to recruit the veteran comedian. "I called Groucho and he seemed willing to testify," Weinglass said. "But [then] he said, 'Hey this judge is sending people to prison. I'm too old to become a homosexual.'" Even without Groucho in his corner, Abbie was optimistic. As Weinglass remembered it, Abbie said, "When I am finished testifying, that jury isn't going to say send that man to prison; they're going to say send that boy to camp."

On December 24, the day he began his testimony, Abbie put on an extraordinary theatrical performance. J. Anthony Lukas noted that Abbie's "eyes mischievously roved over the courtroom." And he added that he couldn't help "winking, sighing, gasping, stretching, waving, making eyes at the judge and the jury, and hugely enjoying the whole thing." When he raised his arm to be sworn in, he made a fist to signify his defiance of authority, and after he took the oath he made a fist again, all the while exchanging furtive glances with friends as though everyone *was* a part of an immense conspiracy. His name was "Abbie," he said; that in itself was a declaration of his independence and a refusal to play by the assistant U.S. attorney's rule that everyone in the courtroom have a last as well as a first name. "It isn't Abbie," Richard Schultz told the judge. "He is a 33-year-old man. His name is Mr. Hoffman." But Judge Hoffman gave up on that point. "There is nothing very much I can do about it at this time," he said. And so Abbie it was.

Abbie explained that he was "a child of the 60s" and "an orphan of America." He lived in Woodstock Nation, which was a country of "alienated young people" that existed as "a state of mind," he said. Borrowing from Malcolm X and black militants in SNCC who had rejected the names that white masters had given their African ancestors, Abbie insisted that Hoffman was his "slave name" and that his "real name" was Shapoznikoff. "I am a cultural revolutionary," he told the court. "A person who tries to shape and participate in the values and mores, the customs, and the styles of living of new people who eventually become inhabitants of a new nation."

On the stand he described his evolution as a cultural revolutionary: his days as a hippie and his meeting with Jerry Rubin, who enabled him to understand that "the war in Vietnam was not just an accident but a direct by-product of the kind of system, a capitalist system in the country." He discussed the formation of Yippie which expressed, he said, "in a kind of slogan and advertising sense the spirit that we wanted to put forth in Chicago, and we adopted that as our password, really." Abbie repeated the gist of his Yippie speeches in Chicago: "I said that fun was very important, too, that it was a direct rebuttal of the kind of ethics and morals that were being put forth in the country to keep people working in a rat race."

Then Abbie recounted the preparations for the Yippie demonstrations in Chicago and described what happened on the streets and in the parks. "The decision to drive people out of the park in order to protect the City was about the dumbest military tactic since the Trojans let the Trojan horse inside the gate," he exclaimed. With great enthusiasm he went on to describe the attack that took place in Lincoln Park on the opening day of the convention, making Chicago sound like an epic battle in which he was the Homeric hero. He was just as comfortable in the New Testament as in the Greek classics. He told the jury that he had explained to a crowd of demonstrators, "you should keep in mind a quote from a two-thousand-year-old Yippie with long hair named Jesus who said that when you march into the dens of wolves you should be as harmless as doves and as cunning as snakes." (The Christ analogy caught on in a big way. "Jesus was very much a Yippie," Philip Slater would write in *The Pursuit of Loneliness.*)

The cross-examination came next, but prosecutors made it seem it wasn't so much Abbie who stood on trial as his book, *Revolution for the Hell of It,* which had been reissued by Dial Press and was selling well, especially with all the free publicity the trial offered. Though Assistant U.S. Attorney Schultz read aloud from *Revolution for the Hell of It,* Judge Hoffman prohibited the jurors from reading it.

Abbie probably exaggerated when he said that "aside from a few obscenity trials . . . *Revolution for the Hell of It* is the only published book in the judicial history of the United States used as prosecution evidence in a criminal case," but he wasn't far off the mark. When Schultz directed his attention to a key passage in the book about the "liberated area" and suggested that the Yippies had meant to start the revolution in the park, and from there gradually take over larger and larger spaces, Abbie exploded. "It's not done in the sinister tone you imply, no," he said. "There's an element of joy. That's what 'revolution for the hell of it' means. That's what celebration means. That's what liberation means."

Schultz continued to read from the book and to wave it in the air as though it was a smoking gun. "You created your Yippie myth, isn't that right?" Schultz asked aggressively. "And part of your myth was 'We'll burn Chicago to the ground,' isn't that right?" If Schultz wanted to talk about fire, Abbie would fight fire with fire. "It was part of the myth that there were trainloads of dynamite headed for Chicago," he said. "It was part of the myth that we were going to form white vigilante groups and round up demonstrators. All these things were part of the myth." In case Schultz didn't understand the terms he was using, Abbie explained, "A myth is a process of telling stories, most of which ain't true. . . . It is a subjective reality; the alliance between what is actually happening and between thoughts and wonders and dreams and projections for the future."

Near the end of his cross-examination, he was asked if he had "announced publicly a plan to kidnap the head pig." He insisted that he had not used the word "pig." What he had said was kidnap the "head cheese." Schultz also asked him if he wanted "to smash the system." "Did I write that?" he asked. "No, did you have that thought?" Schultz added. "Yes, I had that thought," he said. But he explained that he *thought* that American society was "going to wreck itself," much as the Democratic Party had wrecked itself, and much as the conspiracy trial was inevitably going to wreck *itself.*

In January the courtroom became the stage for a mini Festival of Life. Pete Seeger took the stand and swore "to tell the truth, the whole truth, and nothing but the truth" in a voice that sounded "almost liturgical," author John Schultz noted in his book on the trial. Judy Collins recited the words to "Where Have All the Flowers Gone?" Arlo Guthrie sang the opening words to "Alice's Restaurant," but Judge Hoffman shouted "No singing. No singing. No singing, sir." Country Joe McDonald tried to sing the words to his popular antiwar song, "And it's one, two, three, what are we fightin' for?" but the judge stopped him. Norman Mailer testified, and so did historian Staughton Lynd, who said that the events that had taken place in Chicago in 1968 were very much like the protests that had taken place in eighteenth-century Boston before the outbreak of the American Revolution.

Former U.S. Attorney General Ramsey Clark took the witness stand, but Judge Hoffman ruled that the jury could not hear him. Seale was brought back to the courtroom to testify, but the jury was not permitted to hear him, either. And when Ralph Abernathy, who had assumed leadership of the Southern Christian Leadership Conference after the death of Martin Luther King, Jr., arrived late, Judge Hoffman would not allow him to take the witness stand.

On January 27, Abbie and Jerry brought the cultural revolution to the Standard Club, Chicago's most elegant Jewish watering hole, where Judge Hoffman ate lunch. At first Abbie wasn't allowed in because he wasn't dressed properly. So he bought a tie at a haberdasher's and borrowed a coat from the barber at the Standard Club. He was then permitted to join Norman Mailer, Jason Epstein, Jules Feiffer, J. Anthony Lukas, Saul Alinsky, Jerry Rubin, and Gordon Sherman, a liberal Chicago businessman, who were all eating together. Judge Hoffman moved to a table that offered a modicum of privacy.

Total Warfare

In the last weeks of the trial "all hell broke loose," as Abbie put it, and predictably it broke loose on the barricades of language. The clashes that took place in the courtroom—like the original clashes in Chicago—were often clashes about words, about what they meant and how they were used. On February 4, after the defense rested its case, the government offered its rebuttal. James Riordan, deputy chief of police, testified that Dellinger had been at the head of a militant group in Grant Park. To Dellinger it sounded like a blatant untruth, and he shouted, "Oh, bullshit." It was as though he'd fired a shotgun in a small chamber. The ever-vigilant Judge Hoffman turned to the court reporter and asked, "Did you get that?" In his more than fifty years at the bar, he said, he had never heard a man use such profanity. "I've never been in an obscene court, either," Abbie shot back.

Newspaper and television journalists could barely believe what they were hearing. Rennie Davis, who was one of the most polite defendants, exploded. "This court is bullshit!" he shouted. And Jerry Rubin added, "Everything in this court is bullshit." Judge Hoffman pounded the gavel and shouted, "This court is recessed" and "Clear the courtroom." Abbie seemed to have waited for this moment and seemed to know exactly what to say. "You're a disgrace to the Jews," he exclaimed. "You would have served Hitler better." He probably couldn't have said anything more hurtful.

Judge Hoffman revoked Dellinger's bail and "remanded him to the custody of the United States Marshall for the Northern District of Illinois for the remainder of the trial." That night the fifty-five-year-old Dellinger was locked up in Cook County Jail while his codefendants met hurriedly to decide how to respond to the crisis. Hayden was for caution in the courtroom, while Abbie and Jerry wanted to disrupt the proceedings and force Judge Hoffman to put all of them in jail, in the hope that the temple of the law would come crashing down around them.

The next day Abbie launched into a verbal assault in Yiddish. "Your idea of justice is the only obscenity in the room," he told Julius Hoffman. "You *schtunk. Vo den? Shanda fur de goyem?*" which he translated as "Frontman for the gentiles?" He also told the judge that he and his codefendants ought to have disrupted the trial "long ago when you chained and gagged Bobby Seale" and that "it's a shame this building wasn't ripped down."

Judge Hoffman urged the marshals to silence Abbie, but only a gag would stop him up now. "You know you cannot win the fucking case," he retorted. "The only way you can is to put us away for contempt. We have contempt for this Court, and for you, Schultz, and for this whole rotten system." "Order him to remain quiet," Judge Hoffman told the marshal. Abbie replied, "Order us? You got to cut our tongues out to order us, Julie. . . . No, I won't shut up. . . . I don't want to be a tyrant and I don't care for a tyrannical system." He seemed to be drawing upon a deep-seated, long-simmering anger. Judge Hoffman maintained his cool. Instead of revoking Abbie's bail, he merely called for a recess. But that wasn't the end of the culture war.

On the next day Abbie and Jerry came to court in judicial robes that covered Chicago police department shirts. Their message was obvious: Judge Hoffman was a cop in disguise, and the courts were in the business of punishment, not justice. "Even I had to applaud their sense of theatre," Hayden wrote. It was Abbie and Jerry's last major guerrilla theatre performance in the courtroom. Shortly thereafter, Judge Hoffman sentenced all of the defendants and their attorneys to prison terms for contempt of court.

William Kunstler received the longest term—four years and thirteen days—while Lee Weiner received the shortest—two months and eighteen days. When Tom Hayden was sentenced to fourteen months and thirteen days, he told the court that the system was collapsing. "Oh, don't be so pessimistic," Judge Hoffman chided him. "Our system isn't collapsing. Fellows as smart as you could do awfully well under the system." The Judge could be a lot more insightful than the defendants credited him with being.

Abbie was sentenced to eight months for contempt: a surprisingly light sentence considering his verbal outbursts and his guerrilla theatre. Before being sentenced, he announced to the court, "I am going to fight for my right to speak in the same way that I fought for my right to speak and assemble in Lincoln Park. . . . We cannot respect a law that is tyranny, and the courts are in a conspiracy of tyranny. And when the law is in tyranny, the only order is insurrection and disrespect, and that's what we showed, and that's what all honorable men of free will will show."

After Judge Hoffman had sentenced the defendants, Kunstler asked that they be released on bail pending appeal, but his motion was denied. "I find they are dangerous men to be at large," Judge Hoffman declared. And so the Chicago Seven went to jail.

On Valentine's Day the jury began its deliberations on the charges of conspiracy and intent to riot, and on Wednesday, February 18, after hours of bitter negotiation, a verdict was reached. Froines and Weiner were found not guilty. Hoffman, Rubin, Hayden, Dellinger, and Davis were found not guilty of conspiracy, but guilty of crossing state lines with the intention of creating a riot. Julius Hoffman sentenced the defendants to the maximum penalty: five years in prison and five thousand dollars in fines. Emotionally wrought and on the verge of tears, Abbie pointed to the pictures of the founding fathers on the wall and then turned to the judge. "I know them better than you, I feel. I know [Samuel] Adams. . . . I played with Sam Adams on the Concord Bridge. I was there when Paul Revere rode right up on his motorcycle and said, 'The pigs are coming, the pigs are coming.' Right into Lexington."

After the impassioned speeches came slapstick comedy and farce. Abbie tried to bargain with the judge: a $3,500 fine would be far more reasonable than $5,000, he argued. Jerry Rubin tried to hand Julius Hoffman a copy of his new book, *Do It,* in which he had written "To Judge Hoffman, top Yippie, who radicalized more young Americans than we ever could." The judge turned it down.

To his friends Abbie quipped, "I don't mind going to prison, but it would be cruel and unusual punishment to be in the same cell with Tom Hayden." Almost everyone seemed to enjoy the joke, but it wasn't meant to be harmless. Fortunately, Tom and Abbie weren't placed in the same cell; after months of growing animosity, Abbie was now furious with Tom, and indeed they might have come to blows. When Tom's hair was cut, he didn't resist—didn't lift a finger in protest—and Abbie never forgave him for that. When the prison barbers tried to cut Abbie's hair, he fought and fought until they stretched him on the floor, and still he managed to kick and scream.

"It was a scalping of hippies," Hayden wrote in his memoir, *Reunion.* Joseph Woods, the brother of President Nixon's personal secretary, Rosemary Woods, displayed the severed hippie hair at a press conference and at a Republican Party rally. "This is just to show you that we

Republicans get things done," he boasted. The crowd loved it. President Nixon invited Judge Hoffman to the White House for breakfast, and soon afterward the Gridiron Club treated him as an honored guest.

All across America there were "The Day After" demonstrations, or TDAs, organized by the defendants themselves and by members of the Chicago Conspiracy staff, who had maintained an office in Chicago through the trial, raised money, and mobilized the faithful. "One of the time twists was that by the time we were on trial in Chicago, we often were indeed intent on inciting riots and disrupting the system by any means," Abbie wrote in his autobiography. "In fact, we used the trial to organize a coast-to-coast riot on the day after we were found guilty."

The most dramatic protest took place at Isla Vista, near the University of California at Santa Barbara, where William Kunstler gave a speech. Nearby, a local branch of the Bank of America was burned to the ground. "Fill the streets so they can see you," Kunstler told a crowd of students and hippies and radicals. Isla Vista activists felt that Kunstler had contributed to the violence, albeit indirectly. "He was sensitive to our frustration and powerlessness," one protester noted. "He understood the need for people to take to the streets." William Kunstler, the "middleman" for the legal system, as he called himself, had become a street radical. He had become Abbie Hoffman, much as Abbie had become William Kunstler, the advocate of the First Amendment.

After nearly five months, nearly two hundred witnesses, more than twenty thousand pages of transcript, and at least two million dollars in taxpayers' money, the trial was over at long last. But the appeals had just begun. They would continue until the end of November 1972, when the U.S. Court of Appeals for the Seventh Circuit reversed the convictions of Hoffman, Rubin, Hayden, Dellinger, and Davis. In an unusual 121-page opinion, the three judges upbraided Judge Hoffman as well as prosecutors Foran and Schultz for failing to make it possible for the defendants to receive a fair trial. Judge Hoffman's "deprecatory and often antagonistic attitude toward the defense is evident in the record from the very beginning," the appeals court ruled. Rarely had federal judges directed such strong language against one of their own.

However, by a two-to-one margin the appeals court ruled that the anti-riot provisions of the Civil Rights Act of 1968 were constitutional, thus leaving open the possibility of a new trial. At first the Justice Department in Washington announced that no decision had been made on whether the government would return to court. But the defendants and their lawyers knew they wouldn't be back in Chicago, at least not on the same old charges. "I don't think the Government will have the indecency to retry these defendants," Kunstler quipped. To retry the Chicago Eight, the government would have had to disclose all wiretaps and electronic surveillance against the defendants, a disclosure it did not want to make. All charges against Bobby Seale were dropped in 1972, and early in 1973 the convictions for contempt against Abbie and his codefendants were also overturned. For the first time in four years, the Chicago Eight were free men.

In the late eighties, Abbie told college students that there had been "excesses" in the sixties, and that if they wanted to understand the era they would do far better to "forget about the excesses of the people in the streets" and to "focus on the excesses of the government." His comment about "excesses" is certainly relevant to both the disruptions at the 1968 convention and the 1969–1970 trial. The protesters were provocative and confrontational in the streets, just as the defendants were outrageous in the courtroom. But it was the police who rioted, and it was the government who violated the rights of the Chicago Eight to a fair trial. The defendants may have been guilty of bad manners, but Julius Hoffman, Thomas Foran, and Richard Schultz were responsible for the travesty of justice that took place in the federal courtroom.

chapter ten

AMERICAN
ARMAGEDDON

What Goes Up

After the trial ended, conflicts between the movement and the government intensified once again. In April 1970, when the U.S. invaded Cambodia, there were bloody protests nationwide against the widening war in Southeast Asia. All that spring, Abbie seemed to be in a state of perpetual motion: traveling, speaking, and agitating for the permanent revolution. "We defy every law in the world, including the law of gravity," he told students at the University of Maryland. "What goes up doesn't necessarily have to come down."

Throughout 1970 and 1971, he upped his verbal barrage against the old order and its figureheads. After Ohio National Guardsmen killed four students at Kent State University in May 1970, he pointed the finger at President Nixon and insisted that Nixon had "pulled the trigger." At a demonstration in Washington, D.C., the Yippies set up a TV in the streets. When the president appeared on the screen, the crowd chanted "Do it! Do It!" In a frenzy, Abbie smashed the image and the TV itself, as though smashing the image would shatter the reality.

The government fought back with more trials, prosecutions, grand juries, arrests, and a verbal offensive of its own. Nixon's vice president, Spiro Agnew, led the administration's rhetorical barrage against the hippies, the Yippies, SDS, the Black Panthers, and the Weathermen. At the same time, Agnew denounced the media for being far too liberal and blamed the older generation, as well—the "affluent, permissive upper-middle-class parents who learned their Dr. Spock and threw discipline out the window—when they should have done the opposite." (Abbie, of course, had been severely disciplined as a child, refuting Agnew's argument about parental authority and permissiveness.)

Of all the radicals, it was Abbie who directly took up Agnew's rhetorical thunderbolts. He went so far as to say, in a speech he gave at the University of Buffalo, that he had "fucked Kim Agnew," the vice president's teenage daughter. Naturally, the vice president responded with even more attacks on the Yippies and on Hoffman in particular, which was precisely what Abbie wanted. "They used to chase guys like him around with butterfly nets," Agnew quipped. "Now they use television cameras." The vice president could be as sharp and as quick-witted as Abbie.

To Allard Lowenstein, an ex–civil rights activist and liberal Democrat who was trying to build a middle ground that was antiwar but not anti-establishment, it was terrifying to think of Abbie Hoffman and Spiro Agnew engaged in a shouting match that polarized the nation. "You have the whole country thinking it's choosing between Abbie Hoffman and Spiro Agnew," Lowenstein complained in a speech he delivered at Stanford University in May 1970. The speech was given shortly after black students had been shot and killed by police at Jackson State in Mississippi and after the Ohio National Guard had killed four Kent State students who were protesting the U.S. invasion of Cambodia.

America would choose Agnew's brand of repression rather than Abbie's path of insurrection, Lowenstein claimed. It wasn't that simple, however. More often than not, the younger generation followed Abbie, while the parents rallied around the vice president. The polarization, antagonism, and fear that had become apparent during the Democratic National Convention in Chicago in 1968 were now almost routine. Domestic crisis had become an everyday occurrence. Lowenstein was not alone in the belief that violent and bloody events like those at Jackson State and Kent State were the order of the day. It seemed to a great many citizens that America was headed toward Armageddon, toward an immense conflagration that would bring the armies of Abbie Hoffman and Spiro Agnew into a final battle with one another and that would result in the ultimate breakdown of society. In 1969, California governor Ronald Reagan exclaimed, "If it takes a bloodbath, let's get on with it. No more appeasement." That view was becoming increasingly popular in the center of the Republican Party, and it didn't frighten Abbie. "An armed struggle is not only inevitable, it is happening, and the Yippies are part of that," he wrote in 1970.

Immediately after the trial, Abbie's daily life wasn't much different then it had been before the trial, although he was an even bigger media celebrity than he had ever been before. He and Anita socialized with John Lennon and Yoko Ono, and famous figures made the pilgrimage to his apartment and sat at his feet. When celebrated playwright Tennessee Williams and radical author Dotson Rader came to visit him, Abbie regaled them with tales of his own courage in the face of the enemy. He also autographed copies of *Revolution for the Hell of It* and *Woodstock Nation*. "He's accepted his death," Williams observed. "He's been to the mountain." Abbie qualified, in his view, as a "saint."

Almost everywhere that Abbie looked, he saw himself in lights and bigger than life. Jann Weiner gave him major coverage in *Rolling Stone*. A *Mademoiselle* article by David Newman and Robert Benton, entitled "Transitional Sex Figures," described him as the "Rhett Butler of the Revolution." In the *New York Times,* Elenore Lester, an instructor at New York University, argued that Abbie was the contemporary American Shakespeare and that he had created "at least five master works of Theatre of the Apocalypse—the Money-Tearing and Throwing at the Stock Exchange, a farce; . . . the Levitation of the Pentagon, an exercise in ritualistic exorcism; . . . the Grand Central Station Massacre, a blood-and-guts melodrama; . . . the Chicago Confrontation, a powerful drama pitting the forces of youth, light, life and love against age, corruption, hate and death, and its epilogue, the Conspiracy Trial, a metaphysical farce in which the defendants played a complex role as devil-martyrs."

Abbie, of course, didn't want the conspiracy trial to be the coda of his life, and he busily searched for new plots, new personas, and new performances. But much of what he was doing looked like an imitation of what he'd already done. He spoke at Columbia University, for example, and urged students to study chemistry and learn how to make explosives, as they did in the Weather Underground. In New Haven,

Connecticut, where Bobby Seale was on trial for the murder of a fellow Black Panther, Abbie urged thousands of demonstrators to riot and to destroy both government and corporate property. In Boston in the spring of 1970 Abbie reminded a defiant crowd gathered in front of the John Hancock Building that New England was "the cradle of liberty" and that "John Hancock . . . was a revolutionary." He asked the demonstrators "Are you ready to rock that cradle, or are you going to cradle that rock?" Hundreds of protesters threw rocks, tied up traffic, and confronted police.

The more Abbie spoke, the more the authorities banned him from speaking. David Matthews, president of the University of Alabama, refused the school's facilities to Abbie. Rice University in Texas followed suit, and so did several other institutions of higher learning in the West and the South. Soon eleven states had prohibited Abbie Hoffman from speaking in public. In Kansas, he blew his nose so loudly and so rudely into a red, white, and blue handkerchief that he provoked the anger of the governor and state legislators, who charged that he had "unlawfully, willfully and publicly defaced, defiled and cast contempt upon the flag of the United States." When he crossed the border into Texas, he explained to boisterous and volatile crowds that he had only been "blowing in Old Glory."

Everywhere he went he set cultural prairie fires, but he also seemed to be playing with fire in his own psyche. Sue Williamson, an undergraduate at the University of Kansas who skipped classes to roam across the American heartland with Abbie, remembered that young college students "treated Abbie like Jesus, like he was a god," and that he came to see himself as they saw him.

She also remembered phone calls from anonymous vigilantes who promised to snuff him out and silence him forever. Abbie lived in fear of assassination. In May 1970 he told a reporter from *Harry*—an underground newspaper in Baltimore, Maryland—that he was "fatalistic" about his own future and believed that he had "less than two months to stay alive." It wasn't only his own death that concerned him. The movement was dying, too. "It's weirdsville," he exclaimed at the end of 1970. "It's over."

In the winter and spring of 1971, in preparation for the "Mayday" demonstrations scheduled to take place in Washington, D.C., Abbie traveled across the country urging students to protest the war in Vietnam. On April 28, at Oklahoma State University in Stillwater, he insisted that the war in Vietnam was "immoral and illegal," a "racist" war perpetuated by a "decadent empire." In Oklahoma City, on the same day, he urged "rebellion . . . among our units in Vietnam" and announced that the Mayday demonstrations would "begin the process of closing down the Government." The next day, at the University of Oklahoma, he proclaimed "We ain't marching. We are not into that. We're trying to stop the functioning of the government." Mayday would "make Chicago in August 1968 look like a Young Americans for Freedom meeting," he declared. By the time that he arrived in Washington, D.C., he had persuaded himself that Armageddon was at hand. He took LSD and went into the streets, where he and his friends and thousands of other demonstrators overturned cars, blocked traffic, and disrupted the city.

Shortly after the Mayday demonstrations, a federal grand jury indicted him "with intent to organize, promote, encourage, and participate in a riot" and with "obstructing, impeding, and interfering with a law enforcement officer during the commission of a civil disorder." It sounded like the Chicago trial all over again, but this time there was only one conspirator: Abbie Hoffman. On May 6, 1971, federal agents arrested him in New York and took him to FBI headquarters on East Sixty-ninth Street. The next morning they moved him to the Federal House of Detention on West Street. But before long, he was on the streets again.

The Outlaw

By 1971 Abbie was defining himself as an outlaw rather than as an activist or revolutionary. The outlaw persona wasn't entirely new, of course: growing up in Worcester he'd been a "juvenile delinquent"; in college he'd had various scams; and on the Lower East Side he'd been a hustler, a con artist, and a small-time marijuana dealer. In the late sixties, he'd published "Fuck the System," a thirty-two-page illustrated pamphlet on how to survive in New York without money. While he didn't urge criminal activity in the pamphlet, he did suggest ways to get around the law, such as how to ride subways for free and how to use coin-operated telephones without spending a cent.

Immediately after the Chicago Conspiracy Trial, Abbie expanded "Fuck the System" into a full-length book, which he called *Steal This Book*. He hoped the book would provide information on how to live for free, outside the law, all across America. He enlisted the help of several research assistants, including Izak Haber, whom Abbie called his "co-conspirator," and Tom Forcade, a marijuana smuggler and dealer and the founder of *High Times* magazine. Together they assembled *Steal This Book* in about six months. The cutely titled "Table of Discontents" hinted at what was inside: information on free food, free housing, free dope, and free communication. There were chapters on "Guerrilla Broadcasting," "Hip-Pocket Law," and "The Underground." In the introduction, Abbie explained that he wanted readers "to steal from the robber barons who own the castles of capitalism." The only real "crime," he argued, was committed by multinational corporations "against the people as a whole." Moreover, it was "irrelevant" whether his methods were "legal or illegal," he said. Stealing from a "brother or sister" was evil, but *not stealing* from "the Pig Empire" was "immoral."

No publisher accepted the book, and it was not only the title that made it far too hot for most editors to handle. In addition, the chapter entitled "People's Chemistry" provided information on how to make stink, smoke, and pipe bombs, as well as the classic Molotov cocktail. It was not surprising that no one wanted to publish a work that encouraged the use of explosives. So Abbie formed his own company, Pirate Editions, and designed a logo that showed a hippie saboteur blowing up Random House. In 1971 he published the book himself as a $1.95 paperback. He promoted it as "A Handbook of Survival and Warfare for the Citizens of Woodstock Nation." The demand for the book was remarkable, and Abbie was elated. "I can outsell anybody," he boasted. "I can outsell Mailer ten to one." From New York to New Mexico and from Florida to Oregon, tens of thousands of young people as well as members of the respectable middle classes bought (or stole) the book and borrowed many of Abbie's suggestions. They discovered that they could wangle meals, drinks, records, and airplane and movie tickets. Abbie became the guru to a class of Americans who didn't like to work too hard and didn't want to pay for luxury items or even for the necessities of everyday living.

Today the suggestions are largely outdated and impractical. "With all the money in America," Abbie wrote in the chapter entitled "Free

Money," "the only thing you'll have trouble getting is poor." And in the chapter entitled "Free Housing," he noted, "if you're in a city without a place to stay, ask the first group of hip-looking folks where you can crash." *Steal This Book* captured a moment in American history when it was still possible for dropouts from suburbia to find a more or less comfortable "crash pad" in a strange city, get on welfare and obtain food stamps with relative ease, and not worry about being mugged or getting AIDS.

Abbie turned away from the movement and toward family life, though he wasn't happy doing so. Anita wanted very much to have a child. She was, as she herself wrote, "vaguely unhappy, . . . without direction, and lonely." Gradually, Abbie talked himself into fatherhood. At thirty-four it might be a lot more fun and a lot less traumatic, he thought, than it had been at twenty-four. He read Dr. Spock, attended Lamaze classes with Anita to prepare for natural childbirth, and wanted to be part of the birthing process. But Anita's pregnancy often seemed more of an idea to him than flesh-and-blood reality, and so did even the birth itself. "The baby was not something separate from our politics," Abbie wrote. "He was an affirmation." Abbie couldn't simply have a baby. Everything had to be part of the revolution. Accordingly, the boy was named "america," with a lowercase "a." Abbie explained, "We decided to call our kid america because we believe that when the state finally fades, nations will be named after people and people will be nations."

In the fall of 1971, Abbie, Anita, and america moved to St. Thomas in the Virgin Islands and played in paradise. Life on the island, however, wasn't simply a vacation. It was also a rehearsal for the next act in the Abbie Hoffman drama, in which he would appear as cocaine smuggler and dealer. Abbie flew secretly to St. Thomas, where, under the alias Frank Crosetti, he opened a bank account and rented a car as well as an isolated house in the hills. But politics still tugged at him.

A Most Manic-Depressive Society

In 1972 the Democratic and Republican Party conventions both took place in Miami ("the tip of America's phallus," Abbie called it). Miami in 1972 was worlds apart from the turmoil of Chicago in 1968. Even the outrageous Yippies of Chicago were reborn as reasonable citizens. Granted, Abbie designed two zany posters for Miami. In one of them, which borrowed from an Eastern Airlines advertising campaign which had been widely criticized for its sexism, an effeminate-looking Abbie wore a dress and kicked up his heels. "High! I'm Abbie, fly me to Miami," it read. The other poster borrowed from John Reed's classic account of the Russian Revolution and proclaimed "Ten Days to Change the World."

Nevertheless, it wasn't instant revolution that Abbie wanted at the 1972 Democratic National Convention, but rather negotiation, compromise, and reform. The guerrilla was reincarnated as a pundit of caution. "In no sense are we interested in a confrontation," Abbie proclaimed. "We have nothing to gain by a riot." His new persona made sense not only because he was weary of street fighting, but because the movement had lost its aggressive edge. Moreover, Miami didn't seem like a city made for war. In Chicago in 1968, Abbie had felt he was on foreign soil; in Miami in 1972, he felt at home. Anxious to avoid a replay of Chicago, the Miami political establishment opened its doors to Abbie and to Jerry Rubin and treated them like visiting dignitaries. Mayor Chuck Hall and Chief of Police Rocky Pomerance invited Rubin and Hoffman to speak at city council meetings and to address the patrolmen of Miami. They granted permits that allowed the Yippies to camp in Flamingo Park, parade on Collins Avenue, and perform guerrilla theatre almost anywhere. Mayor Hall visited the Yippie office and posed for pictures, while Chief Pomerance urged his deputies to read *Do It!* and *Steal This Book* and to try to understand the motives of the demonstrators. It was a radical about-face from Mayor Daley's position of intransigence.

In Chicago in 1968, Abbie had accentuated the generation gap. In Miami in 1972, he created a bridge between the Yippies and the elderly, especially Miami's Jews. Stew Albert later remembered that Abbie's cry wasn't "Kill Your Parents" but "Love Your Grandparents." Instead of celebrating youth culture and youth rebellion, he acknowledged the importance of older people and their trade union and socialist organizations. He wandered along Collins Avenue, the heart of the Jewish community, shaking hands and talking in Yiddish. He wrote a humorous poem in Yiddish entitled "Nixon Genug!" ("Nixon Enough!"), which he recited at picnics the Yippies held in the parks for the benefit of the retirees. The president was "a good for nothing," Abbie told listeners. He was "a brown-noser of Big Business" and a "slob with Mantovani records" who lived "high on the hog with Pat." The poem ended with the lines "Comes August—you'll get / what's coming to you," which brought laughter and applause.

In *Vote,* a 240-page, pro-McGovern propaganda piece written with Ed Sanders and Stew Albert, Abbie and Jerry claimed that "to glorify youth is to hate yourself." They insisted that in the sixties they had been "responsible for the excesses of youth culture," but that they "had been lured into a Madison Avenue trap: the bourgeois romancing of youth." They sounded practically like academic Marxists. What was important now, they argued, wasn't "do-your-own-thing anarchy" but organizing "a more humanistic society along socialist principles."

In Chicago in 1968, Abbie had insisted on the revolutionary power of television and the importance of the media to create mythic events that blurred the line between reality and myth. "We were the first television news actors," he proudly proclaimed in 1970, when he looked back at Chicago. In Miami in 1972, he continued to argue that radicals ought to use "psychic media terrorism" and create "real life soap opera." Moreover, it was important to develop "media superstars" who could reach the masses, he said. But in Miami he had second thoughts about the media and complained that the Democratic National convention seemed like "a figment of Andy Warhol's imagination." It was a "huge drama where no one knew what was reality and what was theatre, or what was the difference anymore." In Chicago in 1968 Abbie had no great desire to be inside the convention and among the delegates, though he managed to wangle press credentials and sneak inside for a brief visit. In Miami in 1972 he wanted very much to be with the Democrats. Of course, the Democratic Party of '72 was a far cry from the party of '68. There were beards and beads, long hair and Afros, buttons that read "Citizen Power" and T-shirts that read "GAY." Moreover, this time there was a peace candidate and a peace plank. Allen Ginsberg chanted; Dick Gregory told jokes and led the delegates in the singing of "We Shall Overcome." Abbie couldn't afford not to be on the inside, and with the benefit of a more or less legitimate press pass, he made it to the floor, where he rubbed shoulders with Gloria

Steinem, Germaine Greer, Shirley MacLaine, and Norman Mailer. He even approached Hubert Humphrey, who admitted that there had been "problems in Chicago," whereupon Abbie replied, "Yeah, *you, you* were the problem." They were still at odds, but now Abbie was kibitzing with Humphrey.

To many radicals in their late teens and early twenties, Abbie and Jerry were conservative old men. The Zippies, as they called themselves, were a small group of zany activists, mostly Jewish and male and from New York, many of whom had been strongly influenced by Abbie and Jerry. The Zippies knew that the time was ripe to turn on their older, sagging movement brothers. Led by A. J. Weberman, Rex Weiner, and Aaron Kay—who had made a reputation by throwing cream pies in the faces of establishment figures—the Zippies were determined to run the show in Miami. At times they were menacing; at other times they were simply prankish. On Jerry Rubin's birthday they invaded the Albion Hotel, the Yippie hangout, with a cake that read "Never trust anyone over 30."

Jerry admitted in his autobiography, *Growing (Up) at Thirty-Seven*, that by the time of the Miami conventions, he had "become more conservative." Moreover, he astutely noted that many sixties leaders were committing political "suicide," that there was a "tendency of symbolic figures to self-destruct." His own salvation, he claimed, lay in therapy and "the body revolution": rolfing, primal scream, sexual surrogates, bioenergetics, yoga, running, and meditation. He advised Abbie to administer some self-healing and to "forget Abbie Hoffman," change his name, and start life anew.

Besieged by the Zippies, Abbie and Jerry moved closer to one another. For years they'd been in competition as authors, but now they collaborated with one another on *Vote!* They soon discovered how much they had in common emotionally, psychologically, and politically. "History has placed us in the role of models," they wrote of themselves and their contemporaries. "We are a transitional generation, raised in the aftermath of World War II. We carry a mixture of the old and the new into the future without maps or rules."

Casting themselves as social critics, they noted that America was "a most manic-depressive society" and that it had passed through periodic "cycles of hope and despair." In the fifties, there was depression, they explained, whereas in the sixties there was optimism. Now, in the seventies, depression and despair had returned to America, and so had the mind-set of the fifties. Psychoanalysis had replaced radical politics; people were becoming introspective rather than socially conscious or socially active.

In Miami Abbie was both manic *and* depressed, hopeful and despairing. Among observers of Abbie's violent mood swings in the summer of 1972 were Kathie Streem and Gabrielle Schang, two very smart and very attractive young women who had joined the Yippies just as older feminists were evacuating the party. Streem recalled that Abbie was "feeling torn apart" and became "really distant." Schang remembered that when the Democrats were in Miami and it seemed as though Senator George McGovern had a chance to become president, Abbie was "energetic" and "elated," but when Nixon and the Republicans arrived and Abbie realized that they were going to win in November, he "changed from manic to depressive." Ed Sanders remembered that Abbie was "wounded, damaged, upset, troubled over his marriage, not knowing what to do."

Indeed, he and Anita were separated, and their relationship was in trouble. Anita had been in Chicago in 1968, but there was no way she would go to Miami in 1972. In fact, she had taken their son america and had moved from the Lower East Side into her mother's house on Long Island. To Abbie, their apartment now felt like an "oasis of despair," as he put it. Moreover, he was beginning to think and to write extensively about suicide in a manuscript he called "Kiss and Tell." To lift his spirits, he began to snort cocaine; he made contact with dealers who provided him with all the Bolivian powder he wanted. He also smoked marijuana and dropped Quaaludes, which he washed down with whiskey. Inside the Democratic Convention itself, he distributed hash oil to delegates.

According to friends, he spent much of his time with a young woman who called herself "Velocity." He fed her drugs and had sex with her, but she hardly satisfied his lust or his hunger for unending and uninterrupted human contact. In Miami, Gabrielle Schang said, Abbie was "the male version of a nymphomaniac." She remembered that "he would sleep with almost anybody" and that "it was right out in the open."

Chicago and Miami. Manic and depressive. Optimistic and pessimistic. Abbie had come a long, long way; in four years, he seemed to have turned himself inside out and upside down.

The Fall Guy

As the movement fell apart, Abbie started his own private enterprise, but kept it a secret since it consisted of smuggling and selling cocaine. Later on he would describe his group as the outlaw equivalent of the "Watergate operation." In his clandestine group there was equal sharing, he claimed, which is what made it superior to the "plumbers" who broke into the Democratic National Headquarters. "The Watergate operation was not communal," he wrote. "It was not done primarily for the benefit of those carrying out the operation."

In *Steal This Book,* Abbie warned readers that "sniffing cocaine can perforate your nasal passages, so be super-moderate," and he added, "Too much will kill you." On the subject of buying drugs, he observed "arrests are not a problem unless you're the fall guy." In the underworld of dealers and smugglers, it was essential to be eternally vigilant and always on the move. "If you ever have the slightest doubt about the person with whom you are dealing—DON'T," he concluded. How long and how deeply Abbie was involved in the cocaine trade is difficult to say because he never publicly discussed the depth of his own involvement, and because most of the individuals with whom he was involved have never talked openly. But interviews with those who were part of his operation suggest that he was part of a group that was smuggling cocaine from South America via Puerto Rico to Florida. He was selling cocaine, his friends say, mostly because he wanted the money, but also because he thrived on the adventure and the excitement—the high that the lifestyle produced. Living on the edge had become an addiction.

How he was getting the cocaine into the country isn't clear, but those who were involved say there was an ingenious method. For at least a year, Abbie and his clandestine unit were successful. Increasingly, however, he was not following his own advice about the use of cocaine. He was snorting more and more of the drug. He also had increasing doubts about the individuals with whom he was dealing. But he continued, and eventually he became the "fall guy" he had warned readers of *Steal This Book* not to become.

On August 28, 1973, he was arrested in room 1015 of the Hotel Diplomat. Three other members of the group—Carole Ramer, Diane Peterson, and Michael Drosnan—were apprehended as well. Some members of Abbie's operation who smuggled the cocaine into the country have never been arrested. It was three and half years into the seventies when the sixties finally ended for Abbie and for many of his fans. The bust was front-page news in New York, and it was shocking to almost everyone in the movement, including Allen Ginsberg, who included it among other catastrophes in the poem "News Bulletin": "Abbie Hoffman just got busted / million pounds of Cocaine."

It must have seemed like a million pounds to Johnnie Hoffman, who suffered a heart attack and died soon after he heard the news that his oldest son had been arrested. Abbie himself was devastated by the bust. Two undercover officers, Arthur Nascarella and Robert Sasso, as well as six other police officers took part in the arrest. Abbie was handcuffed, taken into custody, and charged with selling three pounds of cocaine—a felony that carried with it a maximum penalty of fifteen years to life in prison.

In his autobiography and in other writings, Abbie offered a variety of comments about the affair. "It wasn't my coke," he said. He "was just curious, that's all." Close friends say that he was profoundly ashamed. As an outlaw he was a complete failure. He had been caught with the evidence in hand. And as a radical opponent to materialism, he'd been exposed as a man who cared about money. He would insist that he had been gathering material for a book about cocaine, that he'd been an observer rather than a participant, and there was an element of truth in that tale. But he could never reveal the fundamental truth—which was, of course, that he'd plotted to bring cocaine into the United States and sell it at a profit. The cultural revolutionary had become a businessman, albeit with a pirate stripe. From 1973 until 1989, the year he died, Abbie would lie about his cocaine involvement, and the lying, his friends say, had a devastating impact on his emotional and psychological life. He himself admitted as much; the "cocaine bust," he wrote in 1987 in Steal This Urine Test, is "still a vulnerable wound." He never recovered from it and was never able to heal the wound in his own psyche.

Immediately after the arrest, friends and family members rushed to Abbie's defense. Some of them participated, knowingly or not, in a cover-up. Those who had worked with Abbie in the cocaine trade as-sumed that the truth could not be told because it would damage the movement as a whole, or so they've said. Anita Hoffman wrote and published an article entitled "On the Disappearance of Abbie," in which she insisted "Abbie is innocent." The *Village Voice* ran two ar-ticles by Ron Rosenbaum which suggested that there was a deep and profound "mystery" and implied that there had been a miscarriage of justice. Veteran reporter and columnist Murray Kempton wrote that "the Abbie Hoffman I know is no seller." Even the *New Yorker* was sympathetic to his plight; the anonymous writer of the "Talk of the Town" column observed that "many medical authorities regard cocaine as a non-narcotic drug, relatively innocuous in comparison to heroin." (This was long before the crack epidemic in the U.S.) Moreover, the *New Yorker* let Anita Hoffman have the last word; Abbie's arrest was "an obvious case of political harassment," she said.

Court records and interviews with several of the participants indicate that Abbie had willingly participated in cocaine dealing. Long before the night of August 28, he had sent out word that he had top-grade cocaine to sell. Carole Ramer, who later spent time in jail for her part in the operation, had told a friend named John Rinaldi that Abbie was anxious to sell cocaine. Rinaldi made connections with a man who posed as a Mafia member but in fact was a police informer, who in turn brought in undercover officers Nascarella and Sasso. The night before his arrest, Abbie met them and negotiated with them about the amount and price of the cocaine. He provided a sample and agreed to meet again on August 28, when he would provide three pounds of cocaine in exchange for thirty-six thousand dollars.

Some of Abbie's friends say he thought that Nascarella and Sasso were in the Mafia (who else would be dealing cocaine? he wondered), so he decided to get the satisfaction of cheating them. He removed a quantity of pure cocaine and put it aside for himself and for Diane Peterson, whom he had recently begun to date and with whom he was apparently planning a night of sex and drugs. Then he cut the remain-ing portion of the cocaine with a baby laxative and placed it in a plastic bag, ready for delivery. On August 28, Peterson met Sasso in the Dip-lomat Hotel. She noticed that he was wearing a gun under his shirt, and on the phone she told Abbie as much. Naturally, Abbie was suspicious. He wondered if Sasso might be a cop, and half-jokingly he suggested that Peterson hug him to find out if he was wired. Still, in spite of all his doubts and reservations, he gave the go-ahead. Peterson and Ramer met the undercover agents in the street and counted the cash, then went to room 1015 to wait for Abbie to arrive with the cocaine.

When he entered the Hotel Diplomat with a paper shopping bag containing three small bags of cocaine and a scale, all of which were concealed by groceries, neither the air-conditioning nor the elevator was working. Everything seemed to be falling apart. In the lobby Abbie bumped into Arthur Nascarella, and began to feel paranoid and queasy. But once again he decided to proceed, and he climbed the stairs to the tenth floor, sweating profusely the entire way.

He opened the door to room 1015 and immediately began to make jokes about the heat and the electrical breakdown. Then he opened the shopping bag, reached inside for the scale, and set it down on the table. He weighed out the cocaine and made sure that Sasso saw it was three pounds. Now he was nervous, indeed. He couldn't stop shaking, and he was unable to transfer the cocaine from the plastic bag to a glass jar; he spilled much of it on the table. But finally he handed over the cocaine. "This is yours," he said. "Give me mine."

Sasso gave him the money; Abbie counted it, put it away, and started to leave. Sasso then drew his gun, pointed it at Abbie, and said, "You're under arrest." Handcuffed behind his back, he was driven to Midtown South Precinct and booked. When allowed his one phone call, he reached Gerald Lefcourt, who rushed to see him. "I almost didn't recognize him," Lefcourt remembered. "He was in a total whacked-out state . . . like somebody dressed up to look grotesque."

A defense committee quickly formed. Norman Mailer lent his name and his credibility and worked diligently for the cause. Money was raised, and Abbie was bailed out. Briefly he considered going to court and putting New York State's drug laws on trial. He thought that he might use a variation on the traditional insanity defense, Lefcourt later remembered. He would take the witness stand and testify that "the government drove me crazy." He would tell the jury, he said, that ten years of harassment by police agents, judges, and prosecutors had taken their toll on him and had deprived him of his sanity. Moreover, he would say that he had lost the ability to distinguish between the reality that was around him and the movie that was in his own head. In his scenario, he was the "victim" of the "same wonderful people who brought us Watergate."

There were, of course, partial truths in this tale. Ten years of defiance and confrontation had taken their toll. Abbie was indeed "coming apart," as Lefcourt noted when he visited him in jail the night of his arrest. He'd lost his ability to read situations and people, and he seems to have become unconscious of the implications of his own actions. But he chose what he did every step of the way—from bringing the cocaine to the hotel, to climbing the stairs to the tenth floor. In this light, his day at the Hotel Diplomat takes on the dimensions of tragedy. Abbie was a free and willing participant in the trap that had been set by the police and from which there proved to be no escape. He had undertaken the very "sacrificial trip" that he had warned his readers about in *Steal This Book*.

When the seventies had started, Abbie had believed he was possessed of godlike invincibility. He could defy every law in the book—even the law of gravity: "What goes up doesn't necessarily have to come down." Now, in 1973, the laws had caught up with him, and he was as down as he'd ever been before. He was a mere mortal, who had lost his imagined magical powers and was trapped in a web of circumstances. He could cry all he wanted about how unfair and unjust society was. The government was engaged in illegal operations, and it was the little guy who was arrested and who went to jail. But it didn't do him any good anymore. He was facing fifteen years to life in prison.

chapter eleven

THE LONGEST
GOOD-BYE

1974 – 1989

Back to the Future

A hefty book could easily be written *just* about the last fifteen years of Abbie's dramatic life. The book would describe his adventures on the road in Canada, Mexico, and the United States as the underground fugitive "Barry Freed." It would recount the story of his political activism as an environmentalist; his ongoing struggle with manic-depressive illness; his romance with and subsequent separation from his third wife, Johanna Lawrenson; his further encounters with the media; and, of course, his suicide. It might be entitled "The Longest Good-bye" because the last fifteen years of his life seem like an extended farewell to the world.

Abbie's story in the seventies and eighties was unique, of course; probably no sixties personality covered as much territory as quickly as he did. And probably few were on the edge so often. Still, his tale is emblematic of the larger story of his contemporaries. His identity crisis in the underground and his quest for a new, post-sixties persona in the seventies serve as metaphors for a larger, generational identity crisis and a search for alternative roles. Likewise, in the eighties his personal conflicts mirrored the social contradictions of the decade. Abbie insisted that he was a Yippie to the core and at war with the counterrevolutionary Yuppies, but when you peered behind the scenes you discovered Abbie the Yuppie. He was still a genuine political activist and troublemaker, but he was also very much a Reagan-era materialist and consumer. He often made as much as a hundred thousand dollars a year from lecturing on college campuses and from debating Jerry Rubin, whom he loved to hate more than anyone else in America—even Ronald Reagan. And he spent his money on all kinds of goodies, from speedboats to computers. He kept his finances a secret, of course, because revealing them would have undermined his reputation and destroyed his image. In fact, he bought and sold commodities, including crude oil, on the Chicago Mercantile Exchange. Steve Tappis, a sixties radical who became a commodities trader and made investments for Abbie, noted that Abbie "loved the idea of making more money than Jerry Rubin, of being more Yuppie and at the same time more Yippie." Indeed, this straddling of identities was characteristic of Abbie, who continued to create new roles and personas.

At many of the best European and American restaurants, he ate nouvelle cuisine as well as traditional French cooking. He traveled to Latin America as an ecotourist, journeyed down the Amazon, and explored the Galapagos. He went into psychoanalysis and tried to work out his troubled relationship with Johanna Lawrenson, whom he met shortly after he went underground. Like many men of his generation, he worried about his financial future, his physical health, his wayward children and their uncertain careers, as well as his own aging, dying, and death.

All of this would make for an entertaining tale, but it would also be a postscript to the main text: his experience in the sixties. Abbie himself clearly understood that the sixties had been *his* time and that everything that came afterward was anticlimactic. The sixties had been "the best years" of his life, he wrote in his autobiography. When he looked back at the past, he decided "the sixties were so earth-shaking that the seventies can only be defined in contrast"; that is, "the seventies were *not* the sixties."

In *It Seemed Like Nothing Happened: The Tragedy and Promise of America in the 1970s* (1982), Peter Carroll argued that the seventies had been a far more important decade than they appeared to be at first glance. "A quiet, almost subliminal revolution was altering the contours of the cultural landscape," he wrote. In many ways the "subliminal revolution" of the seventies was an extension of the cultural revolution that Abbie had helped to bring about. And yet Abbie refused to see it while it was happening. "There's nothing there," he said of the seventies in an interview he did with the *Yipster Times* in 1978. "This has been the quickest decade in history; this is premature ejaculation."

In the eighties he kept hoping and promising that the sixties were going to make a comeback, just as surely as he'd made a personal comeback. If all else failed, he would *will* the sixties back. In 1986, at long last, he insisted that they *had* finally returned, though he couldn't convince the country as a whole. "Back to the future!" he exclaimed. "It's 1968 out there!" On a deeper level he knew that the sixties, and especially 1968—for him, "the greatest year" of them all—would never return, and that the eighties would disappoint him.

"The music is never going to be *that* good, the sex is never going to be *that* free, the dope is never going to be *that* cheap," he said. Despite all his efforts to resist sixties nostalgia, and despite his insistence that nostalgia was a "form of depression," he was filled with nostalgia for the sixties, and was depressed for much of the eighties. In the eighties the gods of the revolution were dead. The time of the hero had come and gone. "We worship heroes and then we knock them down," Abbie told Abe Peck shortly after surfacing. "Eventually we will find out that Elvis Presley was a fuckin' freak and John Lennon was weird and a maniac and probably slugged the shit out of Yoko Ono." It seems likely he was afraid that his own worshippers would see that his feet were made of clay and would topple him from his exalted position.

Again and again he tried to recapture an ideal version of the sixties. He wanted to resurrect it or recreate it, and he wasn't alone. Year after year more books and movies about the sixties were produced, as though America couldn't get enough of the era and was still struggling to come to terms with it. Like so many other sixties radicals in the eighties, Abbie wrote about the sixties, talked about the sixties, and revisited sixties places, from Woodstock and Grant Park in Chicago to the campus of Columbia University. Like Marcel Proust's hero in *Remembrance of Things Past,* he was in search of lost time, which continually evaded him.

Moreover, he treated the eighties as a stage on which he could recycle the dramas of the sixties, writing new lines and wearing new costumes. In 1986, when he was arrested along with President Carter's daughter Amy at the University of Massachusetts for interfering with CIA recruitment, he insisted that their trial not duplicate the Chicago Conspiracy Trial. This time he planned to do the exact opposite: dress conservatively, act properly, respect the judge, and represent himself, rather than allow lawyers to handle his case.

In the sixties, unlike many antiwar activists, including Tom Hayden, Bernardine Dohrn, Rennie Davis, and Dave Dellinger, Abbie had never traveled to Vietnam, Cuba, or any of the other Third World countries that inspired the New Left. In the eighties, he made a point of moving into the international scene. He visited Nicaragua, which he praised in public and criticized in private; he met with Sandinista President Daniel Ortega and insisted that Central America was the Southeast Asia of the Reagan era. From his point of view the sixties were a yardstick for measuring almost every other time and place. In a way he never gave the eighties a chance, never allowing himself to see them without the filter of the sixties and never allowing himself to break out of the sixties mold that had shaped him.

The Fugitive

When he went underground in the winter of 1974, it seemed that he might very well leave the sixties behind him and explore new territories. Indeed, that was the impression he aimed to create. "I like the person I am now," he told reporter Ron Rosenbaum in a mythologizing article published in *New Times* not long after he went underground. "I mean even better than old Abbie." And he added, "Even if they dropped the charges against me back in New York and I could walk free, I don't think I'd wanna go back. I'm almost grateful to the cops who busted me for making me get off my ass. What's there to go back for anyway. You get tired sitting around telling the same old stories." Of course, from the moment he went on the lam, he was determined to return to New York and to cut a deal with law enforcement officials that would require of him the minimum prison time.

As a fugitive, Abbie rarely worried about money; he had considerable savings, partly from dealing cocaine in the early seventies, and he had financial support from Hollywood friends like producer Bert Schneider. He made money writing for *Penthouse* and *Crawdaddy*. It didn't hurt, either, that he had access to Johanna Lawrenson's apartment on

East Thirty-fourth Street in Manhattan and her house on Wellesley Island in the St. Lawrence Seaway in upstate New York, where he could live rent-free.

For Abbie, survival as a fugitive was a psychological rather than an economic problem, though he often insisted that he was psychologically stable in the underground. In his autobiography, for example, he wrote that, "forced to be an outlaw, I never had to face the life crisis confronting my comrades." Nothing could be further from the truth. Like most fugitives, Abbie was paranoid; he was afraid that a friend, an acquaintance, or a stranger would betray him, and he was constantly fearful that he'd be captured and imprisoned. All too often he believed that the police were closing in on him and he would have to make a run for it.

There is no evidence, however, that the FBI was ever breathing down his neck. Indeed, it may be that the Bureau knew more or less where he was but decided not to apprehend him because it wasn't worth the money, the manpower, or the trouble. Jack Tubert, a columnist for the *Worcester Telegram and Gazette* who followed Abbie's career for more than two decades, insists that a Boston FBI agent told him that Abbie's haunts were no secret.

According to Tubert, the FBI knew, for example, that he showed up from time to time at El Morocco, one of Worcester's more exotic restaurants, which was owned by his old friend Joe Aboody. They knew, too, that Abbie threw a fortieth birthday party for himself at a swank Chinese restaurant on the Upper East Side of Manhattan. The FBI gathered the names of the guests and questioned them, but the investigation never amounted to much; the agents apparently had more urgent matters to attend to. FBI documents obtained under the Freedom of Information Act also suggest that the Bureau believed that Abbie was in Mexico in the mid-seventies. Agents knew that Abbie's sister, Phyllis, lived there and that Jack Hoffman arrived there shortly after Abbie vanished. Moreover, the FBI suspected that Johanna Lawrenson was harboring a sixties fugitive on the St. Lawrence, but once again, no manhunt was mounted.

Abbie played with the FBI. When he was underground he sent a letter, on stationery he'd borrowed from the Hotel McAlpin in New York, to the deputy attorney general, requesting his files. "I really am anxious to see your report on my father's funeral, the copy of my father's will in your possession, interrogation of my mother-in-law, and just exactly what was in my wife's refrigerator when you opened the door," he wrote. In the final paragraph of the letter, he quipped, "Well I gotta run now, so send everything to my counsel of record, Gerald Lefcourt, 299 Broadway, N.Y. N.Y. and I'll drop by & pick it up next time I'm in the city."

But Abbie Hoffman, not the FBI, was Abbie Hoffman's own worst enemy in the underground. In his 1980 book *Soon to Be a Major Motion Picture,* for example, he described how he "took a dangerous chance" by attending a memorial concert in New York in the mid-seventies for Phil Ochs, who had committed suicide by hanging himself in a garage. Moreover, he explained that he had approached police officers on street corners and asked for information. "I took so many needless chances that I must have desired to be caught or killed," he concluded. He also describes a "psychotic" episode in a "strange city" where he was alone and without any money: "I craved death but lacked the energy or initiative to do the deed. . . . Every day began with thoughts of suicide and turning myself in." Many of his closest friends testify to his self-destructiveness while he was underground.

Local Insurgent, Again

Several factors saved him from suicide in the seventies: writing articles about his real and make-believe fugitive adventures in what he called "this gorgeous plastic wonderland called America"; working on his autobiography, which took him back to the sixties in memory and in fantasy; visiting with friends and family members, including Anita, america, Andrew, his old nemesis Jerry Rubin, and his new hero Dave Dellinger; and the day-in and day-out presence of Johanna Lawrenson, whom he described as his "Angel" and his "bodyguard" and who indeed protected him, nurtured him, and saved him again and again for most of the six and a half years he was a fugitive. "I get withdrawal symptoms if I don't see her for about four hours," Abbie told reporter Charlotte Cohen; he was more dependent on Johanna than on any one else he'd ever known.

Most of all, his political activism on the St. Lawrence River kept him alive, making him feel that he had a new lease on life. In the late seventies, he was the kind of local insurgent that he had been in Worcester in the early sixties, only now he was even more effective. In the sixties the issue had been civil rights; in the seventies it was ecology. But Abbie's grassroots style of organizing was very much the same. When the U.S. Army Corps of Engineers came up with a plan to dredge the St. Lawrence River so that it would be navigable during winter, Abbie Hoffman—or rather Barry Freed, as he was calling himself—joined with other members of the community to stop it. The organization that he helped to found was called "Save the River." He insisted on that name, rather than "Save the St. Lawrence River," as others had suggested. Barry Freed was "thinking globally and acting locally," as the slogan went, and he was thinking, too, on a symbolic level. It wasn't one river that he wanted to save, but all rivers, and when he was asked his occupation, he would say "River Saver."

He was an amazing organizer, and local residents were awed by his manic energy and seemingly limitless talents. Karen Lago, for example, an artist who later became the director of Save the River, remembered that she asked the man she knew as Barry Freed, "Who the hell are you?" and "What do you really do?" One day he finally admitted, "I'm Abbie Hoffman." Karen Lago didn't believe him. "Yeah, and I'm Angela Davis," she replied.

When he wasn't suicidal, depressed, or unable to get out of bed, Abbie was having the time of his life. He was no longer cowering in a dark corner of the underground but walking boldly in the sunlight. He played bridge with the locals, hung out at the docks along the river, went fishing, and raced his gaudy speedboat, which many people called a "pimpmobile." Most of all he took immense delight in the creation of Barry Freed as a genuine character who took on his own identity, independent of Abbie. With Barry as a kind of front man to protect him, Abbie became confident, funny, and swaggering. On one occasion when the Save the River softball team trounced the U.S. Border Patrol team, he quipped, "no wonder you guys can never catch anybody."

In October 1978, Barry Freed appeared before the Board of Supervisors of Jefferson County, New York. He called the supervisors "gentlemen"and thanked them for allowing him the opportunity to address them. "We are not protesting anything," he said. "We like the river the way it is." The *Watertown Times* covered the meeting and described Barry Freed as the "fast-talking, ambitious public relations chairman of Save the River." In December 1978 he took members of the group to lobby at the state capitol in Albany, and in March 1979 he led a delegation to visit Congressman Robert McEwen in Washington, D.C.

But the major event in the campaign to save the river took place on August 27, 1979, when the U.S. Senate held a field hearing in Alexandria Bay, under the chairmanship of Senator Daniel Patrick Moynihan. A bearded, bespectacled citizen took the podium and read a prepared speech to an audience of more than eight hundred citizens. "My name is Barry Freed," he said. "My wife and I are property owners in Fineview, New York, on Wellesley Island." He was concerned with the potential danger to his "own land," he said, and with the harm to "investment dollars." All traces of the wild Yippie had vanished; now he was a Yuppie environmentalist. At the end of the hearings, he and Senator Moynihan posed for photos. "Everyone in New York State owes Barry Freed a debt of gratitude for his organizing ability," Moynihan said. Governor Hugh Carey sent a telegram in which he thanked Mr. Freed for his "keen public service in providing leadership" and praised Save the River for its "excellent accomplishments . . . to preserve and protect the environment and economic resources of the North County."

Abbie fervently believed in the cause of saving the St. Lawrence River, but he believed just as fervently in the cause of saving himself, both from a long life of isolation in the underground and from a long prison term on drug trafficking charges. Long before he surfaced, he began to spread the word of his good deeds, and old friends, many of whom had given up on him, found their faith restored. "Purifying the water was a way of simultaneously purifying himself," Ed Sanders remembered. And Jay Levin, a close friend from the sixties who'd stood by him when he cracked up as a fugitive, remembered, "Having the river to save saved him."

While Barry Freed was organizing on the St. Lawrence, Abbie Hoffman was directing a campaign to bring himself in from the cold. He persuaded his sixties pals, as well as media celebrities and literary luminaries like William Burroughs and Allen Ginsberg, to appear at a benefit for him in August 1978 at Madison Square Garden's Felt Forum. From underground, Abbie sent a tape-recorded message that was broadcast to the audience. "I don't wanna go to jail," he pleaded. "I just wanna come home." There was an edge of urgency in his voice, but he clearly hadn't lost his sense of irreverent humor, either. "I've always had a need to be wanted, but this takes the coke. Excuse me, Judge, I mean the cake," he said.

In December 1979, four months after his triumphant "save the river" speech in Alexandria Bay, he made the first of nearly a dozen visits to Dr. Oscar Janiger in Los Angeles. Dr. Janiger examined the patient and, in documents that were later submitted in a petition for pardon to the governor of the State of New York, noted that Abbie "evidences mental and motor retardation," that his "every move seems painfully slow," and that "he speaks in such a low voice that one finds oneself moving closer to hear." It didn't seem possible that he was talking about the same person who'd impressed Senator Moynihan and the crowd of eight hundred local residents in Alexandria Bay. Dr. Janiger concluded that Hoffman was "suffering from Bipolar Disorder, Depressed." To lift him out of his depression, he prescribed lithium, and before long he saw signs that his patient was responding well. But his client wasn't out of danger. He recommended that Hoffman "continue psychiatric care for a yet undetermined period of time."

As the seventies drew to a close, Abbie became increasingly itchy to surrender to the authorities because he believed that Ronald Reagan was sure to be the next president of the United States. The political atmosphere would become more conservative, he felt. Fifties-style conformity and repression would return, and it would be highly unlikely that cocaine dealers would receive lenient prison terms. He met with his lawyers, especially Gerald Lefcourt, and they mapped a complex strategy and a variety of lobbying tactics to persuade Robert Morgenthau, the Manhattan district attorney, not to prosecute the case with guns blazing.

The only person close to Abbie who was opposed to his surrender was Johanna Lawrenson. Afraid that she'd lose him to an adoring public, and afraid too that his bipolar disorder would be aggravated when he was once again in the public eye, she argued that he ought to remain a fugitive. But she was fighting a losing battle. Almost everyone else, including Anita and his lawyers, wanted him to surface, though Anita made it clear she didn't want him back in *her* life. In Los Angeles in

1980 she filed for divorce, and because she didn't want the media to get a hold of the story, she listed her name on the official documents as A. Suzanne Hoffman and her husband's name as Abbott Howard Hoffman.

Many of the meetings to discuss Abbie's surfacing took place in Beverly Hills at the home of Bert Schneider, who had produced the sixties movies *Easy Rider* (1969) and *Five Easy Pieces* (1970). On one occasion, Huey Newton of the Black Panthers was there. "There was high tension," Schneider's ex-wife Greta Finger remembered. "The men were in the bedroom, the women were in the kitchen. Huey and Abbie were both manic, both wild. Johanna was pissed off at Abbie. 'He can't do anything without me,' she insisted. Turning to Gwen Newton, Huey's wife, she asked, 'How do you put up with all this?' All that Gwen could say was 'Stand by your man.'"

After nearly six years of continuous writing and rewriting, Abbie was putting the finishing touches to *Soon to Be a Major Motion Picture,* which he hoped would establish his literary reputation, and would help, too, when he had to face a judge in court. His autobiography, which was published at the same time that he surfaced, managed to smooth out most of his rough edges, and to make him seem like an intellectual, a responsible husband and father, and a cute rather than a dangerous revolutionary. He was a genuine patriot, he insisted. He loved America: "Cornfields. Town meetings. Niagara Falls. Hot dogs. Parades. Red Sox double headers." Moreover, in retelling the story of the sixties as he experienced it, he made it appear to be a lot less messy and a lot less crazy than it really was.

He took a few pot shots at ex-comrades and former acquaintances: Tom Hayden was "Uncle Tom"; Jann Wenner of *Rolling Stone* was "the Benedict Arnold of the Sixties." But mostly he wanted everyone to like him and to support him in his legal battle, so he handed out compliments all around. Dave Dellinger was the "anchorman" of the anti-war movement, Huey Newton was "a gentleman and a scholar," Norman Mailer was "America's greatest journalist, a real, honest-to-goodness truth seeker."

Then, too, in *Soon to Be a Major Motion Picture,* he minimized the conflicts in his own family, and made it appear as though everyone was supportive and nurturing. His own father, he said, had taught him that "there is no contradiction between being a good businessman, a good guy, and a good revolutionary." He still loved all of his wives—Sheila, Anita, and Johanna—and all his children, too, he insisted.

Norman Mailer wrote an introduction in which he described the author as "a crazy maniac of a revolutionary." That didn't bother Abbie. What angered him, however, was Mailer's assertion that he had little if any sense of irony. "His heart beats too fiercely," Mailer noted. "He cares too much. He still loves himself too much." Abbie wanted to omit those lines. "I invented fuckin' irony," he exclaimed, but Fred Jordan, his editor, explained that one couldn't simply rewrite Norman Mailer, at least not without consulting him first.

The final chapter in Hoffman's underground journey was an appearance on the ABC television series *20/20*. Confident that Barbara Walters wouldn't present him as a "criminal-drug addict," and thereby endanger his plan to surrender, he invited her to his home in the Thousand Islands and told her about his identity as Barry Freed. On camera, Walters was clearly impressed by what she called "the amazing double life of Abbie Hoffman." Walters allowed him to shape his own image, and to turn the program into a vehicle for his cause. David Fenton, who helped arrange the meeting, remembered that "It was love at first sight. It was like the Jewish mother meets the Jewish son." Abbie's appearance on *20/20* was masterful. Barbara Walters tried him on the court of TV, and not only judged him not guilty, but saw him as a likable fellow as well.

"Organizer, Organize Thyself"

On September 4, 1980, Abbie turned himself into the authorities in Manhattan. Over a hundred reporters and photographers were on hand to capture the event, and, at the time, it seemed like "the ultimate media event," to borrow David Fenton's phrase. Gerald Lefcourt was at Abbie's side as he was taken from the prosecutor's office to the courtroom. "I've never had a walk like that," Lefcourt remembered. "I've never been so crunched by the press. It was a total riot."

The prosecutor asked for one hundred thousand dollars bail, but Lefcourt described his client as a "hero to the people" and asked that he be released on his own recognizance. Judge Williams observed, "I can't overlook the fact that he has been missing for six and a half years," but he added, "I am going to parole you." Abbie smiled, gave the "V" for victory sign, and went from the eleventh floor of the Criminal Court Building to the sixteenth floor of the building owned by his publisher, G. P. Putnam, to hold a press conference about his autobiography.

Four months after he surfaced, on January 23, 1981, he pleaded guilty to possession of cocaine; in return, the prosecution dropped the charges of sale of drugs and jumping bail. In April, Abbie was sentenced to three years in prison. "I am guilty," he said in open court, "and I'm sorry for it." The cocaine sale was, in his words, "an act of stupidity, an act of insanity. I didn't have a good time underground. . . . I don't want to go to prison."

Before the month was up, Abbie became prisoner 81A–1671 and began to serve time at the Downstate Correctional Facility, a minimum security penal institution in Fishkill, New York. The prison experience was sobering, to say the least. "Inmates are not like James Cagney or Paul Newman," he wrote in an article collected in *Square Dancing in the Ice Age.* "They are [like] no one you've seen in movies or talk shows or read about." Rarely had he been so disinclined to idealize the downtrodden and the oppressed. He noted that prison was a place where "you learn jealousy, suspicion and hatred" and that the inmates "go out worse than they come in."

After only two months at Fishkill, he was allowed to participate in a work-release program and was transferred to the Lincoln Correctional Facility in Manhattan, which was known as "The Cotton Club" because it was cushy as penal institutions went. At night Abbie was locked up; during the day he worked as a counselor at the Veritas Therapeutic Community, a drug treatment center for heroin addicts. He also raised nearly fifty thousand dollars for Veritas at a raucous party at Studio 54. The New York state commissioner of prisons put in an appearance, as did Roy Cohn, Norman Mailer, and Robert De Niro.

It was a crazy scene. Here was a man who'd served time for possession of cocaine staging a benefit for a heroin treatment center at a disco where cocaine use by the elite had been so rampant that arrests had been made and the place had been closed down. Drug dealers and cops both showed up at what Abbie called his "little shin-dig." Guests snorted cocaine and smoked pot. Abbie took the stage with singer Carly Simon and actress Karen Black and joined them in singing the Beatles' lyrics "I get high with a little help from my friends, I get by with a little help from my friends." The message seemed to be "Just Say 'Yes' to Drugs."

When Abbie completed his work-release program at Veritas, he went on a speaking tour across the country. Thousands of college students turned out to hear him, and at first he assumed that their large numbers and their enthusiasm were signs that the revolution was coming back. Soon, however, he realized that their applause at the end of his speeches didn't mean they were ready to follow him into the streets and onto the barricades. "I'm like a Chinese meal to these students," he told *Newsweek* reporter Neal Karlen. "An hour after my talk they're back watching 'Dallas' and playing video games. The situation has been reversed from the '60s. It's now the young people who are cynical and in despair, while the . . . '60s people are the ones working for change."

On campuses he found that the younger generation was ignorant about the war in Vietnam, black power, and the counterculture. It irritated him to no end that students called Malcolm X "Malcolm 10" and asked him about a drug they called "LDS." Even more infuriating, strangers would see him on the streets of New York, yell "Jerry Rubin," shake his hand, and explain that they'd heard he was working as a banker on Wall Street. America seemed to be experiencing collective amnesia, and Abbie was determined to wake it up even if he had to slap its face. Indeed, he believed that his role was to be hostile and confrontational. "I'm here to play the role of the nasty cockroach in the cosmic soup, because I basically don't buy any of the crap," he said in an interview that appeared in the Buddhist newspaper *Vajradhatu Sun.* Sounding like Charles Dickens's mean-spirited character Ebenezer Scrooge, he explained, "I don't buy peace. . . . I don't buy Christmas, I don't buy Easter."

As an organizer he was increasingly dysfunctional, and he was in trouble in almost every other area of his life as well. He was both breaking up with Johanna and unsuccessfully trying to get back together with her. According to Marty Kenner, in private Abbie boasted that manic-depressive illness was the "genius disease" and that he belonged in "The Manic-Depressive Hall of Fame," along with Vincent Van Gogh and Winston Churchill. But he was also profoundly ashamed of being manic-depressive; it was his dark secret, and he was at war with the doctors who wanted him to take lithium to ease his mood swings. Suicide looked more and more like a way out. He wrote to the Hemlock Society for their guidelines and began to stockpile sleeping pills. In the winter of 1983 he descended into a mood of dark despair. Ira Landess, a therapist and an old friend from Brandeis and the civil rights movement, remembered that Abbie said he'd heard "an auditory hallucination, a command hallucination that was telling him to kill himself."

When Johanna was out of their apartment, he apparently took seventy-five Restorils, hoping that they would finish him off before she returned. According to Landess, Abbie drafted a suicide note, then tore it up and scribbled another. With a sense of deadly humor, he wrote that now he wouldn't have to see *Frances,* the film about actress Frances Farmer, who'd achieved Hollywood success in the thirties and forties, but then descended into a life of pain, pills, alcohol, and mental distress. Characteristically, Abbie was seeing his own imminent death—just as he had seen his life—as a movie.

Abbie was taken to Bellevue Hospital, where his stomach was pumped. In a matter of days he was receiving visitors, including Rabbi Alexander Schindler, whom he had first met at Temple Emanuel in Worcester two decades earlier. "I told him that I would be wounded if he committed suicide," Schindler remembered. "I said that he'd be betraying the people who held him up as a fighter, and that suicide would be a blow to all those things he stood for all his life." All too quickly Abbie was looking on the bright side of his suicide attempt. It was a way of performing surgery on himself, he said, of extracting the awful hurt in his own head. Moreover, he knew exactly what he had to do. "Organizer, organize thyself," he wrote in a letter to Anita. He began to read books about manic-depressive illness and to monitor his own mood swings. He often insisted that he was going to write a personal account of the illness, bring the topic into the open, and break the long-standing taboo against admitting to depression.

He meant well, but he was incapable of carrying out his own prescription. Despite his good intentions, he sabotaged his plans for recovery. He took lithium, but he didn't really believe that it or any other medication would work, and before long he was delinquent again. The only way to beat his depression and defeat his urge to commit suicide, he argued, was to *will* it to happen. He was going to take a year off from speaking on college campuses and attend to his own needs, Anita remembered his saying, but about a week after he was released from Bellevue, he was on a speaking tour again.

The task of organizing himself—of making what Gloria Steinem would later call the "revolution from within"—was so overwhelming that he didn't really know where to begin or what steps to take. By comparison, organizing a political battle seemed simple and straightforward. Like so many other movement men of his generation, he could have used a sense of self-esteem. Just beneath the surface of his bravado was a fragile human being who thought of himself as a "fuck-up" and a failure.

No doubt Abbie could have learned a great deal about himself by looking back at his own childhood and reflecting on his personality and experiences. Some of his friends, including Jay Levin, publisher of *L. A. Weekly,* urged him to do just that. Meditation and relaxation would probably have helped, as well as a sense of compassion, of getting beyond his own immensely tortured feelings and understanding how other people felt—especially his brother and sister; his sons and his daughter; his ex-wives, Sheila and Anita; and his wife, Johanna Lawrenson, who had stood by him even though he was physically and verbally abusive to her for years.

Time and time again his friends and loved ones had rescued him, but when they were in emotional pain and needed rescuing, he was nowhere to be found. When Johanna Lawrenson's brother, Kevin, committed suicide, friends say that Abbie wasn't in the least bit compassionate. "Why don't you go there, where all dead brothers go," he snapped, as though he wished she would die, too. Bernardine Dohrn, the Weather Underground leader who'd surfaced in 1980, had driven Abbie from the Lincoln Correctional Facility to Veritas every morning for months. But when she refused to testify before a grand jury and was sentenced to jail for contempt, Abbie made no effort to visit her. He was prepared to save rivers—the St. Lawrence, the Delaware, the Hudson—but not other human beings, including himself.

By the summer of 1984, more than a year after his suicide attempt, he felt like he had his "second wind" and was prepared to do battle with the world again. In an article for *Parade* magazine entitled "How to Fight City Hall," he offered a fourteen-point guide for community activists. "Begin with the proper state of mind," he wrote, suggesting it was essential to "feel strongly that, if you put time and energy into a . . . campaign, you will prevail." Unfortunately, he didn't have this kind of careful strategy to fight the mess in his own head.

Perhaps if he'd been able to write an article entitled "How to Fight Manic-Depressive Illness," he would have begun to come to terms with his own difficulties. A fourteen-point guide would have been a good start. Better still, if he had been able to let go of the whole idea of fighting, he might have been able to survive. But he couldn't get beyond the adversarial and confrontational ways of thinking and being that had carried him through most of his life.

In the late eighties, he called himself "the Jewish Road Warrior" and liked to think of himself as a glutton for punishment. Indeed, he was driven; he managed to accomplish more in the last few years of his life than many people achieve in a lifetime. He returned to college campuses and worked with student radicals of the eighties who wanted to build an SDS-type organization. He protested CIA recruitment at the University of Massachusetts, was arrested for trespassing and disorderly conduct, went on trial with Amy Carter, and was found not guilty. He debated Jerry Rubin, his ex-comrade bent on becoming a millionaire, whom Abbie called "a pimp" and a disgrace to their "collective past." He visited Nicaragua, protested U.S. military intervention in Central America, hosted *Radio Free U.S.A.* on WBAI in New York, condemned the Reagan administration's drug policy, and co-authored *Steal This Urine Test* with Jonathan Silvers. He contributed articles to the *Nation,* hobnobbed with Jimmy Carter, appeared as a sixties radical in Oliver Stone's *Born on the Fourth of July,* and portrayed himself in Nancy Cohen's compelling documentary *My Dinner with Abbie,* which was filmed in Sarge's Deli in Manhattan. When Cohen asked him "Who is Abbie Hoffman?" he replied with hostility, "I don't know what the point of the question is," and added that "the search for a psychoanalytic explanation of life leaves me uneasy." In 1986, at the age of fifty, he was in acute pain and full of self-pity. "I miss my youth," he told a reporter for Knight News Service, whose article was entitled "Hoffman at 50: (We're Talking Midlife Crisis)." "I've got taxes to pay, I've got hemorrhoids. I don't have any real estate, I've got kids and they've got problems."

In 1987 he settled in Bucks County, Pennsylvania, and threw himself into the battle against the Philadelphia Electric Company and the plan to pump water from the Delaware River for a nuclear power plant. "You can save the world," he told the young people he tried to recruit into Democracy Summer, an organizing project that he modeled after Mississippi Freedom Summer. He vowed to "kill the pumping station or to die fighting it," and with his son america he engaged in civil disobedience, chaining himself to a fence at the construction site, where he was promptly arrested.

Along with Jonathan Silvers, Abbie collaborated on an article entitled "An Election Held Hostage," which he felt was so explosive that it would cost George Bush the 1988 election. According to Hoffman and Silvers, Ronald Reagan had made a deal with the Iranians in 1980 to defeat Jimmy Carter in the presidential race. At secret negotiations, Reagan's representatives told Teheran that Carter would not be reelected in November if the hostages were not released. Once Reagan was in the White House, they promised, he'd sell the Iranians all the arms they wanted. The arms-for-hostages deal was a sensational story, indeed, and Abbie insisted on delivering the manuscript in person to his editor at *Playboy*. Eventually he did, but not before narrowly escaping death. On the road from his home in Bucks County to Newark, New Jersey, to catch a flight to Chicago, his car was hit by a truck. Abbie was thrown from the vehicle and rendered unconscious, his feet and his rib cage badly bruised.

When he finally came to, he refused to be taken to the hospital and instead paid a bystander to drive him to the airport. The accident was clearly Abbie's fault: he was exceeding the speed limit and was holding a slippery ice cream cone in one hand while he drove with the other. Nevertheless, he insisted that the CIA had tampered with the brakes of his car and that there was a government plot to assassinate him because his information about the arms-for-hostages deal was so damaging to the Republicans. Maybe he really believed his own story or maybe he thought it was a good story to tell, but there's no evidence of any foul play by the CIA.

"A Drizzle of Horror"

Nineteen eighty-eight was *the* big year for movement reunions, and Abbie made sure to appear at almost all of them, especially at Columbia

University and Chicago. But they only added to his sense of isolation, his bitterness, and his despair. "Jerry Rubin's dead," he exclaimed when he arrived on the Columbia campus. He sat in the audience listening to the speakers, resentful that no one had invited him to be on the stage. "I was the most famous person in the room and I wasn't allowed on any panel," he complained. Suddenly he thought that there was a conspiracy against him, and he went out of his way to pick a fight with ex–SDS leader Mark Rudd, who was now a pacifist, much to Abbie's horror.

At the gathering in Chicago to celebrate and reassess the protests at the Democratic National Convention twenty years earlier, Carl Oglesby, another former member of SDS, insisted that Chicago in 1968 had been a "horrifying" occasion, a moment when the Left had "stared down the throat of nothingness." Radicals had made themselves—not the war in Vietnam—the focus of public debate, and that was a fatal error, Oglesby argued. Once again Abbie felt betrayed and outraged.

The year 1988 was a tough one for Abbie and for unrepentant ex-sixties radicals because they were blamed for the lawlessness and immorality that plagued American society of the eighties. Typically, Abbie made himself into a larger-than-life comic martyr who took the rap for everyone else. "I've been accused of getting Nixon elected, the rise of conservatism, the spread of AIDS and crack terrorists holding Manhattan hostage," *Newsweek* reporter David Gates quoted him as saying. "Now all of this is true," he noted impishly. "But it's only a part of my work."

During the last nine months of his life, Abbie arranged his affairs, made his farewells, and prepared to commit suicide. In September he spoke at Clark University in Worcester, where he told undergraduates, "Now it's your turn to seize the . . . time. . . . It's up to you to save our country." But he had little hope for them or for college students anywhere. At the University of South Carolina, he told the audience, "I feel sad because I look at your generation as possibly the last generation."

Throughout February and March of 1989 he was in a dark depression that he felt would never end. "You are going through a phase," Johanna told him, to lift his spirits. "Yeah, the last phase," he said in all seriousness. Reporter Howard Goodman drove to Bucks County to interview

Hoffman for an article he was writing. He found "the last Yippie" was now a fifty-two-year-old with "an old man's body and poor eye sight" who was lost in the past. He was taking antidepressants, Goodman noted, and it seemed that he had "gone to seed" and was "stranded." Abbie admitted that his political activities had taken a toll on his personal life and that he felt a devastating "kind of emptiness." Moreover, he explained that every morning he woke up and asked the ultimate question: "Do I go out there and protest . . . or do I not?" More often than not it was impossible to get out of bed and walk out the door.

Yet he was still alive and kicking. He admitted that he might "look like Don Quixote," but he added that "the windmills are in pretty bad shape." When Iranian authorities announced a death threat on Salman Rushdie, the author of *Satanic Verses*, Abbie helped to organize a protest. On April 4 he spoke at Vanderbilt University in Tennessee along with Bobby Seale and Tim Leary. It was to be his last public appearance, and it seems that he planned it that way. He shared the stage with the father of the psychedelic revolution and with one of the leading figures of the black power movement in America, as though he, Leary, and Seale were a trinity that together represented the sixties. At Vanderbilt, Abbie had the sixties on his mind, and he wasn't the least bit apologetic about them or about anything he had done during that time. "We were young, we were reckless, arrogant, silly, headstrong—and we were right," he said. "I regret nothing. We ended legal segregation. . . . We ended the idea that you can send a million soldiers ten thousand miles away to fight in a war that people do not support. We ended the idea that women are second-class citizens. The big battles that were won in that period of civil war and strife you cannot reverse."

Now that he'd had his final say on the sixties he could go home to Bucks County and die. Johanna considered committing him to Bellevue, under another name, but she was afraid that the press would find out and that he would be publicly humiliated. Among a small group of friends, it was an open secret that Abbie was suicidal. Paul Krassner remembered that Abbie talked about the suicides of Phil Ochs and Lenny Bruce. Allen Ginsberg heard about Abbie's depressed and suicidal state and made a phone call, but only reached the answering machine. "You will live or you will die—both are good" was the message he left.

On Wednesday, April 12, Abbie locked the door to his apartment—
a converted turkey coop—in Solebury, Pennsylvania. There were no
eyewitnesses, but the available evidence, including the coroner's report,
suggests that he emptied the equivalent of 150 capsules of phenobarbital
into a glass of Glenlivet. He drank the suicide potion, then flushed the
empty capsules down the toilet and rinsed out the glass. He removed
his shoes, climbed into bed fully clothed, and pulled the blanket over
his body. Finally, he folded his hands under his head in a gesture that
some observers interpreted as prayer-like and went into a sleep from
which he would never awaken. His depression had apparently become
so painful that death seemed to offer him a sense of relief. And so it was
his own state of mind and body—his illness—rather than the authoritarian state or the political system, that largely destroyed him.

Abbie left no published record of his manic-depressive illness, and
we can only guess what it was like for him. But perhaps William Styron's description of his psychic darkness, which he taped and sent to
Abbie's memorial at the Palladium in New York, may help us understand what Abbie suffered at the end. "Those who have never experienced depression in its extremist form cannot really know the anguish
it is capable of producing—a drizzle of horror that comes to resemble,
in its exquisite intensity, any physical pain known to man," Styron
wrote. "Abbie was a victim of this anguish, which unlike physical pain
inflicts a final insult on the spirit—there is no opiate to grant relief,
even momentarily. The pain continues hour after hour, day in and day
out, night after sleepless night, until the system can bear it no longer.
Suicide in such an instance is neither the work of a coward, nor an act
of bravery—it arises out of blind necessity."

"The Last Resort"

When he was underground in the mid-seventies, Abbie had written a
letter to Anita in which he'd said "I want to be perfect when I die." On
his tombstone, he said, he wanted the inscription "He died in the
streets." Abbie also told Anita his idea of a place he called "The Last
Resort," an exotic retreat where people could "kill themselves in some
grand style." But when it came time to die, in fact and not in fantasy,
Abbie was far from the streets and a long, long way from perfection.

Moreover, his own converted turkey coop was hardly an "exotic retreat," just as the mixture of phenobarbital and Glenlivet wasn't exactly in the "grand style" of committing suicide.

There was no suicide note, either, but if he had left one it might have read a lot like a poignant passage near the beginning of *Woodstock Nation:* "During the past few years I have straddled the line between 'the movement' and 'the community,' between 'the left' and 'the hip,' between the world of 'the street' and the world of 'media.' I have doubts that I can go on balancing these forces in my head much longer." In 1989 he was still straddling "the line," only this time it was between Yippie and Yuppie, rebellion and conformity, the sixties and the eighties, hope and despair, reality and make-believe, life and death. There were more contradictions now than ever, more forces to hold in his imploding head. There was no way he could balance the dualities any longer, at least not alone.

In the late sixties, Abbie had been more afraid of co-optation than of exile, prison, or death. Co-optation spelled defeat and doom because it meant becoming part of a deadly system. For years he'd toyed with the system: hated it and loved it, defied it and embraced it, seduced it and scorned it. He had a wonderful way of remaining outside and inside at the same time, of keeping himself separate even as he was an integral part of it. For years he worked both sides of the street and knew the best of all possible worlds. He was the revolutionary *and* the capitalist, the bad boy *and* the good citizen.

But by the late eighties, he was increasingly a part of the system and no longer able to criticize it from without. He had become an institution of American democracy: "the Tom Paine of the electronic age," as Ed Sanders put it. He was the revered icon of the iconoclast. As he himself pointed out during a discussion on WBAI in 1986, in the eighties he had been allowed to speak in all eleven states that had banned him from speaking in the early seventies. But he was uncertain what to make of that shift. "I don't know if it's progress or not," he said. In fact, acceptance by the establishment was a double-edged sword. While he had access to a larger and more diverse audience, nothing he said provoked his listeners to action or outrage, and that lack of response was profoundly disturbing to him. Repressive tolerance worked against him and took a toll on his psyche.

He was a published author and highly sought as a public speaker. He was world-famous, and he would have been rich, too, if he hadn't squandered the money he made each year. He was friendly with Amy Carter, the ex-president's daughter, and on speaking terms with Jimmy Carter himself ("Abbie Hoffman is a folk hero," Carter said). Abbie had contacts in Hollywood and on Wall Street, at ABC and the *New York Times*. Abbie Hoffman didn't go by the name "Free" or "Freed" anymore; now almost everything had a price tag, including himself, and the sixties had turned into a cottage industry. He was no longer at liberty, and it seems that he knew it. He knew that his time was up and that the devil had come to collect his due.

In the summer of 1987, while Abbie was fighting nuclear power and the Philadelphia Electric Company in Bucks County, the *New Republic* ran a review article by former sixties radical Paul Berman entitled "Who Killed the Sixties? The Self-Destruction of American Radicalism." Extremism had killed the movement, Berman explained. Organizations like SDS had degenerated into "violence and irrationality" and had embraced "totalitarian doctrines." Much the same might be said about Abbie. Extremism contributed to his self-destruction: too many drugs, too much frenetic activity along the existential edge, and far too little control of his own ever-expanding ego.

It might also be said that Abbie was destroyed by his abiding desire to fit in and be accepted by the establishment. In January 1979, for example, eight months before he returned from the underground, he published an article entitled "I Confess," in which he wrote, "I'm really sorry and I wanna come home. . . . Being a fugitive, I've seen the way normal people live and it's made me realize how wrong I was in the past. I've grown up, too. You know how it is when you're young and not in control. I'd like to go back to school and learn how to be a credit to the community." The article was ironic, but the truth of the matter was that he wanted to a normal person and live among ordinary people. More than anything else, what Abbie sought in the eighties was a pardon from the governor of the state of New York. "He wanted a pardon something fierce," Gerald Lefcourt remembered. Lefcourt filed the necessary papers in 1982, and while he pursued the matter for years, no action was ever taken by Albany.

Abbie had tried to take an impossible position. There was no way that he could be the "nasty cockroach in the cosmic soup" and at the same time a prime candidate for a pardon. He couldn't simultaneously be loved and be hated by the powers that be, though he certainly tried. In a sense, asking for a pardon was self-destructive; it went against the deepest grain of his own history and identity. After all, he was the man who had thrown money on the floor of the New York Stock Exchange. He had tried to levitate the Pentagon, sabotage the Democratic Party, and destroy the Federal courts. He had written "fuck" on his forehead and bought and sold cocaine. And now he wanted a pardon?

The movement and the counterculture were caught up in much the same bind as he was. Most radicals and hippies contributed to their own demise, not so much because they impaled themselves on the barricades as because they avoided the barricades altogether and fell into the ranks of respectability. Many black reformers and revolutionaries— Medgar Evers, Malcolm X, and Martin Luther King, Jr.—were shot and killed. White leftists and nonconformists usually made their separate peace.

The temptations of America have always been great; rebels, outcasts, and nihilists have had a difficult time resisting them. Abbie resisted the temptations longer than most. Of all the leading figures of the sixties, he carried on the tradition of the sixties longer than anyone else, and with more passion. But like almost everyone else, Abbie wanted to come home, to feel safe, to be embraced.

If he willingly took part in his own destruction, society also bears responsibility for his decline and collapse because it dangled its pretty wares, its dangerous pleasures and extravagant rewards, in his eager face. America seduced Abbie Hoffman, turning him into a movie revolutionary and a matinee idol of defiance. In *Revolution for the Hell of It,* he noted that "the institutional machine is a trap of death" and that "tragic figures" like James Dean and Marilyn Monroe had been "born out of rejection of a machine-mad American sterility . . . [and] crushed by plastic Hollywood." He, too, was a tragic figure. He, too, was born out of the rejection of sterility, madness, and deadly technology. Like James Dean and Marilyn Monroe, Abbie Hoffman was a masterful myth-maker as well as a living myth. And like them he was destroyed by myth. It was the "plastic Hollywood" world of images and icons, not police truncheons and prison cells, that crushed his spirit and undermined his resistance. He was in love with and dependent on his own reflection in the media, and once the reflection was tarnished and then nearly disappeared from public view, he had little to fall back on. Without fame, he had almost no currency with which to make his way through the world.

In 1968, in *Revolution for the Hell of It,* Abbie had written that Jerry Rubin "would cry at my funeral and make the right speech." Even then, he sensed that Jerry would outlive him, and he was right (Rubin would die in 1994). Though Jerry didn't cry at the memorial in Worcester, Massachusetts, in 1989, he made a speech that Abbie would have liked. "This is *The Big Chill,*" he observed. In death, Abbie's life had become what he'd wanted for a long, long time: a major motion picture about himself. Only now the movie was real.

In addition to the memorial in Worcester, there were wakes, celebrations, and movement reunions in New York, San Francisco, Chicago, and Los Angeles. Almost everyone showed up, paying tribute to Abbie's power and influence: Pete Seeger, Bill Walton, Tim Leary, Bert Schneider, Dave Dellinger, Whoopi Goldberg, Jackson Browne, Oliver Stone, Ron Kovic, Wavy Gravy, Daniel Ellsberg, William Kunstler, Allen Ginsberg, Amiri Baraka, Ramsey Clark, Norman Mailer, and Bobby Seale, to name just a few. Abbie Hoffman was more than a sixties icon now: he was an American archetype, at least in the eyes of his contemporaries.

Jeremy Larner, who went to college with him at Brandeis, remembered, "There was something Great Gatsbyish about Abbie. He embodied the best and the worst of America. He was a cheater, an opportunist, and a fake, and he had drive, ambition, idealism." Tim Leary, who had first met Abbie on the Lower East Side twenty years earlier, noted that he was "up there in the hall of fame with rebel Huck Finn, rowdy Babe Ruth, crazy Lenny Bruce." A. J. Weberman, who'd been Abbie's foe in Miami and a friend throughout the eighties, said, "If you want to know what Jesus Christ was like, I would say that he was very much like Abbie Hoffman: a left-wing crazy Jew." And Miki Boni, who'd known him on the St. Lawrence River, observed that, "like the character in the book *The Little Prince,* Abbie lived on another planet."

In his own mind, Abbie also inhabited another time: his very own sixties, long after they had vanished. Like so many other American revolutionaries, he couldn't adjust to nonrevolutionary times. "It was fun to have that sense of engagement when you jumped on the earth and the earth jumped back—that sense that you were a part of history," he said shortly before he died. "Can it happen again?" he asked rhetorically. No doubt he wished it could, yet he knew it was impossible. "No way," he said. "It is never going to happen again."

EPILOGUE

A CAUTIONARY NOTE

I've created myself out of left-wing
literature, sperm, licorice and a
little chicken fat.

Abbie Hoffman, 1975

When I was writing this book, Anita Hoffman sent me a copy of *The Troubled Face of Biography,* a collection of first-rate essays by nearly a dozen expert biographers, including Victoria Glendinning (Rebecca West), Michael Holroyd (George Bernard Shaw and Lytton Strachey), Robert Blake (Benjamin Disraeli), Ann Thwaite (A. A. Milne), and Andrew Sinclair (Dylan Thomas and Jack London). In the short hand-written note that accompanied it, Anita expressed the hope that *The Troubled Face of Biography* would help me, and it did—if only by making me realize that my troubles with Abbie's biography were not unlike the troubles that other biographers have faced with their books.

I liked Ann Thwaite's observation that "a biographer has to learn not to worry excessively about the feelings of the living" and Robert Blake's comment that "the problem of interpretation . . . is the first and greatest problem of biography." Most of all I enjoyed Victoria Glendinning's essay, "Lies and Silences," because her experiences as a researcher and her insights as an author came closest to my own. Abbie would have appreciated the title of Glendinning's essay and her observation that "all writers, whether of the so-called fact or so-called fiction, are in the lies and silences business." Glendinning wrote that "The biographer is like a detective, following up clues and making connections." She also observed that "survivors are at once the most valuable sources of information and the least reliable." I, too, felt like a detective: searching for evidence, hunting for hidden motives, and building a case. And I, too, felt that Abbie's survivors—the survivors of the sixties—were both unreliable as sources and essential as eyewitnesses.

I interviewed more than 250 people, some of them again and again over the course of several months and even several years. Many people wanted to know what I was going to say about Abbie and whether my biography was going to be sympathetic before they decided whether or not to talk to me. Some had read Janet Malcolm's *New Yorker* piece about Sylvia Plath, Ted Hughes, and the art of biography and were suspicious of *all* biographers—including me, even though many of them had known me well since the sixties.

Many people couldn't remember the past; a few were honest enough to admit it. When I asked *New York Times* reporter John Kifner if he could remember covering Abbie at the stock exchange, he said, "No. Too much time has gone by." Others made up tales, telling lies and half-truths, whether consciously or unconsciously. Some offered accounts of Abbie that I was unable to verify to my satisfaction and therefore omitted from this account. One story that sounded good but which I decided not to include offered a portrait of Abbie in Mississippi. According to my source, Abbie transported two black SNCC workers from Biloxi to Jackson in the summer of 1964. Using all of his dramatic skills and his sense of theatre, he escaped from a mob and a lynching, the source reported. When Abbie was stopped by deputy sheriffs, he put on a Southern accident, referred to the SNCC workers as "niggers," and offered the officers the name of a whorehouse and a madam in Memphis, Tennessee. While Abbie could have and might have acted in that fashion, something persuaded me that my informant was adding to the legend, not to the historical record.

Often the survivors of the sixties put themselves at the center of the stage and moved Abbie to the wings. Sometimes they had historical axes to grind or wanted to settle scores, such as about Chicago in 1968. Or they were ashamed about what they'd said or done in the sixties, now that they were respectable citizens in the nineties and didn't want to lose their jobs, reputations, or images. I learned to distrust the survivors, and on those occasions when I felt that they were trying to pull the wool of the sixties over my eyes, I felt frustrated, angry, and betrayed. But the survivors were also invaluable sources. They often remembered what Abbie had said or done, and they provided clues about what he was thinking and feeling. Moreover, they helped me to recreate an elusive historical time and place: to conjure up the shifting moods of 1966, 1971, and 1983.

When I finished this book, I went back to *The Troubled Face of Biography* to look for the only sentence in the book that had been highlighted, presumably by Anita and for my eyes. I found it in the introduction by editors Eric Homberger and John Charmley: "There can never be a definitive biography, merely a version, an attempt, an essay which in time reveals how completely all such attempts bear the impress of the age in which it was written." At first this idea made me uncomfortable, mostly because I wanted my biography to last forever. Yet I knew instinctively that my book was but a version of Abbie's life and bore "the impress of the age in which it was written." I started *For the Hell of It* in May 1989, less than a month after Abbie had committed suicide, and though I continued to do research and to write for the next five years, it was his suicide more than any other event in his life that cast a long shadow over this book. Initially, I was angry at Abbie because he'd committed suicide. As that event receded, however, I felt more compassion toward him. I began to understand, I think, the conflicts that tore him apart throughout his life and the manic-depressive illness that became increasingly painful and drove him to suicide. I don't believe that I have allowed Abbie to interpret his own actions, but I have tried as much as possible to let him speak in his own words and to allow the reader to hear his uniquely American voice.

As I began to write this book, a series of memorials were held for Abbie. I attended one in New York and another in Los Angeles, conscious of the fact that Abbie's death had provided an occasion (probably the last) for large numbers of sixties people to gather together to pay homage to and share their memories of him. Writing *For the Hell of It* brought me in contact with these people again, both individually and as a group, sometimes after a long separation. More often than not I became involved in their present lives. I stayed in their homes, met their children, and saw them at work, and I was struck by how much the sixties still reverberated in their lives. I was struck, too, by how much Abbie had stayed with them and shaped their ways of seeing and behaving, and how loyal they were to him. Gerald Lefcourt was still defending him as though they were in a court of law together and Abbie was under indictment. Moreover, his three wives—Sheila, Anita, and Johanna—continued to stand by him, despite the emotional injuries they had sustained in relationship with him.

Although this book is my version of Abbie, it has also been stamped by the perspectives of my contemporaries. Others, no doubt, would write it differently, but I've allowed myself to think of it as "our" book. *For the Hell of It* is a sixties book by a (reluctant) sixties person. I have tried to do justice to the contradictions of the era and to the many people who made it happen. I have also tried to write for those who experienced the era firsthand as well as for those for have learned about the sixties through books and movies.

In May 1989, when I began to write this book, it was the era of Ronald Reagan and George Bush, an era that a great many sixties people hated with a passion because it seemed opposite in spirit to the sixties. In many quarters it was also an open hunting season on the sixties and on unreconstructed sixties people. Initially, it did not appear to be a good time for a favorable book about an iconoclast and a rebel. But as the eighties turned into the nineties and as the mood of the country shifted after the defeat of George Bush and the election of Bill Clinton, the climate for a sympathetic biography improved, or so I felt. I began to write about the sixties with more ideological detachment and less defensiveness, and at the same time with more warmth and appreciation. When characters inspired by Abbie appeared in movies like *Flashback* and *Forrest Gump,* I sensed that there really might be an audience for my biography.

Then along came Newt Gingrich, Pat Buchanan, and other Republicans who defined themselves as revolutionaries and insisted they wanted to shut down the government. Indeed, there was a bizarre sense of déjà vu about the political scene. As Hendrik Hertzberg observed in the *New Yorker* in February 1995, "There hasn't been so much loose talk in Washington about 'revolution' since Abbie Hoffman and Jerry Rubin hit town to testify before the House Un-American Activities Committee." Increasingly in the mid-1990s the conservatives and the Radical Right took over the rhetoric that had once been the preserve of liberals and the Radical Left. One might say that the Right was having its sixties. Pat Buchanan campaigned in an American flag tie and urged his followers not to wait for commands from headquarters but to become freewheeling troublemakers. It all sounded a lot like the Abbie and Jerry of 1968. But it seemed, too, that Abbie had finally become a historical figure whose significance no longer depended on shifting ideological fortunes. I felt that it was even more imperative to describe and understand his unique revolution for the hell of it. I wished, too, that he was still alive and that we might benefit from his insights, his humor, and his way of making us aware of American absurdities.

In the first draft of the book I focused on every detail of Abbie's life and gave relatively little attention to his times, so that one friend—Robert Friedman—observed that reading the manuscript was like watching a movie that had been shot only in close-up. When I rewrote it, I tried to put Abbie into the context of his times ("We're all children of our times," he observed) and his peers (Tom Hayden and Jerry Rubin, for example), and by doing so I came to see him as a more compelling figure. When I began to write this book, I felt that Abbie was the single most representative figure of the sixties, the person who embodied most fully the energy of that time. Having finished the book, I am even more convinced. When I gave a talk on Abbie at a conference on critical thinking at Sonoma State University several years ago, a woman in the audience insisted that Abbie wasn't unique, that he was more or less like everyone else in the sixties. Granted, it was part of Abbie's genius that he succeeded in casting himself as the Everyman of the era: someone who symbolized its conflicts, moods, its rhythms. But Abbie was special; in Worcester, in New York, and in Chicago he was a maker of history. Moreover, from the vantage point of the nineties, Abbie's legacy seems even more profound; his use of the media and his style of cultural warfare have influenced several generations of Americans. As public relations expert David Fenton astutely observed, "Abbie figured out how TV affects politics long before anybody else, with the possible exception of Martin Luther King. . . . He figured it out way before Roger Ailes and the early Nixon people."

Since I knew Abbie, I felt that it was essential to begin this book in the first person and to let readers know my connections to him. But I am relieved that I didn't have to write the whole book in the first person. Using "I" seemed to shift the tone; it made me feel awkward and off-balance. I felt on firmer ground when I dropped out of direct view and Abbie took over. I realize that my hand is here, selecting, shaping, and shifting the material, but this is Abbie's story, not mine—as it should be.

I remember that in New York in the winter of 1990, I talked with Abbie's oldest son, Andrew, who was then almost thirty. While Andrew wasn't eager to talk about his father, he did ask how I was going "to write a happy ending." I didn't know what to say then. I'm still not sure exactly what to say to Andrew and to others with the same question, except to say that Abbie's life provides a cautionary tale about how we live and die. Perhaps we can't change the world, as so many of us believed in the sixties, but we can change our own immediate circumstances, at least some of the time. We are the authors of our own lives; we can make them and reshape them. The choices are up to us. We can create ourselves as well as destroy ourselves. That's what Abbie says to me now. It's what the sixties say, as well. That's not the proverbial happy ending, Andrew, but it's the only optimism I know.

BIBLIOGRAPHIC ESSAY AND ACKNOWLEDGMENTS

Like many biographers, I've had to build my own library and files and find my way through a thicket of information. Over the years I've found that Abbie's books and articles have been the most valuable sources of information about him and his times—despite the fact that he fictionalized his own experiences and mythologized the era in which he lived. Abbie's autobiography, *Soon to Be a Major Motion Picture* (1980), is probably the most misleading of all his books, and anyone who accepts it at face value would be foolish indeed, but it provides insight into his state of mind and his conceptions of himself. *Revolution for the Hell of It* (1968)—Abbie's first book—is his best book, and essential reading for anyone who wants to understand him and the cultural revolution of the sixties. *Woodstock Nation* (1970) describes his contradictory feelings about the celebrated music festival that took place in August 1969 as well as his contradictory feelings about the movement and the counterculture.

To America with Love (1976), a collection of letters between Abbie and his then wife Anita when he was underground, offers a portrait of their complex relationship and Abbie's rich inner life. *Square Dancing in the Ice Age* (1982) brings together most of the articles and essays that he wrote for *Mother Jones, Crawdaddy,* and other publications when he was a fugitive; it shows that he was an able journalist and a keen social critic of American life in the seventies. In his last book, *Steal This Urine*

Test (1987), written with journalist Jonathan Silvers, Abbie lambastes the Reagan administration's war on drugs. He's often dogmatic and occasionally even hysterical, but there are insights into his ideas about human nature, freedom, and psychology.

Shortly before his death, Abbie began to work on a collection of his writings he wanted to call *Abbie's Greatest Hits*. Daniel Simon completed it, and Four Walls Eight Windows published it in 1989 under the title *The Best of Abbie Hoffman*. There are selections from *Revolution for the Hell of It, Woodstock Nation,* and *Steal This Book,* plus talks and essays from the eighties (most of which have been previously published). A great deal of Hoffman's work that originally appeared in underground and radical newspapers, however, is still uncollected. Abbie chose not to collect or reprint many of his articles, including the controversial pieces about SNCC that appeared in the *Village Voice* in 1966. There are more than two dozen significant articles that have never been anthologized, and anyone who wants to read them has to find the original issues of *Catholic Worker, Liberation,* the *East Village Other,* the *Rat, WIN, Ramparts, Esquire, University Review,* the *Berkeley Barb, High Times,* the *L. A. Weekly, Premiere, Playboy,* and the *New York Times.*

Marty Jezer's *Abbie Hoffman: American Rebel* (1992), the first Hoffman biography to appear in print, relies far too heavily on *Soon to Be a Major Motion Picture* and doesn't distinguish enough between fact and legend in the life of Abbie Hoffman, but the chapters on the Lower East Side and the antiwar movement in 1967 are admirable. *Run Run Run: The Lives of Abbie Hoffman* (1994), a gossipy biography of Abbie by Jack Hoffman and Daniel Simon, shows what it was like to live in the shadow of a famous older brother. While Jack is proud of his big brother, he's also resentful. Moreover, the book puts Jack and the Hoffman family at the center of the storm, and Abbie falls by the wayside. "The [cocaine] Drug Bust was the worst thing that ever happened to the Hoffman family," Hoffman and Simon write. Still, there are some useful psychological interpretations.

Not surprisingly, fiction writers have often done a better job than journalists at capturing Abbie in print. Three novels have brought his elusiveness and ambiguity to life: Anita Hoffman's *Trashing* (1970), published under the pen name Ann Fettamen; Ed Sanders's *Shards of God* (1970); and E. L. Doctorow's *The Book of Daniel* (1971). A reading of *How to Talk Dirty and Influence People* (1965) shows how much Abbie drew on Lenny Bruce's sense of humor and his belief that "everything is subjective." The 1992 edition has a remarkable introduction by Eric Bogosian, who offers the trenchant observation that the "saints" of the sixties—Lenny Bruce, Abbie Hoffman, John Lennon, Bob Dylan, and Jim Morrison—were all "white men on drugs with groupies."

William Styron's memoir *Darkness Visible* (1990) provides an understanding of depression and indirectly sheds light on the pain that Abbie must have suffered, which no doubt led to his suicide. Katinka Matson's *Short Lives* (1980) offers a series of portraits of creative artists and writers, including Abbie's hero Antonin Artaud, who committed suicide at the age of fifty-two—the same age as Abbie—which may help to illuminate Abbie's despair.

Unlike Abbie, most of the leading radicals—Rennie Davis, Bernardine Dohrn, and Mario Savio—have not written their autobiographies, but there's still time for that. My favorite sixties autobiography is Emmett Grogan's *Ringolevio* (1972), which was reprinted in 1990 with a new introduction by actor and ex-Digger Peter Coyote, who calls it "part fact, part fiction, a lot of anger and humor, a lot of clear-eyed calls, and some poppycock." The writing, especially in the first chapter, is brilliant, and the unsentimental, sometimes cynical perspective is a welcome antidote to the euphoria of the era. Paul Krassner tells his own bizarre tale in *Confessions of a Raving Unconfined Nut* (1993). Chapter 7, "The Rise and Fall of the Yippie Empire," has useful information about Abbie Hoffman, Jerry Rubin, and company, but it's unclear how much of the story is made-up and how much is true. Krassner presents a quotation from satirist Don Marquis at the start of his book, so readers can't say they weren't forewarned: "It is quite true that I have invented for myself a good many experiences which I never really had. . . . On the other hand, I have suppressed a number of incidents which actually happened."

Dave Dellinger presents his life as a pacifist in *From Yale to Jail* (1993), but the book offers little that's new about the antiwar movement, and it tries to settle ideological scores. Tom Hayden's *Reunion* (1988) contains valuable material about the civil rights movement, SDS, the demonstrations at the 1968 Democratic National Convention, and the Chicago Conspiracy Trial. Hayden also does an effective job of placing the era of protest in the context of the war in Vietnam. Jerry Rubin's books *Do It!* (1970), *We Are Everywhere* (1971), and *Growing (Up) at Thirty-Seven* (1976) are more propagandistic and simplistic than Abbie's. Nevertheless, they present lively portraits of the author in his various incarnations as all-American kid in the fifties, irreverent Yippie in the sixties, and post-sixties man searching for a sense of identity.

Todd Gitlin's *The Sixties* (1987) is probably the best available work on the period, yet Gitlin's perspective is informed mainly by his own experiences in SDS in the early to mid-sixties. Thus, his treatment of Abbie, the Yippies, and like-minded cultural revolutionaries is limited. (Predictably, Abbie himself dismissed Gitlin as "the chronicler of the obvious.") Terry H. Anderson's *The Movement and the Sixties* (1995) is a revisionist work that shifts attention away from organizations, ideologies, and leaders toward grassroots social activism. Anderson is strong on the impact of the war in Vietnam on the movement and is first-rate on Vietnam Veterans Against the War, but he tends to flatten the era, to make everyone and every place seem of equal weight and significance. What's missing is a sense of the highs and lows, the heroes and villains of the sixties. William L. O'Neill's *Coming Apart* (1971) was one of the first books to take in the whole era. Although it's glib in parts, it does justice both to the big historical picture and to smaller, local scenes in the revolution. Marvin Garson's *Inside Dope* (1971), published under the pseudonym Marvin Slobodkin, is a lost classic of the era, a humorous, postmodern work that is packed with wonderful and wacky observations about theatre, media, the news, and the sixties, which the author describes as "entirely staged."

There are several excellent anthologies of writings about the sixties by sixties people, including Mitchell Goodman's *The Movement toward a New America* (1970), Judith Clavir Albert and Stewart Albert's *The Sixties Papers* (1985), and Lynda Rosen Obst's *The Sixties* (1977), which also provides a year-by-year chronology of crucial events in politics, sports, entertainment, and science from 1960 to 1969. Allen Katzman's *Our Time* (1972) brings together interviews with Abbie Hoffman, Jerry Rubin, Allen Ginsberg, Timothy Leary, John Sinclair, and Kate Millett that were first published in the *East Village Other*. Paul Krassner's *Best of the Realist* (1984) offers cartoons, articles, and interviews which originally appeared in Krassner's long-running satirical magazine. *"Takin' It to the Streets": A Sixties Reader,* edited by Alexander Bloom and Wini Breines (1995), has essential documents from SNCC, SDS, the counterculture, and the women's liberation and antiwar movements.

David Horowitz's *Student* (1962) is good on the mood of the protesters at the start of the sixties. Jack Newfield's *A Prophetic Minority* (1966) and Paul Jacobs and Saul Landau's *The New Radicals* (1966) both explain the motives and ideas of SNCC and SDS people in the middle of the era, as does Andrew Kopkind's anthology *Thoughts of the Young Radicals* (1966), which includes essays by Tom Hayden, Casey Hayden, Charlie Cobb, Stokely Carmichael, and Richard Flacks.

There's a long list of books about SNCC, including Clayborne Carson's carefully researched *In Struggle* (1981), but the works I found most helpful were more personal, especially Mary King's controversial *Freedom Song* (1987) and the anthology *Letters from Mississippi* (1965), edited by Elizabeth Sutherland. Kirkpatrick Sale's *SDS* (1973) is the most comprehensive book on the leading New Left organization of the sixties. James O'Brien's much shorter and less detailed *A History of the New Left* (1969) offers a broad historical sweep that's remarkably sensitive to the political shifts of the times. In writing about the antiwar movement of the sixties and the seventies, the book I relied on was Nancy Zaroulis and Gerald Sullivan's highly readable, carefully documented *Who Spoke Up?* (1984). Derek Taylor's *It Was Twenty Years Ago Today* (1987) focuses on the Beatles' breakthrough album *Sergeant Pepper's Lonely Hearts Club Band* but branches out to encompass everything else of significance that took place in 1967, including the Summer of Love, the Yippie levitation of the Pentagon, and the cultural explosion that transformed America.

Nicholas von Hoffman's *We Are the People Our Parents Warned Us Against* (1968) covers the San Francisco hippie and Digger scene, while Don McNeill's *Moving through Here* (1970), a collection of articles from the *Village Voice,* depicts much the same phenomenon as it unfolded in New York and offers glimpses of Abbie before he became famous. Jacob Brackman's *The Put-On* (1971) is indispensable for coming to terms with American postmodernism in the sixties and with Abbie's brand of guerrilla theatre and verbal pyrotechnics.

Sisterhood Is Powerful (1970), edited by Robin Morgan, is an extraordinary collection of essays and poems from the sixties and gives an excellent sense of the women's liberation movement just as it was beginning to feel its power. Included is Marge Piercy's "The Grand Coolie Damn," which created considerable stir when it first appeared because it describes the oppression of women within the movement. The volume also contains important feminist historical documents and a riveting introduction by Robin Morgan, who knew Abbie well and briefly worked with him before a parting of the ways.

Martin Duberman's *Stonewall* (1993) is a wonderful book about gay liberation in the sixties. There are valuable sections on Jim Fouratt, who was for many years a close friend and comrade of Abbie's. They worked together on the theatrical protest at the New York Stock Exchange. Fouratt provides a clear view of Abbie's homophobia in the late sixties; "Hippies are fags," Abbie would say, though he later refrained from such comments and apologized for anti-gay remarks he had made.

Of all the books by black radicals in the sixties, my favorite is Eldridge Cleaver's *Soul on Ice* (1968), despite the deeply flawed misogynist perspective. Cleaver mirrors black rage and at the same time offers a loving perspective on the hippie rebellion and the generational revolt of young whites. Theodore Roszak's *The Making of a Counter Culture* (1969) shows how ancient tribal rituals and customs were reinvented by the marijuana-smoking, longhaired dropouts and foes of modern technology. *Woodstock: The Oral History* (1989) by Joel Makower contains entertaining interviews with almost everyone who played a part at Woodstock. *Acid Dreams* (1985), by Martin A. Lee and Bruce Shlain, describes the significant role LSD played in the sixties and reveals links between political and psychic forms of rebellion. The 1992 edition has a new, electrifying introduction by Andrei Codrescu, who writes that acid led to "an unprecedented vision of a different world."

Jonathan Black's collection of essays *Radical Lawyers* (1971) traces the relationship between activists and their attorneys. Frank Bardacke's essay on the Oakland Seven case in this collection is excellent. There are also solid interviews with William Kunstler and Gerald Lefcourt as well as an informative roundtable discussion between Abbie Hoffman and members of the Law Commune entitled "Insurgency in the Courts."

There are probably more books about 1968 than about any other single year of the sixties (although 1964 runs a close second). David Caute's *The Year of the Barricades* (1988) presents the international ramifications of 1968. Irwin and Debi Unger's *Turning Point: 1968* (1988) is comprehensive but unspectacular about a spectacular time. Hans Koning's *Nineteen Sixty-Eight: A Personal Report* (1987) offers a fast-moving first-person account of the year and its aftermath. "I'd be hard pressed to recommend a better book about the 1960s," Abbie wrote in a generous back-cover blurb. One wonders if he'd read the book at all, especially since Koning notes that "Judge Julius Hoffman and Yippie Abbie Hoffman were not that far apart. They talked the same language, in the sense that they both lived in the universe of expectations and safeguards." Abbie also touted *Chicago: 1968* (1988), though author David Farber wrote that "the Yippies . . . played the game of fascism when they aestheticized politics."

Charles Kaiser's *1968 in America* (1988) serves as a good introduction. My favorite book, David Lewis Stein's *Living the Revolution* (1969), was written shortly after the police riot in Chicago and includes snapshots of Abbie and the Yippies. Daniel Walker's *Rights in Conflict* (1968) gathers indispensable documents on the 1968 Democratic National Convention, and Mike Royko's *Boss* (1971) offers a terrific portrait of Mayor Richard Daley and his fiefdom.

Abbreviated transcripts of the Chicago Conspiracy Trial are available in three different books: *The Tales of Hoffman* (1970), edited by George Levine, George McNamee, and Daniel Greenberg, which has an introduction by Dwight Macdonald that helped me appreciate Abbie's unique role in the courtroom; *Pictures at a Prosecution* (1971), which has the advantage of drawings by Jules Feiffer; and *The Conspiracy Trial* (1970), edited by Judith Clavir and John Spitzer, which includes revealing essays by William Kunstler and Leonard Weinglass. For my chapters on the trial, I drew heavily on the work of three writers of differing perspectives who observed it from beginning to end: Jason Epstein's *The Great Conspiracy Trial* (1970), J. Anthony Lukas's *The Barnyard Epithet and Other Obscenities* (1970), and John Schultz's *Motion Will Be Denied* (1972), which was reissued as *The Chicago Conspiracy Trial* in 1993 with a new introduction by former SDS leader Carl Oglesby.

Abbie's free-wheeling testimony to the House Un-American Activities Committee, which investigated the Chicago riots, is contained in *The Conspiracy* (1969), edited by Peter Babcox, Deborah Babcox, and Bob Abel; Noam Chomsky wrote the introduction. For the seventies, I relied heavily on Peter Carroll's *It Seemed Like Nothing Happened*

(1982), which shows how much did happen. The 1990 edition has a thoughtful new preface by the author in which he argues persuasively that the "separation of time into decades" generates a sense of "the discontinuity of historical time." Moreover, Carroll points out, "the invention of the 'seventies'" was intended to bury the sixties and "thus carried an essentially conservative message."

Several outstanding reporters, including J. Anthony Lukas, Nicholas von Hoffman, and John Kifner, consistently covered the key events and people of the sixties, and their articles helped me enormously. Robert Friedman, special projects editor at *Newsday* in the early nineties, provided access to his newspaper's files on Abbie. The *Watertown Daily Times* allowed me to read and photocopy their Abbie files. The *Worcester Telegram and Gazette* opened their files to me and made it possible to understand more fully Abbie's role in his hometown. The librarians at Sonoma State University in Rohnert Park and at the Santa Rosa, California, public library aided me all along the way; I owe them a great deal.

I want to thank Sonoma State University for a Research, Scholarship, and Creative Activity Program (RSCAP) Grant to conduct research about Abbie in the summer of 1993. Over the years, the students in my communication studies classes have helped me clarify my ideas about Abbie and the media. Anita Hoffman handed over more than twenty years of clippings about Abbie. Dozens of people gave me original or photocopied letters Abbie wrote from the mid-sixties to the late eighties; I want to thank all of them. A number of people deserve special mention: Dr. Lucy Candib, Anita Monga, Peter Moore, Jerome Ford, Edward Greer, J. J. Wilson, Ellen Meyers, Gus Reichbach, Michael Kennedy, Martin Kenner, Karen McCormack, Karen MacNamara, Kathryn Chaisson, Benét Lauren Leigh, Phil Peterson, Dianne Romaine, Dr. Fred Quitkin, Jack Ritchie, Claire Wachtel, Tim Ware, Frank Albers, Vicki Carpenter, Sandra Dijkstra, Eric Foner, Malcolm Falk, C. J. Grossman, Nancy Stein, Elizabeth Martinez, Katrien Jacobs, Michael Klare, Don Patterson, Melinda Barnard, David Walls, Karen Petersen, Barry Willdorf, and Bonnie Willdorf. Finally, I've enjoyed working with everyone at the University of California Press, especially Naomi Schneider, Erika Büky, William Murphy, and the copy editor, Liz Gold, whose close reading improved the book immensely.

BIBLIOGRAPHY

WORKS BY ABBIE HOFFMAN

Abbie wrote and published material under several different names. The names he used have been indicated throughout the bibliography.

Unpublished Manuscripts (in approximate chronological order)

Hoffman, Abbott. "A Theory of Motivation by Erich Fromm." Unpublished paper for Psychology 107, Brandeis University, n.d.

———. "'Help' and 'Hinder' in a GESP-PK test: A Pilot Study." Unpublished abstract of experiment in parapsychology, University of California, Berkeley, 1960.

Phillips, Jean [pseud. for AH]. "La Chef Extraordinaire." Twelve-page article on Dominique Nahmias and her restaurant, Olympe.

Hoffman, Abbie. Letter on electronic voting, n.d.

———. "Kiss and Tell: A True Story of Love and Sex in the New Age." Forty-page first draft of autobiography, n.d.

———. "Abbie's Quickest Spanish Lesson in History." N.d.

Hoffman, Abbott Howard. "Last Will and Testament." 4 July 1983.

Hoffman, Abbie. "Memorandum on U.S. Public Relations." Plan for a public relations tour of the U.S. by Nicaraguan president Daniel Ortega, 29 July 1985.

Books (in chronological order)

Hoffman, Abbie. *Revolution for the Hell of It.* New York: Dial, 1968. Reprint, New York: Pocket Books, 1970.

―――――. *Woodstock Nation: A Talk-Rock Album.* New York: Vintage, 1969.

―――――. *Steal This Book.* New York: Pirate Editions, 1971.

Hoffman, Abbie, Jerry Rubin, and Ed Sanders. *Vote!* New York: Warner Paperback Library, 1972.

Hoffman, Abbie, and Anita Hoffman. *To America with Love: Letters from the Underground.* New York: Stonehill, 1976.

Hoffman, Abbie. *Soon to Be a Major Motion Picture.* Introduction by Norman Mailer. New York: Putnam, 1980.

―――――. *Square Dancing in the Ice Age: Underground Writings.* New York: Putnam, 1982.

Hoffman, Abbie, and Jonathan Silvers. *Steal This Urine Test: Fighting Drug Hysteria in America.* New York: Penguin, 1987.

Hoffman, Abbie. *The Best of Abbie Hoffman.* Edited by Daniel Simon and Abbie Hoffman. New York: Four Walls Eight Windows, 1989.

Articles, Poems, Talks, and Letters (in chronological order)

Hoffman, Abbott. *The Drum.* Newsletter written and edited by Abbott Hoffman, Worcester, Mass., 1964.

―――――. Letter. *Worcester Telegram and Gazette,* 4 May 1965.

―――――. Letter. *Worcester Telegram and Gazette,* 12 Aug. 1965.

―――――. Letter. *Worcester Telegram and Gazette,* 4 Oct. 1965.

―――――. Letter. *Worcester Telegram and Gazette,* 7 Dec. 1965.

―――――. Letter. *Worcester Telegram and Gazette,* 20 Jan. 1966.

―――――. Letter. *Worcester Telegram and Gazette,* 6 Aug. 1966.

―――――. "The Crafts of Freedom." *Catholic Worker,* Oct.–Nov. 1966: 1+.

Hoffman, Abbie. *Noww.* Newsletter written and edited by Abbie Hoffman, Worcester, MA, 1966.

―――――. "SNCC: The Desecration of a Delayed Dream." *Village Voice,* 15 Dec. 1966: 6.

―――――. "Another Look at the Movement." *Village Voice,* 22 Dec. 1966: 5+.

Hoffman, Abbott. "View from Canal 11th." Poem. *Punch,* Apr. 1967: 8.

―――――. "Venceremos!" Poem. *Punch,* Apr. 1967: 8.

Hoffman, Abbie. "Liberty House/Poor People's Corporation." *Liberation,* Apr. 1967: 20–21.

―――――. "Love and Hate on 5th Avenue." *WIN,* 16 June 1967: 8.

Metesky, George [pseud. for AH]. "Diggery is Niggery." *WIN,* 15 Sept. 1967: 8–10.

Hoffman, Abbie. "The 1968 Election?" (Hoffman's comments on a panel that included Staughton Lynd, Dr. Spock, and Jack Newfield.) *WIN,* 15 Mar. 1968: 4–5.

―――――. "Creating a Perfect Mess." *Other Scenes,* Oct. 1968: unpaged. (Reprinted as "Creating the Perfect Mess" in *Revolution for the Hell of It.*)

―――. "My Life to Live." *New York Free Press*, 3–9 Oct. 1968: 4–5.

―――. Letter. *Punch*, 4 Nov. 1968: 5.

―――. "The Doctor's Revolt." *WIN*, 15 Feb. 1969. (Reprinted in *The Movement toward a New America*, ed. Mitchell Goodman.)

Hoffman, Abbott. "Fuck the Vanguard, Power to the People." *East Village Other*, 30 Apr. 1969: 3+.

Hoffman, Abbie. Review of *Die Nigger Die!* by H. Rap Brown. *East Village Other*, 15 May 1969: 19.

―――. Letter. *East Village Other*, 18 June 1969: 2.

―――. "Media Freaking." Talk given in Lincoln Park, Chicago, 27 Aug. 1968. *Tulane Drama Review*, Summer 1969: 46–51.

―――. "Commuter Protest." *New York Rat*, 3–16 Dec. 1969: 7+.

―――. "Sami and the Golden Yo-Yo." Short story. *Eye*, Jan. 1969: 67.

―――. Letter. Dated 22 Feb. 1970. *Punch*, 12–24 Mar. 1970: 9.

―――. "Chicago: Two Years After." Introduction to reprint of *Revolution for the Hell of It*. New York: Pocket Books: 1970.

―――. "America on $0 a Day." *Ramparts*, Feb. 1971: 48–55.

―――. Transcript. Untitled audio tape from "Tribunal for *Steal This Book*," 1971.

―――. "I Quit." *WIN*, Sept. 1971: 18–19.

―――. "Yo-Yo Power!" *Esquire*, Oct. 1971: 106+.

―――. "Fire in the Lake: The Image of Revolution." Letter. *East Village Other*, 23 Dec. 1971: 8+.

―――. "The Eyes of Cronkite." *Esquire*, Apr. 1973: 85.

―――. "Book-of-the-Month-Club Selection." *University Review*, June 1974: 12–14.

―――. "Renewing a Revolution." *Berkeley Barb*, 12–18 Dec. 1975: 7.

―――. "Breaking Control and Getting in Tune." *Berkeley Barb*, 19–25 Dec. 1975: 5.

―――. "My Life on the Lam." *Oui*, June 1977: 79+.

―――. "Inside the FBI (Or, How One of the Most Wanted Fugitives Goosed the Ghost of J. Edgar Hoover)." *Penthouse*, Oct. 1977: 142+.

―――. "Abbie: In His Own Defense." Transcript of taped speech from underground to audience at Madison Square Garden Felt Forum. *Yipster Times*, 10 Mar. 1978: 3.

Freed, Barry [pseud. for AH]. "Statement to Jefferson County Board of Supervisors." *Thousand Islands* (New York), 3 Oct. 1978.

―――. "The Facts about Save the River Committee and Winter Navigation." Pamphlet, n.d.

―――. "Statement of Barry Freed, Save the River." United States Senate Subcommittee on Water Resources of the Committee on Environment and Public Works. Field Hearing, Alexandria Bay, New York, 27 Aug. 1979.

Hoffman, Abbie. "My Life as a Fugitive." *Parade,* 14 Dec. 1980: 8–10.

———. Letter. *Harper's,* Dec. 1980: 4.

———. "The Great St. Lawrence River War." *Village Voice,* 1–7 Apr. 1981: 16–17.

———. Letter. Veritas letterhead. 25 June 1981. Photocopied.

———. Talk given at Clark University, Worcester, Mass., 28 Mar. 1982.

———. "Fifties, Sixties, Seventies, Eighties." Talk given at University of Colorado at Boulder, 26 July 1982.

———. "Nuclear Waste Upstate." Op-ed piece. *New York Times,* 27 Sept. 1982.

———. "Steal This Meal." *High Times,* Jan. 1983: 41+.

———. "No Lack of Civil Liberties in Nicaragua." *Post-Standard* (Syracuse, New York), 29 July 1985: A13.

———. "Woodstock: Love It or Leave It." *L. A. Weekly,* 16–22 Aug. 1985: 39.

———. "Steal This Campus: A Report on the Mood of the Colleges from a Veteran Rabble-Rouser." *L. A. Weekly,* 16–22 May 1986: 18.

———. "Students Deserve Truth about the CIA." Guest editorial. *Worcester Telegram and Gazette.* 10 Dec. 1986.

———. Talk given at "The Sixties" conference, San Francisco, Feb. 1987.

———. "Democracy Summer." Public statement on plan to combat the Philadelphia Electric Company, Bucks County, Penn., 7 July 1987.

———. Talk given at Cody's Bookstore, Berkeley, California, to promote *Steal This Urine Test,* 17 Oct. 1987.

———. "Reefer Madness." *Nation,* 21 Nov. 1987: 580–81.

———. "AIDS and Responsible Drug Education." *City Lights Review* 2 (1988): 14–16.

———. "Running on Empty." Review of Naomi Foner's film *Running on Empty. Premiere,* Sept. 1988: 90.

———. "Deers and Cars." Letter to the editor. *New Hope Gazette,* 29 Dec. 1988: 10.

———. "The Young Have to Be There." *Progressive,* June 1989: 15.

———. "The Value of Conflict." Talk given at Naropa Institute peace conference, 19 June 1986. *Vajradhatu Sun,* Oct.–Nov. 1989: 1+.

——— "Reflections on the Dialogue with [Jesse] Jackson." *Tikkun,* Nov./ Dec. 1987. Reprinted in *Tikkun . . . To Heal, Repair and Transform the World: An Anthology,* ed. Michael Lerner, 81–83. Oakland: Tikkun Books, 1992.

———. "Bye-Bye Sixties, Hollywood-Style." Reprinted in Abbie Hoffman, *Square Dancing in the Ice Age.* New York: Putnam, 1982.

Hoffman, Abbie, and Jonathan Silvers. "An Election Held Hostage." *Playboy,* Oct. 1988: 73+.

SECONDARY SOURCES

Books (in alphabetical order)

Adelson, Alan. *SDS.* New York: Scribner's, 1972.

Albert, Judith Clavir, and Stewart Edward Albert, eds. *The Sixties Papers.* New York: Praeger, 1985.

Alinsky, Saul D. *Reveille for Radicals.* 1946. New York: Vintage, 1969.

Anderson, Terry H. *The Movement and the Sixties.* New York: Oxford University Press, 1995.

Arendt, Hannah. *Hannah Arendt/Karl Jaspers Correspondence, 1926–1969.* Edited by Lotte Kohler and Hans Saner. Translated by Robert and Rita Kimber. New York: Harcourt Brace Jovanovich, 1992.

Artaud, Antonin. *The Theatre and Its Double.* Originally publilshed 1938. Reprinted in *Antonin Artaud, Selected Writings,* ed. Susan Sontag, trans. Helen Weaver. Berkeley and Los Angeles: University of California Press, 1988.

Babcox, Peter, Deborah Babcox, and Bob Abel, eds. *The Conspiracy.* Introduction by Noam Chomsky. New York: Dell, 1969.

Becker, Theodore L., and Anthony L. Dodson. *Live This Book: Abbie Hoffman's Philosophy for a Free and Green America.* Foreword by Jack Hoffman. Chicago: Noble, 1991.

Belfrage, Sally, *Freedom Summer.* New York: Viking, 1965.

Bernard, Sidney. *This Way to the Apocalypse: The '60's.* New York: The Smith, 1969.

Bernstein, Fred. *The Jewish Mothers' Hall of Fame.* New York: Doubleday, 1986.

Black, Jonathan, ed. *Radical Lawyers: Their Role in the Movement and in the Courts.* New York: Avon, 1971.

Bloom, Alexander, and Wini Breines. *"Takin' It to the Streets": A Sixties Reader.* New York: Oxford, 1995.

Bockris, Victor. *The Life and Death of Andy Warhol.* New York: Bantam, 1989.

Brackman, Jacob. *The Put On: Modern Fooling and Modern Mistrust.* Chicago: H. Regnery, 1971.

Breines, Wini. *Community and Organization in the New Left: 1962–1968.* New York: Praeger, 1982.

Brinkley, Douglas. *Jimmy Carter: The Post Presidential Years.* New York: Random House, 1996.

Brooks, Thomas R. *Walls Come Tumbling Down: A History of the Civil Rights Movement, 1940–1970.* Englewood Cliffs, N.J.: Prentice-Hall, 1974.

Brown, H. Rap. *Die Nigger Die!* New York: Dial, 1969.

Bruce, Lenny. *How to Talk Dirty and Influence People: An Autobiography.*

Originally published Chicago: Playboy, 1965. Reprint, with introduction by Eric Bogosian, New York: Fireside, 1992.

Bunzel, John H., ed. *Political Passages: Journeys of Change through Two Decades, 1968–1988.* New York: Macmillan, 1988.

Cagin, Seth, and Philip Dray. *We Are Not Afraid: The Story of Goodman, Schwerner and Chaney and the Civil Rights Campaign for Mississippi.* New York: Macmillan, 1988.

Carmichael, Stokely, and Charles V. Hamilton. *Black Power: The Politics of Liberation in America.* New York: Random House, 1967.

Carroll, Peter. *It Seemed Like Nothing Happened: The Tragedy and Promise of America in the 1970s.* New York: Holt, Rinehart & Winston, 1982. Reprint, with new preface, New Brunswick, N.J.: Rutgers University Press, 1990.

Carson, Clayborne. *In Struggle: SNCC and the Black Awakening of the 1960s.* Cambridge, Mass.: Harvard University Press, 1981.

Caute, David. *The Year of the Barricades: A Journey through 1968.* New York: Harper & Row, 1988.

Chicago Conspiracy Trial: Official Pogrom. New York: Domesday, 1969.

Clavir, Judy, and John Spitzer, eds. *The Conspiracy Trial.* Indianapolis: Bobbs-Merrill, 1970.

Cleaver, Eldridge. *Soul on Ice.* Originally published New York: McGraw-Hill, 1968. Reprint, New York: Dell, 1992.

Cohen, John. *The Essential Lenny Bruce.* New York: Ballantine, 1967.

Coleman, Ray. *Lennon.* New York: McGraw-Hill, 1984.

Collier, Peter, and David Horowitz. *Destructive Generation: Second Thoughts about the Sixties.* New York: Summit, 1990.

Cuddihy, John Murray. *The Ordeal of Civility: Freud, Marx, Lévi-Strauss, and the Jewish Struggle with Modernity.* New York: Basic, 1974.

Cummings, Richard. *The Pied Piper: Allard K. Lowenstein and the Liberal Dream.* New York: Grove, 1985.

Dellinger, David. *From Yale to Jail: The Life Story of a Moral Dissenter.* New York: Pantheon, 1993.

Diggins, John Patrick. *The Rise and Fall of the American Left.* New York: Norton, 1992.

Doctorow, E. L. *The Book of Daniel.* Originally published New York: Random House, 1971. Reprint, New York: New American Library, 1972.

Draper, Hal. *Berkeley: The New Student Revolt.* New York: Grove, 1965.

Duberman, Martin. *Stonewall.* New York: Dutton, 1993.

Dylan, Bob. *Lyrics, 1962–1985.* New York: Knopf, 1985.

Eliot, Marc. *Death of a Rebel.* New York: Anchor, 1979.

Epstein, Jason. *The Great Conspiracy Trial: An Essay on Law, Liberty, and the Constitution.* New York: Random House, 1970.

Farber, David. *Chicago: 1968.* Chicago: University of Chicago Press, 1988.

Farmer, James. *Freedom—When?* New York: Random House, 1968.

Feiffer, Jules. *Pictures at a Prosecution: Drawings and Text from the Chicago Conspiracy Trial.* New York: Grove, 1971.

Feigelson, Naomi. *The Underground Revolution: Hippies, Yippies, and Others.* New York: Funk & Wagnalls, 1970.

Fettamen, Ann [pseud. for Anita Hoffman]. *Trashing.* San Francisco: Straight Arrow Books, 1970.

Feuer, Lewis S. *The Conflict of Generations: The Character and Significance of Student Movements.* New York: Basic, 1969.

Fieve, Ronald R. *Moodswing.* Originally published New York: Morrow, 1975. Reprint, New York: Bantam, 1976.

Ginsberg, Allen. *Allen Verbatim: Lectures on Poetry, Politics, Consciousness.* Ed. Gordon Ball. New York: McGraw-Hill, 1974.

Gitlin, Todd. *The Sixties: Years of Hope, Days of Rage.* New York: Bantam, 1987.

———. *The Whole World Is Watching: Mass Media in the Making and Unmaking of the New Left.* Berkeley and Los Angeles: University of California Press, 1980.

Goldman, Eric F. *The Crucial Decade—And After: America, 1945–1960.* New York: Random House, 1960.

Good, Paul. *The Trouble I've Seen: White Journalist/Black Movement.* Washington, D.C.: Howard University Press, 1975.

Goodman, Mitchell, ed. *The Movement toward a New America.* Philadelphia: Pilgrim, 1970.

Goodwin, Richard N. *Remembering America: A Voice from the Sixties.* Boston: Little, Brown, 1988.

Gottlieb, Annie. *Do You Believe in Magic? The Second Coming of the 60's Generation.* New York: Times Books, 1987.

Grant, Joanne, ed. *Black Protest.* New York: Fawcett World, 1968.

Gravy, Wavy. *The Hog Farm and Friends.* New York: Links, 1974.

Grogan, Emmett. *Ringolevio: A Life Played for Keeps.* Boston: Little, Brown, 1972. Reprint, with introduction by Peter Coyote, New York: Citadel, 1990.

Hayden, Tom. *Rebellion and Repression.* Testimony by Tom Hayden before the National Commission on the Causes and Prevention of Violence, and before the House Un-American Activities Committee. New York: World, 1969.

———. *Reunion: A Memoir.* New York: Random House, 1988.

Heirich, Max. *The Beginning: Berkeley, 1964.* New York: Columbia University Press, 1970.

Hill, Christopher. *Lenin.* New York: Macmillan, 1950.

Hoffman, Jack, and Daniel Simon. *Run Run Run: The Lives of Abbie Hoffman.* New York: Tarcher/Putnam, 1994.

Holt, Len. *The Summer That Didn't End.* Originally published New York: Morrow, 1965. New York: Da Capo, 1992.

Homberger, Eric, and John Charmley, eds. *The Troubled Face of Biography.* New York: St. Martin's, 1988.

Horowitz, David. *Student.* New York: Ballantine, 1962.

Horowitz, David, and Peter Collier. *Deconstructing the Left: From Vietnam to the Persian Gulf.* Lanham, Md.: Second Thoughts Books, 1991.

Horwitt, Sanford D. *Let Them Call Me Rebel: Saul Alinsky—His Life and Legacy.* New York: Knopf, 1989.

Howe, Irving. *A Margin of Hope: An Intellectual Autobiography.* New York: Harcourt Brace Jovanovich, 1982.

————, ed. *Beyond the New Left.* New York: McCall, 1970.

Jacobs, Paul, and Saul Landau. *The New Radicals: A Report with Documents.* New York: Random House, 1966.

Jamison, Kay Redfield. *Touched with Fire: Manic-Depressive Illness and the Artistic Temperament.* New York: Free Press, 1993.

Jay, Karla, and Allen Young, eds. *Out of the Closets: Voices of Gay Liberation.* New York: New York University Press, 1992.

Jezer, Marty. *Abbie Hoffman: American Rebel.* New Brunswick: Rutgers University Press, 1992.

Kaiser, Charles. *1968 in America.* New York: Weidenfeld & Nicholson, 1988.

Katzman, Allen. *Our Time: An Anthology of Interviews from the "East Village Other."* New York: Dial, 1972.

Keen, Sam. *Fire in the Belly.* New York: Bantam, 1991.

————. *Hymns to an Unknown God.* New York: Bantam, 1994.

Keniston, Kenneth. *The Young Radicals.* New York: Harcourt Brace and World, 1969.

King, Mary. *Freedom Song: A Personal Story of the 1960s Civil Rights Movement.* New York: Morrow, 1987.

Kinoy, Arthur. *Rights on Trial: The Odyssey of a People's Lawyer.* Cambridge: Harvard University Press, 1983.

Klein, Donald F. *Psychiatric Case Studies: Treatment, Drugs and Outcome.* Baltimore: Williams & Wilkins, 1972.

Kline, Nathan S. *From Sad to Glad.* Originally published New York: Putnam, 1974. New York: Ballantine, 1981.

Koning, Hans. *Nineteen Sixty-Eight: A Personal Report.* New York: Norton, 1987.

Kopkind, Andrew, ed. *Thoughts of the Young Radicals.* New York: Pitman, 1966.

Krassner, Paul. *Confessions of a Raving Unconfined Nut: Misadventures in the Counter-culture.* New York: Simon & Schuster, 1993.

————, ed. *Best of the Realist.* Philadelphia: Running Press, 1984.

Kunstler, William. *Beyond a Reasonable Doubt? The Original Trial of Caryl Chessman.* New York: Morrow, 1961.

———. *My Life as a Radical Lawyer.* New York: Birch Lane, 1994.

———. *Trials and Tribulations.* New York: Grove, 1985.

Larner, Jeremy. *Nobody Knows: Reflections on the McCarthy Campaign.* New York: Macmillan, 1969.

Lawrenson, Helen. *Stranger at the Party: A Memoir.* New York: Random House, 1975.

Leamer, Laurence. *The Paper Revolutionaries: The Rise of the Underground Press.* New York: Simon and Schuster, 1972.

Leary, Timothy. *Flashbacks.* New York: Putnam's, 1990.

Lee, Martin A., and Bruce Shlain. *Acid Dreams, The Complete History of LSD: The CIA, the Sixties and Beyond.* Originally published New York: Grove Weidenfeld, 1985. Reprint, with introduction by Andrei Codrescu, New York: Grove Weidenfeld, 1992.

Levine, Mark L., George C. McNamee, and Daniel Greenberg, eds. *The Tales of Hoffman.* Introduction by Dwight Macdonald. New York: Bantam Books, 1970.

Lewis, Oscar. *La Vida: A Puerto Rican Family in the Culture of Poverty.* New York: Random House, 1966.

Lukas, J. Anthony. *The Barnyard Epithet and Other Obscenities: Notes on the Chicago Conspiracy Trial.* New York: Harper & Row, 1970.

Mailer, Norman. *The Armies of the Night: History as a Novel, The Novel as History.* New York: New American Library, 1968.

———. *Miami and the Siege of Chicago.* New York: New American Library, 1968.

Makower, Joel. *Woodstock: The Oral History.* New York: Doubleday, 1989.

Marcuse, Herbert. *Counter-Revolution and Revolt.* Boston: Beacon, 1972.

———. *Eros and Civilization: A Philosophical Inquiry into Freud.* Boston: Beacon, 1955.

Maslow, Abraham H. *The Journals of A. H. Maslow.* Ed. Richard J. Lowry. 2 vols. Monterey: Brooks/Cole, 1979.

———. *Toward a Psychology of Being.* 2d ed. New York: Van Nostrand Reinhold, 1968.

Matson, Katinka. *Short Lives: Portraits in Creativity and Self-Destruction.* New York: Morrow, 1980.

McAdam, Doug. *Freedom Summer.* New York: Oxford University Press, 1988.

McCord, William. *Mississippi: The Long, Hot Summer.* New York: Norton, 1965.

McLuhan, Marshall. *Understanding Media: The Extensions of Man.* New York: McGraw-Hill, 1964.

McNeill, Don. *Moving through Here.* New York: Knopf, 1970. Reprint, with introductions by Todd Gitlin and Allen Ginsberg, New York: Citadel Press, 1990.

Meier, August, and Elliott Rudwick. *CORE: A Study in the Civil Rights Movement, 1942–1968,* New York: Oxford University Press, 1973.

Meltzer, Milton. *Starting from Home: A Writer's Beginnings.* New York: Viking Kestrel, 1988.

Miller, Alice. *For Your Own Good: Hidden Cruelty in Child-Rearing and the Roots of Violence.* New York: Farrar, Straus, Giroux, 1984.

Miller, James. *"Democracy Is in the Streets": From Port Huron to the Siege of Chicago.* New York: Simon & Schuster, 1987.

Mills, Nicolaus. *Like a Holy Crusade: Mississippi 1964—The Turning of the Civil Rights Movement in America.* Chicago: Ivan R. Dee, 1992.

Mitford, Jessica. *The Trial of Dr. Spock.* New York: Knopf, 1969.

Moody, Anne. *Coming of Age in Mississippi.* New York: Dial, 1968.

Morgan, Bill, and Bob Rosenthal, eds. *Best Minds: A Tribute to Allen Ginsberg.* New York: Lospecchio Press, 1986.

Morgan, Robin, ed. *Sisterhood Is Powerful.* New York: Random House, 1970.

Morrison, Joan, and Robert K. Morrison. *From Camelot to Kent State: The Sixties Experience in the Words of Those Who Lived It.* New York: Times Books, 1987.

Mungo, Ray. *Beyond the Revolution: My Life and Times Since Famous Long Ago.* Chicago: Contemporary Books, 1990.

Neville, Richard. *Power Play: Exploring the International Underground.* New York: Random House, 1970.

Newfield, Jack. *A Prophetic Minority.* New York: New American Library, 1966.

O'Brien, James. *A History of the New Left, 1960–1968.* Boston: New England Free Press, 1969.

Obst, Lynda Rosen, ed. *The Sixties: The Decade Remembered by the People Who Lived It Then.* New York: Random House/Rolling Stone, 1977.

O'Neill, William L. *Coming Apart: An Informal History of America in the 1960s.* Chicago: Quadrangle, 1971.

———. *The Last Romantic: A Life of Max Eastman.* New York: Oxford University Press, 1978.

Paglia, Camille. *Sex, Art, and American Culture.* New York: Vintage, 1992.

The Pentagon Papers: The Defense Department History of U.S. Decision Making on Vietnam. 5 vols. Boston: Beacon, 1971–1972.

Rader, Dotson. *Blood Dues.* New York: Knopf, 1973.

Roche, John P. *Sentenced to Life.* New York: Macmillan, 1974.

Rorabaugh, W. J. *Berkeley at War: The 1960s.* New York: Oxford University Press, 1989.

Rosenman, Joel, John Roberts, and Robert Pilpel. *Young Men with Unlimited Capital.* New York: Harcourt Brace Jovanovich, 1974.

Rossman, Michael. *The Wedding within the War.* New York: Doubleday, 1971.

Roszak, Theodore. *The Making of a Counter Culture: Reflections on the Technocratic Society and Its Youthful Opposition.* New York: Doubleday, 1969.

Royko, Mike. *Boss: Richard J. Daley of Chicago.* New York: New American Library, 1971.

Rubin, Jerry. *Do It! Scenarios of the Revolution.* New York: Simon and Schuster, 1970.

———. *Growing (Up) at Thirty-Seven.* New York: M. Evans, 1976.

———. *We Are Everywhere.* New York: Harper & Row, 1971.

Sale, Kirkpatrick. *SDS.* New York: Random House, 1973.

Sander, Ellen. *Trips: Rock Life in the Sixties.* New York: Scribner's, 1973.

Sanders, Ed. *Shards of God.* New York: Grove, 1970.

Sayres, Sohnya, Anders Stephanson, Stanley Aronowitz, and Fredric Jameson, eds. *The Sixties without Apology.* Minneapolis: University of Minnesota Press, 1984.

Schrecker, Ellen W. *No Ivory Tower: McCarthyism and the Universities.* New York: Oxford University Press, 1986.

Schultz, John. *The Chicago Conspiracy Trial.* Originally published as *Motion Will Be Denied,* New York: Morrow, 1972. Reprint, with introduction by Carl Oglesby, New York: Da Capo, 1993.

Seaver, Richard, Terry Southern, and Alexander Trocchi, eds. *Writers in Revolt: An Anthology.* New York: Frederick Fell, 1963.

Sellers, Cleveland, and Robert Terrell. *The River of No Return: The Autobiography of a Black Militant and the Life and Death of SNCC.* New York: Morrow, 1973.

Slater, Philip. *The Pursuit of Loneliness: American Culture at the Breaking Point.* Boston: Beacon, 1970.

Slobodkin, Marvin [pseud. for Marvin Garson]. *Inside Dope.* New York: Dutton, 1971.

Sorel, George. *Reflections on Violence.* Glencoe, N.Y.: Free Press, 1950.

Stein, David Lewis. *Living the Revolution: The Yippies in Chicago.* Indianapolis: Bobbs-Merrill, 1969.

Steinem, Gloria. *Revolution from Within: A Book of Self-Esteem.* Boston: Little, Brown, 1992.

Stone, Gregory, and Douglas Lowenstein, eds. *Lowenstein: Acts of Courage and Belief.* New York: Harcourt Brace Jovanovich, 1983.

Styron, William. *Darkness Visible: A Memoir of Madness.* New York: Random House, 1990.

Sugarman, Tracy. *Stranger at the Gates: A Summer in Mississippi.* Foreword by Fannie Lou Hamer. New York: Hill & Wang, 1966.

Sutherland, Elizabeth, ed. *Letters from Mississippi.* New York: McGraw-Hill, 1965.

Taylor, Derek. *It Was Twenty Years Ago Today.* New York: Simon & Schuster, 1987.

Unger, Irwin. *The Movement: A History of the American New Left, 1959–1972.* New York: Dodd, Mead, 1974.

Unger, Irwin, and Debi Unger. *Turning Point: 1968.* New York: Scribner's, 1988.

Vellela, Tony. *New Voices: Student Political Activism in the '80s and '90s.* Boston: South End Press, 1988.

Ventura, Michael. *Shadow Dancing in the USA.* Los Angeles: Jeremy P. Tarcher, 1985.

Viorst, Milton. *Fire in the Streets: America in the 1960s.* New York: Simon and Schuster, 1979.

von Hoffman, Nicholas. *Left at the Post.* Chicago: Quadrangle, 1970.

———. *Mississippi Notebook.* New York: David White, 1964.

———. *We Are the People Our Parents Warned Us Against.* Originally published Chicago: Quadrangle, 1968. Reprint, Chicago: Ivan R. Dee, 1989.

Walker, Daniel. *Rights in Conflict.* Report submitted by the Chicago Study Team to the National Commission on the Causes and Prevention of Violence. New York: Dutton, 1968.

Weiner, Rex, and Deanne Stillman. *Woodstock Census: The Nationwide Survey of the Sixties Generation.* New York: Viking, 1979.

Whalen, Jack, and Richard Flacks. *Beyond the Barricades: The Sixties Generation Grows Up.* Philadelphia: Temple University Press, 1989.

Wicker, Tom. *One of Us: Richard Nixon and the American Dream.* New York: Random House, 1991.

Wiener, Jon. *Come Together: John Lennon in His Time.* New York: Random House, 1984.

Witcover, Jules. *White Knight: The Rise of Spiro Agnew.* New York: Random House, 1972.

Wolf, Leonard, ed. *Voices from the Love Generation.* Boston: Little, Brown, 1968.

Worcester Academy Yearbook: 1954. Worcester, Mass.: 1954.

Worcester Academy Yearbook: 1955. Worcester, Mass.: 1954.

Zaroulis, Nancy, and Gerald Sullivan. *Who Spoke Up? American Protest against the War in Vietnam 1963–1975.* New York: Doubleday, 1984.

Zinn, Howard. *The Southern Mystique.* New York: Knopf, 1964.

Articles (in alphabetical order)

"Abbie Hoffman Pays a Call at the Kennedy Library and Basks in Bamboozling of the Feds." *People,* 19 Nov. 1979: 74.

"Bags Yippies Can Get Into in Your Home Town." *Chicago Seed*, 2 (1968), no. 5: 3.

Bardacke, Frank. "The Oakland 7." In *Radical Lawyers: Their Role in the Movement and in the Courts*, ed. Jonathan Black. New York: Avon Books, 1971.

Berman, Dave. "The Battle for the Bridge." *Syracuse New Times*, 14 July 1982: 1+.

Berman, Paul. "Who Killed the Sixties?" *New Republic*, 10–17 Aug. 1987: 28–35.

———. "Yippie Redux." Review of *Soon to Be a Major Motion Picture*. *Village Voice*, 12 May 1980: 43+.

Bilsey, Manasha. "The Conspiracy Comes Home." *Worcester Punch*, Dec. 1969: 3.

Bowart, Walter. "Casting the Money Throwers from the Temple." *East Village Other*, 1–15 Sept. 1967: 3.

Breslin, Jimmy. "The Yippie Myth." *New York Post*, 6 Sept. 1968: 16.

Browne, Paul J. "Abbie Hoffman Ends Fast after Bobby Sands Dies." *Watertown Daily Times*, 5 May 1981:10.

Buchalter, Gail, Cherie Burns, and Davis Bushnell. "The Women in Abbie Hoffman's Life Contemplate His Return from Six Years as a Fugitive." *People*, 20 Sept. 1980: 40–42.

Burgess, Anthony. "Is America Falling Apart?" *New York Times*, 7 Nov. 1971. (Reprinted in *The Norton Reader*, 8th ed. New York: Norton, 1992.)

Cakars, Maris. "New York Resistance, R.I.P." *WIN*, 15 Nov. 1969: 27–28.

Carey, Martin. "Mystic, Saints, Artists, Holymen, Astrologers, Witches, Sorcerers, Warlocks, Druids, Hippies, Priests, Shamen, Ministers, Rabbis, Troubadours, Prophets, Minstrels, Bards, Roadmen Come to Exorcise the Pentagon, Washington, Oct. 21." *East Village Other*, 15 Sept. 1967: 15.

"Cleaver at the Algonquin." *East Village Other*, 18 Oct. 1968: 5.

Cockburn, Alexander. "Convulsions in California." *Times Literary Supplement*, 3–9 Nov. 1989: 1210.

Colander, Pat. "The Woman Abbie Hoffman Left Behind." *Chicago Tribune*, 25 May 1976, sec. 3: 1+.

Cole, Larry. "Writer Leads Opposition to Winter Navigation." *Watertown Daily Times*, 7 Oct. 1978.

Collier, Geraldine A. "Police Beatings Claimed by SNCC." *Worcester Telegram and Gazette*, 25 July 1966.

Collins, Bud. "Reminiscence." *Sports Illustrated*, 17 Sept. 1979: 81.

———. "One Day They Were Gone, But Their Spirit Remains." *Boston Globe*, 28 Apr. 1989: 87.

Connolly, Timothy J. "Remembering Abbie." *Worcester Telegram and Gazette*, 17 Nov. 1992.

Corn, David. "The Abbie and Jerry Show." *Mother Jones,* Feb./Mar. 1985: 16–17.

Cornell, Tom. "Draft Cards Are for Burning." Quoted in Nancy Zaroulis and Gerald Sullivan, *Who Spoke Up?* New York: Doubleday, 1984.

Cott, Jonathan. "A Talk with Pete Townshend." *Rolling Stone,* 14 May 1970: 34.

Crouch, Stanley. "When Watts Burned." Reprinted in *The Sixties: The Decade Remembered by the People Who Lived It Then,* ed. Lynda Rosen Obst. New York: Random House/Rolling Stone, 1977.

"The Crowd in the Cage." *Newsweek,* 17 May 1971: 26–27.

Damon, Gladys. "Fugitive with a Jewish Soul, Abbie Hoffman Is Dead." *Jewish Advocate,* 27 Apr. 1989.

Dancis, Bruce. "Abbie Hoffman: Yesterday and Today." *San Francisco Bay Guardian,* 5–12 May 1982: 7+.

Darlington, Sandy. "River." *Good Times,* 2 Oct. 1970: 16.

Dellinger, Dave. *The Yippie Way.* Commentary on *Revolution for the Hell of It. Liberation,* Mar./Apr. 1969: 45.

"Demonstrations Are a Drag and Besides We're Much Too High." *East Village Other,* 1–7 Mar. 1968: 16.

"The Digger Papers." *Realist,* Aug. 1968.

Doctorow, E. L. "The Brandeis Papers: 'A Gangsterdom of the Spirit.'" *Nation,* 2 Oct. 1989: 348+.

———. "False Documents." Originally published 1977. Reprinted in E. L. Doctorow, *Jack London, Hemingway, and the Constitution: Selected Essays 1977–1992.* New York: Random House, 1993.

"Documents from the Jack Kerouac Conference." Boulder, Colorado, July 1982. *Friction,* 1, No. 2–3 (n.d.).

Dudar, Helen. "Fugitive Abbie Hoffman: The Underground Author." *Los Angeles Times,* 4 May 1980, "Calendar" sec.: 5.

Duran, Kristen. "Abbie Hoffman: 20 Years and Rebelling." *Nightfall,* June 1987: 11–13.

Ehrenreich, Barbara. "Living Out the Wars of 1968." *Time,* 7 June 1993: 74.

Espen, Hal. "The Woodstock Wars." *New Yorker,* 15 Aug. 1994: 70–74.

Fenton, David. "The Press Riots over Abbie." *Village Voice,* 17–23 Sept. 1980: 16+.

Ferullo, Joseph. "Now, Ladies and Gentlemen, the Abbie and Jerry Show. . . ." *New Age Journal,* Feb. 1985: 60+.

Firestone, David. "Radical Cheek." *New York Newsday,* 14 Apr. 1989.

Firstman, Richard C. "Yip vs. Yup: A Post-'60s Road Show." *New York Newsday,* 30 Oct. 1984.

"400 Cops Battle Mob at City Hall." *San Francisco Chronicle,* 14 May 1960: 1–2.

Frain, Mary. "Family, Friends Remember Abbie." *Worcester Telegram and Gazette,* 20 Apr. 1990: A6.

Frankel, Max. "U.S. Study Scores Chicago Violence as 'A Police Riot.'" *New York Times,* 2 Dec. 1968: 1+.

"Funds Asked to Aid Trio in Mississippi." *Worcester Telegram and Gazette,* 24 June 1964.

Furlong, William Barry. "The Straights vs. the Chicago 8." *Life,* 10 Oct. 1969: 28–31.

Gaines, Judith. "Friends Bid Farewell to Abbie Hoffman." *Boston Globe,* 20 Apr. 1989.

Garabedian, John. "Enter Laughing, the Psychedelic Left." *New York Post,* 8 Mar. 1968: 6.

Garrity, John. "David Harris: First Views from the Outside." *Rolling Stone,* 15 Apr. 1971: 8.

Gates, David. "A Lifelong Rebel with a Cause." *Newsweek,* 24 Apr. 1989: 42.

Gilgun. Bernard E. "A Song for Me and Abbie Hoffman." Poem (written in 1965). *Punch,* Feb. 1969: 10.

Gillespie, Elgy. "Don't Drop Your Zipper for the Gipper." *New Statesman,* 18/ 25 Dec. 1987–1 Jan. 1988: xix–xx.

Giordano, Al. "Abbie's Road." *Valley Advocate,* 24 Apr. 1989.

———. "Tales of Hoffman." *Metroland,* 4–10 May 1989.

Girard, Raymond. "Brother Defends Abbie's Position." *Worcester Telegram and Gazette,* 9 Oct. 1968.

Gitlin, Todd. "Hip-Deep in Post-modernism." *New York Times Book Review,* 6 Nov. 1988: 1+.

Goldberg, Art. "Negro Self-Help." *New Republic,* 10 June 1967: 6.

Golden, Stephen A. O. "What Is a Hippie? A Hippie Tells." *New York Times,* 22 Aug. 1967: 36.

Goldman, John J. "'60s Radical Hoffman Turns Himself In, Is Freed without Bond, Plugs New Book." *Los Angeles Times,* 5 Sept. 1980, sec. 1: 12.

———. "Radicals, Friends Bid Hoffman Farewell." *Los Angeles Times,* 20 April 1989.

Goldstein, Richard. "Chicago—Wild in the Streets." *New York Magazine,* 2 Sept. 1968: 30–33.

———. "In Search of George Metesky." *Village Voice,* 16 Mar. 1967: 5+.

Goodman, Ellen. "From Icon to Anachronism." *Boston Globe,* 27 Apr. 1989.

Goodman, Howard. "The Last Yippie." *Inside Summer,* 1985: 61+.

Gould, Jack. "TV: A Chilling Spectacle in Chicago." *New York Times,* 29 Aug. 1968: 71.

Gourgouras, James A. "Heartache Real for Hoffmans." *Worcester Telegram and Gazette,* 8 Oct. 1968.

Greene, Bob. "Yippie, Yuppie, Agent." *San Francisco Examiner,* 14 Oct. 1984, "This World" sec.: 11.

Greene, Daniel. "As Yippie Bait System, 'It's All a Myth, Man'." *National Observer,* 7 Oct. 1968: 24.

Greenspan, Arthur. "Yippies Say Cops Turned 'Love Feast' into a Riot." *New York Post,* 25 Mar. 1968: 2.

Grogan, Emmett. Letter. *East Village Other,* 5–12 Apr. 1968: 5.

Gross, Kenneth. "On the Outside." *Newsday,* 9 May 1970.

Grow, Julian F. "Good Evening." *Worcester Telegram and Gazette,* 15 Oct. 1966: 7.

Gumbiner, Richard. "The Diggers: Who or What?" *Innerspace,* no. 3 (n.d.).

Haber, Izak. "An Amerika Dream: A True Yippie's Sentimental Education or How Abbie Hoffman Won My Heart and Stole 'Steal This Book.'" *Rolling Stone,* 30 Sept. 1971: 32–33.

Hamill, Denis. "A Life and Death Played for Keeps." *Los Angeles Herald Examiner:* 7 Apr. 1978.

Handelman, David. "Abbie Hoffman." *Rolling Stone,* 1 June 1989: 49.

Hansen, Wayne. "Abbie Hoffman in Boston." *Avatar,* Mar. 1968: 9.

Hayden, Tom. "Compared with 1989 in Beijing, Chicago '68 Was a Pacifist Tea Party." *Los Angeles Times,* 18 June 1989, sec. 5: 2.

———. "Why This Erupting Generation?" *Michigan Daily,* 22 Sept. 1960.

Henderson, Randi. "When the Counterculture Becomes a Desperate, Necessary Way of Life." *Baltimore Morning Sun,* 25 May 1976: B1+.

Hentoff, Nat. "Amy and Abbie vs. Free Speech." *Washington Post,* 9 May 1987: A23.

Hertzberg, Hendrik. "Marxism: The Sequel." *New Yorker,* 13 Feb. 1995: 6+.

"The Hippies." *Time,* 7 July 1967: 18–22.

Hoffman, Anita. "Diary of a Revolutionary's Wife." *Eye,* Jan. 1969: 33+.

———. "Life without Abbie." *Village Voice,* 3 Oct. 1974: 10+.

———. "On the Disappearance of Abbie." *University Review,* June 1974: 11.

———. "Trip to Algeria." Unpublished article. Written ca. 1990, Los Angeles.

"Hoffman at 50: 'We're Talking Midlife Crisis.'" *Watertown Daily Times,* 1 Dec. 1986.

"Hoffman Says SNCC to Sue Officials in Newport Melee." *Worcester Telegram and Gazette,* 26 July 1966.

Hughes, H. Stuart. "On Being a Candidate." *Commentary,* Feb. 1963: 123–131.

Hunter, Marjorie. "HUAC and the Yippies Do Their Thing." *New York Times,* 6 Oct. 1968.

———. "War Foes Evicted at House Hearing." *New York Times,* 2 Oct. 1968: 1+.

Janson, Donald. "8 Leaders of Protest during the Democratic Convention Plead Not Guilty to Incite a Riot." *New York Times,* 10 Apr. 1969: 28.

Jezer, Marty. "Abbie in His Time." *Zeta Magazine,* June 1989: 12+.

———. "The Yippie Way." Review of *Revolution for the Hell of It. Liberation,* Mar./Apr. 1969: 43–44.

"John Hoffman, 66: Medical Supply Company Founder." Obituary. *Worcester Telegram and Gazette,* 28 Mar. 1974.

Johnston, Laurie. "Helen Lawrenson, 74, Wrote about Notable Social Affairs." *New York Times,* 8 Apr. 1982: B12.

Jones, Jeff. "Abbie's Legacy." *Guardian,* 26 Apr. 1989.

———. "Abbie's Road." *Metroland,* 4–10 May 1989.

———. "Three Days that Shook the World." *Metroland,* 10–16 Aug. 1989: 10–12.

Kalish, Jon. "No-Nuke Nation." *Overthrow,* June 1976: 6.

Karlen, Neal. "Abbie Hoffman's Second Stage." *Newsweek,* 20 Aug. 1984: 110.

Katzman, Allan. "Alice's Restaurant." *East Village Other,* 1–15 Jan. 1968: 3.

———. "Bandages and Stitches Tell the Story." *East Village Other,* 6 Sept. 1968: 5.

———. "Poor Paranoids Almanac." (Irregularly appearing column.) *East Village Other,* 1968.

———. "Stone and Spirit." *East Village Other,* 23–29 Feb. 1968: 3.

———. "Two Tales from Poor Paranoid." *East Village Other,* 4 Oct. 1968: 3+.

Kelley, Ken. "Riding the Underground Range with Abbie." *Playboy,* May 1976: 67–69.

———. "Playboy Interview: Abbie Hoffman." *Playboy,* May 1976: 57+.

Kempton, Sally. "Yippies Anti-Organize a Groovy Revolution." *Village Voice,* 21 March 1968: 5+.

Kifner, John. "Chicago Protesters Say Police Action on Television Will 'Radicalize' Many Viewers." *New York Times,* 30 Aug. 1968: 14.

———. "Court Voids 5 Convictions in 1968 Convention Case." *New York Times,* 22 Nov. 1972: 1+.

———. "Hippies Shower $1 Bills on Stock Exchange Floor." *New York Times,* 25 Aug. 1967.

———. "Principals in Chicago Trial Still at Odds, but Some Are Less Active." *New York Times,* 30 Nov. 1972: 39.

King, Wayne. "Abbie Hoffman Committed Suicide Using Barbiturates, Autopsy Shows." *New York Times,* 19 Apr. 1989.

———. "Mourning, and Celebrating, a Radical." *New York Times,* 20 Apr. 1989.

Kleinfield, N. R. "Abbie, Eldridge and RFK: Heavy Flashback, Man." *New York Times,* 3 Jan. 1993: E3.

Kohn, Jaakov. "I Saw the Best Minds of My Generation." *East Village Other,* 14 Mar. 1969: 6+.

Krassner, Paul. "Abbie." *Nation,* 8 May 1989.

———. "The Professional." *Village Voice,* 25 Apr. 1989: 1+.

Kunen, James S., Andrea Fine, Ken Gross, Victoria Balfour, Jacqueline Savaiano, and Gayle Verner. "A Troubled Rebel Chooses a Silent Death." *People,* 1 May 1989.

Kunstler, William M. "'Ruckuses' Abbie Hoffman Raised Were Part of the Greening of America." *Los Angeles Times,* 19 Apr. 1989.

Lampe, Keith. "From Dissent to Parody." *Liberation,* Nov. 1967: 20.

———. "The Honkie Rebellion." *Liberation,* Aug. 1967: 14.

Leo, John. "A Lesson from the Deep, Dark '60s." *U.S. News and World Report,* 15 May 1989.

Leonard, John. Review of *Soon to Be a Major Motion Picture. New York Times,* 1 Sept. 1980.

"Lessons of the '60s." *Bill of Rights Journal,* 21 (Winter 1988).

Lester, Elenore. "Is Abbie Hoffman the Will Shakespeare of the 1970's?" *New York Times,* 11 Oct. 1970: D3+.

Lester, Julius. "From the Other Side of the Tracks." *Chicago Seed,* 2 (1968), no. 6. Reprinted from *Guardian* [New York].

Lewis, Dale. "Digging the Diggers: The New Left at Bay." *Village Voice,* 6 July 1967: 11+.

Lincoln, Margaret. "'Art' Films Psychologist's Hobby." *Worcester Telegram and Gazette,* 30 Oct. 1961.

Locke, Michelle. "Florence Hoffman's Son Didn't Become a Doctor." *Athol Daily News,* 15 Apr. 1989.

Long, Gerald. "Radicals and/or Hippies?" *National Guardian,* 16 Sept. 1967: 6.

Lord, M. G. "Aging 1960s Activists." *New York Newsday,* 11 May 1989.

Lowenstein, Allard. "Mississippi Freedom Summer Revisited." Reprinted in *Lowenstein: Acts of Courage and Belief,* ed. Gregroy Stone and Douglas Lowenstein. New York: Harcourt Brace Jovanovich, 1983.

Lukas, J. Anthony. "Disorder Erupts at Chicago Trial After Judge Jails a Defendant for Using a Vulgarity." *New York Times,* 5 Feb. 1970: 8.

———. "Johnson Mocked as a 'Freak' at 'Unbirthday Party.'" *New York Times,* 28 Aug. 1968: 31.

———. "The Making of a Yippie." *Esquire,* Nov. 1969: 126+.

———. "The Second Confrontation in Chicago." *New York Times Magazine,* 29 March 1970: 10+.

———. "Yippies' Leader Tells the Judge Just What His 'Party' Believes." *New York Times* 30 Dec. 1969:14.

Lyon, Jeff. "The World Is Still Watching: After the 1968 Democratic Convention, Nothing in Chicago Was Quite the Same Again." *Chicago Tribune,* 24 July 1988:8.

Marchocki, Kathryn A. "Hoffman: Issues Today Similar to Those of '60s." *Worcester Telegram and Gazette,* 29 Apr. 1988.

Marcuse, Herbert. "Marcuse on the Hippie Revolution." *Berkeley Barb,* 4–10 Aug. 1967: 9.

Marine, Gene. "Chicago." *Rolling Stone,* 2 Apr. 1970: 38+.

Martello, Thomas J. "Abbie Tells 'Truth' about Nicaraguans." *Watertown Daily Times,* 20 Aug. 1984: 11–12.

Martin, Douglas. "Abbie Hoffman Does Stand-Up for His Beliefs." *New York Times,* 31 Aug. 1988: B1.

Maslow, Abraham. "Health as Transcendence of Environment." Originally published 1960. Reprinted in Abraham Maslow, *Toward a Psychology of Being.* New York: Van Nostrand Reinhold, 1968.

McCabe, Bruce. "Why Did Abbie Hoffman Die?" *Boston Globe,* 27 Apr. 1989: 82.

McCabe, Peter. "Radio Hanoi Goes Progressive Rock." *Rolling Stone,* 18 Mar. 1971: 8.

McCormack, Ed. "The Yippie and the Yuppie." *Daily News Magazine,* 20 Jan. 1985: 4+.

McCrary, Lacy. "Abbie Hoffman Changed the World." *Philadelphia Inquirer,* 14 Apr. 1989.

McNeill, Don. "The Grand Central Riot: Yippie Meets the Man." *Village Voice,* 28 Mar. 1968: 1+.

McQuiston, John T. "Abbie Hoffman, 60's Icon, Dies; Yippie Movement Founder Was 52." *New York Times,* 4 Apr. 1989.

Metesky, George. "Awakening of the Pentagon." *East Village Other,* 15 Oct.–1 Nov. 1967: 2.

Miller, Jim. Untitled article on Abbie Hoffman. *L. A. Weekly,* 21–27 Apr. 1989: 22.

Mills, C. Wright. "Letter to the New Left." *New Left Review,* Sept./Oct. 1960: 18+. Reprinted in *Power, Politics and People: The Collected Essays of C. Wright Mills,* ed. Irving Louis Horowitz. New York: Oxford, 1963.

Monahan, John. "Hail and Farewell, Abbie." *Worcester Telegram and Gazette,* 20 Apr. 1989.

Morrow, Lance. "1968: The Year That Shaped a Generation." *Time,* 11 Jan. 1988: 16–27.

Newman, David, and Robert Benton. "Transitional Sex Figures." *Mademoiselle,* July 1970: 102–103.

Nightbyrd, Jeff. "Abbie Talks Before Vanishing." *Village Voice,* 3 May 1976: 18+.

———. "Love and Pain in the Underground." *Austin Sun,* 11–17 Dec. 1975: 8+.

————. "On the Run: Conversation with Abbie Hoffman." *Austin Sun,* Dec. 4–10, 1975: 5–7, 22.

————. "With Nothing More to Say, Abbie Hoffman Went Gently into the Good Night." *Innerview,* June 1989: 2–3.

"Park Plans Foreign Film Shows." *Worcester Telegram and Gazette,* 25 Sept. 1961: 5.

Parshall, Gerald. "The Abbie and Amy Show." *U.S. News and World Report,* 8 Dec. 1986: 7.

Peck, Abe. "Abbie in Chicago: 'Good to Be Home.'" *Chicago Sun-Times,* 31 Dec. 1978: 7.

————. "Abbie's Back, and It's Just Like Yesterday." *Chicago Sun-Times,* 4 Sept. 1980: 1+.

————. "America's Pet Fugitive: Two Years of Movin' On." *Chicago Tribune,* 25 May 1976, sec. 3: 1+.

Pelletiere, Steve. "Diggery." *WIN,* 13 Juy 1967: 13.

"Pictures from an Exhibitionist: The Secret Life of Abbie Hoffman." *Takeover,* 12–26 June 1975: 5.

"Protest March Staged against Nuclear Testing." *Worcester Telegram and Gazette,* 30 Jan. 1962.

Pyne, Anne Forer. "A Relationship Based on Thin Air." Unpublished article. Written ca. 1990, New York.

"Random Notes." *Rolling Stone,* 28 May 1970: 4.

Raphael, Lennox. "Take the A Train to Auschwitz." *East Village Other,* 29 Mar.–4 Apr. 1968: 2–3.

————. "2c Plain Barbarians." *East Village Other,* 7 June 1968: 6+.

Ravo, Nick. "Radical's Memorial: Videos, T-Shirts, 'No Regrets.'" *New York Times,* 18 June 1989: Y21.

Riley, John. "I Wanted Abbie to Be Free." *Worcester Magazine,* 17 Sept. 1980.

"Rocky's Big Stick." *Newsweek,* 10 Sept. 1973: 46.

Rosenbaum, David E. "Yippie Leader Arrested on Flag-Desecration Charge Outside House Hearing." *New York Times,* 4 Oct. 1968.

Rosenbaum, Ron. "The Abbie Hoffman Bust: The Mystery Deepens." *Village Voice,* 16 Dec. 1974 : 24+.

————. "The Abbie Hoffman Bust: Was It the Real Thing?" *Village Voice,* 9 Dec. 1974: 7–8.

————. "On Board the Underground Railroad." *New Times,* 30 May 1975: 14+.

————. "Wavy Gravy." *High Times,* June 1979: 36+.

————. "What Makes Abbie Run?" *New Times,* 13 June 1975: 32+.

Rosenthal, Marshall. "Bringing It All Back Home: An Interview with Saul Alinsky." *Rolling Stone,* 4 March 1971: 34–35.

Royko, Mike. "Abbie Hoffman Really an OK Guy." *Chicago Tribune,* 19 Apr. 1989: 3.

Rubin, Jerry. "Guess Who's Coming to Wall Street." *New York Times,* 30 July 1980: A21.

———. "I Accept! I Accept! I Accept!" *New York Rat,* 21–27 Mar. 1969.

———. "My Hope for America." *Oui,* July 1977: 49+.

———. "A Yippie Goes to Washington." Reprinted in *The Sixties: The Decade Remembered by the People Who Lived It Then,* ed. Lynda Rosen Obst. New York: Random House/Rolling Stone, 1977.

———. "The Yippies in Chicago." *Chicago Seed,* 2 (1968), no. 3: 8.

Samstein, Mendy. "Problems of Freedom School Teaching." Originally published 1965. Reprinted in *The Summer That Didn't End,* ed. Len Holt. New York: Morrow, 1992.

Schwartz, Tony. "Abbie Hoffman Plans Surrender on a 1974 Cocaine Charge Today." *New York Times,* 4 Sept. 1980: A1+.

Seabrook, John. "Abbie Hoffman's Final Days." *7 Days,* 17 May 1989: 22+.

Shampine, David C. "With Abbie, Escape Winter to Nicaragua." *Watertown Times,* 6 Oct. 1984.

"Sheila Hoffman Is Wed to Abbott H. Hoffman." *Worcester Telegram and Gazette,* 18 July 1960.

Shero, Jeff. "Echoes in the Asylum: SDS and Abbie Hoffman." *New York Rat,* 25 Apr.–1 May 1969: 2+.

Shevey, Sandra. "Is Abbie Hoffman Over the Hill?" *Newsday,* 6 Nov. 1971.

Silvers, Jonathan. "Dear Abbie." *In These Times,* 10–16 May 1989.

Smith, Howard. "scenes." *Village Voice,* 8 June and 15 June 1967.

Snider, Burr. "Yuppie vs. Yippie (Rubin and Hoffman) Fight to a Draw." *San Francisco Examiner,* 22 Sept. 1984: A2.

Stern, Michael. "Political Activism New Hippie 'Thing.'" *New York Times,* 24 Mar. 1968: 1+.

Stokes, Geoffrey. "The Last Patriot." *Village Voice,* 25 Apr. 1989.

Stone, Judy. "Some Comedy, Commentary, and a Hyped Up 'Big Fix.'" *San Francisco Examiner Datebook,* 15 Oct. 1978: 21.

"Strange Things in Chicago." Editorial. *New York Times,* 22 Mar. 1969.

Student Nonviolent Coordinating Committee. "Founding Statement." Reprinted in Alexander Bloom and Wini Breines, *"Takin' It to the Streets": A Sixties Reader.* New York: Oxford University Press, 1995.

Taubman, Bryna. "Yippie Easter Bunny Planning a Hip-Hop." *New York Post,* 11 Apr. 1968: 60.

Taylor, Maxwell. "The Cause in Vietnam Is Being Won." *New York Times Magazine,* 15 Oct. 1967: 36+.

"The Trial of Abbie Hoffman's Shirt." *Realist,* Nov. 1968: 1+.

Tubert, Jack. "'Black Power' Is Discussed Here." *Worcester Telegram and Gazette,* 26 July 1966.

Vaskas, Paul D. "Hoffman Starting National Tour." *Worcester Telegram and Gazette,* 28 Mar. 1982.

Viva [pseud. for Susan Hoffmann]. "Abbie's Road: On the Run with Barry and Johanna." *Soho News,* 24 Sept. 1980: 12–13.

Wald, Matthew L. "Hoffman: A Radical in All Ages." *New York Times,* 1 Feb. 1987: L24.

Waldman, Myron. "Yippies Do Their Thing at House Panel Hearing." *Newsday,* 3 Oct. 1968: 3.

Waite, Bob. "Abbie Hoffman: Buck's Dollar a Year Dissident." *Delaware Valley Magazine,* Oct. 1987: 51–57.

Waite, Elmont. "City Hall Crowd in Angry Protest of Red Probe." *San Francisco Chronicle,* 13 May 1960: 1+.

Warren, Robert Penn. "Two for SNCC." *Commentary,* Apr. 1965: 38–45.

Wasserman, Harvey, and Mike Chance. "Abbie Days Are Here Again!" *Takeover* (Madison), October 1978: 16+.

Wechsler, James A. "Thoughts on a Fugitive." *New York Post,* 12 May 1976.

Weiner, Rex. "Caution on the Left." Op-ed piece. *New York Times,* 27 July 1972.

Weinglass, Leonard. Foreword to *The Conspiracy Trial,* ed. Judy Clavir and John Spitzer. Indianapolis: Bobbs-Merrill, 1970.

Whitfield, Stephen A. "The Stunt Man: Abbie Hoffman (1936–1989)." *Virginia Quarterly Review,* Autumn 1990: 365+.

Wicker, Tom. "The Place Where All America Was Radicalized." *New York Times Magazine,* 24 Aug. 1969: 26+.

Wieder, Robert S. "Jerry and Abbie, Untogether Again." *San Francisco Examiner,* 14 Oct. 1984, "This World" sect.: 10–11.

Wiener, Jon. "Abbie Hoffman, 1937[sic]–1989." *Radical History Review,* Aug. 1989: 194–195.

Yippie, Abraham [pseud. for Abraham Peck]. "Yippie—Where It's At." *Chicago Seed,* 15–29 Mar. 1968: 3.

"Yippie Call." *New York Free Press,* 31 Oct. 1968: 13.

"A Yippie Comes In from the Damp: Abbie Hoffman Surrenders on a 1973 Drug Charge." *Time,* 15 Sept. 1980: 22.

"Yippie Leader Held in Raid on Lower East Side." *New York Times,* 24 Mar. 1969: 32C.

"Yippie Leader Outlines Anarchy." *Worcester Telegram and Gazette,* 12 Sept. 1968.

"Yip Women." Leaflet by women in Yippie. N.d.

"Youth Battles against the War." *Time,* 27 Oct. 1967: 29.

Zuckerman, Amy. "On the Road." *Worcester Magazine,* 26 Apr. 1989.

Interviews with Abbie Hoffman (in chronological order)

Wilcox, John. "Conventional Chaos." Interview with Abbie Hoffman, Paul Krassner, and Jerry Rubin. *Scenes and the New York Seer* [later *Other Scenes*], Mar. 1968: unpaged.

Kohn, Jaakov. "Abbie." *East Village Other,* 14–21 May 1969. (Reprinted in *Our Time,* ed. Allen Katzman.)

Katz, David. "An Interview with Abbie." *A Rebirth of Wonder,* June 1969: 8–14.

Fass, Bob. Interview. WBAI (New York), 24 Sept. 1969.

Bergman, Lincoln. Interview. KPFA (Berkeley), 13 Dec. 1969.

Forcade, Thomas. "Abbie Hoffman on Media." *Georgia Straight,* 21–27 Aug. 1969:8.

Carliner, Michael. "Abbie Hoffman for the Hell of It." *Harry,* 15 May 1970: 11.

McLeod, Dan. "It's Going to be Right in Public." *Georgia Straight,* 6–13 Aug. 1969:11+.

Meehan, Byrn, and John Eskow. "Heaven Is a Rational Demand: An Interview with Abbie Hoffman." *Cradle Song,* n.d. [1970?]: 1+.

Kraus, Steve. "Revolution for the Smell of It: An Interview with Abbie Hoffman." *East Village Other,* 25 May 1971: 3.

"The Man Who Cried 'I Am Abbie Hoffman.'" *Takeover,* 4–22 Sept. 1976.

Beal, Dana, and A. J. Weberman. "Abbie Hoffman: An Interview." *Yipster Times,* June and Aug. 1978. (Reprinted in *Blacklisted News,* 558–571. New York: Bleecker Publishing: 1983.)

Hamil, Denis. "Fugitive Abbie Hoffman Surfaces in L.A." *L.A. Herald Examiner,* 15 Dec. 1978:A1+.

Werbe, Peter. "Interview with Abbie." [Fictional interview.] *Fifth Estate,* 19 June 1979:5.

Schechter, Danny. "Interview with Abbie." WBCN (Boston), 1 Nov. 1979.

Rubin, Jerry. "Abbie Hoffman's Last Underground Interview." *High Times,* Feb. 1980:34–41.

Walters, Barbara. "Abbie Hoffman: Life on the Run." *20/20* (ABC), 4 Sept. 1980.

Kleiner, Richard, and Lawrence Wechsler. "Going for Broke." *L.A. Weekly* 26 Sept.–2 Oct. 1980:6+.

Cohen, Charlotte. "Abbie's Road." *Reader* (Chicago), 12 Dec. 1980: 8+.

Peck, Abe. Transcript of unpublished interview. Dec. 1981.

Samuels, Mark [pseud. for AH]. "Abbie Hoffman: Steal This Interview." *Oui,* Mar 1982: 27+.

Wasserman, Harvey. "Abbie Hoffman, 'Never Trust Anyone under Thirty!'" *New Age,* Mar. 1983: 30–35.

Kallen, Ben. "Beaker Madness: An Interview with Abbie Hoffman." *L.A. Weekly,* 16–22 Oct. 1987: 36+.

Anvi, Benny. "An Interview with Abbie Hoffman." *Tikkun,* 4 (1989), no. 4: 15–19.

Blume, Harvey. "Interview with Abbie Hoffman." Unpublished. Boston, Summer 1988.

"Abbie Hoffman: 'An American Dissident.'" *Business Today,* Fall 1988: 35–37.

Ganymedean Slime Mold [video group]. "Interview with Abbie Hoffman." *Wired Journal,* Winter 1989: 15–25.

Goldstein, Al. "Rebel without a Pulse: An Interview with Abbie Hoffman." *Screw,* 15 May 1989: 4–7.

Holmstrom, John. "Interview: Abbie Hoffman." *High Times,* Part 1, May 1989: 35+; Part 2, June 1989: 43+; Part 3, July 1989: 35+.

Films (in alphabetical order)

Aronson, Jerry, director. *The Life and Times of Allen Ginsberg.* First Run Features, 1994.

Benz, Obie, and Josh Waletzky, directors. *Heavy Petting.* Skouras Pictures, 1988.

Cohen, Nancy, director. *My Dinner with Abbie.* MDWA Productions, 1989.

Kitchell, Mark, director. *Berkeley in the '60s.* First Run Features, 1990.

Lanzenberg, Nicolai, director. *My Name Is Abbie, Orphan of America.* First Run Features, 1981.

Markson, Morley, director. *Growing Up in America.* Cinephile, 1988.

Stone, Oliver, director. *Born on the Fourth of July.* Universal, 1989.

INDEX

Perry, Charles, 91
Peter, Paul, and Mary, 206
Peterson, Diane, 230, 231–32
Philadelphia Electric Company, 249–50, 255
Phillips, George W., 184
Phoenix, 37, 56
Pierson, Robert L., 178
Pigasus, 151, 156–57, 180
Pirate Editions, 223
Planet of the Apes, 43
Playboy, xxiv, 250
Police violence: "Black Friday," 33–34, 35; civil rights movement, 47; and Democratic National Convention demonstration planning, 143–44; Democratic National Convention demonstrations, 142–43, 151, 158–63, 165–67, 170, 179–80, 188; Flower Brigade, 96; Hampton-Clark murders, xx, 206–7; Mississippi Freedom Summer, 51–52; Newport Folk Festival, 70; Pentagon demonstration, 122–23; Yip-In, 134–35
Pomerance, Rocky, 225
Poor People's Corporation, 65–66, 68, 72, 73–74, 87–90, 102
Postmodernism, xvii–xviii
Potemkin (Eisenstein), 34
Presley, Elvis, 2, 13, 16, 47
Price, Betty, 48
Price, Cecil, 55
Priest, Terri, 87
Probus Club, 39
Prospect House, 56
Proust, Marcel, 236
Punch, 86–87, 175
Pursuit of Loneliness, The (Slater), 211
Pynchon, Thomas, 2

Quicksilver Messenger Service, 91

Rader, Dotson, 103–4, 111–12, 220
Rader, Gary, 122

Radical Lawyers (Black), 202
Radio Free U.S.A., 249
Rainey, Laurence, 55
"Rainy Day Women #12 & 35" (Dylan), 87
Ramer, Carole, 230, 231
Rashomon, 60–61
Raskin, Jonah: process of writing AH's biography, 259–64; relationship to AH, xviii–xxxii
Reagan, Ronald, 99, 182, 220, 242, 250
Realist, The, 104, 127, 137, 145, 173
Rebel without a Cause, 16
Rebirth of Wonder, A (Katz), 109
Remembering America (Goodwin), 146
Remembrance of Things Past (Proust), 236
Reunion (Hayden), xxx, 215
Reveille for Radicals (Alinsky), 71
Revere, Paul, 215
Revolution, AH's idea of, xxii, xxxii, 63, 109, 174, 191, 194–95, 209
Revolution for the Hell of It, 4, 71, 109, 110, 129, 191, 256; and Chicago Conspiracy Trial, 209, 211; on Democratic National Convention demonstration planning, 140–41, 143, 144, 145, 146, 147, 149, 152, 153–54; on Democratic National Convention demonstrations, 161, 162, 163–64, 167–69; on FBI encounter, 172; on Flower Brigade demonstration, 96; on hippie movement, 91, 100; on HUAC hearings, 178; on Pentagon demonstration, 119, 120, 123, 124–25; on pool hall culture, 15; publication of, xvii, xxii; on Rusk demonstration, 126; on SDS Denton conference, 104; on Sheila Kushner marriage, 92; on stock exchange demonstration, 113, 114, 116; writing process, 173–75; on Yip-In, 135
Ribicoff, Abraham, 166

Compositor:	G&S Typesetters, Inc.
Text:	Adobe Garamond
Display:	Franklin Gothic
Printer and Binder:	Data Reproductions Corporation